Mountaineering in Scotland

Years of Change

Ken Crocket

SCOTTISH MOUNTAINEERING TRUST

Published in Great Britain by the Scottish Mountaineering Trust, 2017

First published 2017

ISBN 978-1-907233-24-1
A catalogue record for this book is available from the British Library

This book is published by the Scottish Mountaineering Trust, a charitable
trust. Revenue from all books published by the Trust is used for the continuation of its publishing programme and for charitable purposes associated
with Scottish mountains and mountaineering. For more information see
<www.smc.org.uk/trust/trust.htm>

Illustrations
Front cover: The Three-Tier Chimney on Cir Mhòr. (© SMC). Climbers
Geoffrey Curtis and Gordon Townend. Photograph Ken Moneypenny.

Production: Scottish Mountaineering Trust (Publications) Ltd
Design: Ken Crocket & Rob Lovell
Typesetting: Ken Crocket
Set in Adobe Caslon Pro 11 on 13

Printed & bound in Spain by Novoprint S.A., Barcelona, Spain

Distributed by Cordee, 11 Jacknell Road • Dodwells Bridge Industrial
Estate • Hinckley • LE10 3BS • UK
Tel: +44 (0) 1455 611185 • Fax: +44 (0) 1455 635687
(w) www.cordee.co.uk

Contents

SMT/SMC Publications List **Inside Rear Endpaper**

Introduction

This volume is the middle of three covering the rise and continuing development of mountaineering in Scotland. As the subtitle would indicate, the period covered, from 1914 through 1971, was one of many changes, both in the practice of climbing, and the equipment used.

Two world wars were major features during this period. The period following World War I saw much economic misery, but also a growing taste for the outdoors, developing eventually in the formation of mountaineering clubs which were open to all and any

World War II had the beneficial side effect of promoting improved clothing and ropes and making these available cheaply in the post-war years. There is good evidence that healthier diets during the second war and of course exercise for those in the armed forces resulted in a population generally fitter and healthier than before. For some time however, equipment and protection could not match the quality and difficulty of climbs being recorded by those at the leading edge.

We look back in a sport and wonder at how much its practice has evolved. Its improvements have often come from the needs of those pioneers pushing out the envelope, occasionally accepting risks which today would be regarded as beyond the pale. That was part of its history in the making, and we can respect it and enjoy its story.

Some of these pioneers will be found here, with an indication of how they were making history in the sport. Through necessity, there is a limit as to how many, and how deeply, this story could cover. It does not include the lower outcrops, nor a few less mountainous areas. It should, however, remain a reasonable introduction to a remarkable epoch.

Inevitably, some of the arguments and conclusions reached here are mine alone. I have strived to remain objective throughout, and where possible have used the words of the climbers involved or of their contemporaries.

This history pauses in 1971, by which time the radical change in the practice of winter climbing, the use of front-pointing with a pair of tools incorporating inclined picks, had begun. The majority of climbers today will not know any other way of climbing steep snow and ice, and will certainly not wish to revert to that way.

The new technique has allowed a huge leap in performance, making possible safe ascents of climbs only dreamed of before. It has also provided access to winter routes for many more climbers who earlier would not have countenanced the gruelling technique of step-cutting. The third volume, to be written by Simon Richardson, will pick up the continuing story from then on to the present time.

Ken Crocket, 2017, Menstrie

Acknowledgments

Once again I must thank the Scottish Mountaineering Trust for their commitment in publishing this volume; without their confident support behind me any wavering of doubt on my part was removed. As with the first volume, published in 2015, Dr Robin Campbell was there to keep me on track, and patiently answer any queries I raised. As the current Librarian and Archivist of the Scottish Mountaineering Club, his knowledge of Scottish mountaineering history is surely unique, and again he was generous with his help.

I must also thank Dave Hewitt for editing my manuscript and tidying the considerable amount of textual flotsam and jetsam I probably left on many pages. To my surprise, finding suitable photographs from the period covered in this book was to some degree more difficult than it was in the first volume. Many of the years covered here would have been years of economic hardship, with many not owning a camera. Even then, gone were the large format models of brass and mahogany of past years, to be replaced with smaller, often cheaper cameras with much reduced negative sizes.

It would have been even harder but for the support again of the SMC Custodian of Images David Stone, who combed through that collection and produced a good number of photographs. Here I must extend my deep gratitude to John Cleare, who freely made his superb portfolio of photographs available.

It will be obvious that some photographs of climbers slightly postdate the period described, but where possible modern images were avoided and the keen eye should note that many show climbers taken before harnesses and other paraphernalia were available, so the march of progress is visible even there.

Anyone who has been interested in the climbing from this time will of course be aware of the contribution to climbing in Scotland by the members of the Creagh Dhu M.C. I received much help from past member Eric Taylor, who helped organise their club web site and built up a fascinating video slide show therein. Also encouraging was 'Big' Ian Nicolson, current President of that Ulyssean crew.

The massive archive of climbing on Skye, compiled by Stuart Pedlar, was again referred to, and I am grateful for his generous cooperation here.

As with the first volume, I am grateful for the work of the various Editors of the major club journals. In particular the FRCC has been a pioneering example in their work to place their scanned journals online. SMCJ Editor Peter Biggar and past SMCJ Editors were holders of the Grail, while SMC Secretary John Fowler was, as always, helpful. New Routes Editor Andy

Nisbet, surely a phenomenon in his own right, continues to make route information and guide book production possible.

Inevitably a few names may go astray, but I owe a debt to all who were without exception helpful. They include, in no particular order: Hamish MacInnes, John Higham, Harold Gillespie, Ken Spence, Allen Fyffe, Ian Fulton, Bob Richardson, Diana Djknaak, Peter Macdonald, Roger Robb, Anne Bennet, Audrey Scott, Ian Crofton, Andrew James, Ed Pirie, Graeme Hunter, Greg Strange, Stuart Pedlar, and others. Scottish mountaineering has lost several good names recently, and I am saddened that they will not be here to read about their contributions to the game.

The first volume was made possible and received its final polishing thanks to Tom Prentice, who recently demitted office as Production Manager for the Publications wing of the Scottish Mountainering Trust. This second volume was overseen by his successor, Rob Lovell, and I thank him here for his patient assistance.

There is, as before, one name above all, who endured the many days of book production, and made it all possible. I thank my wife Aysel again for showing patience and support far beyond the normal.

Table of current SMC guidebooks as used in this history

Title	Author	ISBN	Published
Inner Hebrides & Arran	Colin Moody & Graham Little	9781907233173	2014
Skye The Cuillin	Mike Lates	9781907233135	2011
The Cairngorms	Andy Nisbet, Allen Fyffe, Simon Richardson, Wilson Moir & John Lyall	978-0-907521-96-9	2007
Northern Highlands South	Edited by Andy Nisbet	978-0-907521-97-6	2007
Northern Highlands Central	Edited by Andy Nisbet	0 907521 89 4	2006
Northern Highlands North	Edited by Andy Nisbet	0 907521 80 0	2004
Ben Nevis	Simon Richardson	0 907521 73 8	2002
Glen Coe	Rab Anderson, Ken Crocket, Dave Cuthbertson	0 907521 70 3	2001
Arran, Arrochar and the Southern Highlands	Graham Little, Tom Prentice, Ken Crocket	0 907521 49 5	1997 Note: The Arran section has been superseded by the Inner Hebrides & Arran guide of 2014

Foreword

Our new computerised world has changed completely since 1971. But climber v. rock is still the same game as it was in the early days, or is it? Well, it isn't really, and this book covers the period of most change in climbing history, from the First World War when climbing was effectively Victorian, to 1971 when steep ice and E2 rock were becoming common. So what changed? Read and find out!

My first climb was in 1972. I may feel old but do I make it into this book's era? Not quite, but I'm certainly not a modern climber, so there must be room for a third volume to complete Scotland's Mountaineering History. The first in the series covered 'The Early Years' until 1914. This second volume continues until a major shift in climbing techniques, to modern shoes on rock and front pointing technique in winter. I was lucky that I started with these new advantages and quickly progressed into climbing the harder winter routes of the time.

Ken Crocket is meticulous with historical detail. He used to email me, usually with details of an earlier ascent of some route in one of my guidebooks. My first thought was usually, 'how did he find that out?' Ken was editor of the SMC Journal for many years when I was the new routes editor, and we've continued to be very involved with SMC publications to this day. And we've climbed many new routes ourselves over that period.

The book starts in 1914 when getting to a cliff could take days of travel. What would they have thought about seeing live pictures on Facebook, or hundreds of ascents and grade opinions logged on UKclimbing. And weather forecasts every hour on each hill. Harold Raeburn was the star in the early days; now he could have made a living out of it but modesty was the norm and maybe he climbed even more routes than Ken was able to retrieve.

Mixed in with details of the routes of increasing difficulty are anecdotes which I particularly like. One in the early 1920s was a description of ice axe braking technique by Willie Naismith. I was prepared to laugh, but actually it's the method that is taught nowadays. And of course Naismith's rule is still used for timing hillwalks; nowadays he'd be called a geek.

Jim Bell soon took over as the new king of the crag as standards crept up and more remote crags were first visited. I particularly enjoyed the story of multiple attempts to improve the line of The Long Climb on Ben Nevis, modestly graded Severe at the time, but maybe that was the highest grade Bell used. This summer's accidents prove that it's still a route to be respected.

Soon Bill Murray was involved, and these two wrote books about their climbing exploits, so experience of the sport was no longer exclusively for the wealthy. And from that time on, there were always good stories about the climbs. This became increasingly so after the war with the likes of Brooker, Cunningham, MacInnes, Marshall and Smith, each tending to climb with their own group from their own city. During the 50s and into the 60s, many of today's great classics were climbed by these talented climbers. Nowadays, these are the routes many of us aspire to.

So enjoy this book of how your sport has developed, and the intricacies of the early ascents of the routes you hope to cruise up (but you may find the early climbers were tougher than you think).

Andy Nisbet

1

The Shadow of War (1914–1921)

THE ORIGINS AND EARLY DEVELOPMENT of mountaineering in Scotland have been examined in some detail in an earlier volume.[1] Over the course of a period starting around 1880 and leading up to World War I, the sport in Scotland developed through the efforts of a small but energetic band of enthusiasts, based mainly in Glasgow and Edinburgh, a few of whom had Alpine experience. During this phase, the exploration of–and climbing on–Scotland's mountains, was largely dominated by the Scottish Mountaineering Club (SMC), founded in Glasgow in 1889.

The dominance of the SMC would begin to wane somewhat in the 20th century, due to social changes and the increasing popularity of the sport, but the club has grown and continues to the present day as the publisher of definitive guidebooks for climbing and walking in Scotland.

The years 1894–1898 saw a peak of activity, following which fewer new climbs were pioneered, though technical standards continued to rise slowly. There were several reasons for this change of pace. The weather often played havoc at New Year and Easter, which for many climbers were the two most prominent calendar dates. Other than a few informal meets during the early years of the SMC, and of course private trips organised by climbers among their friends, the only formal meets held were at New Year and Easter.

Also, although several outstanding mountaineers had raised the quality and difficulty of routes, the continuing lack of protection and slow rate of innovation in equipment doubtless proved a significant barrier to progress. These points will be touched on later as changes in technique or equipment are seen to occur.

Many of the pioneering SMC members were now too old to be risking life and limb on rock or snow, and some had merely formed part of the first wave of enthusiasm in order to encourage others, after which they resigned from the club or took a back seat. A trickle of new climbers was appearing, but it would be some years before they were ready to make a significant impact.

A few easy summer routes were recorded in Scotland during 1914, but on the whole the uncertainty of world events stifled many plans. At the end of May 1914, the SMC held a meet in the North–West Highlands, at Inchnadamph and Achiltibuie. The occasion was notable for an attempt by Willie Ling and George Sang to climb Sgùrr an Fhidhleir, the dramatically pointed peak just north–west of Ben Mòr Coigach and with a prominent crest known as the Nose. On Sunday 31 May they approached the cliff.

> Much water was running down the cliff face, and its universal presence made climbing more dangerous than difficult. A long climb from the first terrace, using an intricate series of ledges, brought the leader to a most evil chimney with little but juicy and unsubstantial holds. A certain distance up this unpleasant vent revealed the fact that it gave out suddenly on the face of a hundred–foot slab, and perspecting operations were suspended in that direction, and a descent of some difficulty negotiated by a different route.[2]

In fact, as Ling's diary for that day revealed, they had climbed up part of the wet chimney before reaching an overhang, forcing a retreat to the ledge at the foot where they lunched. *'Then we followed the ledge and went up a grass gully and out on the face up wet steep grass and ledges,'* he wrote, *'then up a long slanting gully and up to the summit 3.30.'*[3] Reference to the current guide would suggest that Ling and Sang had attempted a direct ascent of the Nose, which was not climbed until 1962 and then at a grade of Hard Very Severe. In 1914, Sang was aged 39 and Ling 41, and their attempt on this spectacular route was bold in the extreme. Both were active members of the SMC and experienced Alpinists.

Great Britain declared war on Germany on 4 August 1914. This affected many Alpinists who were climbing in Europe and other mountain ranges including the Caucasus, but by various routes and stratagems they struggled home with many stories to tell, mostly of inconvenience and travel disruption.

There was a strong sense of patriotic duty to serve in the military, especially in the early phase of the war, and an indication of this within the mountaineering fraternity is shown by figures from SMC records. In 1914, the club was 199 strong. Some 60 members, 22%, joined the armed forces, a strong representation for a club with an ageing membership, and 13 of these subsequently died. The Cairngorm Club had 41 members enlisted, almost a quarter of its membership, of whom nine were killed or died later of wounds, although that membership was not all eligible since it included women, albeit not many. [4]

Dundee was particularly hard hit when at least four members of the Dundee Rambling Club, three of them also SMC members, were killed at the Battle of Loos in September 1915, including Harry Walker, lieutenant colonel in the 4th Battalion The Black Watch and a man who had been identified as a likely future President of the SMC. This battalion, very largely drawn from Dundee, suffered appalling casualties at Loos.

Overall, by the end of the war in 1918, almost one in four of the total male population of the United Kingdom of Great Britain and Ireland had joined up. There has been much confusion in general regarding fatalities during the war, particularly when comparing Scottish levels with the British average. What is not in doubt however is that Scotland supported the war effort with widespread enthusiasm, specialising in the provision of manpower, ships, machinery and food, particularly fish. [5]

Recent figures from the Scottish Military Research Group indicate that the Scottish fatality rate of about 12% during World War I was probably close to the British average. [6] The 22% of enlisted SMC members who died is slightly higher than the national average of 17% for officers (12% for other ranks). While admittedly a small sample, this probably reflects the fact that most members were infantry field officers who suffered a higher mortality rate given that their task was to lead men into battle—and with the enemy, when circumstances allowed, being very keen to target officers. In 1915, several letters were sent from the western front to the SMC Editor, Frank Sidney Goggs (1871–1941), describing experiences. One unnamed officer remarked that of 30 officers who had gone out with him, only seven remained. [7]

Not all could enlist, for example the elderly or unfit, or those in a reserved industry. Sang's war efforts involved munitions, and he would be awarded the Edward Medal for his part in rescuing workers from an explosion and fire at Roslin, south of Edinburgh. Ling, being a grain merchant, was probably also exempt from active service—and would in any case have been too old when the Military Service Act 1916 came into force.

All British males were now deemed to have enlisted on 2 March 1916 —that is, they were *conscripted*—if aged between 19 and 41 and residing in Great Britain (excluding Ireland) and were unmarried or a widower as of 2 November 1915. From May 1916, married men were also included.

In 1916, Harold Raeburn, the most outstanding Scottish mountaineer of this period, was 50 years old and beyond conscription age. He nonetheless made determined efforts to join the Royal Flying Corps, the precursor of the Royal Air Force. Prevented from enlisting, he eventually worked in an aeroplane factory in Glasgow where, as his climbing partner and friend Ling later noted, each day he would put in 15 or 16 hours of effort. [8]

Given his age and experience as a brewery owner, Raeburn was probably in a supervisory position with William Beardmore and Company, or one of a number of subcontractors. During World War I, around 500 aircraft were built at the Dalmuir factory on the north bank of the Clyde, and test sites included Inchinnan and Renfrew across the river. It may be fanciful, but one could argue that it was Raeburn's passion for ornithology which led him to aeroplanes.

Initially, travel in Scotland was officially unhindered, but on 11 July 1916, an amendment to the Defence of the Realm Act 1914, the North of Scotland was declared a Special Military Area (SPA). As the Act read, this included:

> The Burgh of INVERNESS as also the whole of the mainland of Scotland which is situated to the North and West of RIVER NESS, LOCH NESS, the road leading from INVERMORISTON PIER by GLEN MORIS-TON, STRATHCLUNIE, and the RIVER SHIEL, to SHIEL BRIDGE, LOCH DUICH, LOCH ALSH and the KYLE OF LOCHALSH.

This clearly covered the North–West Highlands and thus cramped the style of any mountaineer able and eager to climb in that area. Perhaps in compensation, two special weekends were provided by Hugh Thomas Munro (by now Sir Hugh, his father having passed away in June 1913), the 4th Baronet of Lindertis (1856–1919) and SMC member. Munro is an iconic figure for hillwalkers, having produced his famous list of Scottish mountains of over 3,000ft. He hosted the first meet, starting on 22 January 1915, at Lindertis, his home near Kirriemuir in Angus. The SMC President, William Inglis Clark, penned a report, and five others were also present, including Ling and James Alexander Parker (1864–1946), a civil engineer from Glasgow who had moved to Aberdeen while directing the construction of the city's main railway station and then lived in the city for the rest of his life.

Parker—who was to become the third known Munroist with an ascent of Ben Hope on 19 July 1927—had opened up the nearby area of Glen Clova with a couple of routes in 1910, including Backdoor Gully (200m, II). It was of this enjoyable meet that Ling remarked 'We are like pigs in clover', suggesting the article name with its title a pun on one of the main Angus glens. [9] Three main glens penetrate the southern side of the area to the south–east of Cairngorms, namely Glen Prosen, Glen Clova and Glen Esk. Glen Clova, arguably the most popular of the three, is formed from two subsidiary upper glens: Glen Doll and the valley of the Upper South Esk.

Also present on the Saturday of that January meet was Munro's son, Thomas Torquil Alphonso Munro, then aged 14. With his father, he walked to Driesh by the steep slopes of The Scorrie.

The second weekend, 28–31 May 1915, was also held at Lindertis. SMC members present included William Inglis Clark, who remained in his presidential post throughout the war years, Ling, Sang, James Craig, William A Galbraith, JN Marshall, Raeburn, Walter Reid and James Rennie.

For someone such as Raeburn, time and energy were extremely limited, and it is telling that throughout the war years he recorded only two routes, both during the second of Munro's weekends. These were achieved with Galbraith, a solicitor from Edinburgh, and Reid, a chartered accountant from Aberdeen, when they visited Corrie Fee in Glen Doll, climbing *B Gully Buttress* (Moderate) and *B Gully* (200m, II). The article describing the gathering was written by Reid. [10]

Munro proved to be a generous host, providing motor transport each day, the first time to Glen Doll, the second to Glen Isla, some distance further west. Other than the easy climbing done by Raeburn's party, hill-walking and relaxing lower–level walks were the order of their stay, with the constant background of the war never far from minds.

Sir Hugh Munro must have had a reasonably comfortable bank balance, as the car in which he drove his fellow club members was a Delaunay–Belleville, built by a French luxury automobile company at Saint–Denis, north of Paris, at the beginning of the century, and regarded as being among the most prestigious of cars. As a rough guide, in 1913 Delaunay–Belleville cars retailed in Europe for about £800–£900, a figure well beyond the means of all but the wealthiest.

❋❋❋

In 1915, the only other Scottish routes recorded were on Skye. In April, Everard Wilfred Steeple and Guy Barlow were back in the Cuillin, continuing explorations that had begun before the war. As Stuart Pedlar notes in his research into climbing on Skye: *'After the Abraham brothers it was Barlow's partnership with EW Steeple that made the greatest impact on the climbing history of the Cuillin.'* [11]

At Easter 1915, which fell in the first week of April, Steeple and Barlow made a very wintry ascent of *The Chasm* (120m, III) on the Coruisk face of Sgurr nan Eag. This gully had given its name to the mountain, *peak of the notch*, and had been remarked on by James Rennie in 1896. The gully is popular, with remarkable rock scenery, and there is a good winter photograph in the current SMC climbers' guide to Skye. The pair were so pleased with the climb that they returned in August 1919 to make the first summer ascent, at a grade of Very Difficult. On this occasion they were accompanied by an old friend, Arnold Henry (Harry) Doughty (1882–1971). Doughty had enlisted in the Royal Army Medical Corps in 1914, was captured and imprisoned by the Germans in 1918, before being demobilised in 1919.

Two other climbs were recorded on Skye in 1915. On 14 September, *Wallwork's Route* (50m Very Difficult) was completed on Upper Cioch Buttress by William Wallwork (1887–1919), Harry M Kelly and John Wilding. For many years this was markedly under–graded at Difficult, causing considerable anguish to many a roped party. It has one belay on an edge notable for its exposure, and overall provides a superb climb on excellent rock. Wallwork's party were all members of the Fell and Rock Climbing Club (FRCC), the premier Lake District club, and they climbed the line while attempting to find *Archer Thomson's Route* of 1911.

The other climb was *Central Buttress* (600m Difficult) on Clach Glas, by Ling and Edward Backhouse, on 5 July. Backhouse (1876–1922), a bank manager, joined the Alpine Club in 1904 and the SMC in 1907. He has the melancholy distinction of being the first SMC member to die in the mountains, when he and his guide were killed on the Leiterspitz near Zermatt in September 1922.

By 1915, the grim facts about the war were becoming known to the British population; all was not done and dusted by Christmas 1914 as some had thought. Many climbers, particularly those too old to enlist and who could have continued climbing to some extent, found themselves caught up in the mood which now enveloped the country and either stayed at home or worked even harder to support the war effort. There were a few exceptions, and Ling seems to have continued walking and climbing whenever he found partners, usually hillwalking in the Scottish Highlands or rock climbing in the Lake District.

No more routes would be achieved until 1918, when on 26 July a strong quartet arrived on Skye and were responsible for recording three routes on the Cuillin in various combinations. The party included David Randall Pye (1886–1960), an engineer who specialised in the development of the internal combustion engine. During World War II he became research director for the RAF, and was knighted in 1952.

Leslie Garnet Shadbolt (1883–1973), a manufacturer first of cement and later of brushes, had been born in Uxbridge. An Alpine Club member, he joined the SMC in 1911, proposed by Ling and John Bell. Serving in the Royal Navy, he was wounded at Gallipoli. The remaining pair were Ruth and George Mallory, who met the others at Inverness. Of the four, only Shadbolt had been on Skye before. Pye and George Mallory had met at Cambridge, and Pye was to write a seven–chapter memoir of Mallory, published in 1927 and reprinted in 2002. [12]

An account of their climbing can be found in Peter and Leni Gillman's own biography of Mallory, *The Wildest Dream*. [13] On Sunday 28 July, the quartet went to the north face of Sgùrr a' Mhadaidh where they spotted an unclimbed line. As the account in the Sligachan climbers' book details, *'This climb is of moderate difficulty but very interesting throughout, steep and exposed.'* The description finishes by mentioning that there were not many belays.

Pye and Mallory's Route (225m Very Difficult) is described in the current guide as having intriguing route–finding. [14] Conditions were perfect, although throughout their stay on Skye, the midge was rampant. The Mallorys lodged in the Glen Brittle post office for two nights, after which Geoffrey Bartrum (1881–1960), a merchant, and Alastair McLaren would arrive to replace them. McLaren however had been badly wounded at Arras in 1917, where his left ankle was shattered; though he kept his foot, his left leg became stiff and his serious climbing days were over.

Pye penned a long and detailed article for the SMC Journal (SMCJ), describing their climbing over the fortnight–long holiday. [15] The Mallorys left Skye on 1 August, but not before George Mallory and Shadbolt climbed a route of some difficulty on the Cioch Upper Buttress. This was on Monday, 30 July. Pye sunbathed on the Cioch, a spectator while Mallory led Shadbolt on what they thought was a new route. At the finish they came across a cairn, but of this line there was no mention in the Sligachan climbers' book. In 1911, the first ascent party on Archer Thomson's Route on this same buttress also found a cairn at the finish, which they subsequently learned had been left by a surveying party. Perhaps the cairn found by Mallory and Shadbolt was also from such a source.

The line itself is marked on a photograph of the buttress in Pye's SMCJ article, and would seem to lie to the left of Archer Thomson's Route. This can be a difficult buttress to portray in a guidebook – but, when comparing the photograph with the 1996 SMC Rock and Ice Guide by JW Simpson, Pedlar makes an intriguing suggestion.

> Mallory and Shadbolt probably climbed the first pitch of Fidelity (Crocket and Jenkins, June 1970) then traversed left across, and possibly up, part of Walsh and Mackay's Trophy Crack (1956) to join the second, and final, pitch of Haworth and Hughes magnificent classic route Integrity. (1949) As these three climbs are graded E3, E1, and Mild VS respectively, one can only wonder at the sheer technical brilliance of Mallory as a leader. [16]

In fact *Fidelity, Trophy Crack* and *Integrity* are graded in the current guide as VS, E1, and VS respectively, with possible pitches at 4c, 4b, 4c, but even so, and assuming this suggestion is correct, it was indeed a superb lead in nails by Mallory. Pye had plenty of time to watch the ascent and there are several prominent rock features as landmarks, so the photograph, although not taken along the same line of view, shows the face clearly and in good light. Mallory took the opportunity to sneak a look at a prominent curving crack which cut through the buttress behind the Cioch, and considered it to be very hard. As will be seen shortly, this crack would be climbed the following week, but not by Mallory.

On Tuesday 31 July, the huge Western Buttress of the Sròn na Ciche face was attempted, taking at first a steep crack leading to slabs. George Mallory kept running into difficulties on water–worn slabby rock where holds were either absent or sloped the wrong way. Attempts at three different places were all thwarted, and eventually the trio (Ruth Mallory being absent) had to start up the gully for some 75ft or so until they could break out right to continue straight up the face. The crux was probably a section where the leader was 60ft out, on the minimum of holds, and not visible to the second man. Six hours of climbing eventually saw them on top, but behind schedule for their meeting with their friends at Sligachan.

The route was *Mallory's Slab and Groove* (200m Very Difficult). In common with other areas in Scotland described in this book, the grade is from the current relevant guidebook. From the finish of the route, another 300ft of climbing is required to gain the ridge. After descending, the party quickly moved on up the glen, stopping en route for a bathe in the Red Burn, along with a mention of the midges –

> It was scarcely possible to cope with these fiends for five seconds at a time; the only chance was to remain almost continuously under water, or run about at full speed; both of them methods of self–protection of limited usefulness.[17]

The next day, Bartrum, Pye and Shadbolt made for Waterpipe Gully, the Mallorys having left for home. Despite six days without rain, soakings in the gully were unavoidable, as was loose rock. After their ascent, Pye strongly disagreed with the comments on this route in Ashley Abraham's book *Rock–climbing in Skye,* finding that the gully called for '*skill and judgment out of all proportion greater than is required for [as an example] … the direct climb up the Cioch from the Coire.'*[18] [Cioch Direct]. Pye found that the amount of loose rock, often climbed while being distracted by lashings of cold water, added a need for extreme care which contrasted with the glossy praise given to the route by Abraham.

It was on 6 August, however, that Pye and Shadbolt had their day of triumph. They climbed Cioch Direct in an hour and a quarter, avoiding the sensational swing at the crux by climbing the right–hand crack direct, a possibly easier variation. The route then led them, after a scramble, to the great curving crack which Mallory had looked at the previous week, now known as the Crack of Doom. They knew from the earlier examination, and from its appearance now, that the top section was probably going to be the hard part, and so it turned out to be. Bartrum, meanwhile, had walked up and was waving to them from the top of the mountain, prompting a comment by Pye – '*We decided to risk his wrath. After all, he could ask for few better places than the top of Sròn na Ciche for a midday snooze…'*

Pye set off, finding a chockstone halfway up the crack. He saw a possible stance just above this, and continuing found that although there was no belay, the stance was comfortable. He brought up Shadbolt to belay on what he referred to as *'the first chockstone'*. Above, the right wall was slimy and holdless, with the way up calling for a back against the right wall and the use of small holds on the left. (Pye used left and right when looking up the face. Older descriptions often used 'true' left and right, which were based on water–flow, looking downstream.)

> The left wall is dry, and it is possible to find just sufficient hold on it to raise oneself steadily and positively by the feet, with no wriggling. It will be interesting to learn how the pitch strikes other parties, and oneself on a second acquaintance. My present impression on looking back is that holds for hands and feet are excessively small, but that if they are used to the best advantage the place is not really very difficult; on the other hand, a failure to make the best use of what holds there are, and any resort to wriggling tactics might leave one very soon exhausted, and with little chance of winning through. [19]

This description has proved accurate for those who followed and either missed the holds on the left or lost their nerve and resorted to trying to wriggle their way up. *Crack of Doom* (80m Hard Severe 4b) is described in the current guide as being an *'...insecure thrutch, memorable for its polish'*. Perhaps nailed boots, as used by Pye, would have found holds that modern footwear could not use, or possibly the chimney crack has now been polished by countless wriggling pilgrims. The crack had been attempted on 5 May 1909, by HB Buckle, Barlow and AH Doughty, and though unsuccessful they had named it Hanging Gully. A *Direct Finish* (60m Hard Severe) was added on 27 June 1921, by AS Pigott and J Wilding.

One small, but important improvement in climbing technology had appeared by that time, namely the introduction of Tricouni nails in boots.[20] The Tricouni nail was invented in 1912 by a jeweller from Geneva, Félix–Valentin Genecand, nicknamed 'Tricouni' (1878–1957). An experienced Alpinist and a member of the Swiss Alpine Club, he has several mountains named after him, for instance Mount Genecand in Antarctica.

As described in an SMC note, the suggested layout involved 20 nails per boot: six in the heel, eleven round the edge and three in the middle. This arrangement was designed to avoid side–slips and to provide a hold on narrow ledges and projections. The hardened steel made the nails durable; even with wear they retained a sharp edge and the position at the edge of the sole provided a firmer stance. It is possible that Pye was using a set of these boots during this trip. (There is a suggestion elsewhere, however, that they made glissading harder, as they more readily bit into hard snow.)

Boots have been transformed from those used a century ago, and on the Skye Cuillin even the famous guide John Mackenzie almost came to grief through inadequate footwear. The following account was written by William Wickham King, who had joined the SMC in 1891. On Skye, sometime before May 1890, King made an ascent of Clach Glas and Blà Bheinn with Norman Collie and Mackenzie.

> On the slabs leading to Clach Glas we were not roped. J. Mackenzie was the last man. His unsuitable shepherd's boots caused him to slip, and then he slid with face to rock for some distance. He arrested his descent himself. He needed my aid to reach a safe resting place, for he was much shaken. The drink in the rucksack on his back was intact. After a good rest we ascended both peaks, with Mackenzie roped up, till we reached the valley. Collie soon after gave him proper climbing boots. [21]

It was not recorded whether the bottle contained wine or, more likely, the local, full–bodied malt whisky Talisker, distilled at Carbost. As to the date, although King thought this was in 1891, Pedlar notes that another reference to Mackenzie records him wearing new boots in May 1890. [22]

The day after Crack of Doom was climbed, an easy new route was found on the crag visible from Sligachan, Nead na h–Iolaire (Eagle's Nest). *Left Rib* (60m Very Difficult) was climbed by E Robertson Lamb and a Welsh climber, M Gelding Bradley, on 7 August 1918. Lamb (1877–1927), a Liverpool climber and Alpinist, was a timber merchant who joined the SMC in 1922. He was also a member of the Wayfarers' Club (their hut in Langdale is named after him), the Climbers' Club, the Rucksack Club and possibly the Alpine Club.

❄❄❄

Fighting on the western front ceased on 11 November 1918, but there would be no immediate rush of climbers hungry for release in the mountains: the country and its population was exhausted. Many in the armed forces faced delays in being demobilised, after which there were more pressing problems to be addressed at home. Virtually every city, town and village in Scotland had seen men go off to war, and of course women worked in the ancillary services such as nursing and transport. Many men did not return. The major Scottish clubs lost members, as described at the start of this chapter. No official meets were arranged by the Cairngorm Club during the war, though some members did manage a few outings.

Two familiar names in Scottish mountaineering died in relation to the war. Charles Inglis Clark was killed by a sniper in what is now Iraq, then part of Mesopotamia, on 6 March 1918. He was a captain in the Army Service Corps, maintaining transport facilities, and was buried in Baghdad (North Gate) War Cemetery, an area which his parents visited in 1924 during a touring holiday. After the death of her husband in 1932, Jane Inglis Clark, Charles's mother, wrote a book commemorating their family life and including anecdotes from this holiday. [23] Between Palmyra and Baghdad, she wrote–

...a fully–armed, lusty young Arab, pistols in belt, suddenly sprang with a flash of white teeth on to our footboard. Our Syrian chauffeur, hair bristling, but with admirable presence of mind, aimed the car at a large boulder, which it took with so violent a shudder that our assailant was shaken off. Down went the accelerator, pressed home with the strength of a strong and terror–stricken man.

Elsewhere in the same part of the world, Thomas Edward Goodeve, a major in the Royal Engineers and serving in Palestine, was killed on 26 January 1919 somewhere north of Baghdad. A railway locomotive engineer in both his professional and military careers, there was bitter irony in his being accidentally run over by a locomotive after hostilities had ended. He was buried in the Damascus Commonwealth War Cemetery, Syria. Both would no doubt have continued to be prominent and valuable mountaineers in Scotland after the war. That they had shared a Tower Ridge epic on Ben Nevis and died in the same geographical area may be a suggestion of incipient synchronicity.

In March 1919 Sir Hugh Munro died aged 63 in Tarascon, France, where with his sister and two daughters he had been working at the canteen for French soldiers which he had set up and paid for personally. Munro contracted a chill which ended with pneumonia, his health having already been impacted in 1916 by malarial fever contracted in Malta where he had been working for the Red Cross.

His remains were returned to Scotland, and he was buried alongside his wife at Lindertis. Munro may have been one of the many victims of the influenza pandemic of 1918–1920 which killed between 50 million and 100 million people worldwide. It was probably the worst ever natural disaster for humankind, striking quickly with an unusually high mortality rate. In Britain, more than 250,000 died; in France, 400,000.

❋ ❋ ❋

In late August 1919, a fine route was made on the Lower Cioch Buttress on Skye. *Cioch West* (215m Severe) was climbed by Cecil Frederick Holland (1886–1986), Herbert Reginald Culling Carr (1896–1986) and Dorothea Richards, *née* Pilley, (1894–1986). All three were good mountaineers. Holland had survived the war with a Military Cross and Bar and a badly wounded arm; he produced the first Scafell rock guide in 1924 and went on to become President of the FRCC from 1937–1939. Carr, brother–in–law of Gelding Bradley, edited a new edition of the Climbers' Club guide to Snowdon and Beddgelert in 1926. After reviving the Oxford University Mountaineering Club, he was invited to do the same for the Climbers' Club, which resulted in their first hut, at Helyg at Ogwyn in Snowdonia. Carr was a member of the SMC from 1921–1924. In 1925, following an accident in Cwm Glas when his companion was killed, he lay severely injured in the open for two days and nights before being found by chance by a shepherd.

Dorothea Pilley had joined the FRCC in 1918 and the Ladies' Alpine Club in 1920. A founder member of the Pinnacle Club, she was also an expert on all things Chinese. She married the Cambridge professor Ivor Richards in 1926, and both were on an ascent of the North Ridge of the Dent Blanche in July 1928. Pilley kept a diary, which polished her writing and probably led to her classic book *Climbing Days*, published in 1935. [24]

In August 1919, during their month–long holiday on Skye, Holland, Carr and Pilley climbed Cioch Direct and, just as Pye and Shadbolt had done the previous summer, avoided the Abraham cracks at the crux by a deviation to the right. This, they admitted, lowered the climb's standard appreciably, and marks seen on the rocks showed that other climbers had made a similar variation. Despite this, it was still a very good climb.

The next afternoon, following a proposal by Holland, they returned to the Lower Cioch Buttress, taking an easy chimney between Cioch Direct and Cioch Gully. Above lay a 75ft hard pitch followed by a further 100ft. A slab on the right then led to a short vertical crack, above which was a comfortable ledge below the great wall forming a seemingly impossible barrier, except where cut by the chimneys used on Cioch Direct. The party walked right some distance, then climbed up rock which had, though steep, plenty of holds. The leader, Holland, was tied on to 120ft of Alpine line as he set out from a good belay. A pinnacle at the top of an easy chimney allowed him to run the line over this as a runner as he set out on an exposed leftwards traverse. One or two places gave him pause for thought, before he reappeared 30ft higher and could bring up first Carr, then Pilley.

The ascent was described by Carr in a 1920 RCJ article. Easier rock then led to the terrace running below the Cioch and, as Carr remarked– '...*at the top of the difficult part of our route, we built a cairn and congratulated our leader. He decided to call it the West Face Climb.*'

Pilley's book reveals that there was, however, still a final pitch to climb: '*One day we were back in the Cioch Gully again, trying the top pitch, which we had cut on our first visit as seeming distinctly severe, though our only literature made nothing of it.*' [25] Here Holland tried to pull himself up on greasy holds, with the floor of the pitch, comprising large angular scree, 20ft or so below. His arms began to lose their strength and from above his surprisingly calm and impersonal voice remarked: '*I'll be off in a minute.*' Falling off with grace and little injury seemed to have been a personal skill of Holland, and so it was on this occasion. He managed to turn and perform a sitting glissade on the big slab, landing on the scree unhurt, with the laughter of his companions no doubt masking their relief.

❄❄❄

Harold Raeburn had been conspicuous by his absence due to his factory work, though he attended the SMC 1918–1919 meet at Tyndrum, where on arrival on New Year's Day – and having failed to persuade anyone in the hotel to accompany him – he went out alone on skis and gained the 2200ft summit of Beinn Bheag, just north–west of Tyndrum. This was, as the meet report by George Sang noted– '...*at the cost of who can say what energy and great perseverance.*' [26]

On 2 January 1919, a better day, Raeburn went out with the Reverend Ronald Burn and climbed North Rib on the north–east face of Ben Lui in poor snow conditions. The Reverend Aubrey Ronald Graham Burn (1887–1972) was principally a hillwalker, completing the Munros with Beinn a' Chroin, on 20 July 1923. He was, as Bob Aitken notes in his database of early SMC members–

> '...the first to do the tops, and possibly the first to do the Munros properly, though his navigation was so ludicrously erratic that a degree of scepticism about that may be justified.' [27]

Burn has a mention in the classic book by JHB Bell, '*A Progress in Mountaineering*', when, in June 1923, both were present on an SMC Meet based at Sligachan. Burn, he noted, was not an expert on rocks, and had to make an ascent of that nemesis for many hillwalkers, the Inaccessible Pinnacle. In a party of four, led by Bell, Burn was persuaded that in order to fully complete his Munros, he had to stand on the very topmost block, a very exposed position and one most avoid. This he did fairly, so adding to his Munros in good style. [28]

Raeburn was not present at the 1919 SMC Easter Meet at Braemar, a successful gathering at least in terms of weather and social ambience, nor was he on Skye in June when the weather was of the gale and rain variety. It may have been, of course, that Raeburn was still working at the aeroplane factory on Clydeside, as the production of armaments did not cease immediately following the Armistice. He was, however, about to bring to fruition two of his best routes, one in the Alps, one in Scotland. At the same time he would have been working hard on the rewriting of his book, the manuscript of which had been lost during the upheaval of the war.

The Alpine route was a solo traverse of the Meije, a long, high ridge in the Massif des Écrins, just south–west of the Mont Blanc massif. It is a major route with complex sections of rock and ice in extremely exposed positions, including numerous towers demanding technical descents as well as solid climbing. A roped party would normally take about ten hours, with the necessity for strong rock climbing abilities.

Raeburn's book includes a section on guideless climbing, in which he blames the early members of the AC for instigating their ban on climbing without a professional guide. It may well have been that it was not an outright ban, but there was certainly much negativity and outright prejudice emanating from some of the more crusty AC members at the time.

> I cannot help thinking that those members of the Alpine Club responsible for this attitude, however high and admirable might have been their motives, displayed a great lack both of wisdom and foresight. [29]

Raeburn felt that guideless climbing was an inevitable development of the sport, and that by banning or ignoring it they merely took up the proverbially futile and foolish attitude of Mrs Partington and her mop.

Dame Partington was an elderly Sidmouth lady who, if the story is true, was seen during the great storm of November 1824 at the door of her house trying in vain to keep out the waters of the Atlantic Ocean with a mop. It was probably first recounted by the cleric and author Sydney Smith. [30]

There is also a reference to the Meije in the same section of Raeburn's book, where he provides evidence for his argument.

> It was perhaps the successful ascent, only the fourth, of that extremely difficult mountain, La Meije in Dauphiné, in 1879, by the Messrs. Pilkington and Mr. F. Gardiner, which most largely contributed to the breaking down of the British prejudice against guideless climbing. Messrs. Pilkington and Hulton also ascended the Disgrazia "By a new Route and without Guides" a few years later.

The Meije traverse was evidently a prized route. That early SMC tiger, John Gibson, had made the first full west–east traverse in 1891 with Ulrich Almer and Fritz Boss, and within the SMC, King, Rennie and Douglas had climbed it in 1899. Douglas was back again in 1906, with an English friend and two guides, while in 1907 Raeburn and Ling made an attempt but were caught by a blizzard and had to retreat. [In 1910, Raeburn, climbing with Ling, made a first ascent of the now classic Spigolo Inglese on the North Face of the Disgrazia.]

For Raeburn, the solo ascent may in part have been a vindication of guideless climbing – but aged 54 and frustrated in his attempts to join the armed forces, it could also have been a defiant gesture. His friend Ling was climbing in the Alps that season, but Raeburn does not seem to have joined him. Whatever the reasons—and they may have been none of the above—it was a superb demonstration, if one was needed, that Raeburn was still very much a leading mountaineer. As for his confidence and boldness, Raeburn had also made a solo descent of Crowberry Ridge Direct. [31]

George Sutcliffe Bower (1891–1953) was a Yorkshire–born engineer with a doctorate from London. His profession seeped into his climbing, with an interest in ropes, belaying and protection. Early climbing on gritstone and war work with Vickers at Barrow–in–Furness led to much Lake

District exploration, with eight routes on Dow Crag alone. He wrote the FRCC guide to Dow Crag, while his first ascent of Innominate Crack on Kern Knotts on Great Gable at VS 4b has become a classic.

In a brief note in the FRCC Journal, Bower discussed ropes and belaying, suggesting that the use of light Alpine line on some routes could allow for a belay to be found where a full–sized rope would not fit. [32] Additionally, he suggested that an Alpine line should be adequate for protecting a second. He described the correct method for belaying the leader, as it did not seem to be universally known. The second should use his end of the rope to belay to the rocks, then pass the rope over his shoulder. With both hands, the second can then control the rope in a leader fall, utilising friction to absorb the shock gradually, so that only when all slack has been taken up would the rock belay take the strain.

In a holiday in July 1919 with John Bernard Meldrum (1885–1992), a route was climbed on the West Buttress of Beinn Eighe, the lower sandstone tier at Severe and the upper quartzite at Difficult. *West Buttress* (300m) was one of the early routes on this magnificent face. Other routes by Bower and Meldrum on this trip included second ascents of Mallory's Route on Sròn na Ciche, along with the Crack of Doom. On the latter climb, the leader was probably Bower, a climber who often pushed himself nervously into the lead but usually succeeded. In his notes, Bower indicates the leader's state of mind on the crux. The party left the second man to belay where the crucial crack bore to the right and steepened, leaving the leader to climb the severe section in one run out.

> After leaving the chockstone no real rest could be had, for the stance above was disappointing, and the moral strain of the situation unique. Facing towards the left, it was found necessary to wedge for a foot or two before the left foot could reach the first of the small holds on the left wall. Then a hurried pull up on the small holds above, a frantic grip of a wobbly damp chockstone at the top, a loving embrace of a real, hefty, chockstone on the left, and the deed was done, much to the leader's relief. [33]

Bower had prefaced his description of the Crack of Doom by stating it was, without doubt, the most difficult climb on their holiday, the sort of climb one vows never to revisit except in nightmares. And this from a gritstone–trained climber! As for Meldrum, another engineer, he died at the age of 107. A bachelor until the age of 90 (when marriage necessitated his first purchase of a house), he interested the media after having had a minor road accident at the age of 100.

❀❀❀

Raeburn's outstanding post–war Scottish climb was the first winter ascent of *Observatory Ridge* (420m IV,4) on Ben Nevis. Indeed, it is the personal opinion of the author that this was Raeburn's finest winter ascent in Scotland, closely followed by Green Gully. Raeburn had made the first summer ascent, solo, on 22 June 1901. Ben Nevis had been neglected due to the war, and it was with the pleasure of many that the SMC committee decided to hold the Easter 1920 meet of the club at Fort William. The attendance was slightly less than expected, leading to a comment in the subsequent report:

> It is, of course, natural that the decreasing locks and increasing girth of members should make it more and more difficult for them to summon up the necessary energy to put in an appearance at Meets...[34]

With several of Raeburn's finest routes, often due to his modesty the modern researcher has little information to go on, but in this instance his fellow SMC member Frank Goggs described the ascent in an article. Goggs recalled that the last time he had been on Ben Nevis was at the Easter Meet in 1914, when he had enjoyed an ascent with Harry Walker, not knowing that it would be the last time they would meet, as Walker was to be killed in the war. [35]

In 1920, Raeburn had spent Easter Saturday with the Ladies' Scottish Climbing Club, which was holding its own meet at Tyndrum. Cold weather had set in the previous weekend, with fresh snow from Friday to Sunday afternoon, by which time there was a six–inch covering down to the 1500ft level. On Sunday 4 April, Castle Ridge had two ascents, while Raeburn's Easy Route had its first winter ascent (by an unnamed party).

Although the report by Goggs did not say what Raeburn climbed that day, the odds are that he climbed it—and others named it—but there is no other evidence either way. The next day, Raeburn, Ling and Goggs went up Observatory Gully, then made the exposed traverse from east to west across the Great Tower of Tower Ridge, before gaining its summit by the Recess Route on the west face.

On the Tuesday, Raeburn took his motorcycle to Achintee in Glen Nevis, while Goggs and Wilfred Arthur Mounsey (1871–1950) walked from the Alexandra Hotel. Mounsey was a banker from Sunderland. The trio took the bridle path, then traversed between the halfway hut which existed at that time and the lochan to drop into the Allt a' Mhuilinn glen. As Goggs wrote–

> If you can keep close to Raeburn as he skims along and down the slope, now on turf, now on scree, and now on boulders, with the perfect balance of the born hill man, you are in good training.

Some new snow had fallen overnight, but not enough to cause anxiety to the climbers. Cloud was down on the upper 1000ft, and there was little wind. After some food by the burn, the cloud had risen somewhat and the new snow on the upper cliffs looked light, so Raeburn decided that most routes would go. All three had climbed North–East Buttress previously, Raeburn and Goggs were on the upper part of Tower Ridge the previous day, while only Raeburn had climbed Observatory Ridge, and then in summer. The first winter ascent of the ridge sounded tempting and was voted for unanimously.

At the foot of the ridge they roped up, Raeburn leading, Goggs in the middle and Mounsey, who was the heaviest, as third man. They were all on a 100ft rope, with Raeburn as leader being given a generous share of this. Putting Mounsey last was one of the few token offerings to safety, as techniques were still as they had been for decades, the only change being a slight increase in rope length. Belays would be either an ice axe driven in, if sufficient depth of snow could be found, or any spike of rock which they might be lucky enough to encounter. The climbers of the day were well aware of the lack of protection and the illusory strength of the rope—a heavy leader falling was the stuff of nightmares.

At 12.30pm they started to climb. The first 200ft went well, with broken rocks, room enough on stances and no strenuous moves. Then they arrived at a slabby section.

> Raeburn examined the slabs more carefully and suddenly exclaimed, "I have it." It was ten years or more since he had visited the spot under summer conditions, and to solve the problem so quickly was good evidence as to the reliability of his memory. You clamber up a slight recess on the right, then when you can get no further and feel uncomfortable, you see a narrow ledge on your left, but out of reach; however, with the aid of a niche for the toe of your boot, and not much more than a balancing hand on the smooth rock face above, you manage to get your knees on the ledge. Here I seemed most delicately poised, and felt that I might come off my perch if Raeburn merely shook the rope. The problem was to get my feet where my knees were, but there was absolutely no hold above.

Goggs somehow succeeded, and gained the stance above. Mounsey, meanwhile, had carefully observed Goggs, and climbed in fine style. On and upwards they continued, with never more than two slippery ledges visible when they looked down. Looking up, steep rocks were succeeded by steep snow slopes, disappearing into the mist.

As they realised that they were in for a long climb, a lunch stop was suggested, and Raeburn cast around looking for a suitable spot. A traverse right towards what looked like a suitable snow ledge brought hard, steep snow. Raeburn then climbed a short steep gully to regain the ridge; Goggs found getting into the gully difficult and accepted a shoulder from Mounsey to gain a narrow arête beside Raeburn. Mounsey required a direct pull on the rope, but Goggs could only use one arm for this (he was almost certainly holding on to the rock with his other) and there was much kicking and struggling before Mounsey's head appeared above the ridge.

It had been snowing on and off for some time and conditions were worsening, with rocks that were easy in summer becoming the reverse under snow. A direct ascent was obviously impossible, so Raeburn stepped down slightly to the left and found a curious spike of rock some 20 inches long, over which he ran the rope before disappearing round the edge. He soon returned, seeking another way. On their right, smooth rocky faces went directly down to an open snow gully which, although looking steep, hard and icy in places, seemed to lead to an edge at the top, perhaps a cornice blocking access to the plateau.

Raeburn was not worried by that possibility, and fixed his attention to the immediate problem. A band of snow traversed the smooth rock from the ridge to the snow gully; if it concealed a ledge, the route would go. He scraped the surface with the adze of his axe: no ledge, merely a depression holding some snow. Defeat was staring them in the face.

> Once again Raeburn turned to the left, saying, 'It's got to go." I stood at the rock spike with Mounsey a yard or two away, Raeburn disappeared round the corner, and for the next quarter of an hour we saw nothing of him, but heard and saw hard snow and ice hurtling down. The rope went out very slowly, but it went, and that was the chief thing.

When Goggs followed, he found a clamber over rounded and holdless rocks comparatively easy for the second with cleared snow, but a very unpleasant place for a leader. They could now take to the snow gully, broad and open. The snow was hard *névé*, and not enough of it. Often they could only get the ice axe in about six inches, while steps had to be cut in two small icefalls. The angle was steep, on average 45°, with an occasional increase to 60°.

> Raeburn ran out length after length of rope, only one man moved at a time, and rarely was our leader able to say he had his ice axe well in. Our conversation seemed to consist in the following repetition:– Goggs to Raeburn, "Last six feet." Raeburn to Goggs, "You must come: I have no hitch." Every now and then a *tourmente* would sweep round us, and our steps would be filled in, but on the whole the weather improved as we mounted and the clouds rose.

As they slowly gained height they could judge their progress by surrounding hills, with the cairn and ridge of Càrn Mòr Dearg seeming to become lower. The higher they rose, the less desirable a descent became.

> There was a strange, almost weird absence of life: we never disturbed a ptarmigan or a hare; no bird flew over us to see how we were progressing–not even the hum of an insect was heard–solitude reigned here supreme.

Luckily for the climbers there was little wind and the temperature was not low, so that Goggs thought none of the party was ever really chilled.

> The only thing I feared was cramp: the steps were perforce small, the angle steep, the ice axe could rarely be depended on to give a satisfying sense of security, the leader had to take his time, and occasionally we had to wait, not at the most convenient stances, but just where we happened to be at the moment: the strain on our leg muscles (after five war years) was therefore considerable. As under the conditions described, physical failure on the part of any of us would have been distinctly unpleasant.

They found the route remarkably scarce of any comfortable stopping places, while the angle never seemed to ease, but eventually Raeburn was able to assure his friends that the cornice would not be a problem and that victory was at hand. A short icefall was cut up and after another slope of hard snow Raeburn landed on snow–covered flat rocks and the other two followed.

> I brought Mounsey up the steep staircase to where I stood; he put the shaft of his axe in the hole which Raeburn's and mine had successively occupied, and then I started to join Raeburn. At the ice fall a few rocks jutted out on the right, and I remember the feeling of security and satisfaction there was in gripping a rough rock surface: it was literally the first rock which could be described as in any way useful we had seen for some hours.

The cornice above the party was easily overcome, and they landed on the summit plateau. The sun, which had been threatening to break through the scurrying clouds, bathed them in light just as they finished the climb. Goggs and Mounsey congratulated Raeburn heartily on his success—he had led throughout and done all the work. It was 6.15pm, some 5¾ hours from the start. At 8.30pm, just 12 hours after setting out, they were back at the Alexandra Hotel, announcing to Harry MacRobert that his guidebook to Ben Nevis required amendment.

Observatory Ridge is the hardest of the Ben Nevis ridges; although listed in the current guidebook as IV, 4, depending on conditions it can easily be considered a grade V by hard–pressed climbers. It is as near an Alpine a climb as can be found in Scotland, and was a superb addition to Raeburn's portfolio. In three months' time he would be 56, but had demonstrated that he remained the best mountaineer Scotland had thus far produced.

The reference to MacRobert's guidebook was due to the recent publication by the SMC of the update to William Inglis Clark's guide to the mountain, first published in the SMCJ of September 1902. The new guide of 1920 was edited by MacRobert and James Reid Young. The SMC had copies for sale in a local bookseller and stationer during the Easter

Meet, with rumours of a daily queue waiting to see a highly artistic poster advertising the *'New Guide–Book to Ben Nevis.'* Young died suddenly soon afterwards, his end possibly hastened by over–strenuous editing work. The obituary in the SMCJ, pertaining to his editing, mentions *'almost pagan thoroughness'*, and *'incessant labour'*. [36]

The SMC's general Climbing Guide had a slow start, mainly due to lack of funds, having been first mooted in 1894. To allow publication, it was included, section by section, in the SMCJ. The MacRobert update for Ben Nevis, itself delayed by the war, added little to the original guide. A total of 1000 copies were printed, with 600 sold in the first year.

In June 1920, the Cuillin ridge on Skye received its second one–day traverse, by Theodore Howard Somervell (1890–1975), a missionary doctor who had joined the SMC the previous December. A member of the AC, and its President 1962–1965 as well as President of the FRCC 1954–1956, Somervell was an experienced alpinist and was also on the 1922 Everest expedition. His comment on the Cuillin traverse, which took 10 hours and 49 minutes from end summit to end summit, was – *'...another time, with a water bottle and a pound of raisins, I think I could knock another hour off the time – but the chief disability was thirst and unappetising bannock!'*

Somervell was less fortunate with his attempts on new Scottish rocks during a holiday in June 1920 with his brother and others. He made an ascent of the Douglas Boulder, a climb on the West Face of Aonach Dubh in Glen Coe, and a route on Knight's Peak in Skye, but all three routes were ignored by guidebook authors, the first two certainly due to the amount of poor rock, a feature admitted by Somervell in his article in the FRCC Journal. [37]

❅ ❅ ❅

In the summer of 1920, Raeburn turned his gaze to higher ranges. He went to the Himalayas to explore the possibility of climbing Kangchenjunga, a project that had been on his mind for some time. He also had a second project, to see if he could approach Everest. With Colonel HW Tobin (an AC member), a sirdar, cook and 21 porters, Raeburn set out on 22 July to explore the south–east approach to Kangchenjunga. There had been earlier expeditions, including that of the Scottish chemist and scientist Dr Alexander Kellas in 1911, and Raeburn was able to clarify much of the early mapping.

During the return journey, while descending the gorge of the Rinpiram River, he suffered his only loss, though a severe one personally – *'My ice–axe, a faithful friend of a dozen years, doubly valued as a gift of the late Harry Walker, AC, was swept away by one of these flooded torrents.'* [38] This comment is of special interest to the SMC, as one of the three items passed from President to President is an ice axe which once belonged to Raeburn. The current axe is evidently the successor to that lost in the Himalayas, and with which Raeburn had presumably climbed such routes as Observatory Ridge.

A second expedition was made in September of the same year, with CG Crawford of the AC. On this occasion they were to approach Kangchenjunga from the south–west, and Raeburn reached an altitude of 20,000ft. His previous high–altitude experience had seen him at around 18,000ft on Elbrus in the Caucasus. Again, Raeburn improved the mapping knowledge of the area, and succeeded in finding and crossing the direct pass between the Yalung and Rathong valleys.

In many ways, 1920 stands out as the zenith of his mountaineering career: he recorded two outstanding ascents and undertook two good and useful expeditions. His book, delayed by the war and hindered by the loss of the manuscript, was finally published. Aged 56, he still had one more grand mountaineering expedition ahead – but it would not be a happy one.

References

1. Crocket, Ken. *Mountaineering in Scotland – The Early Years. (SMT, 2015.)*
2. Proceedings of the Club. *Whitsuntide 1914 Meet at Inchnadamph and Achiltibuie.* SMCJ 13, 75, October 1914, 166–174, p.169.
3. Ling's Diary, May 31, 1914, p. 57.
4. Murray, Sheila. *The Cairngorm Club 1887–1987.* (1987. The Cairngorm Club, Aberdeen), 82.
5. Coetzee, D. *"Measures of enthusiasm: new avenues in quantifying variations in voluntary enlistment in Scotland, August 1914–December 1915",* Local Population Studies, Spring 2005, Issue 74, pp. 16–35 <goo.gl/JxFGmP>. Accessed April 2015.
6. The Scottish Military Research Group. *Celebrating Scotland's disproportionate WW1 deaths.* <goo.gl/EPFq7x>. Accessed April 2015.
7. *Members' War Experiences.* SMCJ 13, 78, October 1915, 349–350.
8. Ling, W.N. *In Memorium – Harold Raeburn.* SMCJ 18, 103, April 1927, 26–31.
9. Clark, W Inglis. *The S.M.C. in Clover.* SMCJ 13, 77, June 1915, 268–272.
10. Reid, Walter A. *The S.M.C. in Clover Again.* SMCJ 13, 78, October 1915, 337–340.
11. Pedlar, Stuart. *Across Unmeasured Space – A History of Climbing in the Cuillin.* Unpublished MS 2010.
12. Pye, David. *George Leigh Mallory: A Memoir.* (2002, Orchid Press. ISBN 9789745240100.)
13. Gillman, Peter and Leni. *The Wildest Dream – The Biography of George Mallory.* (2000, Mountaineers Books. ISBN 978–0898867411.)
14. Lates, Mike. *Skye – The Cuillin. Rock and Ice Climbs.* (2011. SMC. ISBN 978–1–907233–13–5)

15. Pye, D.R. *A Fortnight in Skye.* SMCJ 15, 87, April 1919, 132–149.

16. Pedlar, Stuart. *Op.cit.*

17. Ibid. 17. p.140.

18. Abraham, Ashley Perry. *Rock–climbing in Skye.* (1908, Longmans, Green & Co. London.) p. 105.

19. Ibid. 17. p. 144.

20. Galbraith, W. *Nails Tricouni. In: Excursions and Notes.* SMCJ 13, 73, February 1914, 62–63.

21. King, W Wickham. *Some Early Climbs in the Cuillin.* SMCJ 26, 147, May 1956, p. 37–39.

22. Pedlar, Stuart. Op.cit. 18. Chapter 6, *Tormaid agus Mhic Choinnich, p.391.*

23. Clark, Jane Inglis. *Pictures and Memories.* (1938. The Moray Press, Edinburgh & London.)

24. Pilley, Dorothy. *Climbing Days.* (London: Bell, 1935).

25. Ibid. pp.102–103.

26. Proceedings of the Club. *1918–19 New Year Meet at Tyndrum.* SMCJ 15, 87, April 1919, 172–178, p.177.

27. Aitken, Robert. *Personal communication.*

28. Bell, J.H.B. *A Progress in Mountaineering.* (1950, Oliver & Boyd, Edinburgh & London.) pp.175-176.

29. Raeburn, Harold. *Mountaineering Art.* (1920, T. Fisher Unwin Ltd, London.) pp. 9–11.

30. Smith, Sydney. *Speech given in Taunton, October 1831.*

31. MacRobert, H. Addendum in: Garrick, J.A. *The North Wall Variation of The Crowberry Ridge.* SMCJ 17, 97, April 1924, pp.1–10.

32. G.S.B. (George Bower). *Ropes and Belays.* FRCCJ, 4, No.2, 1917–18, p.117.

33. Bower, George. In: Excursions and Notes. SMCJ 15, 89, April 1920, pp.284–286.

34. F.S.G. [Frank Sidney Goggs]. Proceedings of the Club. *Easter Meet at Fort William and Spean Bridge, 1920.* SMCJ 15, 90, October 1920, pp. 327–333.

35. Goggs, F.S. *Ben Nevis: Observatory Ridge.* SMCJ 15, 90, October 1920, pp. 310–318.

36. J.C.T. [JC Thomson]. *In Memoriam. James Reid Young.* SMCJ 15, 90, October 1920, pp.335–338.

37. Somervell, T. Howard. *Climbing in the North–West Highlands.* FRCCJ, 5, No.2, 1920, pp.111–119.

38. Raeburn, H. *The Southerly Walls of Kanchenjunga and the Rathong Pass.* Alpine Journal (Vol. 34, p.33.)

2

Watery Rocks & Emerald Turf (1920-1924)

WILLIE NAISMITH, one of the founders of the SMC, continued in his unofficial role as an expert on winter techniques with a short article on how to stop a fall on hard snow or ice. [1] He had, as he stated, undertaken many experiments on snow–and, finding that such advice was rarely found in mountaineering books–was happy as an old climber to pass on his findings.

Basically, his advice was that in the event of a fall, the climber should immediately turn face into the slope and dig their toes into the slope. Next, holding the shaft of the axe with one hand, the other hand should grasp the head of the axe by the adze and then, bringing it down to the level of his breast-bone, the pick should be pressed into the snow, at first gradually but ultimately with the weight of the body behind it.

The climber, he continued, will then be supported on a tripod formed by the axe-head and the toes of the boots, which will be ploughing parallel furrows down the slope. Holding the axe in this fashion would quickly bring the climber 'right end up', even if they had been sliding down sideways.

Even without an axe, Naismith wrote, by turning face-inwards one has the best chance of arresting a slide downhill on a moderate snow slope. He recalled proving that on hard-frozen snow at a measured 32°, it was just possible to stop with the toes alone; but when the angle steepened to 35°, the help of the axe was needed. One should bear in mind that this technique relied on nailed boots; with modern vibram-soled boots it might not work so well, while attempting it when wearing crampons could very easily lead to injuries.

❄❄❄

As in the years before World War I, Skye continued to draw climbers like a moth to a candle, albeit at a quieter pace than before. The energetic trio of

Everard Wilfred Steeple, Guy Barlow and Arnold Harry Doughty had last been on Skye in 1915; they returned in late August and early September 1920, and again in the summers of 1921 and 1922, climbing 11 new routes, the best of which include *Terrace Gully* (210m Severe) on the Coruisk Face of Sgùrr a' Ghreadaidh, *Parallel Cracks Route* (150m Very Difficult) on the Western Buttress of Sròn na Cìche and *Stack Buttress Direct* (150m Difficult) on North Crag, Upper Coire a' Ghrunnda. Fortunately for Scottish mountaineers, Steeple was a good communicator, writing up these routes in the SMCJ.[2]

Indeed, so detailed were the descriptions, accompanied by photographs, that the SMC invited Steeple and Barlow to write its first guide to Skye; this was eventually published in 1923, with diagrams by Steeple. The guide would in due course lead to the series known as the District Guides, pre-dating the separately published climbing guides which concentrated on rock and ice climbs and excluded sections on an area's history, geology, natural history and so on. The District Guides were published for many years in what was to become familiar red, stippled cloth covers.

In these three idyllic summer visits, Steeple and his friends camped in the corries and explored the lower crags of Coir' a' Ghrunnda. The routes they climbed were described, complete with a diagram, in the April 1923 issue of the SMCJ.[3] In the current guidebook to the Cuillin, five of the Coir' a' Ghrunnda routes have star gradings, with *Central Buttress* (210m Difficult) and *Stack Buttress Direct* (150m Difficult) being two-starred. For Scotland, it was an unusual burst of activity.

Steeple's friend Barlow was busy in another way on Skye, assessing the heights of the main Cuillin peaks. A physicist, he had been alerted some years before by Colin B Phillip that the height of Sgùrr Theàrlaich was still very uncertain, so in July 1921, on the last day of a holiday, he set about measuring the height difference between it and Sgùrr Alasdair. Using a surveying aneroid (with an accuracy of two feet) and an Abney-type level, Barlow determined a difference of 49ft, making Theàrlaich the second-highest peak in the Cuillin.

When he looked at an aneroid reading of Sgumain taken the same day, he found an Alasdair-Sgumain difference of 156ft. This was widely at odds with the OS, which gave a difference of 205ft. Norman Collie's work some years earlier had calculated a difference of 171ft.

Scientific curiosity aroused, Barlow returned in 1922, armed with a light mountain theodolite, two pocket levels, a new aneroid, a steel tape and other accessories. One of the latter was crucial, being a five-foot jointed rod of bamboo with a pocket level screwed on to the top. Using this equipment, Barlow hopped around Theàrlaich, Alasdair and Sgumain over three days, taking aneroid readings but also using a self-devised method based around the bamboo rod.

First, he carefully found the point (X) on Sgùrr Alasdair level with the summit of Sgùrr Theàrlaich, using visual sightings. He then needed to measure the vertical height from that point to the summit of Sgùrr Alasdair, which he did by placing the rod on point X and sighting with the level to some easily distinguishable point (Y) on the slope above. This would be repeated, using point Y for the next reading.

Moving up the slope in these steps, each with a rise of exactly five feet and each marked with chalk and recorded immediately, he estimated that in a rise of 100ft the error should only amount to a few inches. He repeated this procedure on the south-west ridge of Sgùrr Alasdair, starting at a point level with the summit of Sgùrr Sgumain. In summary, he confirmed his readings of the previous year: the Alasdair-Sgumain difference was 147ft, and not the 205ft of the OS.

Barlow now approached Sgùrr Sgumain as a target, and decided to use Sgùrr Dearg as a final reference point. The Inaccessible Pinnacle was a nuisance here, as it blocked the view to many of the southern peaks, but this was sidestepped by taking readings from a point on the ridge 60ft away from the cairn. He found a Sgumain-Dearg height difference of 28ft between his readings and those of the OS. Worse still, readings from Sgùrr Dearg to all the other peaks gave significant deviations from the OS heights.

These discrepancies were resolved by taking the simple assumption that Sgùrr Dearg was actually 3,206ft in height, and not the accepted OS value of 3,234ft. Sgùrr Alasdair therefore had to suffer a reduction in height of some 58ft, becoming 3,251ft. As Barlow pointed out, this was almost identical to the height of 3,255ft given in the original version of Munro's Tables, a height probably provided by Collie. Other heights worked out by Collie were close to Barlow's, vindicating, not that this was really needed, that pioneer's work.

As the peaks of Bidein Druim nan Ràmh and Sgùrr a' Mhadaidh were also wrongly located on the OS map, Barlow concluded –

'...the additional heights given in the Second Edition of the O.S. map are mostly defective, and there is a general tendency to return to the values given by Dr Collie, Mr Harker, and other members of the Club.' [4]

✳✳✳

Across on the eastern side of Scotland, as Greg Strange noted –

'...by 1929, no real technical advances had been made in the Cairngorms beyond that achieved by Raeburn before the war [...] Apart from the ascents of easy gullies like the Black Spout on Lochnagar, winter climbing had virtually ceased for the time being.' [5]

There was some modest exploratory activity in the east, however, notably by James Alexander Parker, who served as president of both the SMC

(1924–1926) and the Cairngorm Club (1928–1930). In addition to his professional engineering skills, he was also an enthusiastic builder of mountain view indicators or toposcopes, including those on the summits of Ben Nevis, Ben Macdui and Lochnagar. It is sad to relate however, knowing how much effort went into erecting these indicators, that most would be vandalised, leading to their eventual disappearance. Their appearance probably resulted from an attempt to moderate the numerous arguments heard on summits over the identification of distant peaks. With modern technology, there are now numerous apps for mobile phones which can do the same task, given a signal.

Parker was a lover of mountain architecture, so he and his companions Howard Drummond and Henry Kellas (younger brother of Alexander Kellas) were delighted when, after a long trek into the remote Garbh Choire on Beinn a' Bhùird in July 1921, they saw a spectacular rocky ridge. They explored its upper part as far as they could before retreating to the plateau, assisted by a top rope from Kellas. Parker returned the following June with Henry Alexander. On prospecting the ridge, they thought it looked very difficult, but this did not prevent Parker from naming it. As seen from the corrie floor, the ridge showed two peaks of similar height – and that part of the hill was called Cnap a' Chléirich, meaning cleric's stone or hillock. Parker therefore gave it the name of Mitre Ridge, after a bishop's ceremonial hat.

On this trip Parker and Alexander had not brought a rope, but in an article describing the geography and the buttress Parker described a possible route. He calculated the height (using an aneroid) as being 600ft, and wrote that it was made of dark weathered granite. The east face consisted of great unclimbable slabs, while the west face *'...is just a great and almost vertical precipice, down which a stone thrown from the highest point falls five seconds before touching bottom.'* [6]

While not wishing to deflate Parker's obvious delight at this discovery, the stone would have travelled some 400ft (122m) vertically in five seconds, but the current guidebook gives most routes on the crag lengths of from about 200m to 250m. Leaving aside questions of height and length, it would be another 11 years before Parker's Mitre Ridge would be climbed.

Henry Alexander (1875-1940), later Sir Henry, was born in Aberdeen to a family which for many years was prominent in the public life of the city. In 1914, he succeeded his father as editor of the *Aberdeen Free Press*, was Lord Provost (1932-1935), and was heavily involved in a long list of organisations. He was chairman of the local town planning committee which prepared a scheme enfolding some 96 square miles or 25,000 hectares and which, on its approval in 1933, was regarded both at home and internationally as a major pioneering study in town planning.

A lover of the Scottish hills, Alexander's major contribution was the *SMC Guide to the Cairngorms* in 1928. As William Garden wrote in his obituary note–

> This book contains a most exhaustive and minutely accurate mass of information with regard to these important mountains, and has so far been one of the best-sellers of all the Club guide books yet issued. [7]

Parker and Alexander were evidently under the spell of their Mitre Ridge discovery, as they were back there again on 20 July 1924, this time carrying ice axes. They found a huge area of snow in the north-west corner of the corrie and to the right of the easternmost tongue of snow they saw two pinnacles. They immediately set these as targets, and started by climbing the main snow patch and crossing a bergschrund at the top of this. After a failed attempt on the lower pinnacle, they continued up an easy gully and thus made the first known route in the Garbh Choire, *Pinnacle Gully* (150m Easy). The buttress on its left then became named as Pinnacle Buttress. [8]

Tentative explorations continued in 1925, when Alexander (Sandy) Harrison (1889-1988) and Louis St Clair Bartholomew (1897-1952), both members of the SMC, walked in to Coire Bhrochain of Braeriach. Harrison was an SMC member for a record 71 years, serving as President from 1945-1948. An experienced alpinist, he was an early exponent of guideless climbing and a sometime partner of Frank Smythe. He must have lived a charmed life, as in World War I he was a Major in the Royal Scots attached to the Machine Gun Corps (the infamous 'Suicide Corps'), and was one of its few officers to survive.

Also, on 22 May 1915, at the last minute he was not obliged to travel on a southbound troop train carrying half of the 7th (Leith) Battalion, the Royal Scots. This was involved in Britain's worst railway accident when it collided head-on with a halted local train at Quintinshill, just north of Gretna and a Glasgow express then ploughed into the wreckage. Some 216 soldiers were killed in the collisions and ensuing fire.

Many will know the maps published by the Bartholomew family, of whom St Clair, as he was known, was a member. His climbing record was a modest one, and his life was probably cut short by an illness contracted while working in Uganda in 1952. Harrison and Bartholomew, both from Edinburgh, made the first ascent of the West Buttress of Coire Bhrochain by *Pioneers' Recess Route* (200m Moderate), more often climbed as a Grade III in winter.

The first real signs of a blossoming in Cairngorms climbing came courtesy of a 20-year-old engineering student at Aberdeen University. Godfrey Roy Symmers had already found an interest in the hills and was introduced to climbing by Parker and Bill Malcolm, who also encouraged him to join the Cairngorm Club. [9]

Symmers began his personal siege of Lochnagar in August 1926, when with F King he made the first snow-free ascent of the Left Hand Branch of the Black Spout, employing a threaded rope and combined tactics at the huge chockstone (or chokestone, as Cairngorm climbers tend to call such obstacles). Four years later, Nesta Bruce discovered a through-route here, but the line which was on the mind of Symmers and others was Raeburn's Gully, first climbed by Raeburn's party in November 1898 and still awaiting a second ascent. Symmers attempted this in July 1927, but failed at the great overhanging chockstone which Raeburn had overcome by using an ice axe for a crucial hold–see Volume One for more on this.

Symmers returned for another attempt in August with J Silver, but was tempted instead to climb a 60° crack which sprang up from the foot of the gully. This gave Symmers' first virgin route on Lochnagar: *Pinnacle Gully 1* (200m Moderate), and as with most of the early routes here it is best climbed in winter conditions. In September 1927, Symmers climbed Black Spout Buttress (250m Difficult) with Bill Ewen, being unaware of the 1908 ascent by Raeburn. It is one of the better early summer routes.

Symmers' attempts were attracting interest from other climbers, with Raeburn's Gully becoming the route to do. Finally, in August 1929, accompanied by Bruce, a prolonged dry spell helped bring a successful second ascent of Raeburn's Gully, with the chockstone being overcome using a threaded sling as a foothold. The gully received a third ascent a month later, but the crux pitch, a twin cave with the huge chockstone as a finish, was obliterated by a rockfall in 1940. The route is currently a Hard Severe.

Nesta Bruce had so far limited her climbing to the granite tors of Clachnaben and Ben Rinnes, but on Lochnagar she bloomed in partnership with Symmers. She led the 30ft cave pitch on the second ascent of West Gully in very wet conditions, and was instrumental in making the first ascent of Central Buttress in August 1928. In 1932, she led the first ascent of *Shallow Gully* (300m Very Difficult) with HA Macrae, where loose rock had earlier defeated her and Symmers.

Symmers made other ascents on Lochnagar, with several partners, but despite there being plenty of solid, cleaner buttresses, and with no fewer than five of the major gullies still unclimbed, he seems to have persisted in tackling the wet, loose and vegetatious routes. By 1928, he had repeated all the summer lines, with the exception of Tough-Brown Route. His efforts, with various partners, helped to raise the awareness that in Lochnagar there was a vast and virtually untapped source of routes.

❈❈❈

As mentioned in the previous chapter, Harold Raeburn had made the first winter ascent of Observatory Ridge on Ben Nevis in April 1920–an outstanding feat, with Raeburn leading the entire route. That same year he made two reconnaissance expeditions to the Himalayas, reaching 20,000ft. These exploits could hardly be missed by the organisers of the next British Himalayan assault, the Everest Reconnaissance Expedition of 1921, and Raeburn was chosen as the climbing leader. The overall leader was Lieu-tenant-Colonel Charles K Howard-Bury, DSO; George Mallory and Guy Bullock were also selected, though neither had any Himalayan experience.

A valuable member was Alexander Mitchell Kellas (1868-1921), an Aberdonian who had not only amassed Himalayan experience from eight expeditions, but had studied the physiology of oxygen deprivation at high altitudes and had himself reached 23,400ft on Mount Kamet. [10] On that expedition, he determined that the extra weight of the oxygen apparatus counteracted the benefit of the oxygen itself.

Kellas was an SMC member, having joined in 1898, proposed by Norman Collie, and his life is also detailed in the history of the early Everest expeditions, *Into The Silence*.[11] Kellas was aged 53, Raeburn 56; both were probably too old for any difficult high-altitude climbing.

This expedition has been widely described in print, and there are many useful summaries. [12] During the expedition, which began in April and was over by October, Mallory and Howard-Bury developed a mutual dislike, Mallory did not think much of Raeburn, and several of the personnel suffered from food poisoning and dysentery. Those afflicted included Raeburn and Kellas, especially the latter, who fell severely ill with dysentery and died of a heart attack on 6 June.

Raeburn was obliged to return to Sikkim to recuperate on 7 June and from then on was effectively a spent force, after which Mallory became the *de facto* climbing leader. Unfortunately, it appears that Raeburn left no record of any sort, so historians have to rely on the writings of Howard-Bury and Mallory for any insight.

Much to everyone's surprise, Raeburn reappeared on 1 September, having braved monsoon conditions, but events following the expedition's return to Britain conspired to dishearten him, and on returning to Edinburgh his doctor advised him to recuperate in a nursing home.

He probably had not allowed himself to fully recover from the dysentery. There is also the possibility that Raeburn had never fully recovered internally from his accident on Stùc a' Chroin in February 1910 (see Volume One).[13]

In his book on Mallory, Wade Davis is particularly brutal in his references to Raeburn in relation to the 1921 Everest expedition. In one passage, Davis mentions Raeburn's 1910 fall and states that it '...*robbed him of courage and nerve*'. This of a man who in 1920 had made the first winter ascent of Observatory Ridge, a route which demanded of the leader a continuous supply of courage and nerve, and who in 1913 and 1914 had put up nine new routes in the Caucasus.

There is a medical note indicating that in 1911 or 1912 Raeburn suffered an attack of melancholia, which could well have been a reaction to his injuries from the 1910 accident. On the 1921 expedition his illness and temporary retreat were major setbacks that possibly led to an attack of depression. In 1922 he threw himself in front of a cab, hoping to die. He was hospitalised, where his condition slowly worsened, leading to his being force-fed on occasions. By April 1926 he had lost much weight and was down to seven stones (45kg). He died just before Christmas 1926 and was buried in the family grave in Warriston Cemetery, Edinburgh. [14,15]

Raeburn had been the leading climber in Scotland for several decades, helping to raise standards and leaving behind a legacy of good routes such as Raeburn's Arete, Green Gully and Observatory Ridge and Buttress on Nevis, the second ascent of Crowberry Direct (and a solo descent of that route's crux pitch) on the Buachaille in Glen Coe, and Barrel Buttress on Quinag. From several descriptions there was no doubting his assertive nature and indomitable will–character traits which could be useful in a tight climbing situation, but which perhaps should be reined-in during an expedition situation.

Lord Mackay wrote almost a quarter-century after Raeburn's death– *'Something, I sometimes thought, of Stalin was in his make-up.'* Mackay none-theless considered Raeburn –

> ...the best all-round equipped man on the mountains that Scotland produced. When he proceeded [...] to join an Everest Expedition, I have always felt sure that, had he been younger, his method and special knowledge might well have led to its conquest. [16]

It is right and certainly good to finish here on a positive note, and for that there is the description of Raeburn from his close friend and climbing partner, Willie Ling–

> Few have had a wider knowledge, or a more intense love of Nature in all its aspects – birds and beasts, flowers and rocks, the natural features of the countryside – all attracted his keen observation, and to a nature such as his the call of the mountain was irresistible [...] Light, wiry and active, with supple limbs and a beautiful balance, he added to his physical gifts an indomitable will, a sound judgment as to routes and possibilities, and a fearless self-reliance. [17]

❖❖❖

Exploratory climbing was patchy throughout the 1920s, but one moun-taineer was to provide an interesting picture of Scotland through foreign eyes. In the summer of 1920, Dr Ery Lüscher, a reader in physiology at Berne University, Switzerland, took six weeks' holiday starting at the end of July. Lüscher appears to have had an interest in biochemistry, and had at least one paper published while working in Cambridge. Knowing little of British climbs, he was grateful when Collie pointed him toward Skye, and he arrived at Sligachan one fine evening–

> It was not quite as I had imagined. I thought that the hills would be higher and nearer, the valleys cut deeper, and I found a wide, lonely island. But I felt the singular charm and I liked it at once. The fine evening was followed by a rainy day, and so it remained for the first ten days. Any serious climbing seemed to me impossible. [18]

Although climbing on his own, Lüscher was clearly very competent. After a period spent walking and scrambling, once the weather improved he had gathered some knowledge of the corries and the ridge and felt ready for more difficult problems. He began with the Pinnacle Ridge of Sgùrr nan Gillean, descending the west ridge with its 'policeman' or 'gendarme'. He then visited Coruisk, when the rain began again, but he was by now accustomed to it, even liking it, as, he thought, clouds and mist made the rocks blacker, the ridges steeper and higher and gave a feeling of extreme loneliness.

He decided to walk over the tops to Glen Brittle, and despite the mist and rain he gained the summits of Gars-bheinn and Sgùrr nan Eag, descended into Coir' a' Ghrunnda, and reached Mrs Chisholm's post office in time for dinner. The following day he climbed the Inaccessible Pinnacle by its western side, lowering his rope for two young men who had turned up at the same time. They descended the eastern ridge.

With the sun shining, next day he headed for Cìoch Gully and gained the Cìoch by that route, then did the round of Coire Lagan, finishing with another solo climb up the Inaccessible Pinnacle as he felt like smoking his pipe on its summit. He had a look at the South Crack, a Hard Very Difficult, and when he had regained the foot of the Pinnacle he soloed this to reach the top again and finally enjoy his smoke.

Two days later Waterpipe Gully on Sgùrr an Fheadain was on his agenda. Against expectations, a small burn was flowing through the deep, dark chasm, and a combination of wet skin and common sense saw Dr Lüscher avoid the 80ft pitch. He then followed the right edge of the gully, glad to be in the sun again. More routes followed, and the more he went out, the more he liked these hills. He remembered with special pleasure the climbs he did with a Mr Bell–John Hart Bell, who was to become President of the SMC in 1922. John Bell and Mrs Bell also enjoyed a summer holiday on Skye in 1921, which Bell wrote up as a series of diary entries for the SMCJ. [19]

In 1920, Dr Lüscher descended the precipitous nose of the central peak of Bidein Druim nan Ràmh, abseiling down two pitches. At the beginning of September he moved to Fort William, with Ben Nevis as the target.

Mist and rain again concealed much of the topography, but when empty boxes and broken bottles indicated Gardyloo Gully was above, he knew he had found the beginning of North-East Buttress. This he climbed, despite the conditions. The next day, in strong wind and mist, he probably made a first ascent in the Castle Corrie somewhere between Staircase Climb and Cousins' Buttress – but as Dr Lüscher himself acknowledged, it was difficult to provide a clear description while alone and concentrating on finding a way up.

G Graham Macphee, who wrote the first climbers' guide to Ben Nevis, could not find the route with certainty, even though it is marked on a diagram in the guide. It may well share a short section with the later *Macphee's Climb* (now named *Macphee's Route*, 165m Very Difficult), and Macphee described it as being probably Severe.

The route does not appear in the current guide, as it's line remains uncertain, and Dr Lüscher regarded the climb as having been serious, with the crux a traverse across a wet slab with few and small handholds. He carried a rope, which he trailed behind him, with his sack tied on at the end. He then pulled this up after climbing a section. Dr Lüscher appears to be unjustly underrated, as he was certainly a competent and thoughtful climber with a genuine fondness for the Scottish hills.

❄❄❄

As mentioned earlier, Charles Inglis Clark, son of prominent Edinburghers William and Jane Clark, had been killed in 1918 on active service in what was then Mesopotamia (now Iraq). Seven years later, Ernest Maylard, a consultant surgeon in Glasgow and prime architect in the foundation of the SMC, was attending the 1925 Easter Meet of the club in Fort William. On a walk up the path on Ben Nevis, he came across the old Half-Way Hut near Lochan Meall an t-Suidhe, once used as part of the meteorological infrastructure but now disintegrating. Two younger members of the club, AJ Rusk and RN Rutherford, were using it as a refuge.

Maylard, while admiring the enthusiasm of the climbers, was not impressed by the amenities provided by the disintegrating wooden structure– *'I recognised the risk they were running in damaging their health [...] by sleeping in such a hovel with wet and wind creeping through innumerable crevices.'* [20] At dinner in the Alexandra Hotel, Maylard noticed that Sang, then SMC Secretary, was sitting with his guest who was the factor for the estate. Maylard raised his idea, which was that a hut could be built on the mountain. The factor was cooperative, and agreed to pass on the idea. Maylard also proposed that a suitable *raison d'être* for its construction would be as a war memorial. He wrote to the Inglis Clark family, outlining his suggestion, and they responded by saying it would be a fitting memorial for their son.

Construction began beside the Allt a' Mhuilinn at an altitude of 679m, in May 1928. The hut was completed and the opening ceremony held on 1 April 1929, with the party including Charles Inglis Clark's parents. An 18-minute cine film was made of the ceremony–in black and white with no audio–and is available for viewing at the Scottish Screen Archive.[21] The CIC Hut–or the Charles Inglis Clark Memorial Hut, to give the structure its full name–has been renovated several times and has, especially in winter, proved to be a highly popular base for climbing on Ben Nevis and a useful mountain rescue facility. Climbing clubs may book spaces (for winter usually at least a year in advance) through the SMC website. [22] (The CIC Hut story has been more fully described in *Ben Nevis - Britain's Highest Mountain.* [23])

❆❆❆

The slow if steady increase in the appearance of younger climbers in Scotland continued through the 1920s, starting in 1920 itself when a 26-year-old joined the SMC. Joseph Alan Garrick (1894–1996) was already a member of the FRCC, and an assistant lecturer in mechanical engineering at the Royal Technical College in Glasgow. Born in Sunderland, much of his climbing had been in the Lake District, with ascents such as Eagle's Nest Direct and Kern Knotts Crack. Garrick was an authority on alpine plants and must have also been interested in geology, as the Hunterian Museum at Glasgow University has a small collection of his rocks and minerals.

Garrick took up his position in Glasgow in 1920, working there until retirement in 1960 as senior lecturer in the Department of Heat Engineering. His knowledge of Norway led him to work in Naval Intelligence during World War II, and he provided photographic analysis of V-2 rocket sites prior to D-Day. A very private man, he married Isabelle Mitchell, also a climber, in 1926, and died just short of his 102nd birthday. [24]

As Garrick noted in an article written in 1924, he had only two months in the year when he could indulge in climbing, presumably due to work commitments at weekends. [25] As a consequence, he sometimes went for months without seeing a mountain, except perhaps at long range–and so, at the end of May 1923 and with a programme of Alpine climbs looming, he was very keen for some exercise.

He often climbed with a friend, D Biggart, for example in 1921 on a new route on Creag Tharsuinn near Arrochar (*Garrick's Route* 200m Very Difficult). In 1923, however, they made for the Buachaille, despite poor weather. On Crowberry Ridge, the pair backed off the Direct Route, continuing up what they thought would lead to a traverse line back left. Faced with two steep ramps, they chose the cleaner, right-hand line, with Biggart making an exciting crux move.

Garrick thought he had pioneered a new route. A few days later he talked to Harry MacRobert, finding that the latter had failed on a winter attempt in 1910 at the same difficult pitch; MacRobert added a useful addendum to Garrick's article on the climb. Murray, MacAlpine and Dunn also attempted a winter ascent in 1936, oblivious to the earlier efforts, and also failing high up. The following year, Murray and Mackenzie returned to make the first winter ascent. The first summer ascent was by the English climbers Fred Pigott and John Wilding, in September 1920, who had not sent any information to the SMCJ.

❆❆❆

Pigott and Wilding were perhaps being a bit naughty in not promulgating news of the route north of the border, much like the Hopkinson family in earlier years. Garrick's Shelf Route, as it was known at first, was renamed plain Shelf Route in Murray's guide of 1949. A loose Difficult in summer, *Shelf Route* (165m IV,6) is best kept for a winter experience, the grading a warning that high technical difficulties will be found.

Pigott produced more than just this route on Crowberry Ridge. That same 1920 holiday saw the first ascent of *Crypt Route* (135m Very Difficult) on Church Door Buttress of Bidean nam Bian on 15 September, with Wilding and Morley Wood, a route with extraordinary rock architecture including the option of a subterranean section. In his article Pigott considered that their ascent had 'considerably improved' the original route. [26] Also with Wilding and Wood, two days earlier he had made an early ascent of Shadbolt's Chimney on Am Basteir, finding it loose and vegetatious:

> Climbing up steep grass, we found on entering the gully that its floor consisted of steepening slabs with loose, flaky holds, and with vegetation sprouting from the interstices for all the world like an old paved garden path reared on end.

On 17 September, the trio climbed Crowberry Direct, which gave them an 'exhilarating climb'. The Stockport sugar merchant Alfred Sefton Pigott (1895-1979) was a prominent gritstone-trained climber. World War I left him with a slightly dysfunctional arm, but this does not seem to have impaired his climbing, as he recorded a fair number of new gritstone routes in the early 1920s.

On 24 September 1920, Pigott and Wilding made an ascent of The Comb on Ben Nevis with *Pigott's Route* (250m Severe). Raeburn had explored this area in 1903, but rejected it, partly due to poor rock. It is now virtually ignored in summer but on rare occasions with sufficient ice it allows access to the steep buttress. (The author attempted the winter route several times but never found the right conditions.) On 21 September the two men had climbed Raeburn's Route; snow had fallen two days earlier, with three inches of snow coating the top of the mountain for several hundred feet. On 23 September they were on Tower Ridge, finding a variation to the Great Tower. *Pigott's Route* (45m Very Difficult) starts up the north-east arête of the Tower, and from below looks very imposing.

Pigott's Route on The Comb came on their last day on Ben Nevis –

> A farewell peep into the Observatory; a dash across to Carn Dearg; and a last, long look out to the west, where, for a glorious moment, the rugged tops of Skye were bathed in liquid gold; then a race down the pony track to Mrs. Macpherson's generous welcome.

Pigott's trips to Scotland continued for a few more years. On 27 June 1921, he and Wilding climbed the *Direct Finish to Crack of Doom* (60m Hard Severe) on Sròn na Cìche, and the following day two routes were added on the south face of the Inaccessible Pinnacle: *Route I* (30m VS 4b) and *Route II* (30m VS 4b).

In the summer of 1922, Pigott and Wood laid down the direct route on the Central Buttress of Beinn Eighe. Yet another line known as *Pigott's Route* (270m Severe 4b), it starts up the sandstone tier with some wet and vegetated sections before continuing up the quartzite via a succession of ledges. In summer it is a classic, while in winter it is promoted into a superb climb, long and hard at VI, 7 with the crux at the top.

Pigott was instrumental in advancing protection for climbers – *Pigott's Climb* (VS, 5a, 1924) on the East Buttress of Clogwyn Du'r Arddu involved the use of a natural stone inserted into a crack, with a rope sling looped round this allowing the rope to be threaded through the sling to form a running belay. He was also a founder member of the Mountain Rescue Committee and its chairman from 1956-1972. Older climbers will recall the Pigott stretcher, an emergency improvisation made from a climbing rope.

Unsurprisingly, advances in protection techniques for mountaineering were driven by climbers from the Lake District and North Wales. Climbing in these centres was mainly on rock, the structure of which lent itself more readily to protection than that found in Scotland. As early as 1886, Owen Glynne Jones used a threaded belay, while George Abraham, in his 1916 book, describes how a leader could use a jammed stone in a crack by untying the rope from the waist, pushing the rope up behind the stone, and retying it round the waist. [27]

Geoffrey Winthrop Young, in his 1920 book *Mountain Craft*, describes methods of belaying and points out the danger of the rope breaking due to insufficient allowance for its inherent elasticity. The technical input for the book's section on climbing equipment (which was of course almost entirely limited to ropes) was supplied by John Percy Farrar (1857-1929), president of the AC (1917-1919). He mentioned the importance of elasticity in ropes for absorbing energy generated during a fall, but may have been unaware of the earlier research by SMC member John Hart Bell, who had a note published in the September 1897 edition of the SMCJ. [28] The research by Bell was alarming, indicating that even a very short fall by a leader could see the rope break–assuming, of course, that the second climber could hold the fall.

❊❊❊

The early history of The Chasm on Buachaille Etive Mor was outlined in the earlier volume. On 12 April 1920, three climbers had probed its defences and left a rope on the 100ft pitch, halfway up the gully. An account of their partial ascent of the gully the next day was recorded by one of the party, Ralph Forester Stobart (1889-1979), an engineer from Cornwall. [29] He was to join the SMC at the end of that year, along with Garrick and ten others. Also present were Noel Ewart Odell (1890-1987) and his wife Mona. Stobart's nickname was '*The Belay*', due to his steady nature as a second man. [30]

Odell was a geologist and would become associated with Himalayan climbing through the 1924 Everest expedition, where he was probably the last person to see Mallory and Irvine during their summit attempt. He also made the first ascent of Nanda Devi in 1936, with Bill Tilman, when it was the highest peak thus far climbed, a record which remained until the 1950 ascent of Annapurna.

The ascent on the Buachaille was partial, as in the strictest sense the actual finish of *The Chasm* (450m VS 4c) is always wet, with water spilling over the narrow exit of the last major feature in the gully, The Cauldron. Very few climbers have succeeded in this uncomfortable final pitch, with most taking the South Wall exit at the foot of The Cauldron. The exit route taken by the 1920 party was by the South Chimney: dirty, steep, and loose. At the time of their visit, snow and ice masked the upper section of the gully.

The 1920 routes by Odell and Pigott marked a brief return to climbing in the Glen Coe area and the first for a decade on the Buachaille, the previous route having been the first summer ascent of Crowberry Gully by Raeburn's party in September 1910.

❊❊❊

Easter 1922 saw both the SMC and the Cairngorm Club hold meets at Aviemore, and a convivial time was had by a total of 51 members and guests. One interesting occurrence was the production of a new Ordnance Survey map showing the Cairngorms, at a scale of one inch to the mile. This followed a suggestion to the OS by James Parker, and apparently its production had been rushed in order to catch the meet. Parker brought with him three dozen copies and had no difficulty in disposing of them.

The map, as the account of the SMC Meet indicated, was excellent – *'one of the best pieces of cartography produced in this country–but, of course, nobody was going to admit this in Parker's presence, and he was rudely asked what commission he was making.'* [31] Parker then reviewed the map for the SMCJ. [32] The Cairngorm Club had published a special map in 1895, which reproduced the necessary parts of four other maps, but this was not extensive enough and was in any case out of print.

One of the new map's features was that contour lines appeared at 50ft intervals, with every fifth contour being slightly thicker than the others. This replaced the older format, which had contours at 100ft intervals up to 1,000ft, and at 250ft intervals above that height. The new map was printed in four colours, with green and brown shades indicating surfaces at various levels; the combined effect indicating the relief as never before.

❊❊❊

The SMC continued to hold regular meets through the early 1920s, usually attended by well-known names of the earlier generation plus a few younger climbers. One such gathering was based at Sligachan, in May and June 1923. Those present included John Hart Bell and the unrelated James Horst Brunneman Bell (1896-1976). The former was one of the early tigers of the club, while Jim Bell was destined to be prominent throughout the middle part of the 20th century.

Another SMC member present was the Reverend Aubrey Ronald Graham Burn (1887-1972), from Chichester. While a modest mountaineer, he was certainly an enthusiastic Munro bagger and on 20 July 1923, with an ascent of the two tops of Beinn a' Chròin, he recorded that he had:

> ...completed all the hills over 3,000 feet, i.e., all the mountains and tops contained in both editions of Munro's Tables, 558 in all (including, therefore, those omitted from revised tables). I believe I am the first and only one to have done everything. [33]

There are however, several indications that cast some doubt on this claim. Bob Aitken notes in his database of SMC members that '...[Burn's] *navigation was so ludicrously erratic that a degree of scepticism about that may be justified'*, while a biography by Elizabeth Allan suggests that Burn was a fairly hapless character. [34] He was popular and welcome enough on club meets, where one of the jokes was his being the first known case of a burn running up a hill.

Hapless or not, along with Sang on the same meet, Burn found a new climb on the north face of Blà Bheinn, *North Face Direct* (470m Difficult). Chockstones required some combined tactics on a day of mist and strong wind, with several pitches involving streams of water. The route also gives a good winter climb.

Born in Auchtermuchty, Fife, Jim Bell was the son of a Scottish Presbyterian minister and a German mother. He was educated at Bell Baxter High School in Cupar, followed in 1916 by taking an MA at Edinburgh University (Honours in Mathematics and Natural Philosophy), then a BSc in 1918 and a doctorate in 1934.

Bell was in the Officers' Training Corps infantry in 1913 as a cadet, and in the Middlesex Regiment as a private for a few months in 1917. He worked as a chemist in explosives factories for the latter half of the war, which would have classified him as being in a 'reserved occupation', and hence ineligible for combat. [35]

He joined the SMC in 1922. Physically a small man, he was nonetheless imbued with remarkable stamina, possibly helped by having cycled long distances as a youth. He began by exploring his local hills such as the Lomonds of Fife, where West Lomond gave him a taste for rock climbing on its dolerite crags. He also recorded routes on the ghastly basaltic agglomerate of Dumyat in the Ochils, and it could have been these experiences of climbing poor rock that would instil his seeming indifference to vegetated, loose horrors on steep ground.

In 1924 he met Frank Smythe, the two hitting it off and climbing successfully in the Alps. Together they made the fourth traverse of the Cuillin Ridge and recorded several climbs on Skye, including *West Ridge of the Cioch* (140m Severe) and *West Trap Route* (240m Severe) on 17 and 22 July 1924 respectively. The first of these routes was originally named Cìoch West Buttress before being renamed to avoid confusion with *Cìoch West*, which it joins higher up.

After World War I, Jim Bell became an industrial chemist in the paper manufacturing trade–the dissertation for his doctorate entitled *The effects of beating on fibrous cellulose*. A major influence in Scottish mountaineering over several decades, Bell would edit the SMCJ from 1935 to 1959, while *A Progress in Mountaineering* would become a classic book, providing a mix of personal experiences and helpful knowledge, still readable today. [36] In the multi-authored obituary note in the SMCJ, WH Murray regarded Bell as the best and most influential mountaineer that Scotland produced between 1930 and 1950.[37] His friends Alex Small and Colin Allan praised his personal qualities, not least of which were his knowledge of music, philosophy and political theory, while Geoff Dutton, himself a scientist and a highly regarded editor of the SMCJ, highlighted his kindness and true humility. Running through all accounts of Bell was his inner toughness and great sense of humour.

It will come as no surprise to anyone who knew Bell that his skill on dangerous and loose ground could on occasion be converted, on perfect rock, into a disregard for such trivia as ropes, for example when climbing

Raeburn's Arête on Ben Nevis without a rope while his companions stuck with convention and tied on.

As for Bell's greatest service to mountaineering in Scotland, it could well have been his recognition of the state of climbing in Scotland at the time, and which activists were best placed to improve matters. Using the pages of the SMCJ, he actively sought out those who could write well, and who were able to provide useful comment or information on the current state of play.

Bell also climbed with a vast range of people, young and old. Another way in which he helped to resurrect mountaineering in Scotland was by proposing suitable candidates for the SMC–at least seven, including WH Murray and Alex Small. Scottish mountaineering might have been spluttering along on three cylinders at this time, but Jim Bell would keep the engine firing, look under its bonnet and make suitable and improving modifications.

Scottish mountaineering in the early 1920s tends to be regarded as having been at a very low point of activity–but, as will be seen shortly, several key events over the next few years would help to provide a new and badly needed impetus.

References

1. Naismith, W.W. *How to stop a fall on hard snow or ice.* SMCJ 15, 90, October 1920, pp.323-324.
2. Steeple, E.W. *Some new climbs from Glen Brittle.* SMCJ 16, 94, October 1922, p.154-160.
3. Steeple, E.W. *The Lower Crags of Coir' a' Ghrunnda.* SMCJ 16, 95, April 1923, pp.233-241.
4. Barlow, G. *The Relative Heights of the Cuillin Peaks.* SMCJ 16, 95, April 1923, pp.244-249.
5. Strange, Greg. *The Cairngorms - 100 Years of mountaineering.* (2010, SMT.), p.31.
6. Parker, James A. *The Mitre Ridge - Beinn a' Bhùird.* SMCJ, 16, 95, April 1923, pp.211-215.
7. Garden, W. *In Memoriam. Sir Henry Alexander, LL.D., 1875-1940.* SMCJ 22, 130, November 1940, pp.255-257.
8. Cairngorm Club Journal, no.63, p.143.
9. Strange, Greg. *The Cairngorms - 100 Years of Mountaineering.* (2010, SMT.) p.27.
10. Mitchell, Ian R and Rodway, George W. *Prelude to Everest: Alexander Kellas, Himalayan Mountaineer.* (Edinburgh: Luath Press, 2014.)
11. Davis, Wade. *Into the Silence: The Great War, Mallory and the Conquest of Everest.* (2011. Knopf Canada. ISBN 067697919X.)

12. 1921 British Mount Everest reconnaissance expedition. Wikipedia. <goo.gl/kzDDdW> Accessed March 2017.

13. Crocket, Ken. *Mountaineering in Scotland - The Early Years.* (2015, SMT.) pp.305-307.

14. Jacob, Mike. *Harold Raeburn - The Final Journey.* SMCJ 40, 199, 2008, pp.41-51.

15. K.V. Crocket & J.R.R. Fowler. *Of Beer and Boats.* In: Miscellaneous Notes, SMCJ 36, 1997, pp.380-383.

16. Mackay, Lord. *Vignettes of Earlier Climbers.'* SMCJ, 24, 141, April 1950, pp.169-180.

17. Ling, W.N. *In Memorium, Harold Raeburn.* SMCJ 18, 103, April 1927, pp.26-31.

18. Lüscher, E. *A Summer Holiday in Skye.* SMCJ 16, 93, April 1922, pp.99-108.

19 Bell, J.H. *Skye.* In: Excursions and Notes, SMCJ16, 92, October 1921, pp.88-90.

20. Maylard, A. Ernest. *The Club In Retrospect I. - Its Origins and Growth.* SMCJ, 22, 127, April 1939, pp.6-13.

21. Scottish Screen Archive <http://ssa.nls.uk/film/7702>

22. CIC web page <http://www.smc.org.uk/huts/cic>

23. Crocket, Ken and Richardson, Simon. *Ben Nevis - Britain's Highest Mountain.* (Scottish Mountaineering Trust, 2nd edition 2009).

24. Gold, Fraser. *Who was Garrick of Garrick's Shelf?* SMCJ 36, 189, 1998, pp.539-542.

25. Garrick, J.A. *The North Wall Variation of The Crowberry Ridge.* SMCJ 17, 97, April 1924, pp.1-10.

26. Pigott, A.S. *Notes on some Scottish Climbs.* Rucksack Club Journal 4, 1921, No.15, pp.185-193.

27. Abraham, G.D. *On Alpine Heights and British Crags.* (1916, Methuen, London)

28. Bell, J.H. *The Strength of Climbing Rope.* In: Correspondence, SMCJ 4, 24, September 1897, pp.347-349.

29. Stobart, R.F. *The Chasm - Buchaille Etive.* SMCJ 16, 92, October 1921, pp.62-64.

30. Odell, N. *Obituary for Ralph Forester Stobart.* ACJ, 1980, 85, No. 329, p.267.

31. H.A. [Henry Alexander]. *Easter Meet, 1922 - Aviemore.* In: Proceedings of the Club. SMCJ 16, No.94, October 1922, pp.194-200.

32. J.A.P. [James Alexander Parker]. *New Ordnance Survey Map of the Cairngorms.* In: Reviews. SMCJ 16, No.94, October 1922, pp. 202-203.

33. Burn, Rev. Ronald. In: Excursions and Notes. SMCJ 16, 96, October 1923, p.329.

34. Allan, Elizabeth. *Burn On The Hill: The Story of the First Compleat Munroist.* (1995, Bidean Books.)

35. Edinburgh University, Roll of Honour 1914-1919.

36. Bell, J.H.B. *A Progress in Mountaineering - Scottish Bens to Alpine Peaks.* (1950, Oliver & Boyd, Edinburgh & London).

37. *In Memorium - J.H.B. Bell D.Sc.* SMCJ 31, 167, 1976, pp.80-89.

3

New Clubs (1925-1940)

Mountaineering is normally an activity carried out by two or more climbers; there are a few who prefer to solo, but on the whole it is a sport which works better in company. Two climbers on a rope will have a safer day on the hill than one, while sharing transport is cheaper for two or more. There is also the social benefit of having like-minded companions, and so there was an inevitability that, historically, mountaineering clubs would be formed.

This chapter examines the significant expansion of Scottish clubs between the two world wars, a phenomenon which played an integral and important role in the growth of mountaineering. This is not a complete account, however; for every mainstream club, there was, and is, a number of smaller, informal clubs which for the most part have no need of the trappings that accompany their bigger counterparts: constitution, secretary, president, journal and so on. Some of these are mentioned.

Often, members of these less formal clubs have also been members of a mainstream club. For some, this setup provides the best of worlds: the standard conveniences of a large club, including hut access, an annual dinner, a published journal, and several meets through the year, while an informal club can use a bothy, perhaps hidden away in a popular area and unencumbered with building regulations, council rates, heating bills and so on.

As an example from one popular area, the author knows of at least six informal venues in Glen Coe and has stayed in several over the decades, in various degrees of comfort. In a few cases a gamekeeper might allow a disused barn to be used – one well-known example was the roadside barn of Dan MacKay at Altnafeadh, at the head of Glen Coe, used for a number of years by climbers and other travellers.

MacKay had been a stalker on the Strathcona Estate. In the mid-1930s he was succeeded by Dodie Cameron, with the temporary residence becoming known as Cameron's Barn. Several informal clubs came and went here, and in the days before organised mountain rescue teams became prevalent, the police and locals knew they could call on such bothies and pluck out climbers to help with a rescue, even if only for hard work on a stretcher-carry. Alastair Borthwick's classic book *Always a Little Further* tells of an evening in Dan Mackay's Barn, during a fierce storm on the weekend of the Glasgow September holiday in 1934. [1]

Further west in Glen Coe was the roadman's cottage at Allt-na-reigh, facing the Lost Valley. It was to here that Bob Downie, then roadman in Glen Coe, moved in 1939 from Lagangarbh. Allt-na-reigh had an adjoining barn, used as a woodshed by the Downies and often as a doss by climbers. In later years, the mountaineer, inventor and mountain rescue pioneer Hamish MacInnes would live in this cottage.

The Cairngorms, where climbers were faced with long approach marches, rapidly developed a number of informal shelters, often rough howffs which used boulders as part of their structure. Many of these were built in secret, particularly on estates where stalking and shooting were strong features and gamekeepers were diligent. One keeper in particular must be singled out for his cooperation and generosity at making available space in his outhouses for climbers and that was Bob Scott at Luibeg Cottage, who looked after the Derry beat. Many a new route started from the bothy here.

The numbers in these clubs was small, often from a nucleus of half a dozen to perhaps a score of active participants. The clubs rose, grew, flourished and faded, often leaving no record other than the important one, the efforts of their members on the cliffs and corries of Scotland.

All sources covering mountaineering in Scotland in the 1920s agree that to all appearances nothing of importance was occurring, and it is certainly difficult to dispute this sentiment. However, there were a few stirrings and twitchings, including the new SMC Skye guidebook mentioned earlier. By itself, this book produced no surge of activity; for that to happen there had to be climbers and those climbers had to have time, energy and access to transport. The guidebook would be ready and waiting for this hoped-for new wave of climbers.

❋❋❋

Before the mid-1920s, mountaineering clubs in Scotland comprised the established clubs in the four principal cities: the Dundee Rambling Club (formed 1886); the Cairngorm Club (1889) in Aberdeen; the Scottish Mountaineering Club (1889), formed in Glasgow and initially with a mainly Glasgow-Edinburgh axis of membership; and the Ladies' Scottish Climbing Club (1908), which likewise had a mainly Glasgow-Edinburgh membership. The Aberdeen climber Malcolm 'Mac' Smith, writing in the Etchachan Club Journal of 1959, described these clubs as: *'...all full of professional men and women* [excepting the SMC of course, which had no women members at that time], *relatively expensive and, although active, rather staid and conservative in outlook.'* [2]

Dundee had plenty of energetic outdoor people, perhaps a consequence of its marine exploration and whaling days, with an agricultural hinterland, and the Dundee Rambling Club (DRC) was formed on 28 April 1886. It was basically a social club for walking, though many of its members had qualified for the SMC. During the First World War, four DRC members were killed while serving in the 4th Battalion The Black Watch, including Harry Walker, Charles Air and THB Rorie, all of whom were SMC members. The DRC no longer exists, but was still extant in 1939, with 44 members.

The earliest of the new wave of clubs was the Rucksack Club of University College, Dundee, formed 7 December 1923, *'to further the interests of members in all matters appertaining to the open-air life'*. From its beginning, the Rucksack Club seems to have been popular – and this continues today, with membership numbering around 150. It maintains an open bothy on the Balmoral Estate at Glas-allt-Shiel on the shore of Loch Muick. [3] There was also a Glasgow-based Rucksack Club, which had two small wooden shelters, one at Kinlochard, the other in Glen Loin near Arrochar. Both of these structures were acquired by the Scottish Youth Hostels Association after its formation in 1931.

❊❊❊

Even those fortunate enough to own a car found access to the further-flung hills difficult. The roads were very poor, as tarmacadam had not yet stretched beyond the Great Glen, and in most areas the surface consisted of two stony tracks where the wheels of motor vehicles and carts had gone, with grass and weeds in the middle. For example, the high and exposed section of road crossing the eastern edge of the Blackmount and leading to Glen Coe and beyond could be particularly difficult in winter conditions. It was partly for this reason that early tourists preferred to take the boat up Loch Etive, and continue their sightseeing from the head of the loch by horse-drawn coach.

The new road to Glen Coe has a surprising history, in that it was not universally wanted. Indeed, there was much hostility towards its proposal, partly because some of the pressure for it was due to the increase in tourism, something which many local inhabitants had no wish to see. The editor of the SMCJ, John 'Jack' MacRobert (brother of Harry MacRobert and editor from 1927-1932) went so far as to ask Sir John Stirling-Maxwell to contribute an article detailing its genesis. [4] Maxwell (1866-1956) was the 10th Baronet of Pollok, a Scottish Conservative politician who was the MP for the College Division of Glasgow from 1895 to 1906 and a founder member of the National Trust for Scotland (NTS).

With his sense that green spaces were important for city dwellers, Stirling-Maxwell regarded the new road as an error, spoiling the fine scenery through which it passed. It reached from Tyndrum to the foot of Glen Coe, some 30 miles, and although only it was 18ft wide, bridges and culverts were built to carry 20-ton loads. The road would follow an entirely new line from Bridge of Orchy to Kings House, bypassing the inns and houses on the old route. Most of its line was to the east of the old road, which in part followed the even older military road. The cost was an estimated £512,000, equivalent to roughly £206 million in present-day terms.

The required engineering was even more drastic than for the new road driven through the middle of Highland Scotland, from Blair Atholl to Kingussie. That road – the modern A9 over Drumochter – despite its effect on the landscape, was recognised as being necessary. By contrast, Stirling-Maxwell outlined his feelings on the western project:

> My own view, if I may venture to give it, is that this road ought to have been frankly treated as a tourist road and improved so as to provide reasonable facilities for vehicles of such weight as the existing culverts and bridges would carry. Even in its present state the road has in recent years been used every day by scores of cars all through the summer and autumn. The steep gradient at the Studdie could have been reduced by cutting the rock at the summit and increasing the length of the hairpin bends, yet left steep enough to add a spice of adventure to the journey. The Alpine character of the road which contributes more than some people realise to the majesty of the scene would thus have been retained. The gorge at the Studdie would have remained untouched. The tourist would still have enjoyed the striking view from the shoulder of Clachlet and the charming drive round the shore of Loch Tulla.

Stirling-Maxwell made some valid points regarding the design of the road, and the newly formed Association for the Preservation (later Protection) of Rural Scotland intervened regarding the section through the gorge at 'the Studdie' in Glen Coe, suggesting certain modifications. Stirling-Maxwell preferred the Highlands to be kept as they were, with their wildness and comparative remoteness being important assets to an industrial country. He wished the road only to be improved to carry tourist traffic.

> This tripping may be only a phase. As education grows in the best sense and with it a true appreciation of the gifts of Nature, the genuine tourists will more and more secede from the ranks of the mere trippers. Our generation inherited the Highlands unspoilt. The changes of our time have already deprived great areas of their pristine bloom. It is surely our duty to

protect what remains (and especially places of special beauty and interest like Glen Coe) from changes which will diminish their value for those, an ever-increasing number, who are by tradition and training fitted to draw the highest kind of enjoyment from them.

One example of the 1920s being a period in Scotland marked by poor road connections came in June 1925 when four SMC members – LS Bartholomew, GM Lawson and the Scott brothers, JA and WP – set off for a meet on Skye. They arrived at Sligachan on the first of the month, having taken three days to travel by road from Edinburgh. The car had suffered obscure and noisy complaints from the rear axle and was left with a local plumber at Kyleakin for repairs, the quartet finishing the trip by hire car.

World War I had of course brought changes in Scotland, and many industries were nationalised, including munitions, railways and coalfields. Post-war, their return to private hands worsened their already fragile state, as subsidies were removed and competition increased.

Heavy industry in Scotland was a major sector, and as the economy entered a depression in 1920 unemployment rose as shipbuilding and steel-making, along with textiles, contracted. The west of Scotland was especially hard hit, as was Dundee. The unemployment level throughout Scotland in the 1920s was continually 14 per cent or more, with several blackspots being higher.

This was bad enough, but unemployment soared following the Wall Street Crash of 1929, leading to a quarter of the workforce in the west of Scotland being out of work in the early 1930s. The Scottish economy was worse off than the rest of the UK and would not start to recover until rearmament ahead of World War II. Housing was expensive in the 1920s, and this led to an expansion of public sector building. Even so, most of the urban population in Scotland was still living in houses with just one or two rooms.

Increased social tensions had several unplanned outcomes: professional boxing and football increased in popularity, while – slowly at first – there was also a growth in recreational walking. Although there would have been some pressure from the establishment, for example the church, as a way of diverting unemployed men from the streets and pubs, there is no doubt these early escapees from the cities found the freedom of the countryside liberating. If employed, someone wishing a taste of the landscape could make his or her way out of the city late on a Saturday and meet with similar-minded souls.

❈❈❈

A manifestation of these early escapes, in particular from the great city of Glasgow, came in the form of the Craigallian Fire. This was not a destructive fire, razing some tenement to the ground; rather it was a formative beacon, one which burned almost continuously for many years.

On the north side of Glasgow lies the sprawling, mainly middle-class commuter satellite of Milngavie. A few miles further north and scattered over the post-glacial landscape are some small lochs filling the ice-scooped basins. One of these, Craigallian Loch, became a meeting place for the unemployed and others in the early 1920s. A country track led north from Milngavie to continue along the loch's west side, at the foot of Carbeth Hill. It was here, halfway along the loch, that like-minded escapees from a dreary urban existence would meet, heading to the campfire in the trees like moths to a candle.

A number of these 'fire-sitters' became mountaineers or conservationists, including John 'Jock' Nimlin and Bob, later Sir Robert, Grieve. Perhaps the most prominent from a climbing point of view was Nimlin (1908-1988), who owed his light-coloured hair and blue eyes to his Finnish grandfather Johann Niemelin, who came to Scotland and married a Scots lass, Catherine Stewart. The family modified the family name to make it more easily pronounced.

The grandfather worked in the Kelvingrove Galleries and was a crucial influence in educating Jock and his brother Eric to the natural world around them. Another important influence on Nimlin was climbing and playing on the walls to be found around the back courts of Glasgow tenements, an understated source of climbing skills in many an early West of Scotland mountaineer. Allied to Nimlin's interest in the outdoors was a later enthusiasm for geology: he would write a booklet on Scottish gemstones and came to know much about amethysts and agates. [5] He also became a field officer for the NTS, in which capacity he was active for some time on St Kilda.

Nimlin left school aged 14, as the family were not well off enough for him to continue his formal education, even though he was a good pupil and particularly adept at English. He found a job at Biggars, a music shop on Sauchiehall Street, which had the downside that on Saturdays it stayed open until 9pm. By now Nimlin was exploring the hills, so this made weekend activities something of an obstacle course. Any modern climber who regards himself as being 'tough', should ponder the following excerpt from an article by Nimlin, where he describes a typical trip, leaving work late on a Saturday evening and heading for a day's climbing at Arrochar, via Loch Lomond –

> One bus got to Balmaha for midnight. From there we could reach Rowardennan before 2 a.m., but sometimes we arranged for a rowing-boat to be ready at Balmaha jetty and rowing with two pairs of oars in two-hour shifts we would cover the fourteen miles to Tarbet by 4 a.m., snatch a few hours' sleep under the trees and walk to Arrochar for a fair day's climbing before facing the return trip to Balmaha. [6]

There was an alternative route to Arrochar, and it is a moot point which of the two was better as both involved much effort. This second route involved a rush to catch the last bus to Garelochhead for midnight, then climbing the hill to Whistlefield and walking along the railway track to reach Arrochar in the small hours. As Nimlin noted, *'One always touched down on the Arrochar road with a mincing gait after long attunement to the spacing of the sleepers.'*

It was during an ascent of Ben Lomond that Nimlin met two others who announced themselves as 'Craigallian Boys', and thus was he introduced to the motley crew who met by the side of Craigallian Loch to light a fire, brew up tea, discuss politics and sing songs before falling asleep under the stars. Like his companions, Nimlin would travel very light, with an ex-army knapsack containing some food and perhaps a spare sweater. Settling down for the night, usually with no sleeping bag, entailed putting on the spare sweater and sticking feet into the sack. This was the reason for keeping the fire going all night if possible: to stay warm enough to sleep. If it rained, they got wet.

Another Maryhill man who was a fire-sitter was Bob Grieve (1910-1995). Later Professor Sir Robert Grieve, he held many senior government posts, including the first Professor of Town and Regional Planning at Glasgow University, first chairman of the Highlands and Islands Development Board and chief planning officer at the Scottish Office.

It was his early experiences at Craigallian and round the Loch Lomond basin which opened Grieve's eyes to nature in general. As an apprentice civil engineer, one of his subjects was geology and he began to recognise how the landscape had been formed. He became unemployed in the late 1920s on completion of his apprenticeship, but this afforded him the time for countryside experience.

As Nimlin wrote–

In time the faces became names. Christian names, nicknames, but rarely surnames. Through the years came a great roll of names, some forgotten, some unforgettable. Starry, Bones, Sparrow, Peaheid, Scrubbernut, where are you now? Simple-lifers. Not for them the Ramblers' Federation and the Youth Hostels. *Under the wide and starry sky. There's the wind on the heath, Brother.* We quoted Stevenson and Borrow at length. We had an analytical appreciation of Stevenson's *Night Under the Stars,* which expresses the very essence of sleeping out.

> Under the wide and starry sky
> Dig the grave and let me lie:
> Glad did I live and gladly die
> And I laid me down with a will.

(Robert Louis Stevenson, *Requiem. I*)

There's night and day, brother, both sweet things; sun, moon, and stars, brother, all sweet things; there's likewise a wind on the heath. Life is very sweet, brother; who would wish to die?

(George Borrow. *Lavengro* (1851, Ch.25).

❊❊❊

New clubs which would lead to a significant increase in the number of mountaineers originated when three young members of the SMC met for a holiday in the Bernese Oberland in July 1924. Archibald George Hutchison (1903-1983), Arthur John Rusk (18??-1965) and Richard Napier Rutherfurd (1902-1994) were to start a club in which the interested could meet fellow climbers, learn the basics and, possibly, create an easier route for those wishing to join the SMC.

Rusk seems to have been the initial instigator. A civil engineer from Edinburgh, he had joined the SMC in 1921. Hutchison and Rutherfurd were engineering students at Glasgow University and had been introduced to rock climbing while at school by GF Woodhouse, a Fell and Rock Climbing Club (FRCC) member. In May 1921, the pair began to visit the Arrochar Alps on a regular basis, finishing a week's work at noon on a Saturday in their Govan and Bridgeton works, cycling to their respective homes then loading their bicycles with a home-made tent, groundsheet, sleeping bags, a primus stove and so on, and setting off for Arrochar, 37 miles away. [7]

Sunday morning at their camp, beside the Sugach Burn in Glen Loin, comprised porridge, bacon and eggs, fuel for a good day's climbing on the Cobbler's jagged peaks. A brew of tea once back at camp was followed by the return cycle home, before work on Monday morning.

Holidays allowed more remote areas to be explored, though as with many climbers from Glasgow the Arrochar hills were their first love. Equipment remained rudimentary: no pegs or harness, and they attached themselves directly to the rope with a bowline or middleman's knot. They were imbued with the fitness of young men and buoyed with the excitement that all such beginnings provide. Many other young climbers lacked even a bicycle, and very few stretched to owning or having access to a car.

During their Alpine holiday in 1924, Hutchison, Rusk and Rutherfurd became stormbound in the Mutthorn Hut at the head of the Lauterbrunnen valley. They spent their time formulating the constitution for the new club, and it was probably here that its name was agreed on: the Junior Mountaineering Club of Scotland (JMCS). The inaugural meeting was held at the Narnain Boulders, beside the path up the Cobbler, on 29 August 1925, when 11 climbers were bivouacking or camping on the hill.

The next day was a Sunday, with bad weather enforcing a long lie. They were joined by Charles Edgar (Eddy) Andreae (1902-1977), a civil engineer from London who was working in Glasgow and was elected Glasgow JMCS president, while William Blair Speirs (1907-1997), a company secretary from Glasgow became the secretary.

The 1925 meet spent some time building up a stone wall, but even then only a handful of adventurers could expect to remain dry in the rain, with four lucky ones tucked away in the inner section while three absorbed the moisture in the outer. The best howffs on the Cobbler, unknown at first to the author (who spent a weekend under the dubious shelter of the boulder as a schoolboy), can be found higher up in the corrie, with enough capacity for at least half-a-dozen in total. Like all howffs, their condition depended on when they were last used and whether running repairs (i.e. replacing rocks or divots) had been done.

In a mark of just how popular the JMCS would become, an SMCJ note in November 1925 announcing the formation of the JMCS stated that there was already a membership of 50 or so. [8] A shiver may well have run through the upper echelons of the SMC at this news, though relations between the two clubs were cordial and have remained so. The intentions of the JMCS were laid out for prospective members, with the basics being:

> The object of the Club is to foster the knowledge and love of mountains, and to afford opportunities of climbing and an introduction to mountaineering technique to those to whom the necessary companionship and advice are not available...Membership is confined to those who are not yet qualified for the Scottish Mountaineering Club, and who have reached the age of seventeen...The Club, it is intended, will prove a training ground for men taking up mountaineering, and a source of new members for the Scottish Mountaineering Club.

As the SMC in 1925 remained a club for men only, the JMCS, by positing itself as a feeder for the SMC, logically followed suit. Initially there were two sections, Glasgow and Edinburgh, but Perth was added in 1929, followed by Lochaber, Inverness and London (the latter having members from across England). Alastair Lorimer Cram (1909-1994) was one of the founders of the Perth section and joined the SMC in 1930. He became a prominent member of both clubs and a wartime hero, renowned for multiple escape attempts after being captured. His Military Cross, unusually, was awarded mainly for efforts to escape and rejoin the war. Another member of the Perth section, JD Sturrock, moved to Inverness where he initiated that section. The Perth JMCS later became the Perth Mountaineering Club, while the Inverness section is no more.

At the AGM of the Glasgow section in the Kings House Hotel on 9 November 1996, an important amendment to the constitution was implemented, with 'males' replaced by 'persons': *'Membership shall be open to persons who have reached the age of sixteen years and who have attended a minimum of three meets.'* This change of course threw open the JMCS to women, with the AGM of the whole club having made this change possible earlier that year.

As there were sections in different cities, each would hold its own business meetings, followed by an annual whole club AGM. This led to a situation in the early 1980s when the Edinburgh section was almost being thrown out of the JMCS after they proposed to admit women. Other sections, such as Perth, often had women attending meets – and it is worth mentioning that various pubs in cities including Edinburgh banned women for many years.

❆❆❆

Dundee continued its enthusiasm for the outdoors with the formation of the Grampian Club on 19 January 1927, following a letter to the *Dundee Courier*. The founders were George Chalmers and Robert Ower, and membership rose from an initial 26 to 65 in 1939. Currently, this club has about 220 members, many, but not all, based around Tayside. The club website states that *'Nowadays, most of our members are primarily hillwalkers going out into the Scottish mountains in all seasons and weathers'*, and the club has two properties, in Glen Etive and in Torridon, the latter for the sole use of members. Jim Bell was for many years the Grampian Club honorary president.

Two significant events took place in 1929. One was the opening of the CIC Hut on Ben Nevis, described in the previous chapter. The other was the founding of the Ptarmigan Club by Jock Nimlin, as he described in an article in the SMCJ–

> One night by Craigallion [sic] we solemnly enrolled the members of the Ptarmigan Mountaineering Club. We named it not for the spur by that name on Ben Lomond, but for the tough little bird of the high tops whose most southerly outpost is the summit of the Ben itself: We closed the roll at twenty members, thus seeming to ensure a short life for the club, for the high wastage-rate of climbing club membership can only be balanced by a comparable inflow of new recruits. [9]

Bill Dougan was another Ptarmigan Club founder, and there were actually 16 original members, with four joining later. Ian Thomson's biography of Nimlin lists 16 of these, two of whom were women, Isabel Kennedy and Jean Black. [10] (In various accounts of the period, 1929 is usually given as the date for this, although in a later interview for the STV series 'Weir's Way', Nimlin gives 1930, probably a slip of the memory.) Women sometimes stayed at the Craigallian fire, when the conversational tone and content would have been moderated appropriately.

Nimlin was prescient in his comment about a short life for the Ptarmigan Club, as by the mid-1930s it was no longer active. It did, however mark the start of a new climbing panoply, with the following decade seeing almost a dozen new clubs being formed.

As the article in the SMCJ noted, the Ptarmigan Club members –

…would go off on a three week climbing holiday carrying neither tents, sleeping-bags, nor blankets, sleeping in barns, deserted cottages, and caves. Wisely, they did not stint themselves when it came to carrying food. Commandos have been toughened on the hills by similar methods. [11]

According to Thomson, Ptarmigan Club members usually roamed around the Arrochar area, but other than Nimlin, Dougan and John Fox, with whom Nimlin and Bob Ewing made the first complete ascent of Recess Route on the Cobbler, no other members seemed to have been involved in finding new climbs. Records from this period tend to be patchy, however, and the nature of Ptarmigan Club 'holidays' would probably impress current members of the special forces.

With a smaller number of SMC members and their guests using the CIC Hut, they were often outnumbered by the younger climbers of the JMCS, though not necessarily at the same time. With increasing experience they would become a crucial component of the mix of Scottish climbers. The working-class component suffered from high unemployment, which often constrained their activities to the Loch Lomond basin, the Trossachs and the Arrochar area.

It is interesting to contrast the weekend outing by Hutchison and Rutherfurd described above with one experienced by those less well off. If you were working and lucky enough to finish at Saturday lunchtime, it was possible to buy a workman's ticket, allowing easier access by bus to a popular launching spot such as Balloch, Drymen or Helensburgh. From there, one continued by walking through the darkness or gained a lift by hitching. Nimlin described one such walk which might have easily killed someone less tough.

On Saturday 21 February 1931 he caught the last bus to Drymen. An 11-mile trudge through more than two feet of fresh snow led to Rowardennan on the eastern shore of Loch Lomond. Here he slept for four hours on the concrete floor of a corrugated-iron shed, using a large tarpaulin as a blanket. After breakfast he continued to Cailness, meeting Jimmie Stewart and Johnny Evans. The latter decided to take the main road from Inversnaid to Aberfoyle, but Stewart had more ambitious plans and suggested a traverse of Ben Lomond to Glen Dubh, then to the Duchray Pass.

When Nimlin and Stewart gained the open hillside, they realised the plan was over-ambitious. The snow had fallen with no wind and lay uniformly deep with no compaction. They decided to head for the pass north-west of Cruinn a' Bheinn, at around 1,100ft, from where they would drop east then south to Campbell the shepherd's cottage at Comer. The going was desperately strenuous. Stewart was wearing shorts and his knees were cut by a slight crust on the surface of the snow, which meant that Nimlin had to break trail. They gained the pass at 2pm, the wind blasting them with ice crystals. It was three miles to the cottage, and hard work with peat hags, hummocks and deep runnels. They even tried wading down the burn, but pools of freezing water soon drove them out.

Close to exhaustion, they stopped to eat and could feel their wet feet beginning to freeze. Eventually they were close enough to the cottage to hold a shouted conversation with Mrs Campbell, who pressed them to hurry as she was putting the kettle on. At 5pm, in the twilight, they reached the cottage, which had snow up to its eaves. The shepherd, on his day off, was snug by the fire, feet up on the mantelshelf, pipe propped on his chest. They were given a meal of boiled eggs, fresh scones and very hot tea. After an hour, despite the offer of two beds in the attic, they set off again. The last bus was already about to leave Aberfoyle for Glasgow and they still had ten more miles to go.

The sky was now clear with a moon, which with the uniform snow cover gave a brilliant light. After another seven miles of slow trudge, they gained the Duchray Pass. Despite a strong desire to lie down and sleep, they carried on, reaching Kinlochard post office from where they telephoned a reassuring message home, before carrying on to Aberfoyle, gained at 4am. They enjoyed three hours' sleep in a cold doorway, after which the first bus took them to Glasgow, with a full day's work ahead of them.

The obvious differences between Nimlin and his working-class friends, and the middle-class climbers, included the lack of a sleeping bag, tent, bicycle or car. They survived this brutal winter walk due to their innate toughness and fitness.

Elsewhere, the Tricouni Mountaineering Club was formed in 1930 with around 20 members of both sexes. It never exceeded 40 in number, and had as its climbing qualification the ability to traverse the three peaks of the Cobbler. It mattered not in what style this was done, as an agreeable personality was more important than mere climbing ability. The club met on Friday nights in one of Miss Cranston's tea rooms in Glasgow to plan trips, as women were barred from pubs. The Tricouni could claim several well-known climbers as members, including Hamish Hamilton and Alex Small. There was no link with an English club of the same name, and World War II effectively led to the club's demise.

Another club was formed in 1930, one which would, particularly after World War II, make many outstanding contributions to climbing. This was the Creagh Dhu MC, consisting largely of Clydeside shipbuilding workers.

Contrary to general perceptions, it had four women members, all married to members; Elsie Jamieson, Tess Brown, Mary Miller and May MacFarlane. Elsie Jamieson was secretary of the Club for a time in the 1930s. (See Chapter 8 for more of this Club.)

The Elgin-based Moray Mountaineering Club was formed on 15 November 1931 by Finlay Mackenzie (who became its first president), Edwin Davidson (secretary and treasurer) and John Geddes. Its prime objective was to train novices, and by 1935 there were 120 members, rising to 172 by 1939, with Geddes noting that *'A Moray Meet was like a large, happy family party.'* It tended to concentrate on the Cairngorms and Western Highlands, but members now seem to be active around the world.

The Scottish Youth Hostels Association (SYHA) was formed in Edinburgh in 1931. To quote from the minutes of that meeting, chaired by Lord Salvesen, its aims were –

> To help all, but especially young people of limited means living and working in industrial and other areas, to know use and appreciate the Scottish countryside and places of historic and cultural interest in Scotland, and to promote their health, recreation and education, particularly by providing simple hostel accommodation for them on their travels.[12]

The first hostel was opened later that year, at Broadmeadows near Yarrow, and by 1936 there were 48 hostels and a membership of almost 12,000. The hostels were of particular value for visitors from abroad, intent on seeing the Scottish landscape as well as its principal cities. Many members used the hostels to walk and perhaps even climb on the Scottish hills, finding them useful bases with friendly wardens who could hand out good advice, but many impecunious or unemployed explorers continued to sleep out as before or camp closer to their intended destination.

❊❊❊

Social structure was evolving, and with it the variety of places to sleep at night. The use of howffs – a Scots word for a haunt or meeting-place, meaning here a rough shelter in the hills – became widespread. A howff was usually made by improving a natural shelter under a large rock, a practice probably copied from shepherds, and before modern, lightweight tents became affordable such places were used fairly extensively to allow a closer approach to climbing areas. In the southern Highlands for example, the Cobbler and the Brack on opposite sides of Glen Croe each had well-made howffs.

Howffs were even more popular in the Cairngorms, where long approaches were made more bearable by an overnight stop. One of the oldest examples must be the Shelter Stone, at the head of Loch Avon, while the Garbh Choire of Braeriach has its own howff. They vary from large to small, from semi-open to claustrophobic, and accordingly cover a wide spectrum of comfort. Jock Nimlin had a good article on mountain howffs in the SMCJ, where he described Cobbler View, the howff in the lower corrie of the Brack. [13] This proved useful for him, Ben Humble and other climbers while they were researching the 1954 Arrochar guidebook.

Nimlin described the preparation of Cobbler View, where a huge mica-schist block was resting on several square-sided rocks. The base of the main block formed the roof, which luckily sloped down towards the entrance. As was often the case, the formidable-looking rocks on the cave floor were loosely bedded and easy to remove. Lacking axes or picks, the climbers improvised with flattened soup-tins, the work taking three hours:

> Many of the rocks thus excavated weighed several hundredweights, but gravity worked on our behalf. Adopting back-and-knee positions and pushing all together, we soon levered them to the doorway and toppled them down a short slope to the heather. Having thus cleared a space for five or six sleepers, we levelled off the floor, sealed up the apertures at the back of the cave and laid in a foot of heather and moss for bedding. The secret of a draught-proof howff is to baffle the air currents by allowing only one ingress, which should be as small as possible. A ground-sheet hung over a wedged tree-branch or ice-axe will then seal the entrance against driving snow or rain. This howff, "Cobbler View," was well tested for structural defects that same night. A thunderstorm travelled over Glencroe, and we lay securely in our sleeping-bags as the blades of lightning flashed against the dark mass of the Cobbler.

It is of course also possible to prepare a temporary howff in snow, given a sufficient depth and consistency. A good-sized snowbank is usually a prerequisite, allowing a cave-like space to be excavated, and overnighting in a snow-hole is therefore unlikely to be a spur-of-the-moment event. Bridges were also popular, and Nimlin knew of many such shelters, including at least one in Glen Coe. The obvious disadvantages of bridges are traffic noise, running water and the potential for flooding.

❉❉❉

The 1920s had brought difficult living conditions for many, and with the Wall Street Crash matters became worse as the US economy nose-dived into depression. With a mood of alarm setting in, the Americans called in foreign loans and erected customs barriers; the depression became global. In 1931, the UK government raised income tax and cut unemployment benefit by 10 per cent; the reduction in spending power deepened the depression, hitting the lowest-paid the hardest and leading to mass unemployment. This had an impact on Scottish mountaineering.

By the late 1920s, Nimlin had amassed several years of good climbing. His energy and drive, combined with a ferocious fitness, made him a highly competent mountaineer, with a toughness burnished from many a hard outing.

He had also become a proficient writer, and his introduction to the SMCJ article reads as well today as it would have done in 1940. He continued to describe the nature of climbing on the mica-schist of the Cobbler, explaining how a handhold anywhere else would be looked on as jug-handle if found on the Cobbler, as climbing here often requires confidence and a cool head.

Many a good day on its rocks was based from Bruce's Cave in Glen Loin, the western flank of which, under A' Chrois, is a warren of hollows and caves. These would become popular in the 1930s for weekenders seeking shelter from the weather (and perhaps from the law). The 1954 guidebook to rock climbs at Arrochar includes a section on the caves and fissures in the area, of which Bruce's Cave is the largest and most accessible. It can be found about 100m above the floor of Glen Loin, on the west side of the burn which drains the eastern corrie of A' Chrois, Coire nan Each. Above this is another large cave leading to a 30m chimney which can be climbed in semi-darkness by back and foot, emerging on to the hillside above.

Borthwick's classic book *Always a Little Further* gives a vivid description of the entry to what was probably Bruce's Cave, on a January evening in 1933. Borthwick eventually found the entrance after stumbling around the hillside, courtesy of the smell of kippers emanating from a hole in the ground. Inside were three young men by a wood fire, frying the fish and heating a black pudding above the fire. Introductions were informal and food was shared.

That night arrivals kept on coming, until 18 were in the cave. As Borthwick learned, it was the club-room and hotel for the Creagh Dhu Mountaineering Club. There is a darker side to these geological features, however, as there have been several accidents relating to the fissures in this area, including the death (in 2006) of a very experienced mountaineer.

In 1932, John Harvey founded the Lomond Mountaineering Club. Like the Creagh Dhu, this was Glasgow-based, and both clubs seem to have required a six-month apprenticeship. The Lomond club, which continues to this day with a wide range of hill pursuits, was by far the largest and best organised of these inter-war clubs and began bus meets – usually to Glen Coe, but for longer weekends to areas further afield including the Lake District, Fort William and Aviemore.

The Lomond club bus became a popular fixture with climbers, and was used as cheap transport by many. The bus even acquired a name – *The Mountaineer* – and just before the outbreak of World War II it made two trips to Switzerland. By 1939, club membership was about 50. The Lomond club included women members, as noted by Archie Hendry (1919-2013), an Edinburgh schoolmaster and member of the SMC, when describing a Glen Coe holiday trip in July 1940.

He mentions a large encampment near Achtriochtan Cottage, where the Lomond bus had arrived and its passengers were busy setting up tents. The following day Hendry's party and some Lomond members were climbing on Aonach Dubh, and Hendry (described by Robin N Campbell in his obituary as '*...deft, witty, and often barbed*'), noted that '*The feminine contingent very properly stayed by the tents to carry out their domestic duties.*' [14]

Hendry may have written in jest, though the above quote was certainly in appearance barbed, and we will hear more of him later. As for the competence of Lomond club women, routes climbed by them included Clachaig Gully, Raven's Gully, and other good climbs.

Jim Bell wrote two useful surveys of Scottish climbing clubs and rightly singled out Nimlin as being an influential figure at this time–

> If we regard W.W. Naismith as the father of the S.M.C., we might almost look on J.B. Nimlin as the parent of this new type of climber, as he was the founder of the first of these clubs and has had much to do with most of the others. [15,16]

❊❊❊

The latter part of the 1930s and the early war years saw a succession of Scottish university mountaineering clubs being formed: St Andrews (1934), Edinburgh (1939), Aberdeen (as the Lairig Club, 1940) and Glasgow (1941). Many students went on to join one or more of the senior clubs, while in a few cases members of a senior club aided the formation of a student club. As might be expected, the history of these clubs tends to be patchier, as rapid turnover of members and the distracting pressures of undergraduate life made for a reduced continuity of reporting in journals or magazines.

Dundee continued to expand its interest in mountaineering, with the formation of two more clubs in 1937. The Corrie Club started in June that year, founded by Jack Scott, Kenny McLaren and John G Ferguson, with a ladies' section added in 1939. Syd Scroggie – later to become widely known as a blind hillgoer and author– and his brother Jack were members. First ascents were made in Glen Clova and on Lochnagar. A Dundee branch of the Creagh Dhu was also started that same year, and by 1939 it had 20 members before breaking up during the war.

The Etchachan Club, based in Aberdeen, was formed in 1938. This was, as a member admitted when writing a brief history, '*...a breakaway offshoot from the mighty Cairngorm Club*'. It was started by William Lawson, George A Beckslinn and Garth Lorimer, and there were 54 members by 1940.

One of the strengths of the university clubs was that they had a mixed membership. The LSCC continued, but it was an older, established unisex club and not an obvious or convenient route to the mountains for an impecunious female student. Some clubs did not admit women, or at least did not promote their membership, and this narrowed the options even further. Despite this, as will be seen later, good routes were put up which involved women, while further social changes during and after World War II would help to introduce a more democratic atmosphere.

The 1975 issue of the SMCJ has a collection of articles celebrating the 50th anniversary of the JMCS, which had been formed, in its several sections, during a period when the country was still feeling the effects of World War I. [17] There were ongoing changes in society, and subsequent upheavals would affect everyone.

Despite this background, some had the energy and enthusiasm to put their boots on and do something, especially if that something involved the mountains. This energy would see the formation of new climbing clubs, many open to all, with Nimlin and the JMCS being major influences. The importance of events in 1925 cannot be overstated. With hindsight, the period not only brought into play a large number of new participants, it also encouraged others to form their own clubs, and so the sport blossomed.

Arthur Rusk died in 1965. He had been one of the founders of the JMCS. In the leading article of the 1975 collection another of the original members, Archie Hutchison, recalled Rusk's life philosophy, which had led to the club's formation under that wrinkled boulder beside the Buttermilk Burn and hence to the inter-war growth of mountaineering in Scotland. It seems right to finish this chapter with Hutchison's words–

> Rusk looked on mountains as a challenge. Many do. But, to him the challenge did not only provide an opportunity in which he might express himself. He looked on mountains from a wider angle and felt the challenge as something more subtle. They were not chance phenomena. They were there for a purpose and had a part to play in the scheme of things. They influenced the lives of men and pointed a way, endlessly, up and beyond the low levels where, for the most part, man's course is run. Metaphysically speaking, mankind need not live in the valleys. The mountains vision could and should have a wider implication in human events. So, he had a burning urge that men and mountains must meet. I think if he were living now, how much he would rejoice that more and more they do. Over the door of the Town Hall in Sacramento, California, a Legend is engraved:-

> *'Give me men to match my mountains.'*

> Those who go on the mountains might well ponder these words in respect of our responsibilities in today's world. Still more widely, they might provide a clue on how to restore the sense of purpose which the world needs so much.[18]

References

1. Borthwick, Alastair. *Always a Little Further*. (Faber and Faber Limited, London. 1939).
2. Smith, Malcolm. *The Etchachan Club*. In: Kindred Clubs. SMCJ 27, 153, May 1962, pp.250-253). Excerpted from the Etchachan Club Journal, 1959.
3. <http://www.durc.org.uk/> (Accessed March 2016).
4. Maxwell, Sir John Stirling, Bart. *The Glen Coe Road*. SMCJ 18, 105, April 1928, pp.149-165.
5. Nimlin, Jock. *Let's Look at Scottish Gemstones*. (Jarrold Publishing, Sept. 1974. ISBN 9780853064916, 32pp.)
6. Nimlin, John. *May the Fire Be Always Lit*. SMCJ 27, 154, May 1963, pp. 336-342.
7. Rutherfurd, R.N. *More Than Fifty Years Ago*. In: The Formation of the J.M.C.S. SMCJ 30, 166, 1975, pp.310-312.
8. In: Events of Note. SMCJ 17, 100, November 1925, p.236.
9 Nimlin, John. *May the Fire be Always Lit*. SMCJ, 27, 154, May 1963, pp.336-342.
10. Thomson, I.D.S. *May the fire be always lit. A biography of Jock Nimlin*. (The Ernest Press, Glasgow. 1995. ISBN 9-780948-153396.
11. Bell, JHB. *Scottish Climbing Clubs: A Survey. II. The Younger Glasgow Clubs*. SMCJ, 23, 137, April 1946, pp. 300-301.
12. <http://www.nls.uk/catalogues/online/cnmi/inventories/acc13372.pdf> (Accessed December 2015).
13. Nimlin, John B. *Mountain Howffs*. SMCJ 24,139, May 1948, pp.1-8.
14 Campbell, Robin N. *Archie H. Hendry*. In Memorium. SMCJ 42, 204, 2013, pp.613-616.
15. Bell, JHB. *Scottish Climbing Clubs: A Survey. I*. SMCJ, 23, 136, April 1945, pp.252-260.
16. Bell, JHB. *Scottish Climbing Clubs: A Survey. II*. SMCJ, 23, 137, April 1946, pp. 295-308.
17. Various. *The Formation of the J.M.C.S.* SMCJ 30, 166, 1975, pp.309-347.
18. Hutchison, A. G. *The Beginning of the J.M.C.S.* In: The Formation of the JMCS. SMCJ 30, 166, 1975, pp.309-310.

4

Nimlin, Bell & Macphee (1929-1933)

The Skye guidebook, published in 1923, was heavily indebted to Steeple and Barlow, with many of the routes having been climbed by that pair. Harry MacRobert was the general editor, diagrams were by Steeple, with a selection of photographs by the Reverend Archie Robertson. Many of the illustrations were drawn by Eric Greenwood, himself a climber. He had illustrated Slingsby's book *Norway, the Northern Playground*, published in 1904.[1]

One feature of the Skye guide was an attempt to provide grades for the routes. The authors employed a four-level numerical style, from the easiest, 1, to the hardest, 4, along with an adjectival equivalent: *Easy, Moderate* and so on. This grading system would have been based on the guide to Skye published in the 1902 SMCJ and written by William Douglas – who had himself based this system on Owen Glynn Jones' guide to his *Rock Climbing in the English Lake District*, published in 1897. [2,3]

The Jones guide using the following system–

A rough classification is here appended of some sixty of the well-known courses judged under good conditions. They are divided into four sets. The first are easy and adapted for beginners, the second set are moderately stiff, those of the third set rank as the difficult climbs of the district, and the last are of exceptional severity.

These grades were then *Easy, Moderate, Difficult,* and *Exceptionally Severe*. Jones wrote that items in the fourth class were best left alone, and added the words of Charles Pilkington:

The novice must on no account attempt them. He may console himself with the reflection that most of these fancy bits of rock-work are not mountaineering proper, and by remembering that those who first explored these routes, or rather created them, were not only brilliant rock gymnasts but experienced and capable cragsmen.

An interesting and generally well-researched article by Sandy Wedderburn in 1939 stated that the publication of the Skye guidebook seemed to put an end to the period of English activity on the island, even though the following year saw Steeple and Barlow active again, making the book out of date. [4] The only other pair doing new routes in 1924 were Frank Smythe and Jim Bell, with *West Trap Route* (240m Severe) on Sgùrr Sgumain and *West Ridge of the Cìoch* (140m Severe). The years 1925-1926, Wedderburn continued, were blank in Skye, as in the rest of Scotland.

In this he was unaware of a route found by Claude Deane Frankland (1878-1927), which was an oversight, as it had been mentioned in the SMCJ of April 1934. [5] The article described a later ascent, perhaps even a second ascent, of the gully on the North Buttress of Sgùrr Sgumain that had first been climbed in 1925 by a strong English party comprising Frankland, Mary Mabel Barker (1886-1961) and HV Hughes.

Frankland, a schoolmaster and member of both the Yorkshire Ramblers' Club (YRC) and FRCC, was a latecomer to climbing, having taken it up when he was 31. He put up hard climbs at Almscliffe, including Central Route and Green Crack, having learned to climb safely while out of balance on very steep ground by pulling outwards on his hands, a technique not then used by most. He was killed while leading a Very Difficult route, Chantry Buttress on the Napes on Great Gable; it seems that a hold snapped off, with the second unable to hold the fall.

Barker was a geology graduate who went on to gain a PhD in education, setting up an outdoor pursuits centre at Caldbeck in the northern Lake District. In 1926 she became the first woman to traverse the Cuillin ridge, along with Frankland and without use of a rope. Hughes had climbed with Macphee on Nevis.

On 4 August 1925, the trio entered Coire Lagan in thick mist, aiming for the Sgùrr Alasdair face with hopes of either Collie's or Abraham's route. They failed to find a cairn, and Frankland decided to find a way up a wall and so gain the ridge. After passing an evil-looking crack, severely overhung and with a bright green moss patch, they climbed a mantelshelf problem and found themselves in a deep gully. This provided a good climb leading to an easy ridge and so to the top. When the mist cleared they realised they were on Sgùrr Sgumain, not Sgùrr Alasdair.

The gully is briefly noted in an article by Barker in the YRC journal, where she mentions a new climb they did on Sgùrr Sgumain, proposing to call it *'Big Wall Gully.'* [6]

> On the way we encountered a mantelshelf. C.D.F. led up it: I tried to follow.
> H. V. Hughes, who was third, could only see my boots from his stance. He

says he went to sleep, woke up again, and they were still there. However, they are not there now, nor is he, so we all got up somehow in the end, but it was not a star performance, except for the leader.

After Frankland's death, Hughes in 1934 decided to commemorate a '... *fine cragsman and a lover of the Coolin by calling the climb "Frankland's Gully."'* The route was a 300m Hard Severe.

On 24 June 1927, another good route was added on Skye– *West Face Direct* (200m Hard Severe), which climbs the Fourth Pinnacle of Sgùrr nan Gillean, Knight's Peak. The perpetrators were Francis Waldron Giveen (1904-1930), CH Cooper and DR Orr. The description in the *Climbers' Club Bulletin* for November 1927 by Giveen notes *'Rubbers advised. Leader needs 100 Feet of rope. Rock good throughout.'* The current guide has it as an interesting and popular route – and what is certainly interesting is Giveen's life.

An advocate's son, he was thrown out of Oxford, not just Wadham College, but the city as a whole, for the offence of placing a chamber pot on the war memorial. While a member of the Climbers' Club, he and his companion committed what might possibly now be regarded as manslaughter. For the grisly details, see *'Hole in the Mind'* in the blog *Footless Crow* for 9 January 2016.

❄❄❄

On a holiday on Arran in July 1927, Nimlin made an audacious attempt to climb Beinn Nuis Chimney (130m VS), retreating from the third chockstone by fixed rope – but his most happy hunting ground was the Cobbler, where he made at least 11 first ascents –

Route	Climbers	Original Grade	Current Grade
Right-Angled Gully – Direct Finish 1930	Nimlin, Solo	S	S
Right-Angled Groove 1934	Nimlin, Solo	VS	S
Recess Route May 1935	Nimlin, John Fox, Bob Ewing	S	S
Fold Direct June 1936	Nimlin, David Browning	VS	S
North Rib Route 1935	Nimlin, John Fox	V Diff	V Diff
Ardgartan Wall October 1937	Nimlin, Jimmy Wyne, Wattie Neilson, Rab Goldie	S	V Diff

It is worth highlighting Right-Angled Groove, the original description for which includes–

> Stonecrop grows profusely on the lower part. The holds are small and sloping and the whole route very exposed. Awkward bulge at 30 feet and traverse left at 90 feet on minute holds. Dry windless weather essential. Can only be done as a single pitch, balance climbing throughout, so rather hazardous. Climbed in rubbers.

A modern ascent will find protection, bringing the grade down to Severe. The finish is on the steep headwall with an enhanced sense of exposure. The reference to rubbers concerned the increasing use of 'sannies', light canvas shoes with rubber soles called sandshoes and which presumably became associated with holidays and beaches. Another common name is plimsolls. It should be borne in mind that the few small reductions in grade are not surprising, considering that there would be vegetation on the first ascents and that modern footwear makes an ascent much easier.

The grades given above are from the current SMC guidebook, as are other grades in this volume. Over the decades there has been a general upward trend, with some routes originally climbed at, say, V Diff now regarded as Severe. Many of these climbs would have been led in nailed boots or sandshoes. Additionally, the more popular lines such as Recess Route have become polished over time, which may increase their grade.

Ardgartan Wall, another of the 'newer balance' climbs, was, like Right-Angled Groove, cautioned against on a windy day. There is a film in the Scottish Screen Archive taken by Ben Humble in 1946 and showing a traverse of the Cobbler peaks with Nimlin, Harry Grant and David Easson, and including Ardgartan Wall. [7]

Nimlin's explorations in the Arrochar Alps, in which he was joined by members of the Creagh Dhu and others, would lead eventually in 1954 to the first guide to rock climbs in the area, written by Humble and Nimlin. It was published by the SMC, with Bill Smith thanked in the acknowledgments – he was responsible for most of the accounts of Creagh Dhu climbs.

In the guide's historical notes, the authors found it difficult to account for the neglect suffered by the Arrochar area in the period 1906-26, suggesting that the '...*scathing (and quite untrue) reference to The Cobbler in G.D. Abraham's British Mountain Climbs (1909) may have had something to do with it.*' Certainly during the initial phase of climbing in Scotland, before World War I, climbers from the south usually headed for Skye, which had easier travel and access.

In his 1909 guide, George Abraham had described the Cobbler and other Arrochar hills, but he was evidently disgruntled, with the tone of the entire section being negative. Referring to the Cobbler, he noted that it and Glen Croe had the reputation of being one of the wettest districts in Scotland, with the weird summit outline often hidden–

If mist-hidden, the temptation is lacking; truly ignorance is bliss in this case. The writer speaks feelingly in this matter, for during the first visit to Scotland his party were led to curtail their climbing on Ben Nevis in order to spend some days on the Cobbler during the homeward journey. The result was disappointing. Instead of a ridge, the mountain-top proved to be a sort of plateau, with curious outcrops of most unsatisfactory rock forming the skyline. The supporting crags were found to consist of a micaceous schist, unreliable, smooth, and vegetation-draped; moreover, they were set at such angles as usually to be either impossible or ridiculously easy. At the end of a day, despite some unpleasantly exciting moments, there was a feeling that no genuine rock-climbing had been encountered. [8]

Abraham had been one of the foremost climbers of his day. Perhaps he was intent on a new climb, and was unused to the often unnecessary removal of unwanted vegetation – and the rock itself may well have been new to him, with its demanding nature obliging a climber to make a succession of moves in balance, often with an absence of comforting holds.

In an article in the SMCJ of November 1940, Nimlin gave his response and included a list of climbs which had been compiled by George Clarke Williams (1903-1981), a commercial importer from Glasgow who joined the SMC in 1930. Williams was on the first ascent of Route 1 on the Buachaille's Rannoch Wall, and the Cobbler descriptions were to have been included in the Southern Highlands Guide which was delayed by World War II. Eight later routes were added by Humble, along with three photographs, while Small prepared finished diagrams from rough sketches.[9]

Nimlin's words were clearly aimed at the Abraham description, as when he described the Cobbler style of climbing – it may be guessed who was meant by 'spring-cleaning' cragsmen. The italics are Nimlin's–

> Nowadays there is no need to adopt an apologetic note on the introduction of a Cobbler Guide, for this mountain has come into its own. For years it was neglected, sometimes even miscalled, and except for an occasional note contributed by early devotees its climbing potentialities were for the most part unknown.
>
> But this was hardly reason for regret; it meant that the Cobbler could preserve its pristine shagginess and the glamour of the unknown until ten short years ago. Its hanging gardens had a longer immunity from the vandal grasp of "spring-cleaning" cragsmen, and its time-hewn wrinkles were spared the ravages of the ruthless clinker.
>
> For a surprising number of years the Cobbler produced no more than a handful of rather dull routes—mere practice courses for exploits on better peaks. But virtue will out. The restless eye of a later climbing generation found new and worthier routes. Nailmarks multiplied and spread over crags which earlier writers described as impossible, and soon the stigma of *practice*

ground was removed for all time. Indeed, it may now be said that many of the *better* peaks make suitable practice grounds for the Cobbler.

❋❋❋

If the southern Highlands saw little exploration in the 1920s, the northern Highlands were almost completely ignored. The SMC Northern Highlands Guide of 1932, written by Willie Ling, has virtually nothing to say of 1920s exploratory climbing. Jim Bell was on the 1923 SMC Easter Meet which was held at the end of March and based mainly at Kinlochewe. Although blessed with good weather, there was very little snow in what had been a very dry early spring. One gully on An Teallach did hold snow, and was duly climbed on 30 March by Bell and his guest EE Roberts: *Lord's Gully, Right Branch* (400m II).

The second chapter mentioned Pigott's Route on Beinn Eighe, easily the major find of this decade in this area and made by the English climbers Fred Pigott and Morley Wood in the summer of 1922. Other than this, climbers were very thin on the ground and were mostly content to scramble and walk. One exception was during the SMC Easter Meet at the end of March 1926, held in Glen Shiel, when Arthur Rusk, Louis St Clair Bartholomew and John Alexander Scott (1901-1972) found *Big Gully* (200m V Diff) on the Saddle. Climbed in mixed conditions, it provided snow, chockstones and vegetated pitches. Two easy snow gullies were recorded on Liathach in 1928 by elderly SMC members.

Jim Bell had joined the SMC in 1922. By 1927 he was still finding his way, but would become one of the leading mountaineers in Scotland. An early ascent was made on the last day of 1927, during an SMC meet at Loch Awe. The climb, on Beinn Eunaich, was on the right flank of the Black Shoot, *Beaver Buttress* (120m III). This vegetatious horror had been the target for the rope of four; John Rooke Corbett (1876-1949), a district valuer from Manchester, Charles Wynn Parry (1901-1960), a schoolmaster from Surrey, a guest APA Robertson, and Bell. The route's name was a nod to Corbett's magnificent beard.

Corbett was one of the founders of the Rucksack Club and a member of the SMC since 1923. A prodigious walker, in 1930 he became the second person to complete the Munros and Tops, and in addition attempted to climb all Scottish hills from 2,500ft to 2,999ft, leading to the list of hills named after him (though in this last endeavour it isn't certain that he succeeded). On his death his list was passed to the SMC by his sister Dr Catherine Corbett, herself an accomplished climber and founder member of the Pinnacle Club.

The quartet found the route entertaining, with powder snow and a hard frost, and it was climbed as a second choice when the Black Shoot looked uninviting. Various short traverses were made, with Parry leading several hard pitches, one of which forced Bell to use an axe as a foothold while another short section demanded combined tactics. The current guide confesses that the given grade of III is a guess – the route might still be awaiting a second ascent.

By the end of the 1920s, Bell was beginning to make his mark on Scottish mountaineering. Within the SMC he was trying to improve the publication of guidebooks, and suggested that before a new guide was published there should be a good examination of existing routes, with a special committee set up to report to the various editors. He had already written notes commenting on the descriptions of routes and evidently felt that in some cases there was room for improvement. [10]

The existing procedure for guidebooks appeared to be simply one of tacking on new climbs to the existing version and trusting that these were more or less correct. This may well have been acceptable in the early years with slow exploration and few climbers, but circumstances were changing and the old order had to be replaced by those capable of adapting to the changes.

On 6 July 1929, Bell met Alex Harrison at the Kings House and headed for Central Buttress on Buachaille Etive Mor, where they climbed most of what is now the popular *North Face Route* (220m Severe). Bell wrote a description of their weekend of exploration. The pair employed combined tactics at one awkward point, but it was nonetheless a fresh approach, looking for new rock and boldly taking in a steep new buttress. The final section, on excellent, rough rhyolite, making a leftward traverse and taking in slabs, was added in September 1936 by Douglas Scott, JC Henderson, AM MacAlpine and WH Murray. [11]

Harrison, along with Addenbrooke and Bartholomew, also recorded *D Gully Buttress* (150m Difficult/Severe) in July 1929. There was an earlier ascent of this route, with a note by WC Newbigging describing an ascent of the ridge left of D Gully on 13 October 1903. Newbigging left out the lower easy section, perhaps due to the very wet conditions on the day, with the leader (assumed to be Newbigging himself) requiring assistance at two points. [12]

Bell became renowned for his ability to climb in summer where almost no one nowadays would wish to follow. Proof of this lies scattered around Scotland, with examples not only on major mountains and cliffs, but also on lesser hills. As mentioned in chapter two, he learned to climb, alone, on the poor rocks of the Lomond Hills, where handholds were a temporary aberration and vegetation a pleasing decoration. The author has climbed several such routes on the Ochils and can testify to the statement by Bell (as related by Murray), that *'Any fool can climb good rock; but it takes craft and cunning to get up vegetatious schist and granite.'* [13]

The occasion of this Bell quote was on 28 May 1939, when Bell and Murray were en route to make the first ascent of *Parallel Buttress* (280m Severe) on Lochnagar. Murray was astute enough not to disagree with Bell, recalling the old saying that '*...it did not pay to curse the alligator's mother before fording the river*', and he knew full well that Lochnagar '*...was the greatest citadel of vegetatious granite*'. In winter, the route provides an excellent VI, 6 climb, but in summer dry conditions are virtually a necessity. The ascent was made more dramatic at the crux, a steep wall with a thin crack which defeated both climbers until Bell delved into his sack to produce a hammer and two pegs. These he used for handholds to overcome the section, athletically mantelshelfing on to the first peg.

Bell had already made other first ascents, ranging across Scotland but mainly in Glen Coe and on Ben Nevis in the west, and on Lochnagar in the east. Between 1924 and 1950, he recorded about 70 first ascents, summer and winter, several of which have become classic routes.

In Glen Coe, for example, he made two routes on Diamond Buttress of Bidean nam Bian; the second, harder route, *Direct Route* (150m Severe), climbed in August 1931 with Colin M Allan (a JMCS member), was on steep and occasionally vegetated ground that is better saved for a winter ascent (250m VI, 6). Bell was busy that year, as work was ongoing for a guidebook to Glen Coe. Again with Allan on Bidean, he climbed *Summit Buttress* (130m Very Difficult) on 13 September. This was another climb better done in winter, but Bell was opening up new ground.

After lunch, the two climbers set to work on the triple buttresses of Stob Coire nan Lochan, with Bell naming these South, Central and North. Now highly popular, with excellent routes both summer and winter, this fine corrie had been neglected since the early pioneers – Collie and Hastings climbed here in May 1894, while the inimitable Raeburn found the excellent winter route up Central Buttress with the Clarks in April 1907.

Bell and Allan climbed North Buttress on very loose rock. It contained a chimney which was so loose and dangerous that Bell, belaying his companion, wore a large flat rock plate as a headpiece to protect himself from debris. They finished their day with a descent of SC Gully, now a popular winter classic, with Bell recognising that it would make a magnificent climb under snow and ice. (In *The Early Years*, mention was made of the possibility that this gully could have been first climbed in winter in 1906, by Glover and Wordsell. [14])

Many of Bell's routes at this time will have been on mixed ground, with loose rock, tottery sections, wet and slimy rock, vegetation and so on, but he was not afraid to venture on to new, previously bypassed rock. Many of his routes, despite their state in summer, had taken good lines and are now good winter options – and, as will be seen, his explorations would lead to better material soon enough.

In an article entitled *Research in Glencoe,* Bell not only publicised the forthcoming new section of the SMC guidebook, but was open enough to highlight areas of rock which appeared to be promising, an act of generosity which might astound the current generation of climbers. [15] He pointed out that the Chasm had not yet had a complete summer ascent, while *'The great precipice facing Kingshouse is also not in a satisfactory state'* – a reference to what is now known as the Rannoch Wall. Also mentioned on the Buachaille was Central Buttress, which Bell readily admitted needed a direct and central route.

On Bidean nam Bian, the North Face of Aonach Dubh had promising lines, as did Stob Coire nam Beith. It is also interesting what Bell did not mention: the East Face of Aonach Dubh. Three years later, in September 1934, he would record – again with Allan – *Original Route* (90m Severe). It was not on one of the main faces, however, but comprised a good, old-fashioned, boulder-rattling chimney tucked away in a shadowy corner. It was not until 1947 that the face would finally be recognised as a first-class playground of enjoyable rock climbs on good rock.

Elsewhere on Bidean, Bell noted that in October 1930 there had been a failed attempt to climb Eastern Buttress (now known as Diamond Buttress) by a central route. As noted above, he went back in August 1931 and with Allan succeeded. These tantalising admissions, along with the wide knowledge that a guidebook was in preparation, stimulated climbing. The reminder that the Chasm still awaited a direct finish prompted its first complete ascent on 30 August 1931 by Iain Garson Jack (1906-1976) and James Gordon Robinson (1910-199?). Both were JMCS members, and both joined the SMC in 1933.

An attempt was made on Clachaig Gully in September 1931 by the two Speirs brothers, William Blair (1907-1997) and George Ramsay (1908-1983). Again, both were JMCS members, and had joined the SMC in 1927 and 1928 respectively. Despite relatively dry conditions, they were defeated, being forced out of the main gully at the Great Cave Pitch – a barrier to all attempts thus far, starting with Collie, Solly and Collier in March 1894. William Speirs would go on to be SMC president (1956-1958).

❊❊❊

Bell was not the only major character on the stage at this time; a very different man was likewise a rising star. Joining the SMC in 1927 having been proposed by the botanist Professor Fred Bower, George Graham Macphee (1898-1963) was a dentist in Liverpool, having first trained in medicine. Born and educated in Glasgow, he was in many ways a contrast to Bell. He joined the Highland Light Infantry aged 17, then transferred to the Royal Flying Corps and was shot down behind enemy lines in April 1918 and held prisoner.

Although he had made his first ascent of Ben Nevis aged eight, Macphee appears to have had no direct stimulus to take up climbing, and did not begin until aged 28. He was described by Frank Smythe as being not averse to leading, but the ideal second, having a strong build with a watchful nature. Macphee kept a diary from an early age, which, according to Smythe, reflected his *somewhat unimaginative and plodding nature*. Nonetheless, while at Liverpool – where he held an academic post and built up two profitable dental practices – he was supportive of the university mountaineering club. [16]

A biographical article by Ken Smith (1901-2000) in the SMCJ paints a picture of Macphee, warts and all. He is described as having a caustic sense of humour and a superior manner, which coupled with his Kelvinside accent would be enough to set some people off along the wrong road. He certainly had a reputation for bearing grudges, and apart from his having fallen out with Bell, Smith mentions a mutual and intense dislike between Macphee and Alan B Hargreaves of the FRCC (no relation to Albert T Hargreaves), as well as a long-standing feud with Graham Brown. [17]

One can imagine the Bell and Macphee interactions: Bell would bounce ideas off Macphee and seek a discussion about, well, anything, with a heady mix of science, philosophy, politics, music and so on, to which Macphee might well dampen the Fifer's flow with some deflationary remark. They climbed a few routes together, including in the Alps, but it was probably then that each went his own way, following an incident when, in a foursome, Macphee's partner dropped his axe and Macphee insisted on continuing, leaving Bell to descend with the axeless one. Whatever the trigger, the two were ill-matched.

Macphee made several significant ascents while teamed with Albert T Hargreaves. These included, in 1930, the ascent of Deer Bield Crack in Far Easedale, an outstanding early Lakeland route offering sustained chimney climbing with little protection. Originally graded Severe, it was later upgraded to HVS and thought by many to be worth E1. Macphee could evidently climb hard rock, and was about to turn his attention to Ben Nevis.

❀❀❀

The early 1930s were fairly quiet on Skye. In June 1930, four climbers were attempting to follow Steeple and Barlow's Girdle Traverse on Sròn na Cìche and had reached as far as the Cìoch before running short of time and descending to Glen Brittle. Next day, the four – DL Reid, EH Sale, JD Brown and Bill Wood – decided to meet where they had left off and complete the climb. Reid and Sale intended to climb Central Gully, but found themselves in a prominent crack which was harder than Central Gully should have been. No nail marks were visible and they decided to press on so as not to worry their friends.

The following year, Reid, Brown and Sale returned to Skye, determined to clarify just what route had been climbed that day. Both trips were written up by Reid in the SMCJ, who noted that at one time route-naming was easy enough: either it was a route climbed by Collie and sufficiently illustrious to bear his name, or it was christened after one of the points of the compass. [18] Nowadays, however:

> ...things were not so simple, and there was a regrettable *fin de siècle* atmosphere about some of the names allotted by what one might call the left wing of climbers, Hiatus, and Blasphemy Crack, and the Mermaid, that starts well, but tails off. The excuse for our choice, Engineers' Slant, is that of the older school in another branch, the vocational, still not exhausted despite the Doctor's, Professor's, and Smuggler's Chimneys of the English Lake District.

So it was christened *Engineers' Slant* (390m Very Difficult), as Reid, Brown and Sale were engineers with ICI at Billingham. It takes a more interesting line than Central Crack and has become fairly popular.

There were several prominent people on Skye in June 1931. Bell was staying at Cuillin Cottage at the end of the month with two guests– one the physicist Paul Dirac (1902-1984), one of the developers of quantum theory, who had an interest in rock climbing. In 1933 he would share the Nobel Prize in Physics with Erwin Schrödinger.

The other guest was the physicist Igor Yevgenyevich Tamm (1895-1971), from Moscow. He was involved in the Russian development of the atomic bomb and would likewise, in 1958, become a joint-winner of the Nobel Prize in Physics. He was a more accomplished mountaineer than Dirac, with whom he climbed Elbrus in 1936, and Bell would surely have very much enjoyed their company. A son of the Manse and a Fifer, Bell would surely have held his own in their conversations.

❊❊❊

In 1931, Macphee found that an Alpine holiday was not possible, so he decided to spend some time on Ben Nevis, one of his favourite mountains. He went up to the CIC Hut on 13 June, meeting his guests, Albert T Hargreaves and HV Hughes. Hargreaves in particular was a strong climber, considered to be one of the leading Lake District climbers in the early 1930s, having being gritstone-trained. He was killed in 1952 by an avalanche while skiing at Obergurgl in the Austrian Tyrol. Climbing with such a stellar leader, Macphee was content to second. The climbers had mixed weather: it rained on most of their stay from 14 to 24 June – and, as a relief from this, on 19 June it snowed.

On their first day they cleaned out the hut and were surprised by the arrival on ponies of Mrs Inglis Clark and her sister, followed by Mabel

Inglis Jeffries on foot. The women had made their pilgrimage to deliver a new picture of Charles Inglis Clark, to whom the hut had been dedicated two years earlier. Mabel, the daughter of William and Jane Clark, and a good climber herself, joined the three men on an ascent of the direct route on the Douglas Boulder, with Hughes leading.

From the hut, they had spotted a potential line on Càrn Dearg Buttress. On the Monday, the women descended, and when the rain had abated somewhat the climbers went up to investigate the line. It was promising, but they decided to wait for a better day. The Tuesday gave a good ascent of Observatory Ridge, led by Hughes, then Wednesday 17 June dawned clear and so, with Hargreaves leading, they tackled their promising line on the great buttress of Càrn Dearg.

Finishing as the weather turned really bad, they struggled along to the top of No.3 Gully. This looked fearsome in the mist, and Hughes had never done any glissading, so bearing this in mind they went on to the summit and down to the Càrn Mòr Dearg arête and so back to the hut. *The leader christened our climb Route I, to avoid any risk of the obsolete eponymous nomenclature which still persists sometimes.*[19]

Route I (215m Severe) is described in the current guide as – *'One of the finest chimney climbs on Ben Nevis, calling for determined use of an armoury of bridging and back and foot techniques, with the crux right at the top.'* For modern winter tigers it is a superb VI,6, while the first-ascent party faced problems due to wet rock, with the crux pitch being an exposed slab where small holds had to be unearthed from their covering of wet, slimy earth.

The next day it poured, a good excuse for a rest. Part of this was used to examine the hut climbs book, where it was noted that a new SMC member, George Clarke Williams, had made an attempt to climb Observatory Buttress. Hence on the Friday they trudged up Observatory Gully, to *'have a look at it'*.

Hargreaves set off in the lead as usual, climbing progressively more diffi-cult pitches to reach an impasse. A shower of snow, and their chattering teeth, suggested a short descent for lunch to a convenient ledge, where a large slab leaned against the wall and provided a thread belay. By the time lunch was over the snow had stopped and climbing recommenced. An overhang was climbed on the left, where a step on to a foothold led to a removable chockstone, which was used as a thread belay.

Macphee confessed that this pitch was somewhat artificial, as easy rocks lay on the right, but it maintained the direct line of the buttress. Just above, difficulties eased, and 200ft of scrambling led to the final pitches where the crest was regained leading to a finish on the summit, close to the former observatory. They had made the first ascent of *Observatory Buttress Direct* (340m Very Difficult).

❄❄❄

Here pause should be made to discuss what was meant by a 'thread belay'. Modern equipment includes a variety of slings, useful for belays and runners, including spots where one can thread the sling behind a jammed chockstone or behind a good flake of rock. In the 1930s, however, such slings were almost unheard of in Britain, though occasionally a rope sling was used in the Alps for belaying an abseil rope. Raeburn mentions such a sling, used once in the Alps in 1906 and once in Scotland on the first ascent of Barrel Buttress on Quinag in 1907. On both occasions, Raeburn's frequent climbing partner Willie Ling was present, a very experienced alpinist.

By the 1930s, not much had progressed regarding ropes and their use. In 1935, the FRCC Journal published a lengthy article by AT Hargreaves on rope management, recommending that a novice should begin with a full-weight rope, with perhaps a later move to one of three-quarter weight, as sold by Beal. A full-weight rope was normally 1¼ inches (3.18cm) in circumference and was sold by the pound in weight (c. one lb per 20ft.) [20]

Ropes would be made of natural fibres such as hemp or manila: heavy, unwieldy, worse when wet, and with a low breaking strength. Hargreaves recommended 60 feet between climbers. German climbers were often innovative with climbing equipment, and in 1910 Otto Herzog developed the first steel karabiner, basing it on a pear-shaped steel ring he had seen carried by firemen. Hans Fiechtl invented and manufactured pitons which incorporated an eye, replacing those with an attached ring. It took years, however, for such innovations to spread and be accepted.

Hargreaves' article mentions the Munich method whereby climbers used a separate waist-line into which the climbing rope would be tied, using an eye. This avoided the marked reduction in strength which came when using a knot. He also mentions the idea that 100 climbing hours should be accepted as the life of a rope, and that it was better to discard any rope which had held the shock of a falling leader.

To tie on, Hargreaves recommended that the rope be passed round the chest, just under the armpits. Four feet should be left free at the end. The knot should be shifted round the back and the free end should then be tied to the front of the loop. This simple device should prevent the loop slipping down to the waist. On gaining a suitable stance for belaying, the leader should find a means of belaying as high as possible and of course soundly. The leader then pulls up sufficient rope from his waist knot over the belay, usually a notch or projection, such as a flake, and pulls on it down to the waist loop, keeping it taut. He then forms a bight or loop on the part leading away to the next man, passes it through his waist-line, and ties it off round both parts forming the taut part of the belay.

In describing the thread belay, Hargreaves describes the same method as above, indicating in a drawing the belayer tied on to a jammed chockstone. It is not surprising that slings were not in general use; climbers were well aware of the low breaking strength of rope material, and in any case good karabiners were not widely available. Hargreaves mentions the technique whereby a leader unties the rope, then runs it behind some jammed rock, before tying on again and continuing. A better method, Hargreaves wrote, was if the leader carried a five- or six-foot length of spare line, which could be used as a runner. The same loop of line could also be used as a belay to allow an abseil.

There was also a dislike of using equipment additional to the rope, as for many climbers this felt like cheating. Hargreaves describes the older way of belaying a leader, in which the second man merely ran the rope over some projection. In a leader fall, there was a very good chance of the rope breaking. Instead, Hargreaves recommended the system outlined above. In the illustrations, the belayer is shown running the active rope over one shoulder. It would be a few years before the waist belay came into use, adding more safety to the belaying method.

The evolution in climbing equipment was a slow, sporadic process, with pioneers scattered around the world. European climbers were usually the innovators. Advances in equipment often had to await the invention of a new device, with one example being the manufacture of man-made chockstones. (For a useful and fascinating summary of many such advances in equipment, see the article by John Middendorf. [21])

Climbers were beginning to use a jammed rock for a belay or a runner, and in 1927 Pigott was experimenting on the East Buttress of Clogwyn Du'r Arddu, choosing stones of a useful size and shape and placing them in cracks. These in turn would be replaced by machine nuts, with rope-eroding grooves drilled out and a sling fitted. When the author climbed Centurion on Ben Nevis in the early 1970s, an awkward crack on first pitch had a jammed machine nut in place. It may well be there still, a rusting tribute to those early pioneers. Eventually, savvy climbers began to manufacture specially designed shapes of chockstones, leading to the huge range we now enjoy.

❈ ❈ ❈

Back on Ben Nevis in 1931, Macphee and Hargreaves were up early on the morning of 20 June, as Hargreaves had to leave that day. Their target was Raeburn's Arête, the brilliant Severe first climbed by Raeburn and the Inglis Clarks in 1902. Macphee remarked that the severity of the slabs they climbed seemed harder than the guidebook description, and he thought that perhaps they had kept too far to the right of the arête. On one pitch, Hargreaves ran out 130ft of line before gaining even a moderate belay. In summary, Macphee wrote that the quality of the rock was superb and the climbing a sheer delight.

Next day, Hughes and Macphee attempted the Comb direct, finally succeeding after some effort. They must have been disappointed to learn later that it had already been climbed, on 24 September 1920, by Pigott and Wilding. Pigott's Route (250m Severe) is not recommended, with some poor rock in summer, while rare good conditions are needed at the crux for a winter ascent. One thing is evident, however, namely the superb rock architecture of the Comb, a fine buttress at the head of Coire na Ciste, its crest bristling in profile.

The pair had further disappointment two days later. On the previous evening, once the rain had cleared, they went up to Càrn Dearg Buttress to explore a route which, from one or two clues, would appear to have been in the vicinity of Waterfall Gully. On attempting the climb, through lack of time and enthusiasm Macphee decided not to attempt the crux, instead traversing off right to join an easier route to the summit. On the only fine day of their stay, they had chosen a wet line. He may well have failed to climb the route as originally planned, but he left a full description plus a diagram with his article. The climb, *Macphee's Route* (165m Very Difficult, V,6), is again poor in summer but is described in the current guide as an interesting and unusual mixed route in winter, useful in wild weather or deep snow as it does not lead to the top of the mountain.

Hughes was climbing well and was desperate to lead something, so they descended to the foot of the Great Tower, allowing him to lead the direct route up its face. Here is a puzzle, as Macphee refers to a note by Bell in 1929 which mentions climbing the Great Tower direct, with Macphee stating that Bell made a variation to the direct variation by Pigott. However, Bell makes no mention of Pigott's Route, probably due to being unaware of the earlier ascent. Perhaps Bell had left a note in the CIC hut's climbs book, or mentioned it later to Macphee. Pigott described his 1920 climbs on Ben Nevis in an RCJ article the following year, but it would seem that neither Bell nor Macphee was as yet aware of this. [22]

❁❁❁

Macphee's 1931 Ben Nevis trip seems to have coincided with a burst of energy from other climbers. In April, two SMC members were also exploring the Ben Nevis rocks: Herbert Westren Turnbull (1885-1961) was born in Wolverhampton and schooled in Sheffield before becoming a mathematics graduate at Cambridge. He would end up at St Andrews, where he was Regius Professor of Mathematics at United College from 1921-1950. On retirement he began to edit the correspondence of Isaac Newton.

Bell, a climbing friend and one of his obituarists, saw in him something of the noted Victorian mountaineers such as Forbes and Tyndall. Turnbull was president of the SMC 1948-1950. His companion was James Younger

Macdonald (1902-1960). Born in Glasgow and educated at Edinburgh Academy and Trinity College, Oxford, he became a lecturer in physical chemistry at St Andrews, inevitably climbing with Turnbull on many occasions. He joined the JMCS in 1926 and the SMC in 1928. A keen hillwalker, he was an early Munroist, completing the list on 28 August 1958, on Mull. [23]

Turnbull and Macdonald walked up to the CIC Hut on 17 March 1931, then cut steps up Castle Ridge the following day. The day after that was very windy, and they calculated that the most sheltered part of the mountain would be on the west side of Tower Ridge. High on this flank, a great corridor could be seen, the outside wall of which was named the Secondary Tower Ridge. This area was thus far unexplored.

Macdonald described their ascent in the SMCJ. On the initial section, their 80-foot rope was often used to its full extent, with belays poor or non-existent, while a thaw meant wet snow underfoot and dripping ledges. After the initial groove and chimneys, the Secondary Ridge was a delight, with holds and good belays every few yards. The finest part was where it curved in a delicate little snow-crest to join the parent ridge. *1931 Route* (125m Difficult) is also a good winter route at IV, 4 when in condition. [24]

❋❋❋

Other climbers were busy in Glen Coe in 1931, with Stob Coire nam Beith seeing several parties scouring its buttresses for lines. The easy routes were the targets, as climbers attempted to clarify the sometimes puzzling architecture. The pyramidal-shaped mountain changes its visual priorities on approach and it is not uncommon in winter to confuse, for example, North-West Gully with Summit Gully.

The start of the 1930s saw a reassuring rise in the number of younger climbers. Whereas much of the activity described in *The Early Years* took place on club meets, after World War I meets of the senior clubs had essentially been transformed into social gatherings based on hillwalking, with the occasional easy snow ascent. There was some anxiety in the SMC concerning pressures on their traditional club meets. At the 1933 New Year Meet held at Crianlarich, there was discussion concerning the limitation of membership, initiated by Macphee.

Two letters were then published in the following April's SMCJ. The first was from Bell, who was concerned to maintain the spirit of intimacy and informal friendship at meets. He was also of the mind that the SMC should not only maintain, but increase its standard of proficiency in the art of mountaineering. At this time, he continued, the SMC was largely recruited from the JMCS, a body over whose activities the SMC had practically no control. The JMCS had certain advantages, with smaller and more compact groups centred locally and therefore better able to use such opportunities as occasional weekends and holidays. It was suggested that visitors to the CIC Hut were roughly in the proportion of two JMCS to one SMC. Bell's solution was to have two classes of SMC member: full and associate. Only the former would be eligible to attend traditional club events.

This proposed throttling of membership was intended to keep the traditional New Year and Easter Meets down to manageable numbers; many meets were spilling over to several hotels, and their atmosphere had changed. As for maintaining standards of proficiency, this was a red herring, as standards would be raised largely by the young climbers and not by the ageing seniors of the SMC. Doubtless some experience could be handed down by personal contact between the two, but to limit membership in this way would be self-defeating. It was a surprising suggestion from Bell, given his recognised generosity of spirit and openness to younger climbers.

As for the second letter, from Macphee, it stated that the ideal size of a climbing club appeared to be between 200 and 300 members. The SMC was approaching this upper size, and with the limited capacities of most Highland hotels the typical club atmosphere of a meet would be lost. Macphee thought that Bell had made an excellent suggestion in terms of a stiffening of the qualification. He did not think, however, that there should be two classes of membership; this would lead almost inevitably to competitive climbing. Nor did he think it desirable to encroach on the activities of the JMCS. There was no mention from either climber of the eligibility of women to join the SMC.

The discussion reached the next AGM of the SMC, on 1 December 1933, where Bell spoke to his motion –

> The bristling horror of several die-hards who had come to oppose the conversion of the Club into a gymnastic school, into which entrance would be by competitive examination, gradually faded as the speaker developed his theme, and most people at once recognised and sympathised with the points that Mr Bell made regarding the trend of matters. [25]

Bell questioned the adequacy of the present admission qualifications, which did not indicate whether the candidate necessarily possessed any real mountaineering experience. It was recognised that he had made a good case for a thorough investigation, and the matter was eventually passed to a sub-committee for consideration. The president, Harry MacRobert stated that new members came from two main classes: young men with usually very extensive qualifications, and older men who might not have rock-climbing experience. Both types must be equally welcomed.

At the next AGM, the following December, MacRobert reported that the committee had considered the club rules carefully. When Naismith enquired what qualification was now required for admission, the secretary, Alexander Harrison, stated that –

…although the Committee did not bind itself to any definite qualification, candidates were informed that at least forty ascents over 3,000 feet were necessary.

An 'ascent' meant hillwalking. The qualifications had crept up very slowly, by some form of osmosis rather than by any concrete rule. A brief look at various application forms from the early years would see that a dozen or more mountains in summer, and a few in winter, would suffice. In later years summits gained after climbing some technical route would appear. It would be some years before minimum levels of difficulty on climbing routes appeared as a prerequisite for consideration.

Currently, it would be expected that a candidate for SMC membership could lead at least Grade IV in winter, and Very Severe (4c) in summer. At least 50 Munros would be expected, with a good number done in winter conditions. Alpine experience would be taken into consideration. A candidate requires a proposer and three seconders.

In 1934, to the relief of many members of both clubs, the discussion quickly evaporated. For most young climbers, of course, this would all have been an irrelevance: they went out where and when they could, with friends, and climbed what they could. The mountains are oblivious to club memberships.

❄❄❄

Mountaineering activity in the east of Scotland, as in the west, was beginning to show some life. The SMC Guide to the Cairngorms had been published in 1928, written by the Aberdeen climber and journalist Henry (later Sir Henry) Alexander, a member of both the SMC and the Cairngorm Club. With over 200 pages, the guidebook was a good seller – although Cairngorms expert Adam Watson is of the later view that Alexander's guide was not as comprehensive, nor as accurate, as its reputation suggested. Nonetheless, for a mountainous area starved of information, it was welcomed.

In July 1930, Nimlin climbed *Serrated Rib* (135m Moderate) on Stag Rocks above Loch Avon. As Greg Strange points out in his Cairngorms history, this was the first new route since Raeburn's Shelter Stone route some 23 years earlier, and the first on the Stag Rocks. In the same year, Godfrey Roy Symmers had taken up a job with the railway at York. He continued to climb on and off when time and holidays allowed, often with Bill Ewen, an Aberdeen schoolmaster. On 10 and 17 August 1930, Symmers and Ewen made two first ascents on Lochnagar, the first of which, *Giant's Head Chimney* (220m Very Difficult) is wet and grassy, but is transformed in winter into a popular IV,4 . Combined tactics were needed at the crux chockstone. According to Strange, this was probably the most important route on Lochnagar for more than two decades, since Raeburn's Black Spout Buttress. [26]

The second effort was *Parallel Gully A* (270m Severe), when they started up Eagle Buttress and made a rising traverse to enter the gully above its initial pitch. Symmers climbed the Severe upper section in tennis shoes, which he had carried up in preparation for any hard climbing encountered.

Elsewhere, new venues were being explored. Coire an Lochain, one of the three northern corries of Cairn Gorm, is the most popular modern climbing area in the Cairngorms, largely due to the ski road which greatly eases access. *Central Crack Route* (120m Moderate) was the first climb recorded here, by Alexander (Sandy) Harrison and Louis St. Clair Bartholomew. The latter was a JMCS climber from Edinburgh and one of the Bartholomew family firm of cartographers which is credited with the introduction of hypsometric tints, or layer colouring on maps. This indicated low ground in shades of green, and higher ground in shades of brown, leading to still higher ground in purple then white. Leonardo da Vinci was probably the first to produce a map using a basic colour scheme to indicate high ground, with his map of central Italy in the early 16th century. [27,28]

Louis St.Clair Bartholomew appears not to have paid a very active role in the family firm, however, perhaps saving his energy for mountaineering.

❆❆❆

There are a few occasions when a combination of factors produces just the right place and time for a significant event, and one such occurred on 4 July 1933. The place was the Garbh Choire of Beinn a'Bhùird, where conditions were ideal with a dry summer following a lean winter, and a party of fit, young Scottish/Cambridge students entered the upper corrie: EJA (Jock) Leslie, Ernest Alexander (Sandy) Maclagan Wedderburn (1912–1944), Patrick (Pat) Douglas Baird (1912-1984), M Stephen Cumming and John Wenman (later Sir John) Crofton (1912-2009). The latter was a pioneer in the treatment of tuberculosis, at a time when the mortality rate was close to 50%. His son Ian is an author and a member of the SMC.

The students had been climbing for a week in the Cuillin and this had fine-tuned them physically. Their target was the Mitre Ridge, which they had planned since a visit to Wedderburn's rooms, where it transpired that four of the students had their eyes on the ridge. Blame for this can be laid at the feet of Arthur Rusk, who with AG Hutchison in 1930 had explored the possibility of climbing the ridge. They in turn had been inspired by the writings of James Parker. Rusk and Hutchison attempted a route but found the difficulties beyond them. A superb photograph of the ridge by Rusk was published in the SMCJ for 1930, along with a note on their visit, and this immediately attracted Wedderburn and his friends.

They felt that a lack of sufficient ropes had kept back the earlier parties, so they took some 600 feet of rope and line, most of which proved to be superfluous. The approach walk was long, so a bivouac in the corrie was in order. Two ropes were settled on: Wedderburn, Baird and Leslie for the most direct line, and Cumming and Crofton for an interesting alternative line on the north-west flank of the arête.

The first pitch of the direct line turned out to be the most difficult, with smooth, holdless slabs and an overhanging wall on the left. All went well until the top of the fifth pitch led to two slender cracks up the first tower. The leader, Wedderburn, and the second man both tried the left-hand crack but both failed. (Now taken by Mitre Ridge Direct, 1975). Instead, they avoided the tower on the left, then continued up to the foot of the second tower.

Wedderburn launched himself up this, climbing the arête on its right edge, but some 15ft up he *descended with more rapidity than dignity, losing his hat in the process*. In his obituary for Pat Baird, Iain Macleod Campbell described what happened as the party watched Wedderburn nearing the top:

> Edging his way up a steadily increasing overhang which looked to us to be utterly impossible – as indeed it proved. Suddenly, with 15 or 20 feet out, he fell directly on to the rope, 30 or 40 feet; but the imperturbable Pat, firmly ensconced and well belayed, calmly held him, miraculously unhurt. We later picked up his hat 600 feet below. [29,30]

He then looked at the two possible lines of weakness on the second tower, a central one and another on the left. Failing on the central line he took the left-hand option and so gained the top of the second tower. Easier ground finished their ascent.

In the current guide, *Mitre Ridge* (220m Hard Severe) is introduced as *'one of the great classic ridges of the Cairngorms. Although there is some vegetation and a little loose rock, it is a fine natural line with rewarding situations.'* In winter, as with many routes of this period, it is a much sought after climb at V, 6.

As for the other rope, Cumming and Crofton were rewarded with another classic, *Cumming-Crofton Route* (165m Severe). More sustained than its sister route, it climbs a corner well seen in photographs and joins the main ridge below the second tower. Like their companions, Cumming and Crofton tried and failed on the central line, finally climbing the left-hand line. The climbers left the reporting to Leslie, who used their names, a habit of earlier decades but one which was now falling into disuse. As the current guidebook notes, *'This steep and sustained climb is the most outstanding pre-war route in the Cairngorms'*.

Following their ascents, the students splashed about in the small burn in the corrie just to the east of Mitre Ridge, before eating lunch. They then removed their boots and walked to the north summit of Beinn a' Bhùird over a refreshing mossy and well-watered summit plateau. Adam Watson later wrote – *'I have measured their barefoot tramp to Beinn a' Bhuird and back as 3.6km!'* [31]

Two months later, on 9 September 1933, two Aberdeen climbers entered the corrie. Charlie Ludwig and Donald Dawson had no knowledge of the July ascents, and in socks Ludwig led the entire direct route. He must have been very pleased with the climbing, as on 1 October, with three others, he again led the entire route, again in socks. Thinking that his September ascent was the first, he sent a note to Parker, who passed it on to Charles Parry, then editor of the SMCJ. Both accounts were published in the April 1934 edition.

Wedderburn became a solicitor in his native Edinburgh. He worked with Baird and Smythe *inter alia* on mountain training of troops in Canada, and was writing a book entitled *Alpine Climbing on Foot and with Ski* when he had a fatal accident during the campaign in Italy – where he was second in command of the Lovat Scouts – slipping on marble steps and falling over a low banister while inebriated, a testament to unsuitable footwear, perhaps. This happened on Christmas Eve, 1944, and was possibly the greatest single loss of talent to Scottish mountaineering during World War II. His book was revised and finished by C Douglas Milner and HP Spilsbury. [32]

Baird, like many a climber, fell in love with the Arctic, which he first experienced on Baffin Island. He eventually studied glaciers and became a major in the Royal Canadian Artillery. Crofton outlasted all his friends from that group, dying in 2009, aged 97. An eminent professor and head of the medical faculty at Edinburgh University, he was knighted for work on respiratory illness.

Ludwig continued to impress. Three days following his September ascent of Mitre Ridge, he soloed Douglas-Gibson Gully on Lochnagar, wearing gym shoes and with no prior knowledge of the summer horrors he was about to encounter. He survived its wet and unstable environment, and commented in an SMCJ note that *'the rock throughout was so rotten that the climb may be considered as quite unjustifiable'*. He graded it Severe, and no doubt performed a valuable service by dissuading others. He graduated from Aberdeen University in 1934 and became a lecturer in physiology at Leeds University. In January 1942, having volunteered for the RAF, he was killed when his Hampden bomber crashed following a raid on a French port.

An odd omission in the history of mountaineering in Britain by Clark and Pyatt is the complete absence of any mention of the climbs on Mitre Ridge. The authors, in describing climbing in Scotland between the wars, list three rock climbs which they regarded as landmarks: Route 1 and

Rubicon Wall on Ben Nevis, and Route 1 on Rannoch Wall. Perhaps the fact that Albert T Hargreaves was on the first two routes, and Macphee was on both Route 1 climbs, skewed their perception somewhat, but to miss the significance of the Mitre Ridge ascents, given Leslie's article in 1934, is puzzling. [33]

Symmers and Ewen teamed up again to continue their pursuit of Lochnagar routes. In August 1933 they climbed *Gargoyle Chimney* (120m Difficult) on the West Buttress. The toad-like rock feature after which the route was named juts out from the plateau rim. The following month, they climbed *Polyphemus Gully* (200m Severe), the wet, loose gully cutting up Shadow Buttress B. Like the previous route, it is best ignored in summer, and gives what the current guide describes as the *'finest gully climb on the mountain at V, 5 '.*

❀❀❀

MacRobert was invited to give a talk about climbing in Scotland to the Alpine Club, which he did on 7 March 1933. He began by stating that Scotland afforded as good a training ground for Alpine climbing as did Switzerland for Himalayan climbing – which echoed the feelings of the previous generation. He then went on to state, and here he was basically correct, that there was a great gulf between standards of climbing in the Lake District and Scotland. Scotland could not compete overall with the amount of good, accessible rock to be found in the Lake District, nor in the numbers of very competent climbers using that rock. [34]

He emphasised the potential Scotland could provide for practice in navigation and route-finding, and it will be recalled from *The Early Years* that MacRobert had instructed troops in this during World War I. He continued by demolishing the then current thinking that Scotland provided splendid climbing in all sorts of remote areas. This, he stated, was not quite true, with only hill walking or perhaps ridge scrambling to be had outside three or four districts.

He continued negatively by saying that the Cobbler, formed of micaceous schists, was most unpleasant to climb on, especially when wet. At least, he said, the Scots were superior when it came to walking downhill, as on one frosty December day on the Cobbler when the descent from the North Peak, merely a walk, was too much for the rock experts who had the mortification of watching the Scottish group easily trotting and glissading down, while they themselves had to be rescued with a rope.

MacRobert at least warmed to his subject once he moved northwards, and after some praise about Glen Coe and Ben Nevis, he stayed with the Cuillin of Skye for the remainder of his lecture. It is difficult to pin down precisely just where he stood. It is known that he had a dry sense of humour, but quite a few hidden gems of climbing must have been unknown to him, or at least unrecognized for what they were.

In conclusion, he said that due to Scotland often having high winds in fine weather, it was possible to watch windslab being formed on powder snow – and that he had triggered an avalanche on a small slope after observing it for about 90 minutes then cutting across below it, the windslab being barely half an inch in depth. A variation on watching paint dry perhaps.

❄❄❄

The Great Depression was biting deeply by the beginning of the 1930s. Relying for a large part on heavy industry, especially shipbuilding, Scotland suffered badly, and by 1933 around 30 per cent of Glaswegians were out of work. There were queues at soup kitchens, and a Government report in the mid-1930s estimated that upwards of a quarter of the UK's population existed on a subsistence diet. There was also child malnutrition, leading to scurvy, rickets and tuberculosis. When a slow fall in unemployment eventually began, it was mainly in the south. Poor housing in Glasgow resulted in chronically high rates, particularly in tuberculosis.

In such grim conditions, by 1933 it had become seen as unpatriotic to holiday abroad, not that many had the means to do so. Car ownership was still not widespread, and public transport patchy. Many climbers nonetheless headed for Skye, which saw increasing activity, although very little of significance was done. On the positive side, a growing number of younger climbers were now aware that there was much unexplored rock in Scotland. They were also moving out of the wet and vegetated chimneys and gullies, gingerly at first, then with rapidly growing confidence. Over the next few years, standards would gradually return to a level not seen since before World War I.

References

1. <https://archive.org/details/norwaynorthernp00slingoog>
2. W.D. [William Douglas]. SMC Guide Book. *The Island of Skye*. SMCJ 9, 54, Sept. 1907, pp.293-367.
3. Jones, Owen Glynne. *Rock Climbing in the English Lake District.* (1897, Longmans, Green and Co. 39 Paternoster Row, London, New York and Bombay.)
4. Wedderburn, E.A.M. *A Short History of Scottish Climbing.* SMCJ 22, 128, November 1939, pp.97-108.
5. Hughes, H.V. *A New Gully Climb on Sgùrr Sgumain.* SMCJ 20, 117, April 1934, pp.190-191.
6. Barker, Miss M. *Some Severes.* YRCJ, 5, 17, pp.192-197.
7. *A Cragsman's Day by Ben Humble.* Arrochar, Tarbet & Ardlui Heritage website. <http://www.arrocharheritage.com/ACragsmansDay.htm>
8. Abraham, George D. *British Mountain Climbs.* (1909. Mills and Boon.)

9. Nimlin, J.B., Humble, B.H., and Williams, G.C. *Rock Climbs on the Cobbler – A symposium.* SMCJ 22, No. 130, November 1940, pp. 221-233.
10. Bell, J.H.B. *Reflections on Philosophy of Guide Books.* In: Excursions and Notes. SMCJ 18, 104, November 1927, pp.118-119.
11. J.H.B.B. *Central Buttress Buchaille Etive Mor.* In: Notes and Excursions. SMCJ 18, 108, November 1929, p.379
12. Newbigging, W.C. *Beuchaille* [sic] *Etive Mor, 13ᵗʰ October 1903.* In: Excursions. SMCJ 8, 43, January 1904, p.87.
13. Murray, W.H. *Mountaineering in Scotland.* (London: J.M. Dent & Sons, 1947.) In: Chapter XIII, p.122.
14. Bell, Jas. H.B. *The Northern Cliffs of Stob Coire an Lochan.* SMCJ 19, 113, April 1932, pp. 313-317.
15. Bell, J.H.B. *Research in Glencoe.* SMCJ 19, 111, April 1931, pp.190-192.
16. Smythe, Tony. *My Father, Frank: The Forgotten Alpinist (Legends and Lore).* (2015. Mountaineers Books. ISBN 978-1594859144.
17. Smith, Ken. *Graham Macphee.* SMCJ 40, 200, 2009, pp.272-281.
18. Reid, D.L. *Sròn na Cìche – Engineers' Slant.* SMCJ 19, 114, November 1932, pp.382-388.
19. Graham Macphee, G. *Twelve Days in the Hut.* SMCJ 19, 112, November 1931, pp.229-237.
20. Hargreaves, A.T. *Rope Management.* FRCCJ. Vol.10, No.2, 1935, pp.232-242.
21. Middendorf, John. *The Mechanical Advantage.* <Bigwalls.net/climb/mechadv/index.html>
22. J.H.B.B. [JHB Bell]. *Ascent of Tower Ridge on Nevis.* In: Notes and Excursions. SMCJ 18, 108, November 1929, pp.378-379.
23. Bell, J.H.B. *Herbert Westren Turnbull, F.R.S., F.R.S.E., LL.D.* In: In Memorium. SMCJ 27, 153, May 1962, pp.303-304.
24. Macdonald, J.Y. SMCJ 19, 113, April 1932, pp.337-342.
25. J.L.A. [J Logan Aikman]. *Annual Meeting, 1933.* In: SMCJ 20, 117, April 1934, pp.204-209.
26. Strange, Greg. *The Cairngorms – 100 Years of Mountaineering.* (2010. SMT), p.33.
27. <https://en.wikipedia.org/wiki/Collins_Bartholomew>
28. <http://www.royalcollection.org.uk/eGallery/object.asp?maker=12196&object=912277&row=436>
29. Leslie, E.J.A. *The Mitre Ridge.* SMCJ 20, 117, April 1934, pp.183-188.
30. I.C.M. [Iain Macleod Campbell] *P.D. Baird.* In Memorium. SMCJ 33, 175, 1984, pp.91-92.
31. Watson, Adam. *A Zoologist on Baffin Island.* (2011 paperback edition, Paragon Publishing, ISBN 978-1907611704, p.233).
32. Wedderburn, E.A.M. *Alpine Climbing on Foot and With Ski.* (London, Countrygoer Books, 1954).
33. Ronald W. Clark and Edward C. Pyatt, *Mountaineering in Britain* (London: Dent – Phoenix House, 1957).
34. MacRobert, H. *Climbing in Scotland.* ACJ. Vol. XLV (45), No. CCXLVII (247), pp.259-267.

5

Winter Revival (1933-1936)

By 1931, GRAHAM MACPHEE had in all probability been designated as the author of a new guide to Ben Nevis. No new routes were found there in 1932, but by April 1933 climbers were beginning to engage in explorations. The Scottish-Cambridge group of Baird, Cumming and Leslie climbed *Green Hollow Route* (215m Very Difficult) on the first platform of North-East Buttress, and on 13 September 1933 Albert T Hargreaves was back, with Frank and Ruth Heap, husband-and-wife members of the FRCC.

Hargreaves had earlier in the year broken a leg while skating; now clearly recovered, he and the Heaps made their way up the pony track, round to the Allt a' Mhuilinn and so to the CIC Hut. This was, at that time, the only permitted route to the hut from the north side of the hill, and it was not until a few years later that the SMC negotiated permission for climbers wishing to stay at the hut to reach it from the Ben Nevis Distillery.

Frank Gustave Heap had won a scholarship to read history at Cambridge, then won the Military Cross following a tank engagement at the Battle of Cambrai in November 1917 which saw him rescue several of his tank crew from behind enemy lines. (The Germans buried the abandoned tank, perhaps for re-use, and it was discovered and dug up in 1998.)

Hargreaves and the Heaps made for Observatory Buttress, the broad, rocky mass to the right of the more defined Observatory Ridge, and lying between the prominent gash of Point Five Gully and Gardyloo Gully. *Rubicon Wall* (310m Severe), the name given to their route, is now a highly rated ice climb at V,5 , while in summer the guidebook describes it as being a fine route on good rock.

The second summer ascent, in August 1937, was to be vividly described by WH Murray in his classic book *Mountaineering in Scotland*, where he wrote that it was the hardest climb he knew on Ben Nevis. Graded Very Severe in the 1936 Macphee guide, it eventually settled down in later guides as one of the top Severes in terms of difficulty.[1]

In March 1934, SMC members Turnbull and Macdonald spent a week at the CIC Hut. In what seem to have been poor conditions, with a thaw, they climbed *1934 Route* (200m II) on Secondary Tower Ridge, *North Gully* (120m II) on Creag Coire na Ciste, and *South-West Ridge* (180m III) on the Douglas Boulder. The current guide describes the latter as '*A great little climb, good value for money*'. The author's own experience of this route is that every now and again it feels undergraded, with a series of awkward, if interesting, mantelshelves. To back this up, a new book of winter climbs, by the author of the current guide, has belatedly upgraded the route to IV, 5, which is probably about right. [2]

On 16 September 1934, Sandy Wedderburn was on Ben Nevis with two Slovenian climbers, Mira Marko Debelak (1904-1948) and her husband, Edward (Edo) Deržaj. Mira Debelak was a diminutive woman who had, in 1926 with Stanko Tominšek, made the first ascent of the Direct Route on Špik, a 2,472m mountain in the Julian Alps. On Nevis, the trio would make the first ascent of what is now *Slav Route* (420m Severe).

A friendship with Fanny Copeland (1872-1970) had led to this visit to Scotland, with Wedderburn probably designated to escort them on Ben Nevis. (Professor Copeland, another keen alpinist, was a lecturer in English at the University of Ljubljana in Slovenia in the former Yugoslavia, from 1921 until the German invasion in 1941. In 1939 she was awarded the OBE for her 12 years acting in an unofficial role as vice-consul. She loved the area and in 1953 moved there and remained for the rest of her life.)

The story of the route begins as far back as 1925, when Frank Smythe was a guest of Jim Bell on the SMC Easter Meet at Fort William. Smythe suggested to Bell that '*something ought to be done about the two formidable unclimbed gullies running up to the summit plateau*'. These gullies are now named Zero and Point Five, both classic winter climbs and high on many a climber's wish list.

As for the unusual name of Zero Gully, Bell suggested it in an article describing a partial, or perhaps hybrid, ascent in April 1936 –

> This name is suggested by the current numerical nomenclature of the Nevis gullies, for the steep gully between the Observatory Ridge and the flank of the North-East Buttress. It is not a good name, but we have not yet heard of a better. [3]

The earlier gully names on Nevis run left to right from Number 2 to Number 5, with Observatory Gully, the huge, open slope on the east flank of Tower Ridge, also being known as Number 1. The next prominent gully further left, lying between Observatory Ridge and Observatory Buttress, was unclimbed, as was the next gully beyond that, on the east flank of Observatory Ridge. As this latter gully was the first to receive some form of ascent, it was also the first of the two to be named, as Zero. (Observatory Gully forks near its top into two shorter gullies, Tower and Gardyloo, thus missing out on the numbered protocol.)

This left the steep, prominent gully right of Zero lacking a name – but, with mathematical logic, this has become Point Five. Later ascents of the major gullies further left of Zero have led to negative labels; Minus One, Minus Two and Minus Three. Happily, further lessons in mathematics will not be forthcoming, as Ben Nevis has exhausted its potential candidate gullies.

During the 1925 meet, Smythe and Bell attempted Tower Ridge, firstly climbing rock on the Douglas Boulder. On reaching the Great Tower at 5pm they used the Eastern Traverse, taking an hour on hard snow to gain Tower Gap. By now it was snowing. They were ignorant of what lay ahead and could only glimpse a white wall, while they were also unaware of the descents on either side of the Gap, so they decided to retreat down Tower Ridge.

Their own footsteps, luckily, were easily seen, and climbers of this period were very well used to descending routes – indeed often going out of their way to do so. Bell later admitted that had they known the finish of Tower Ridge they would have continued upwards, but he pointed out the wisdom of backing off when encountering the unknown.

During that day, the two climbers could hear the roar and swish of avalanches pouring down the great gullies further left, not an encouraging sound. In early 1932 they returned, but the weather was poor. They discussed 'the project' and revised it to attempt, not the future Zero Gully, but rather a direct ascent from its base to gain the snowfield in the centre of the face left of the gully (the snowfield nowadays called the Basin). A further two years on, and in 1934 Bell was again at the hut, and witnessed the climb put up by Wedderburn and the two Slovenians.

Wedderburn wished to impress his guests with a good, hard climb – and, knowing of their high standard, felt that none of the existing routes were difficult enough. Bell passed on his new idea and so the alarm was set for 5am, although, as Wedderburn's article explained–

> Being a thoroughly experienced clock, however (I dare not suspect foul play), it stopped during the night, and it was not until the relatively civilised hour of 6.30 a.m. that the party began to stir. Two hours later the three of us, Marko, Edo, and myself, moved off up into the mists round the North-East Buttress. [4]

In telling his story, Wedderburn used the literary device of pretending that a fourth climber was on the rope – in itself a recognised mountaineering phenomenon experienced by quite a few parties in difficult circumstances.

> ...a fourth man on the rope who alone would have to account for all that happened. That these words are written without consulting him only goes to show that my high sense of duty overcomes the regard that I have for him and forces me to lay the whole facts before the Club.

Their intention had been to climb Zero Gully, but being neither dry nor filled with snow this did not appeal. They took to a delicate slab on the left, with no belay after 50 feet. Wedderburn was third on the rope, with Edo Deržaj leading.

> A sound as of hammering came from above, but looking round I was able to distinguish the approving smile of the fourth man, and so I held my peace. Then Marko climbed the pitch. In the various articles which have been written about her climbs she has been likened — or rather her method of climbing has — to a squirrel and to a spider. Clad as she was in someone else's trousers, her movements were as striking as they were skilled, but it would be unkind to use any similes. After a wait it was my turn, and as befits the last man on the rope, I made speed my aim; but the pitch was distinctly tricky. Arrived at the piton I hung there until Marko had vacated the only available stance.

A second pitch was also difficult but led to a splendid belay, while a third pitch, including a section without handholds, finished on a ledge large enough for all three climbers. Then it started to rain. An open chimney above ended in a slight overhang with no belay, so the sound of hammering was heard again. Down below, Bell had arrived to spectate. The angle eased above the chimney, but as they were starting the fifth pitch the rain began to intensify, and by the time all three finished this pitch the whole cliff was pouring with water. Worse, stones began to come down, so a slight retreat was made to shelter round an edge.

The mists began to rise and they could see Bell below, sheltering under a large overhang. A miserable half-hour was spent trying to light cigarettes until finally the deluge appeared to abate and they reclimbed the pitch.

> "What would you like most now?" Edo called down. I shivered – "A hot bath." "All right." A movement to the right, and before I could even pull at the rope Edo was plunging through a large waterfall which joined the main gully just below. Although there is a possible route to the left, it is for dry weather only, so we needs must follow.

The climbing eased after this pitch, and they stuck as close as possible to the edge of the gully.

At one place what French climbers most delightfully term a courte échelle was necessary, and, in spite of my innate courtesy, I was thrust forward into second place.

A 'courte échelle' equates to a 'leg-up', but as Wedderburn stated in his article that no combined tactics were necessary, it must be assumed that the term was used in its psychological sense only. Wedderburn also added an interesting footnote on pitons –

On our first pitch we had a choice of three courses: we could have descended and abandoned our route; we could have continued up the difficult and unknown rock without any belay for the second man; we could drive in a piton to be used as a belay.

One must distinguish between two entirely separate ways of using pitons: as direct aids to climbing, as in steeple-jacking, or as safeguards where the natural rock provides no belay. Although the first method has already made its appearance in British climbing (in the Lake District), I can only say that it does not appeal to me. But I have been able to satisfy myself that the use of pitons in the second way, that is, purely to safeguard, is, on new climbs at least, unexceptionable.

For the limited options then available for protecting a climb, Wedderburn's view was a sensible one. On a major cliff, faced with slabby rocks and no natural belays, not only was it courting disaster to climb a difficult pitch, but Wedderburn advised that *parties repeating the climb should take a couple of carabiners*.

Wedderburn added a note on the climb's grade. Judging by the initial harder pitches, he thought it was probably Very Difficult by Welsh standards, or a good '4' by Cuillin grades. In Macphee's 1936 Ben Nevis guide it is high in the Severe category, while the current guide has it as a 420m Severe, *'A pleasant route, but not in the same class as The Long Climb.'* Like many climbs of this period on Ben Nevis, it is superior as a winter climb, at VI, 5 . The grades used in the Macphee guide were Easy, Moderate, Difficult, Very Difficult, Severe and Very Severe.

Two weeks after the ascent, Mira Debelak was interviewed for a Dundee newspaper. [5]

"It is an entirely new ascent of the 'wall', which is 900 feet high. It had been considered absolutely impracticable. We had shocking weather and the climb took four hours."

Climbing is indeed Mrs Debelak's life.

"It gives me my supreme and my most precious moments," she said. Mrs Debelak sees no peril in conquering chasms. "My main dread is of spiders," she declared. "I cannot stand spiders. I do not mind mice. "Once when I had got to the top of a Dolomite peak I found a tiny mountain mouse looking at me. We became good friends, and lunched together.

❊❊❊

There were explorations beyond Ben Nevis, especially in Glen Coe which was easy of access and possessed a hoard of unclimbed rock, waiting for a new breed of climber. One of these was George Clarke Williams (1903-1981), who had been on the first ascent of Route I on Ben Nevis. On that occasion, he had examined the final section on a top rope, and in Glen Coe he would repeat this method. The huge potential of climbs on the south-east flank of Crowberry Ridge–Rannoch Wall–could no longer be ignored, and with the slowly increasing confidence of many of the younger climbers it was becoming a natural target. As Macphee noted in an SMCJ article, an attempt had been made late in 1933. Williams had explored the face and had actually ascended a route, although he used a top rope at the difficult part. [6]

Two visits were made with a view to attempting a first (clean) ascent of this route. The first was probably in early December 1933, but poor weather and snow on the rocks saw the leader, Macphee himself, refuse to go on – *'A hopeful suggestion made to me that I should attempt the climb, having never even seen it before, was treated with the contempt which it deserved.'*

Macphee was now living in Liverpool and had made a round trip of over 600 miles not to do a new climb. The next visit on which he was present was fixed for May 1934, at Whitsuntide, the Sunday falling on 20 May and coinciding with the Glasgow spring holiday. It rained and snowed on the mountains and as a consolation Macphee, George Todd jnr, Williams and Ian Garson Jack (1906-1933) gardened their way up *The Chimney* (Very Difficult) at the left end of Craig a' Bhancair on the Buachaille. They then moved over to the rocky buttress further left, now known as Lagangarbh Buttress, where they found two routes.

The next day was even wetter, and the party ended up on Gearr Aonach on Bidean nam Bian, where Todd led them up *'a conspicuous chimney'* on its north-east corner. The only climb of this type in this area is *Chimney and Face Route* (Severe), recorded in 1949 and probably not the same as the 1934 one, which therefore remains unknown. It was, as Macphee wrote, the second round to Rannoch Wall.

A new guide to Glen Coe was being worked on, and accordingly they were keen to climb the route before the book was published. Then the rumour mill suggested it had already gone to press, which meant that they could put it out of date. The party was back on the Buachaille on 3 June 1934, with Williams finally successful in leading the climb. *Route I* (70m Very Difficult) takes a somewhat vegetated line up the face, with a section of loose rock. Its significance lies in it being a flagship route, climbing a steep face which had seemed out of bounds. It breached a psychological barrier to better routes and further empowered the growing number of young climbers.

In winter, too, events were starting to come to life. On 23 March 1934, the Cambridge students Pat Baird, WJA Leslie and Hugh Arthur Fynes-Clinton (1913-1991) cut their way up *SC Gully* (150m III,3) on Stob Coire nan Lochan, taking five hours. Two days later Wedderburn, Greenwood and AF Bell made the second ascent. Baird described the first ascent in an SMCJ note.[7] As WH Murray observed in his autobiography, the note was too factual, short and dull, and he considered that the description failed to alert the young climbers in Glasgow that changes in Scottish mountaineering were happening.[8]

It is worth reflecting on why Scottish mountaineering was in the state it was in at that time, only slowly regaining the standards and expertise gained by the pioneers before the first world war. Given the amount of information available these days, it might seem almost inconceivable that climbers in the 1920s and 1930s would be ignorant of some of the major routes put up before the war, including such prominent climbs as Green Gully and Crowberry Gully.

There are several explanations for this. First, there was less than perfect communication between the mountaineering groups. By contrast, an enthusiastic modern climber can research a climb by a variety of means, including, increasingly, videos of ascents in glorious colour (but often, unfortunately, accompanied by irritatingly loud and poorly chosen music). Current snow and ice conditions on many mountains can be found, along with weather predictions and avalanche potential. Many of the harder new climbs are written up almost instantly on informative blogs such as scottishwinter.com.[9] Indeed, some have appeared on the internet within a day of their ascent.

Secondly, World War I had a long-lasting and seriously reducing effect on both the numbers of those mountaineering, and on the drive and enthusiasm of those who survived. Many had seen enough terrible things in the war for this to have had a dampening effect on their enthusiasm for sporting and perhaps dangerous excitement on the mountain; they were survivors and wished to keep it that way. There was as yet no formal, medical recognition of post-traumatic stress, and many of those demobilised had a delayed reaction and would have received little or no help.

Thirdly, if the assessment of WH Murray is correct, even if climbers were keen to dive into struggles with icy gullies, the 1920s saw a decade of mild winters. It was only in the 1930s, Murray noted, that hard winters returned – as shown by, for example, the old road over the Blackmount being blocked frequently, at least until the new road came into operation in the mid-1930s. Rock climbing followed a similar trajectory.

Records of weather in Britain include one which concentrates on winters alone. [10] At netweather.tv, there is a listing of the winter data collated by D Fauvell and I Simpson; basically, it is a history of snowfalls in British winters. It shows that the winter of 1931-32 was probably Scotland's most snowless winter in memory, with no real falls of note, and this might explain why no new routes were found on Ben Nevis in 1932.

In the table below, the data should be treated with some caution, referring as it does to an overall impression of snowfall, not one directly linked to measured mountain snow cover.

TABLE BASED ON 'THE HISTORY OF BRITISH WINTERS'. (SEE REF.10)

Winter Year(s)	Snow?	Comment
1920–23	Little or Average	Blizzard at end of March
1923–24	Snowy	30 inches of snow in Braemar in November
1925–26	Snowy	Notable snow mid-January
1927–28	Very Snowy	
1928–29	Snowy	
1930–31	Snowy	
1931–32	Little	Scotland virtually snowless
1932–33	Very Snowy	Late October snow in Scotland
1936–37	Snowy	
1937–42	All Snowy years	Scotland saw severe blizzards

Data from the Met Office would indicate that winters in the 1920s and 1930s seemed to be stormy, with plenty of precipitation, but no colder than average. [11]

As for the lack of information on earlier climbs, it is difficult to fathom why ascents of major routes seemed to fade so quickly. Jim Bell thought he was doing the first ascent of Green Gully in 1937, some 21 years after Raeburn had climbed it. Similarly for Bill Mackenzie, JB Russell, Kenneth Dunn and Hamish Hamilton in 1936 with Crowberry Gully, 27 years after Raeburn had made the first winter ascent.

Murray remarks that they had no knowledge of the Easter 1909 Crowberry Gully ascent, and by way of an explanation states that Easter is normally too late for good ice in Glen Coe. [12] This is a bit facile, as conditions vary almost as much as the actual date of Easter (the Sunday fell on 11 April that year); Murray, Dunn and MacAlpine made a winter ascent of Crowberry Gully on 2 April 1939, and the first winter ascent of Deep-cut Chimney on Stob Coire nam Beith followed five days later.

It is probable of course that many of the younger climbers had no access to the earlier SMC journals, which did not have large publication runs. Several complete sets existed, but these would not be advertised and even then there was no guarantee that these early ascents would have had much impact. Raeburn, for instance, helped to bury the knowledge of his ascent of Green Gully by low-key and opaque reporting.

The youthful, energetic climbers of the pre-war years were either dead or ageing, and although well-known activists continued to attend club meets, for the most part hillwalks and easy snow gullies were dominant. The journals, meanwhile, were short of writing which could inspire a young climber looking for adventure.

In essence there was more than one factor acting to curb the development of mountaineering between the wars. Scotland was not alone in this, of course; climbing in the Lake District, which had led in standards and techniques, was likewise muted for some years. Soon, however, this was to change.

❋❋❋

It is fairly well accepted–or at least several writers have noted–that the starting gun for Scottish winter climbing in the 1930s was fired by the ascent on Ben Nevis of what was then called Tower Gap West Chimney, now known as Glover's Chimney, and named from its first summer ascent by George Glover's party in 1902. The instigator and leader on the winter ascent was Macphee, busy researching for the Ben Nevis guide, backed up by George Clarke Williams and Drummond Henderson (1900-1961). Henderson was an optician from Glasgow, and as Professor Sir Bob Grieve stated in a warm obituary–

> He was one of the first breed of climbers which was not of the more leisured class, and his early forays into Highland country on 10-day holidays were with a 50-lb. rucksack on his back in which food, bed, clothing and climbing impedimenta were packed. Apart from one climbing holiday in the Pyrenees, he was unable to climb abroad until he was 47; before that, financial stringency forbade the Alpine climbing which then was the privilege of the better-off and is now open to almost anyone. [13]

Henderson clearly loved Scotland, and according to Grieve he was a good painter, a good poet, and a superb raconteur. He was also, if a later reference by WH Murray is to be trusted, a *rabid nationalist who represented a very small minority of vociferous Scotsmen'.* This somewhat uncharacteristic comment by Murray is taken from a letter to Edward Pyatt regarding the setting up of the JMCS London section, which Henderson opposed and Murray supported. The quote is found in an article on the early history of that section. [14] Henderson was a JMCS member who would join the SMC in 1936, proposed by Williams. The latter was a commercial importer from Glasgow who died in 1981, but there is no obituary in the SMCJ, perhaps because he outlived many of his club friends. He had extensive rock climbing experience in the Lakes from 1925 onwards, and had been on the first ascent of Route 1 on the Rannoch Wall in June 1934, along with Macphee and two others.

Several commentators, including Murray, Clark and Pyatt, have stated that the first winter ascent of Glover's Chimney, with its account by Williams, was an event which galvanised Scottish winter climbing. [15] There was certainly a readiness for this, with several tentative routes which showed a new boldness slowly emerging. In 1935, Macphee was reaching the zenith of his Ben Nevis explorations: 11 new climbs were recorded that year. He was now living in Liverpool and making roughly monthly visits to Ben Nevis. His normal method, for what was a round trip of just under 700 miles, was to have a companion drive his Bentley from Liverpool to Glasgow, where he would take over for the road to Fort William.

On Sunday, 17 March 1935, Macphee, Williams and Henderson made a late start from the CIC Hut and headed for the Garadh na Ciste, the subsidiary buttress projecting from the west flank of Tower Ridge. For once the weather was good, Macphee having had more than his fair share of wet days on the Ben. Indeed, Williams remarks that days which he did not mind having missed included Macphee's first summer ascent of Gardyloo Gully, a new direct route on the Great Tower, and Observatory Buttress, all of which were climbed in pouring rain.

The trio gained the flat top of the Garadh and roped up with a 200ft length of line. Here an explanation of ropes used for climbing might be useful. As Raeburn's book describes, the best type at the time was thought to be the English Alpine Club rope, made of Manila hemp with a distinguishing red thread in each of its three strands. [16] Flax was another natural fibre used to construct climbing ropes. Both types were used to make laid ropes, in which the strands were twisted or layed, not plaited. Manila rope formed a right-hand helix, being laid from left to right. An easy way to assess this is to hold a length vertically: if the visible fibres run up from left to right, it is a right-handed helix. Another way is if you hold the rope pointing away from you and it twists clockwise moving away, then it is right-handed, otherwise it is left-handed. The helix of normal DNA is right-handed, as are most screws, which close to a point in a clockwise direction.

The Alpine rope described by Raeburn weighed approximately one pound per 20ft, and measured about 1¼ inch in circumference. In the SMC General Guide of 1921, the advice on ropes states that– '*...the most convenient length for a party of two is 50 or 60 feet; 80 feet for three; 100 feet for four. The usual weight is 1 lb. per 20 feet.*'

Raeburn also stated that 80ft for three climbers should be sufficient. Macphee, however, in an article published in 1936, strongly disagreed with this. [17] In fact, as a member of the committee then discussing the revision of the General Guide, he dissented from the inclusion of the above advice. In this, Macphee was certainly right.

> One hundred feet of rope for four climbers is, in my opinion, not only ridiculous but dangerous on any but the easiest climbs. It allows of an average length of only 28 feet of rope between two climbers *at most*, and would not be enough for ascending the Tower Ridge of Ben Nevis in safety. Under difficult winter conditions, at least one climb on Ben Nevis (Tower Gap Chimney) requires 150 feet of line for the leader alone...on any difficult or unknown climb there should always be 100 feet of line between every two climbers. A length of 100 feet of Alpine line weighs less than four pounds, so weight is no excuse for not taking enough.

Macphee was talking from experience. On the first ascent of Glover's Chimney the party had used a 200ft length of line, up to half the weight of the usual Alpine rope of the day. Many a day's outing had been blighted by multiple short pitches, adding much to the time taken on a route.

On the desperate epic in December 1908 which led to the ascent of Goodeve's Route on Ben Nevis, the three climbers used 60ft of rope despite also carrying an 80ft length. With hindsight they realised and admitted how stupid this was, as it slowed their progress dramatically.

The use of longer ropes, and the increasing use of lighter line, indicated an increasing confidence. Although on some climbs this could lead to a longer run-out, it did provide climbers with more flexibility, perhaps allowing a good stance to be gained whereas before the shorter rope might have prevented this.

The downside of using a lighter rope would of course be that in a leader fall there would be much more potential for the weaker rope to break. It is worth quoting some words from the SMC General Guide of 1921, written by Raeburn–

> It should not be forgotten that a twelve-stone [76kg] man falling about ten feet is sufficient to break the best rope which it is practicable to carry, and that, though it forms an almost perfect safeguard in rock climbing for the followers if properly handled, for the leader it is physically a nuisance and practically useless, whatever its moral effect may be. A leader *must* not slip.

In mid-March 1935, Macphee's party duly moved up to the foot of the first pitch of Glover's Chimney, a very steep 120ft icefall, at one point bulging to the vertical and probably just overhanging. For some reason they had made a late start, and began the actual climb at midday. (On an ice pitch, vertical very much feels overhanging.) Macphee began cutting his way upwards with an axe that was almost certainly not one of the shorter styles which had begun to appear. After about 40ft, he came back down for a brief rest, before going up and progressing steadily for about 100ft. Williams then had to unrope to provide the leader with sufficient extra length to gain a safe stance, which he succeeded in doing after two hours of single-handed step-cutting and a run-out of 135ft of line. He probably would have had no protection on this pitch.

Reunited, it was necessary to enter the gully itself by traversing left over ice-sheeted rocks and making a difficult descent into the confines. Here they found soft snow which led to a second, smaller ice pitch. There was more snow above, and a third ice pitch, avoided by taking to iced rocks on the right. This proved to be a difficult pitch, and a lunch stop was decreed. The third man, Henderson, was carrying the rucksack, and with an awkward stance he found it difficult to extract the food, holding on with one hand at the same time. It was then discovered that Macphee had plucked a packet of firelighters off the hut table instead of the sandwiches, meaning that dried bananas and biscuits had to fuel them sufficiently enough to continue the ascent.

> It was now late in the afternoon and beginning to darken. Snow conditions in the gully had now become very difficult—some 18 inches of loose snow had to be cleared in order to cut steps in the underlying ice. As Macphee advanced he sent down showers of snow and huge lumps of ice which, owing to our positions, Henderson and I could not dodge. This section took 1¾ hours, and the leader reached the foot of the final chimney at 7.30 P.M.

By this time it was almost dark, though diffused moonlight helped a little – the moon was three days short of being full and had risen several hours earlier. Macphee entered the chimney, which rears up steeply to finish at the Tower Gap. Every hold had to be cleared, with most of them iced. A chockstone pitch almost defeated the leader, but despite the exhausting step-cutting below he was equal to the task.

> I could now but dimly see him as he moved slowly and steadily upwards. Now and then, when in clearing holds of ice his ice-axe struck the bare rock, I could see sparks fly out. Above the chockstone the conditions, instead of easing off, became harder. The entire chimney was sheeted with ice and

there was no place where the leader could take a proper rest, much less to which he could bring me up. He had now run out over 100 feet of line, and the situation was very sensational. It was a thrilling experience for the second and third, straining their eyes in the darkness watching the leader's figure dimly silhouetted against the sky as he got nearer to the Tower Gap. By superb climbing he reached the Gap and announced his arrival there in no uncertain manner. Henderson and I were very glad to take advantage of a loop of rope let down from the Gap.

A final bout of step-cutting above the Gap and a nasty icy traverse led to the plateau at 10pm, where Macphee, always keen to gain the actual summit, walked over to bag it. Williams noted – *'Henderson and I, not being purists, coiled the line. No. 3 Gully was descended, not without difficulty, and we reached the Hut at midnight.'*

Macphee led the climb all the way, and he has put it down on record as one of the most arduous and exacting expeditions he has ever undertaken. It was a splendid example of what one well-known mountaineer-author has described as "real" mountaineering, and a refutation of the assertion made by another that "alpine" conditions are not to be found in Britain.

Although Murray (who was the first author referred to above) was effusive in promoting this climb as an important influence on him and his contemporaries, there was more muted praise from Wedderburn in an article in 1939.[18] He mentions that 1935 was the busiest year Ben Nevis has known –

Macphee was concerned in no less than eleven new ascents – some fine new routes, others the clearing up of little problems necessitated by the revision of the "Guide Book". With Macphee was often associated G.C. Williams, another member of the Club, and A.G. Murray, as well as several others. Winter climbing on Nevis owes much to Macphee's lead.

Glover's Chimney (250m III,4) is not mentioned by name in the Wedderburn article, nor is *Bayonet Route* (185m Hard Severe), another of Macphee's 1935 climbs with Arthur Goudie Murray (1898-1957), a Glasgow steel merchant who later chaired the executive committee of the Scottish Orchestra. Bayonet Route is listed in the current guide as one of the most enjoyable climbs of its grade on the mountain, and is one of Macphee's best efforts, climbing the First Platform to the right of Raeburn's Arete. Perhaps space was limited in the SMCJ that year.

There can be little doubt that with that stirring paragraph in the article by Williams, describing Macphee's crux moves, in itself a radical change in writing style for the time, many young climbers would have felt the urge to go out and do something exciting. Accounts of earlier climbs were determinedly downbeat and modest, often concentrating on the ambience of the day rather than the physical and mental trials experienced by the climbers. There had been brief flashes of this physical aspect in the past, but too few, and never intense enough to excite the imagination.

❉❉❉

In the spring of 1936, Macphee's Ben Nevis Guide was published by the SMC. It comprised 101 pages: one photogravure from a photograph by Harry MacRobert, 19 other illustrations (mostly photographs by Macphee himself), five line drawings and one map. A bonus was a set of four pull-out panoramas from the summit, drawn by James E Shearer during a week of perfect weather in June 1895.

The guide was a revised edition, the first part following on from William Inglis Clark's original article published in the SMCJ and the moderate revision by Harry MacRobert in 1919. From page 23 onwards, it was completely rewritten by Macphee, including all known routes. It remained the same size of red cloth-bound hard back, 218mm x 144mm, and was of course not the smaller size of climbers' guides which would appear in later years.

It was generously reviewed in the SMCJ by Macphee's contemporary and rival Bell, beginning his long editorial reign which stretched from 1935 to 1959. Bell immediately congratulated Macphee, mentioning the enormous amount of exploration and meticulous revision revealed by even casual scrutiny of the guide. He briefly discussed some of the routes, adding a few notes. Macphee had stuck to naming his climb Tower Gap (West) Chimney, but Bell suggested that a better name would be Glover's Chimney, and so it has remained ever since.

Bell even provided a humorous story regarding the route. Exactly two weeks after Macphee's ascent, Bell had accompanied Colin Allan into Coire na Ciste, looking for No.2 Gully in dense mist. They were actually in No.3 Gully, as they crossed an abominable ice bulge and descended a steep snow slope which terminated in a rocky pitch above a steep, narrow gully. The gully went without much difficulty, ending in a chimney with excellent holds and leading to – Tower Gap. The incident, Bell remarked, was a fitting sequel to two hours of midnight wanderings on the preceding night, attempting to locate the CIC Hut.

Returning to the Wedderburn history, Bell mentioned the publication in 1934 of the Central Highlands Guide, noting that 'summer saw the start of the present [i.e. 1939] alarming series of climbing accidents in Glen Coe'. This may well have reflected both the growing number of young climbers active on the mountains and an increasing tendency to push the limits.

The first route on Rannoch Wall was described earlier and was climbed, as Wedderburn remarked, by a party from the old school. He now noted the rise, in 1935, of a new movement in Scottish climbing, prominent among which was what he called *'the Glasgow ginger group'*. Most of these were JMCS members, with others coming from the numerous small clubs that had appeared in the past decade.

Wedderburn pointed out that Scottish climbing had persisted in its original condition for longer than climbing in the Lakes and Wales. Throughout most of the 1920s, Scotland was mainly regarded as a training-ground for larger mountains, providing practice in the off-season for members of the Alpine Club. This attitude tended to make climbing a sport for the wealthier classes, so that climbers in the *'new movement'* found themselves not so much heirs to a tradition, rather the discoverers of a hitherto secret society, kept hidden from their class.

The upstart newcomers were unlikely to start out for a day on the mountain from some hotel, but from their tent, youth hostel, or even emerge from under some rock. They probably wore ragged Grenfell breeches of closely woven cotton and a miscellaneous collection of sweaters. All the men were beardless, though probably unshaven, and could be met wandering uphill with coils of Alpine line, a hatchet, a few spring-clips and probably a ring spike or two, *'just in case'*, to have a look at some secret project. Gone were the tweed garments, the beards, the pipes. The nights were spent under hedges and rocks, with cigarettes and paraffin stoves. These youthful climbers presciently appeared to Wedderburn to be the future of Scottish climbing.

❄❄❄

Over in the east, however, it could hardly be claimed that a winter revival had taken place. On 27 December 1932, Symmers, Ewen and Sandy Clark made the first winter ascent of *Raeburn's Gully* (200m II,), a route which may be elevated to grade III in lean, early winter conditions, but which fills quickly with snow (and, having a large catchment area, is more avalanche-prone than the other Lochnagar gullies). The following day, Clark and Ewen found a 90m grade II route high up the Black Spout, Left Branch, *Pinnacle Gully 2* – but it would be an astonishing 16 years before the next winter route was recorded on Lochnagar.

In summer 1933, Symmers and Ewen returned to climb *Gargoyle Chimney* (120m Difficult) on 6 August. Their next project was the right-hand gully of the three Shadow Couloir lines, but one attempt fizzled out when they encountered a loose-looking tooth of rock at about 150ft. They returned another day and descended from the top to satisfy themselves as to its stability, before making the first ascent of *Polyphemus Gully* (200m Severe) on 16 September. The gully is left untouched in summer by all sensible climbers, but is recognised as the finest of all Lochnagar gullies in winter.

Back in the west, two formidable English climbers visited Glen Coe in June 1936. Sidney Harold Cross (1913-1998) and Alice M (Jammy) Nelson (1911-2004) were two working class climbers from Kendal. Nelson was nicknamed 'Jammy' after the French *jamais*, or 'never', as she was stubborn in her youth. Colin Wells considers that she was probably the best all-round British female mountaineer between the wars, with career highlights including the first female ascent of Central Buttress on Scafell (E1 5b), the first female winter ascent of Bowfell Buttress (VI, 6) and the second winter ascent, with Cross, of Steep Gill (V) on Scafell. She was also, Wells believes, the first woman in the world to climb grade V. [19]

Cross was trained as a shoemaker and met Nelson while she was working in K Shoes at Kendal. They married in 1939, and in 1949 took over the Old Dungeon Ghyll in Langdale. Cross was also a pioneer in improving mountain rescue.

The couple's first ascent on the Buachaille was *Shackle Route* (75m Severe), taking an imposing crack up the East Face of North Buttress. They had good weather, dry rock and climbed in rubbers. Indeed, their description in the SMCJ stated that it would not have been feasible in nailed boots. The route name is deliberately ironic, as the Edwardian Lakes climber George Bower, patently a misogynist, had advised Cross not to climb with a woman, as he considered them '*shackles*'. It was the first route on this face at perhaps easy to middling Severe standard (Murray gives it Mild Severe in his guide of 1949), and it was also anomalous in being climbed by working class climbers rather than by the generally middle class 'ginger group'. While not yet a breakthrough in difficulty, it was a sign of things to come. [20]

Those wishing to peer further into this period, and to learn more about those who personified the new movement, should read the classic book by Alastair Borthwick. *Always a Little Further* is a wonderful chronicle of mountaineering in the 1930s, with a cast of characters and hilarious escapades made all the better by their veracity. It almost remained unpublished, as Faber and Faber were uncertain until one of their directors, a certain TS Eliot, persuaded them to take it on. [21]

Borthwick (1913-2003) was a Scottish author and broadcaster who recorded the popularisation of climbing as a working class sport in Scotland, and also described World War II from the perspective of an infantryman (he was an intelligence officer attached to the Seaforth Highlanders). A prominent character in *Always a Little Further* is James Felix Hamilton (1912-1991), known in the book and in real life as Jimmy or Hamish. When Hamilton joined the Tricouni Mountaineering Club, one of the increasing number of small clubs springing up between the wars, two women members pointed out that they had two Jimmies already, including another Jimmy Hamilton – '*we'll call you Hamish*', they decided, and that was that. [22]

Many of these new clubs were mixed, in contrast to the bewhiskered SMC. As women then were barred from many pubs, the Tricouni met on Friday nights at one of the Miss Cranston's Tea Rooms in Glasgow, where they hatched plans for the weekend outings.

Hamilton was a salesman by occupation and a mountaineer by disposition, joining the SMC in 1944, and compleating the Munros in 1954. He was by all accounts a superb climber, and as Alex Small wrote in his obituary, he possessed a –

> …lithe, cat-like movement, content mostly to repeat recognised routes, but on occasion he had the inborn prognostic ability to discern a new route and climb it on sight. This he amply demonstrated on Agag's Groove, the South Ridge Direct on Cir Mhor, and the Central Buttress of Coire Mhic Fhearchair.
>
> After climbing, his prowess as a driver of motor bikes and cars was notable, many said notorious [...] He had a private condition of travel when you went on his bike, which was that if he was caught for speeding you paid half the fine. I duly subscribed on several occasions. He had some spectacular car crashes from which he emerged unscathed. Swimming seemed second nature to him and he could cover long distances in chilly water with evident enjoyment. A party of us rowed from Tarbet across Loch Lomond to climb Ben Lomond by way of Ptarmigan. A strong wind was blowing when we came back to return, strong enough to make Bill Mackenzie sling his boots round his neck as a precaution. Hamish just swam back. [23]

Bob Grieve also remembered Hamilton, writing in his obituary that–

> …when Hamish joined the SMC at the end of the War he hardly fitted the Club image; the atmosphere that clung to him was of a cheerful recklessness, a by-passing of the miles. In fact, he was simply reflecting changing times. Other clubs had risen before the War which were based on the easier attitudes of the engineering shops and shipyards of Clydeside. Borthwick's book was closer to that and—as I personally know—portrayed it accurately. Mountaineering was becoming 'democratic' and the Club was inevitably changing, too, whilst holding pride in its own special conventions and history.
>
> Another notable memory is of Arch Gully in hard winter conditions when the rest of the party (since night approached) petulantly wanted to retreat. 'Shower of bloody defeatists' came from on high out of the fearsome dusk— and we meekly followed to a nightmarish but masterly finish in darkness. [24]

The summer of 1936 was not a particularly good one–although, as with many of its type, there were a few good days. On such a day early in May, Small and his friends gathered at the foot of Crowberry Ridge, intent on exploring Rannoch Wall and finding where Route I went. They climbed this (then known as the Rannoch Wall Route) and also enjoyed, as Small had it, *'that more delectable form of climbing, lying on one's back and conquering new routes with the eye of faith and the fancy of a sanguine imagination'.* They had picked out a second, longer fault running up the face of the wall, merging into an overhanging bulge before continuing on to the crest of the ridge. If a way could be found up the bulge, Small thought, a new route seemed possible. [25]

It was not until 16 August that they were back at the foot of Crowberry Ridge. By this time the Buachaille appeared to have become a very popular mountain, and the sun not only shone on Small and his friends–

> …but also on a critical spectating 'gallery' perched at ease on the Curved Ridge [...] the hoarse shouts and the cheerful clatter of falling stones cleared by the swarming parties ringing round with the populous clamour of a cup-tie. Not that a referee would be out of place, for with the simple faith of trusting souls we had mentioned our discovery to others, and the 'gallery' contained not only spectators but competitors who missed priority only by minutes.

The competitors who turned up minutes too late were William Machattie Mackenzie (1908-2003), along with Dunn and MacAlpine. Born in Moray (he played football for Elgin City as a youth), Bill Mackenzie became a banker and accountant, eventually moving to Glasgow where as a member of the JMCS he became a prominent part of the Murray coterie. He was overshadowed by Murray (with whom he began climbing later the same year), mainly due to the latter's writings, but was certainly a better climber in winter (as Murray himself admitted) and at least his equal in summer. Mackenzie joined the SMC in 1937, and as his obituary in *The Scotsman* put it, *'He climbed in his seventies, skied in his eighties and golfed and fished in his nineties'.* All these activities were also practised much earlier of course, and due to his mountain skills he was in the Special Forces during World War II.[26]

Before all that, on Rannoch Wall on that sunny day in August 1936, Mackenzie settled down as a spectator on Curved Ridge as three members of the Tricouni and the JMCS–Hamilton, Alex Anderson, an engineer with Rolls-Royce, and Small, a teacher, set off with 100ft of rope and 100ft of line. The prospective route lay leftwards round the edge from the usual start to Crowberry Ridge, where a slender crack ran up a corner. The effect was like an overlap on the side of an upturned clinker-built boat, with the groove's angle easing after about 90ft to provide a narrow shelf on its left. After three pitches, and at 200ft up, a large block belay was gained, just beyond which was the impending bulge.

Hamilton examined the rocks above and began to move up on sloping holds just left of the groove, which now reared up steeply and oozed with moss, water and mud. It is easy to forget that many a classic route, now clean and shiny, was festooned with vegetation and damp crevices in its virgin state – and this one was no different. After a few moves, Hamilton decided to abandon his sandshoes, peeling them off without letting go of the handholds. Slow and careful climbing in stockinged soles brought him to just below the crux after a further 50ft, where he tied on to a small spike. Anderson then moved up below while Hamilton arranged the belay.

Hamilton now moved up the nose of rock on small holds, using a tiny hidden crack, to reach some loose rock which he threw down, first warning Small on the belay below. A stone plunged downwards and exploded on a ledge, with fragments whizzing past Small's ears, luckily with no contact. Hamilton cleared the nose with a strenuous and difficult pull and settled in above, allowing Small to move up to the spike and Anderson to climb up the crux. While doing so, one of Hamish's sandshoes, which Anderson had stuck under his belt, fell out, bounced off Small and sailed down into Easy Gully below.

Small started up and reached the crux, but just as he was occupied with this, using one sloping foothold and a greasy, finger-wide crack, there was a great crash in the gully below. Glancing down between his legs, Small spotted a climber sprawling on his back as he fell down the gully; '*most reassuring*', was his immediate thought. He continued above the nose, where the groove was now cleaner and where Hamilton had found another spike of rock for a belay.

The final pitch was taken slightly to the left of the crack by a narrow wall, returning to the crack about halfway and finishing abruptly on the right, on the crest of Crowberry Ridge, where the first ascent team built a cairn then sunbathed on Crowberry Tower.

Just below, the second ascent was being made by Mackenzie, Dunn and MacAlpine. Meanwhile, Hamilton was adding another anecdote to his reputation by making the first hopping descent of Curved Ridge on a solitary rubber shoe. Small finished his description by hoping that '*those who repeat this climb will sympathise to a certain degree with the difficulties of the Biblical nomenclator in "treading delicately"*'. [27]

A Biblical name, Agag's Groove,was given to the climb, having been suggested by Small. [28]

> The climb ended as it began – in a smoke room. Stern faces and knit brows glared at a list of names written on different sheets of paper. Our part was in the parental throes of christening the climb. Title after title was suggested only to be rejected until we were heartily sick of names and nomenclature. Disgustedly we made to rise and leave, but at that moment out of the void

there came into my mind the name "Agag." "Agag", I thought, "Agag"–the king that trod delicately and the image of Hamish tip toeing up the climb returned to me.

"Agag's Groove," I announced. They stared. They murmured the syllables over to themselves. We sat down again and called for drinks to toast the first ascent of our new route on the Crowberry Ridge, "Agag's Groove."

As Grieve noted –

Hamish was the most courageous man I have ever climbed with. He gave me back confidence at a crucial period of my life when I badly needed it – this because he also had great human warmth and insight and was, indeed, a genuinely religious man. A day or two before he died he joked to me about meeting on the other side. I do not know what heaven he visualised – the world's history has produced many – but his might be a gentler version of Valhalla.

In the current guide, the climb is *Agag's Groove* (105m Very Difficult), and the SMC does not hand out four stars willy-nilly. In the main, it is highly rated for its position, rather than for any perfection of rock. For its grade, it remains a perennial classic, providing excitingly exposed positions on a quintessential mountain, with a superb outlook.

❊❊❊

The last few years had seen an upshift in mountaineering in Scotland; activity in pursuit of new climbs was on the rise, as was the tentative exploration of new crags and faces. The occasional use of ring spikes or pitons was introduced for protection. A host of new clubs made it easier for young climbers to enter the sport. One of these, the JMCS, was dominant, and in 1936 it celebrated its tenth year. The original membership of 54 had grown to 191 by 1936 and by the outbreak of war to 210. During the club's first decade, 87 members qualified for the SMC, comprising two-thirds of those who joined the senior club in that period. By 1939, the SMC was 307 strong. The senior club had indeed benefited from the formation of the junior, as had mountaineering itself.

Many young climbers were not affiliated to any recognised club, however, and this played a part in the rise of the number of accidents on the mountains. Increasingly, other climbers, local residents and the police were involved in rescues, and the lack of an organised structure was beginning to cause problems. It was not unusual for a rescue to be arranged by telephone between members of the SMC and others, with a party then leaving from one of the cities, usually Glasgow or Edinburgh, and using private transport. Indeed, the SMC maintained stretchers and first-aid kits at Glen Brittle, Fort William, and the Clachaig in Glen Coe.

The SMCJ began to publish basic details of some of these accidents, for example–

27th December 1936 – William Christie (23), of Dunblane, killed on Buchaille Etive Mor. Christie slipped when jumping on to a patch of snow. He had no ice axe. S.M.C. and J.M.C.S. members were called out from Glasgow and Edinburgh. Many answered the call and spent all day on the hill.

8th August 1937 – Charles Paterson (22), Glasgow, killed on Buchaille Etive Mor. Alone and unroped, he followed a climbing party and fell down in the Great Gully.

Accidents received publicity in the press, with the accounts often being exaggerated and sensationalised. Before much could be done about this sorry situation, however, war would intervene – but in the period leading up to conflict some further significant ascents were to be recorded.

References

1. Murray, W.H. *Mountaineering in Scotland.* (London: 1947, J.M. Dent & Sons.)
2. Richardson, Simon. *Chasing the Ephemeral.* (Glasgow & Edinburgh: Mica Publishing, 2016.) South-West Ridge, pp.98-101.
3. Bell, J.H.B. *Zero Gully, Ben Nevis.* In: New Climbs. SMCJ 21, 123, April 1937, pp.200-201.
4. Wedderburn, E.A.M. *A Climb on Ben Nevis.* SMCJ 20, 118, November 1934, pp.233-237.
5. *Mountaineering is her Hobby.* Dundee Evening Telegraph, October 10, 1934.
6. Macphee, G. Graham. *Some Recent Rock Climbs in Scotland.* SMCJ 20, 118, November 34, pp.243-249.
7. P.D.B. [PD Baird]. *Stob Coire nan Lochan – S.C. Gully.* SMCJ 20, 118, November 1934, p.284.
8. Murray, W.H. *The Evidence of Things Not Seen.* (Bâton Wicks. London. 2002.) Chapter 3: Renaissance, p.40.
9. <http://www.scottishwinter.com/> Accessed September 2017.
10. The History of British Winters. <goo.gl/EmaeZg> Accessed March 2017.
11. Davison, Brian. *Personal Communication.* January, 2016.
12. Murray, W.H. *The Evidence of Things Not Seen.* (Bâton Wicks. London. 2002.) Chapter 3: Renaissance, p.41.
13. Grieve, Robert. *Drummond Henderson, F.B.O.A.* In Memorium. SMCJ 27, 153, May 1962, pp.301-302.
14. Jordan, Hugh. *J.M.C.S. – London Section (1) The Early Days.* SMCJ 31, 168, 1977, pp.157-158.
15. Williams G.C. *Days on Ben Nevis.* SMCJ 20, 120, November 1935, pp.394-400.

16. Raeburn, Harold. *Mountaineering Art*. (T. Fisher Unwin. London. 1920). Chapter 2 (Equipment), pp.24-28.

17. Macphee, G. Graham. *Scottish Mountaineering and its Relation to Mountaineering Abroad. II.- Remarks on Snow and Ice Conditions*. SMCJ 21, 122, November 1936, pp.85-92.

18. Wedderburn, E.A.M. *A Short History of Scottish Climbing. II.-From 1918 to the Present Day*. SMCJ 22, 128, November 1939, pp.98-108.

19. Wells, Colin. *A Brief History of British Mountaineering*. (2001. The Mountain Heritage Trust.)

20. Cross, S.H. *Buachaille Etive – North Buttress, "Shackle" Route*. In: New Climbs. SMCJ 22, 127, April 1939, p.73.

21. Borthwick, Alastair. *Always a Little Further*. (Faber and Faber Limited, London. 1939).

22. Borthwick, Alastair. *Battalion: British Infantry Unit's Actions from El Alamein to the Elbe, 1942-45*. (Bâton Wicks Publications, 2000. ISBN 978-1898573357).

23. Small, A.C.D. *James F. Hamilton*. In Memorium. SMCJ 34, 182, 1991, p.718.

24. Ibid. p.719.

25. Small, Alex. C. D. *Agag's Groove*. SMCJ 21, 122, November 1936, pp.112-116.

26. <http://www.scotsman.com/news/obituaries/bill-mackenzie-1-600471> (Accessed March 2016.)

27. King James Bible. 1 Samuel 15:32. 'Then said Samuel, Bring ye hither to me Agag the king of the Amalekites. And Agag came unto him delicately.' [Delicately, as in cautiously. Didn't do him much good however, as Samuel hewed him into little bits.]

28. Small, A.C.D. *First Ascent – A Glencoe Rock Climb*. Unpublished article. NLS.

6

Opening Moves (1937-1940)

THE SMC, though like many clubs somewhat diminished following World War I, maintained its leading role with the publication of guidebooks. The first of these had been the William Inglis Clark guide to *Ben Nevis*, published in the SMCJ in 1902 as a section of what the SMC was to call its *General Guide*. [1] Appearing in 1921, this included the Ben Nevis guide, a revised edition of Munro's Tables, and several chapters on non-climbing aspects of the Scottish mountains written by different authors. (See table below.)

The revision of Munro's Tables was not completed by Sir Hugh Munro himself, as he had died in 1919. The main revision was undertaken by James Reid Young (18??-1920), the SMC general editor of guidebooks and the editor of the *General Guide*, which the club decided to dedicate to those of its members who had been killed in the war. James Gall Inglis, a cousin of Inglis Clark, rearranged the individual Munro Tops, now having the benefit of contour lines and other sources.

The Ben Nevis guide of 1920 was sold to the general public as a separate publication, and was also marked as Section E within the *General Guide*. It may thus be seen as the first SMC guidebook standing on its own and available to the public. Some 4,000 copies were printed and by 1929 these had sold out. The 'General' in the title refers to a compendium, giving various chapters on the flora, meteorology, fauna and geology of the Scottish hills. The author has a bound, separate book of these, including the Ben Nevis Section E. This was probably an individual's copy, privately bound, as the *General Guide* was never published outwith the SMCJ.

Steeple and Barlow's Skye guide may be seen as the first major publication in the series of SMC guidebooks covering the distinct climbing and walking areas of Scotland, a series which would continue for the next eight decades or so (but not including the books covering particular sets of hills, such as the trilogy *The Munros, The Corbetts,* and *The Grahams,* which would be published in due course).

A TABLE OF SOME EARLY SMC GUIDEBOOKS:

Title	Author	Year	Pages
Ben Nevis (in SMCJ)	William Inglis Clark	1902	42
Skye (in SMCJ)	William Douglas	1907	74
Ben Nevis (Section E)	William Inglis Clark	1920	42
General (in SMCJ)	Various	1921	144
Skye	Steeple and Barlow	1923	126
The Cairngorms	Henry Alexander	1928	218
Western Highlands	James Parker	1931	133
Northern Highlands	William Ling	1932	87
Central Highlands	Harry MacRobert	1934	158
The Islands	William Naismith	1934	135
Southern Highlands	John Wilson (editor)	1949	204

Southern Highlands, published in 1949 and edited by John Wilson, had been delayed by World War II. Paradoxically, although this area is the closest to most of Scotland's population, the Southern Highlands have often seemed the most neglected with regard to guidebooks.

In their distinctive red cloth covers (modestly hidden behind dust wrappers), with fold-out maps, photographs and mountain diagrams, this series of guidebooks, initially covering climbs and walks, evolved into district guides – with the emphasis on walking – as specialist climbing guidebooks, describing rock and ice routes, began to be published.

An Alpine Journal review by WH Murray of the 1948 second edition of the Skye guide made an amusing observation regarding the first edition. [2] For the second edition, the red covers had been made waterproof, as the older version *'shed a bloody ooze over damp clothing'.*

Murray took issue with one section of the new guide, where under the heading of *'Advice to Hillwalkers'* it stated that it was best to avoid alcohol on the hill, yet added that a flask may be carried for emergencies. An emergency, suggested Murray, was the worst time to use alcohol. Perhaps the guidebook writer was being humorous.

❆❆❆

By 1937, unemployment in the UK had fallen to 1.5 million. The following January saw a rise to 1.8 million, suggestive of a 'bumping along the bottom' picture rather than a true recovery. The economy was saved temporarily however although not in a pleasant manner, by the rise of Nazi Germany, with a commensurate policy of rearmament by the UK National Government, in preparation for what was seen by many as an inevitable confrontation.

It was still possible for some travel to be made by climbing and walking parties, and several energetic climbers did just that before they joined the armed forces. Virtually no climbing was done in the Northern Highlands, which remained even quieter than in previous years. Indeed, in some cases, decades separated visits to even major cliffs. Prominent climbers during this pre-war period included Mackenzie, Bell, Murray, Henry Iain Ogilvy and, climbing outwith his usual home patch of the Cobbler, Nimlin.

The standard of winter climbing was seemingly advanced another notch in 1937 by Mackenzie and Murray, and the latter describes this phase well in his autobiography. [3] The word *seemingly* is used advisedly, as there is a case to be made that winter climbing standards were merely being returned to where they had been before the Great War. In his chapter *Renaissance: 1930s*, Murray describes how Macphee's ascent of Glover's Chimney inspired him and his Glasgow contemporaries. After ascents of such easy classics as the Upper Couloir of Stob Ghabhar, Arch Gully and Gardyloo Gully, and acclimating themselves to steep ice by practising on ice-coated boulders, they felt ready for something harder.

They found this on the Buachaille, but initially had their overconfidence hammered flat by monumental failure and retreat on *Garrick's Shelf Route* (165m IV, 6) at the end of 1936. Note that this climb is currently named simply *Shelf Route*. Several basic errors had set up the party for nothing less than a winter epic, spanning over 20 hours, 14 of which were in descent. They survived – and learned from their mistakes. The four were Mackenzie, MacAlpine, Dunn and Murray.

Firstly, they attempted the climb on 13 December, when what was almost certain to be a difficult winter route was handicapped by the short hours of daylight. Secondly, they started up the mountain late, having been delayed by one of their number forgetting his boots. Thirdly, the party, with four climbers, was too large for speed. And finally, although carrying sufficient rope, they had no pitons or any other protection equipment such as slings and snap-links, markedly reducing their safety margin and making it very difficult to find good belays should they face difficulties and have to rope off or climb down. The actual moment of failure came high on the climb where Murray, leading, was faced by a move on thinly iced, slabby rock with no handholds and, of course, no protection. He declined the challenge and retreat was begun. The first winter attempt, by MacRobert and Brown in March 1910, should not be forgotten; they failed at the crux. (See *The Early Years* for more details.)

Murray's epic is vividly described in his classic book in the chapter headed *Defeat,* and is fancifully the mountaineering equivalent of Napolean's retreat from Moscow, although thankfully with no deaths. Even that possibility came close, however, when Murray, descending as the last man on one pitch, had the rope roll off the spike it was sitting on, plunging him downwards to fall neatly on to the shoulders of Dunn – who managed to hold him. On reaching the road at dawn they were met by a rescue party, and this led to each of the climbers receiving a written rebuke from the JMCS committee– '...*damning our route as unjustifiable. Desist, said they.*' The climbers had learned a hard-earned lesson, and thereafter in winter carried slings, snap-links and pitons. Fortunately for Scottish mountaineering, they also ignored the command to desist. [4]

Just over 100 days later, on 28 March 1937, Mackenzie and Murray made the first winter ascent of Shelf Route in five hours. They waited until sufficient ice had built up, and after some blizzards in March had been followed by two weeks of sun and frost the time had arrived. When they reached the foot of Crowberry Ridge they saw that Shelf Route was a complete ribbon of ice, with the abandoned ropes from their December defeat visible under two feet of transparent ice columns. Leading alternately, they climbed four hard ice pitches to arrive below the crux at noon. Ice-glazed slabs on the left were deemed impossible, forcing a continuation up rocks on the right, with a huge drop into Crowberry Gully. Delicate moves up thin ice consumed two hours before they could emerge into a broad groove, masked by a 150ft icefall. This gave them two 50ft sections of bulging ice which finally led to the crest of Crowberry Ridge.

Other lessons were learnt around this time. In February 1936, Mackenzie, Dunn and Hamilton climbed Crowberry Gully, believing it was the first winter ascent. Hamilton suffered a fall on one big pitch when the pick of his axe pulled out. Axes then had straight picks, non-inclined, suitable for cutting steps in ice but not for pulling on. In his autobiography, Murray writes that it is a mistake, when nearing the end of a pitch in winter [when a leader may be tired] to simply stick the pick into hard snow and pull on the axe. Fortunately Hamilton was not injured, and this lesson was well heeded by all. Additionally, they were still using long axes, which even having been shortened to about 78-81cm (31-32ins) and weighing 900g (2lb) remained too cumbersome and tiring.

Crampons were rarely employed, as without any front points they were of use only when placed flat; they came into their own on icy glaciers, where a slip could lead to a fall into a crevasse. (When the author was cutting steps during his first few winter years, his wooden-shafted axe was some 54cm (21ins) in length and weighed 900g (2lb). With hindsight, this was too heavy – and also ill-balanced.) What was actually the second winter ascent of Crowberry Gully took the three climbers 12 hours. The first ascents, summer and winter, had been by Harold Raeburn.

Another climber at this time was Douglas Scott (1911-2008), who would become known for his explorations and photography. Scott made the third winter ascent of Crowberry Gully the week after Mackenzie's ascent, with the major difference being that Scott used a short axe. He had picked up this idea from Bill Bennett, a climber who had a slating and plumbing business in Glasgow. When Mackenzie and Murray saw this, they realised that a slater's hammer would be the right length and weight for steep ice work, being some 36cm (14ins) long and weighing 709g (1lb 9oz). At a price of ten shillings (50p), it was also fairly cheap. Using the Retail Price Index as the calculator, 50p in 1936 would equate to about £30 in current money. A 1937 advert for Robert Lawrie of London has various ice axes for sale at 21 shillings (just over £1), but it is doubtful whether many climbers were in the market for the slater's pick, given the small number climbing at this grade in the 1930s.

The slater's hammer was adapted by cutting off the side-claw (used for levering slates from roofs), leaving a weighty and short ice hammer for steep ice cutting. Scott, who on occasion climbed with Murray, had a short axe made by a blacksmith in 1936. There are several points to mention regarding the use of an axe for cutting steps. Length is crucial, with the old-style axes very unwieldy in narrow confines such as those found in gullies, and too long for any real amount of effective step-cutting with one hand on a steeper slope. Long lengths, as used by the early climbers and alpinists, made cutting holds above one's head very strenuous. Additionally, it was difficult to have much finesse, something necessary when crafting a step in ice. At easier angles on snow, support from the knees helps with balance and allows two-handed cutting, but this becomes impossible at steeper angles, when handholds are needed.

Weight and balance are also important, with an axe which is too light becoming ineffective as the ice hardens and the slope steepens. A stronger climber can use a heavier axe, but there will eventually be diminishing returns as fatigue sets in faster. Even with the optimum axe, step-cutting in winter was a strenuous business, where one pitch could easily take an hour or more to lead. It never occurred to anyone at this time, as Murray admitted, that a drop-head ice axe could be useful, so for the next three decades or so the winter game relied on a single axe and an ambidextrous leader with good shoulders.

Murray and his contemporaries were still in their twenties and ignored protests from their club committee and any noises off from the senior club. With their modifications to axes, the carrying of protection gear, longer ropes or line and the use of head torches, they made further advances in standards. The introduction of head torches probably received a boost from MacAlpine, who was a dentist and used one at work. On the second winter ascent of Observatory Ridge, Murray and MacAlpine used lightweight torches clenched between their teeth, while Mackenzie, leading, had a battery in his pocket connected by wire to a reflector and bulb secured on his head by an elastic band. This was similar to a setup described by Macphee in the 1936 SMCJ, and ironically would be a setup used later by many climbers before a good design of head torch came onto the market.[5]

According to Murray, far better climbing was done than records might indicate, as routes could now be attempted even if in difficult or sub-optimal condition. Crampons were still of little use, lacking front points, but this latter feature could now be had at a price and was used in Europe by advanced alpinists. Nailed boots retained some advantages, however, particularly on mixed routes where snow- and ice-covered rock holds could be used.

Murray is on record as dismissing the use of crampons in Scotland – and went further, as seen above when discussing Garrick's Shelf Route, stating that on the first winter ascent with Mackenzie crampons would not have helped. [6] The introduction of tricouni nails, invented in 1912 by a jeweller from Geneva, Félix-Valentin Genecand (1878-1957), made climbing ice-covered rock a little easier, though climbers always preferred snow-ice as the perfect medium. Genecand was a keen mountaineer and admired an Italian climber named Guiseppe Tricouni. Being aware of this, Genecand's friends nicknamed him Tricouni.

The fashioning of holds in winter, ideally sloping slightly inwards and downwards with an outer lip, demanded practice. The tricounis, or 'trikes', were made from hardened steel and their serrated edges could bite securely into hard snow, ice and even small indentations on rock. Like crampons, softer snow could 'ball-up' the tricouni nail; this was a danger to be watched for, dealt with by tapping the boot edge with an axe shaft. The Tricouni Company was established in 1921 in Geneva (but the modern Tricouni Brand is now a privately held British luxury fashion house based in Wiltshire).

In his autobiography, Murray mentions that he and his friends having eyes on new climbs further blackened their poor reputation. Macphee was old and wise, he wrote, and therefore could be allowed his first winter ascent of Glover's with its return to the hut at midnight, but Murray's group could not be excused, being young and of no name. Fortunately for history, these 'Young Turks' ignored their accusers and chased the routes.

One indication of this generation gap can be seen in the CIC Hut logbook, where there is a brief exchange of opinion between Murray's party and Macphee:

April 4th, 1937. W.M. MacKenzie, W.H. Murray, A.M. MacAlpine. Gardyloo Gully + arete to Carn Mor Dearg. The gully was found to be ridiculously easy and is not at present recommended to other than complete novices in snow-climbing.

(This party should try the climb again when there is less or, better still, no snow in the gully. GGM).

(The above party has every intention of climbing the gully again under better conditions. They are not unaware that gully climbs vary enormously in winter. On 4/4/37 Gardyloo Gully was easy. WHM). [7]

Others who were looking for new winter climbs included Jim Bell, editor of the SMCJ and providing a parallel, if different force to Macphee. Bell was aware of routes waiting in Coire Ardair of Creag Meagaidh; Raeburn had nosed around there in 1896 and again in 1903, on both occasions attempting to climb the Centre Post, one of three prominent gullies. Since then, wrote Bell, in an SMCJ article, '...*the Posts [...]* have been neglected by climbing parties, not without good reason perhaps, as the prestige of Raeburn has cast an effective halo of inaccessibility over them'.[8] Bell first attempted the Centre Post in April 1934 with Colin Allan, climbing the gully as far as a bare icefall of excessive steepness. They were forced to traverse left on to B Buttress until iced rocks forced a retreat down the gully. Two later visits that same year persuaded Bell that a summer ascent would be impossible, due to the amount of water coming down.

So to 21 March 1937, when Bell and Allan returned to the Post and good snow allowed steps to be kicked to just below the great pitch. Bell used a clinometer, finding the angle of the gully steepening as they ascended: 55° just below the icefall, then 72° on the upwards traverse to the right which was made to avoid the icefall. Allan led the start of the traverse, the first 30ft of which took an hour. His technique was new:

With his left hand he secured himself with his ice-axe, while his right arm wielded a small hatchet, a most adaptable step cutter in such a position of precarious balance. It proved equally useful for hammering in belays. Allan's lead was a magnificent piece of work.

Ever open to experimentation, Bell also carried a novel ice-axe, one with a compound design and giving them two belays when the upper and lower sections were separated. Bell followed Allan along a thin line of icy notches, which provided him with as much thrill as he wanted. Even then, his mind was calculating the possibility of climbing the icefall:

> A slip by the leader would have been much more serious, as he would have had practically a clean drop down a vertical wall of green icicles to the hard *névé* of the basin—on to a surface inclined at an angle of 55 degrees!

> All this must be taken into account when considering the possibilities of the direct route up the 150-foot icefall. It may be that a larger party, the use of crampons, and a liberal supply of ice ring spikes could render such an attempt a reasonable undertaking.

Bell and Allan finished by following the traverse for a distance then turning straight up, finally making a traverse left on very steep snow to a point above the great pitch. An easy scoop of good, hard snow led to the plateau, where there was a bitter wind and it was snowing hard. Visibility was almost zero as they started to make their way back to Aberarder, grateful that they had left the direct route severely alone. The great pitch would not be climbed until 1964.

As to Bell's futuristic comment about *'ice ring spikes'*, Murray described what then happened, or almost happened, in March 1939. [9] Bell and Murray made a date to attempt the direct route up Centre Post, and Bell brought along a bag full of brass curtain rods, specially prepared, he said, to nail the big pitch. He had ringed the tops and filed the bottoms, having discovered that tubular pitons worked better in ice. Murray was relieved the next morning when they found insufficient ice in the gully. Continuing worry over a possible further attempt the following winter was dispelled by the outbreak of war.

In the east, the 1930s saw slow and patchy development, with routes on Lochnagar and Mitre Ridge on Beinn a' Bhùird being highlights. A chance meeting at Corrour bothy in 1937 led to the first winter ascent of *Chokestone Gully* (150m III), the prominent gully which also gives the name to the corrie and cliff west of Sgòr an Lochain Uaine. Edinburgh climber Archie H Hendry (1919-2013) had cycled from Edinburgh, and on meeting another climber, named Andy, the two joined up to make the ascent. According to Greg Strange, at the time it was the most difficult winter gully in the Cairngorms. [10]

Hendry joined the JMCS about that time, and the SMC in 1944. An accident on Crowberry Ridge on the Buachaille in April 1939, when leading Speirs' Variation, led to a serious leg-break after a loose block was dislodged. This resulted in the removal of a kneecap, which blighted a promising climbing career and exempted him from active war service. His career in foreign-language teaching led to a post at George Watson's College in Edinburgh, where he remained from 1948 teaching German.

He was a mentor to the young Robin Smith, of whom more later. Hendry was SMC president 1960-62.

❊❊❊

Bell persisted with his tubular piton idea the month following his ascent with Allan. On 4 April 1937, he was on Ben Nevis with three English climbers befriended earlier– Dick Morsley, Jack Henson and Percy Small. Morsley was a founder member of the Mountaineering Club of North Wales. The history of Ben Nevis has details of their trip, during which the quartet made a taxing second ascent of Green Gully in good conditions.[11] As the first ascent in 1906 had not made any impact, due mainly to the understated report by Raeburn, the climbers were unaware that it had been climbed.

On the day, Bell led the first ice pitch but became tired further up the gully where a second hard pitch loomed. A rocky arête on the right of the steep ice showed the promise of a few small ledges. Henson, then Bell, failed on this, before Small, the best rock climber in the group, made an attempt. He managed to establish himself on the arête, but could make no further progress and decided to try and reverse his position. Bell described what happened next –

> Soon he reappeared on the edge. He had to descend quickly as his strength was ebbing away. With a final warning that he might come off any minute he started to descend, imploring us for advice where to put his feet. About a quarter of the way he held on, then he came off and fell clear of rock into the gully bed. I felt a tremendous strain on my axe & it was jerked right out. But the second axe held tight and he was brought up on the snow unhurt but a little shaken. A party of two could not have taken this risk. [12]

The climb was now in serious doubt, with only around two hours of light remaining. They decided to allow Henson another attempt, limiting it to 30 minutes. It was one of those classic moments which mountaineering throws up, when circumstances force a difficult decision and the outcome is not guaranteed. Henson attacked the pitch straight up the right-hand corner, on a wall at first of rock with a thin coating of ice, and ultimately on ice.

> Henson was a tall, quiet fellow. His replies were always quiet and deliberate – 'I think it ought to go' – 'I think I can do it' - and then after a long period of hacking with little apparent progress – 'I know I can make it go!' Morsley turned to me in triumph. 'You leave it to Henson. He doesn't say much, but he means what he says.

The pitch was won, and above, hard snow led to the cornice finish, where Henson again took the lead, gaining the plateau at twilight's last glimmer. Bell had met his new friends just two days before.

❀❀❀

Jock Nimlin was encountered in an earlier chapter– Cobbler aficionado
and founding member of the Ptarmigan Mountaineering Club. Although a
highly proficient mountaineer, he seems to have recorded very little outside
the Arrochar area, but this would change on 13 June 1937 when a party of
five climbers entered the deep gully cutting into the Buachaille, between
Slime Wall and Cuneiform Buttress. *Raven's Gully* (135m Hard Very
Severe) took the party ten hours, much of it due to the size of the team and
also the care needed to avoid injuries from loose rock dislodged from scree
in the gully bed.

Nimlin entered the description of the ascent in the SMCJ for April 1938.[13]
The fourth pitch, then as now, was the crux, where a huge chockstone completely
blocks the gully with a cave underneath the overhang. The route takes the left
wall, almost holdless, with an exposed outcome below. Fortunately there is a good
belay at the back of the cave.

> Leader is advised (or compelled) to requisition aid from below. Adhesion
> gained by jambing [sic] shoulder in narrow slot between wall and overhang.
> Key to climb is good hold in bed of continuing groove (not visible). Extra
> strenuous and severe.

The second ascent was made by the JMCS team of Murray, MacAlpine and
Walter George Marskell (19??-1968) on 5 June 1939. Climbing in sandshoes
they took two-and-a-half hours, with Murray commenting that pitch four, the
crux, must be the most strenuous in the whole of the Glen Coe area. Oddly, there
is no mention of this difficult climb in Clark and Pyatt's history.

Nimlin also wrote an article describing the ascent for the magazine *'The Open
Air in Scotland'*. [14] This was published by William Maclellan, Glasgow, and came
out three times a year, Spring, Summer and Winter, from 1945 to 1948. There
were also articles from JHB Bell and WH Murray, with the latter finding his
way as an author. Several of Murray's articles, published for the first time in this
magazine, would appear later as chapters in his two books *'Mountaineering in
Scotland'*, and *'Undiscovered Scotland.'*

Nimlin's party had camped that weekend and on Sunday they made their way
up Great Gully on the Buachaille to gain the foot of Raven's Gully at the late
hour of 1pm. As Nimlin wrote in his Open Air article, they were worried about
the state of the nails on their boots. *'It was that season when thrifty climbers get a
final lease of well-worn nails before having them replaced for the summer holidays.'*
The party of five agreed to be more safety-conscious, and also ignore the late start.

> If darkness found us on the hill it would be no new experience, nor would
> we regard it as benightment, which seems to imply an unforeseen and igno-
> minious situation. Ours was the attitude expressed by Daniel Boone, the
> famous American frontiersman. Asked if he had ever been lost in the back-
> woods Dan replied, "No, but I was once bewildered for a week or two."
> Bewildered we might be be, but never benighted.

The party sorted itself out with Nimlin in the lead, followed by Norman Millar, Barclay Braithwaite, John MacFarlane, and Garry McArtney.

Several steps of waterworn rock led to caves, ending abruptly against the roof of the third and final cave. Above was a huge roof of jammed boulders, projecting beyond the floor and overhanging the lower caves. *'A total overhang. A sight to curb the enthusiasm which had carried us to this point.'* As leader, this barrier fell to Nimlin.

> There was a thin slit between the overhang and the left wall of the gully. Unfortunately that part of the slit accessible from the cave floor was only a few inches in width, and the only part wide enough to admit a body was at the outer edge and hanging in space!

Ninmlin attempted the moves several times, jamming an arm in the slit and wriggling out across the wall, hanging for a few seconds before jumping back to the cave. It was a very strenuous move which he could only sustain for a few seconds. He realised that the time had come for decisive action.

> I stepped off and worked towards the outer edge of the slit. No polished performance this, and best described in braid Scots as peching and sprachling: with feet scrabbling furiously to give the essential lift to an insinuating shoulder-blade and a right hand alarmingly redundant, clawing for a friendly projection on the roof.

> At last I felt myself wedge enough to indulge in a brief rest. One shoulder-blade was jammed in the slit, but legs and right arm hung uselessly. A glance between my knees showed the anxious faces of Mac and Garry peering up at my bootsoles from the second cave. Then another breath, as deep as a constricted chest would allow, and I was sprachling again. This was the crux of the action. Then my right hand found a blessed little wrinkle in the rock, my left worked up to a positive "jug handle," the slit widened and offered a sequence of holds which led me back to the safe floor of the upper gully....One by one the others arrived, soaked in sweat and gully drainage. The query, "How would you grade that pitch?" and the answer "Moderately impossible!" brought no dissent. It was a very strenuous passage indeed.

Higher up they came to another formidable overhang. The left wall was steep but appeared to offer the one hope of advance. On this section Nimlin keenly regretted the state of his nails. His feet kept slipping, leaving him dangling on very poor finger holds. Painful scree ruled out climbing in stockinged or bare feet. Combined tactics were required, and well-nailed boots. *'Barclay was the man who wore the boots. They bristled with a new type of tricouni nail, little saw-toothed ridges of case-hardened steel reputed to bite the hardest rock.'*

Barclay ended up standing not just on Nimlin's shoulders, but his head, protected only with a thick woollen helmet. The move succeeded and Barclay gained rocks which fell back a few degrees from the vertical. It was now 8pm and they had taken seven hours to climb about 300ft. The mist was now falling. Above lay another overhang. The right wall was quite holdless, and Nimlin spent nearly an hour on the left trying to force the difficult rocks below its crest. There remained one last alternative, making a dizzy traverse across a bulge of rock which overlooked the whole line of ascent to gain a scoop. The traverse was thankfully short, but the scoop held the first unsound rock of the day's climbing. In some ways this was the most trying part of the whole gully. Sound belays were hard to find, though they did find the minimum for safety.

> I have heard it said that a piton is now in position to augment the safe passage of this scoop, but we did not leave it. We carried none, being rather inclined to the view that a piton, like the flask of brandy "for emergencies only," creates its own need.

The last pitch remained, a wall looming up dimly in the fading light. Nimlin was now tired, and kept slumping to the scree until Norrie gave him a 'back-up.'

> In a few more minutes, I stepped out on the open shoulder of the mountain to meet the first spatter of a night-long drizzle....A mere five hundred feet of climbing had taken us ten strenuous hours. We were wet, cold, hungry and dog-tired. There was a long descent of a dark and difficult hillside before us, a camp to strike, and an eighty mile car-run to the city. Yet we were quite inordinately happy.
>
> There are other ways of finding happiness, but happiness which can endure in the face of such odds is of no ordinary kind. Which says more than a little for inspired action in wet unknown gullies.

The following year saw the first ascent of *Clachaig Gully* (520m Severe) on 1 May by Murray, MacAlpine, Dunn and Marskell – and that climb does receive a mention by Clark and Pyatt. Perhaps this was due to the latter climb having a history, with Collie and others attempting it, whereas Raven's Gully came out of the blue. Like many a gully, Raven's is more popular in winter, when it is V, 5. Nimlin does at least merit a passing mention by Clark and Pyatt, for his Cobbler climbs, with Recess Route highlighted.

What Clark and Pyatt–and for that matter Murray and his friends–were unaware of, was that Nimlin had already climbed the crux pitch of Clachaig Gully, in September 1937. On a day of continuous rain, a party of Lomond Club climbers, led by Nimlin, made a serious attempt on the gully. On gaining the Great Cave Pitch, the obvious lower line was impossible due to the amount of water coming down. Nimlin spotted another way up, which with a higher traverse was just possible. This was Nimlin's pitch and that he succeeded was due to his leaping for a small rowan tree which gave a handhold, allowing a turfy ledge to be gained. The party abandoned the gully after this pitch, as it was frothy with rain water–and their bus was due to leave in a couple of hours. His companions on this day were Peter McGeoch, Alf Slack, Jimmie Stewart and Danny MacGovern.

Four months after Murray's first ascent, Nimlin was back in the Lomond Club bus, and with his girlfriend Jennie Dryden (whom he later married) plus two other Lomonds, Dick Williamson and Alex Bulloch, they made a complete ascent of the gully, Dryden's being the first lady's ascent.

On the right day, preferably in spring after a dry spell and with no party above, Clachaig Gully can provide a very pleasant outing. There is some loose rock, water will always be present and the protection on some pitches can be difficult to arrange. All attempts before Murray's–Nimlin's excepted–failed at the Great Cave Pitch, from the attempt by Norman Collie's party onwards. Coincidentally, on the day of Murray's success, a party of good climbers from England, accompanied by Alastair Cram, was also attempting the gully. On failing to find a way up the crux pitch, they stepped aside to allow Murray's party to try, and on their success Cram's party descended.

A later landslide badly affected the gully below this pitch, and this lower stretch is now not recommended. Consult the current guidebook for the best descent routes, and certainly avoid the slope immediately west of the gully, now badly eroded and dangerously loose. It is worth reading the chapter in *Call-Out: Mountain Rescue* by Hamish MacInnes, where he describes various rescues in Clachaig Gully. [15]

❊❊❊

On Ben Nevis, Bell opened up yet another face when with Hamilton he succeeded at the second attempt to climb the steep rocks left of Point Five Gully, putting up *West Face Upper Route* (300m Severe). [16] The date was 11 July 1937. The pair had looked at the line the previous September, but retreated in the face of bad weather. After an abortive start adjacent to the gully, finding slabby rocks that were not only wet but also very hard, they moved further left where a small chimney was a useful launching point. A somewhat jinking line followed, with several traverses and steep chimneys, one of which took the leader into a precarious position, forcing him to drive in a ring-spike and pass the rope through a spring-hook as protection. A few moves further saw boots and socks removed *'and a delicate friction glide on a smooth slab led to assured safety'*.

Bell finished his note by suggesting that there were surely a number of other routes to be found on this great face– *'Some may be more direct than ours, but all will be difficult. We can only claim to have made the opening move of the game.'* Like many of Bell's explorations, his *'opening move'* would lead to a good number of hard and popular winter climbs. This face is now known as Observatory Ridge West Face.

Limited activity on Skye saw Mackenzie, MacAlpine and Oxley climb *South Gully* (210m Severe) on the Glaic Moire Face of Sgùrr a' Mhadaidh. The current guide provides a good write-up for this route, making mention of continuous, clean, solid rock and challenging route-finding.

❉ ❉ ❉

As described in *The Early Years*, the first traverse of the Cuillin Ridge on Skye was that by Leslie Garnet Shadbolt (1883-1973) and Alastair Campbell McLaren (1880-1950) on 10 June 1911, with a peak-to-peak time (Gars-bheinn to Sgùrr nan Gillean) of 12 hours 18 minutes. Both men were SMC members.

The first largely solo traverse was by Theodore Howard Somervell (1890-1975), a London surgeon, on 15 June 1920. A good Alpinist, with two Everest expeditions to his credit (1922 and 1924) and also an SMC and AC member, Somervell was president of the latter club in 1926. He did have company for part of the ridge in the form of Graham Wilson, who went as far as Sgùrr na Banachdich, at which point he stated that '*he was "done"'*. Somervell's peak-to-peak time was 10 hours 49 minutes.

Going against what had become the convention, the first north-to-south traverse was made on 17 July 1924 by BR Goodfellow and F Yates of the Rucksack Club, taking 12 hours 50 minutes. Towards the end, a navigational error on Sgùrr nan Eag lost them 35 minutes. Two days later, Frank Smythe and Jim Bell enjoyed their own traverse in 11 hours 37 minutes.

The first female traverse was by Mabel Barker on 11 August 1926, on her third attempt, accompanied by Claude Dean Frankland. They had weather of all types, as befits the Cuillin, with rainbows, hailstorms and sunshine. Their time was 13 hours 30 minutes. Barker returned in 1931 to make a second traverse, having in 1925 led Frankland up the crux pitch on Central Buttress of Scafell, the fourth ascent and the first by a woman.

The Greater Traverse was the next target for the record-makers and breakers. This involves the normal traverse of the Black Cuillin ridge, plus the two peaks of Clach Glas and Blàbheinn. The crossing of the latter two alone is recognised as one of the finest outings in Scotland, with the current guidebook suggesting seven hours at Grade 3/Difficult . The Greater Traverse became a topic of conversation in the 1930s and soon attracted two JMCS members, one of whom, Ian G Charleson (1925-1974), grew up in Oban before making a career with the Bank of Scotland. He joined the SMC in 1938 and was president 1960-1962.

His partner in the Cuillin project was Woodhurst Edward Forde (1911-1990), born in Carmunnock to the south of Glasgow and joining the SMC in 1946. He eventually worked in the publishing company of Oliver and Boyd, where he assisted Bell with his 1950 book. In preparation for the traverse, Charleson and Forde stashed food under the Inaccessible Pinnacle and put up a tent containing more food in Harta Corrie.

On 12 June 1939, there was some mist and drizzle, with morning frost on the hill and a fresh, northerly wind as the pair left their tent below Garsbheinn. They were pleased when the mist cleared on the Sgùrr a' Mhadaidh section, especially as a recent fall of snow had hidden the nailmarks on the rocks, sometimes a useful clue to the route. The drizzle returned on Sgùrr nan Gillean. On gaining their tent in Harta Corrie they ate and rested for 75 minutes before climbing into mist on Clach Glas, which they left as twilight descended. The first summit of Blàbheinn was gained at 11.15pm, and the second a few minutes later. Their full traverse had taken the pair 20 hours and seven minutes.

Those wishing more details can find an article by Forde's daughter Helen (herself an SMC member), which includes the two-part article on the traverse which Forde had published in the *Weekly Scotsman* in August 1939.[17] Charleson recorded his own account in the SMCJ.[18] On 24 August 1939, with war looming, Murray and RG Donaldson made the second Greater Traverse, taking 19 hours. They enjoyed sunshine most of the way – too much, in fact.

❄❄❄

Edmund A Whittaker Hodge (1901-1979) was a member of the SMC, the Rucksack Club and the Wayfarers' Club, joining the first in 1936. He seems to have been mainly a walker (becoming an early Munroist, in 1938), and he lived for many years in Elterwater Hall near Ambleside. Described in his Rucksack Club obituary as '*...a legal man and property owner*', he spent what must have been enjoyable summer holidays exploring the Western Isles, hiring a 34ft motor cruiser with friends and going where they fancied and the weather and seas permitted. He made four or five such trips between 1936 and 1939, with the one in June 1937, of three weeks' duration, providing material for an article in the SMCJ.[19] While the landings produced no climbs, scrambles were enjoyed and many summits gained, including Conachair on St Kilda. He did however note potential cliffs on the way.

Hodge edited the SMC Islands guide which saw the light of day in 1953. He was still exploring the islands and had a sailing trip in August 1954, which was duly written up for the SMCJ.[20] He also used this article for answering some critical remarks received regarding the guidebook. One reviewer had blamed him for interpreting the interest of mountaineering too widely, to which Hodge responded–

> Let me say candidly I do not regard a mountain as merely a collection of climbing routes 'made' (as the quaint phrase goes) and still more quaintly named by various individuals, but as an affair of a few billion tons of rock; I like to view its shape from below, above, and the flanks, and to know what

lives on it, what it is made of, and its place in the life of the countryside. I agree, therefore, with W.H. Murray that the heart of mountaineering lies in exploration.

At this time only a handful of climbing guides was available, as distinct from the more general guides such as the one to the Islands and others which would include any climbing routes as an appendix. It would be a few more years until the separation became near-complete, with the district guides covering areas such as the Southern Highlands and the Cairngorms, and separate climbing guides for summer and winter routes. It is ironic that it took until 2014 to see publication of a climbing guide which includes climbs in the Inner Hebrides (incorporated with Arran), but this is partly explained by the slow pace of exploration on the islands, excepting Skye.[21] Hodge and his *'sea-mountaineering'* recalls an earlier odyssey, when the SMC set out by the steam yacht *Erne* at Easter 1897, intent on mounting a sea-borne invasion of Rum and Skye.

❊❊❊

In the current guide, Crowberry Ridge Direct is graded VII,6. It is also given two dates for winter ascents: 1938 and 1953. The second date is for the first complete ascent by Hamish MacInnes and Chris Bonington, while the earlier one has to date gone virtually unrecognised. On 3 April 1938, Alex Small and his companion Jim Wood headed up the Buachaille with Crowberry Ridge in mind. They had one borrowed axe between them. The day was squally, with cumulus against a bright sky. The snow and ice was plentiful above 2,000ft, enough to make the approach via the early part of Curved Ridge messy and tiresome. Easy climbing led to Abraham's Traverse.

> I cleared the snow off as far as I could then took off my boots before making an attempt proper. Passing the bad bit was not too bad but the broader scoops above held snow and on these I found it difficult to advance. While clearing snow with my hand I slipped back & got rather a fright but the finger tips of my left hand bit through snow on to a rock wrinkle and I stayed put. Cautious work got me up to the halfway part of the pitch but nerves & ice took some time before I completed the pitch.

> I hauled up the boots & the axe (Bill Neil's) and Jim came up by Greig's – taking rather a time. [22]

(The reference to Greig's is the easier variation which avoids the crux moves on Crowberry Direct by climbing up from the right end of Abraham's Ledge, before moving left again to join the Direct Route.) Small found the move in the square corner of the next pitch difficult, after which easier ground led to the slabs. These looked so formidable that they moved

The great line of cliffs of Sròn na Ciche on Skye. The shadow of The Cioch prominent on the left. © John Cleare

Crack of Doom. This Hard Severe classic on Sròn na Ciche, Skye, remains a formidable test piece. © Roger Robb

Cioch Direct, late 1950s. Roger Robb & Jim Simpson. A Severe from 1907, there have been recent rockfalls. © Roger Robb

Wallwork's Route above the Cioch. Two unknown climbers appear to be off-route, with the second in difficulty. © Ken Crocket

A studio portrait of Harold Raeburn, SMC. The most prominent Scottish mountaineer of the early 20th Century. © SMC

North-East Buttress on Ben Nevis from Càrn Dearg, with Observatory Ridge starting bottom right, first climbed in winter by Raeburn. © John Cleare

The cliffs of Mitre Ridge on Beinn a'Bhùird, Cairngorms. Photo: Donald Bennet.
© Anne Bennet

A winter meet of the Tricouni MC, formed in 1930. © SMC

A rare photo of Percy Unna in July 1925, an SMC climber prominent in helping to buy part of Glen Coe for the NTS. Taken sneakily while he was sleeping. © SMC

Swiss scientist and mountaineer Dr Ery Lüscher who had a solo climbing holiday in Scotland in 1920

Davy's Bourach. A tiny but occasionally lifesaving shelter, built by Davy Glen in 1966 by the side of Jock's Road. © Peter F Macdonald

The very first meet of the JMCS, under the Narnain Boulder, The Cobbler, September 1925. L to R: W Speirs, JA Stevens, G Robertson, AJ Rusk, R Waddington, CW Parry, RN Rutherford, GR Speirs, AG Hutchison.

A JMCS built bothy in Coire Ardair, Creag Meagaidh, built in the 1960s and now defunct. © Andrew James

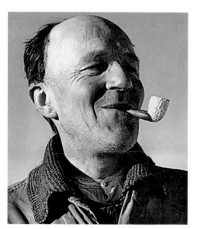

JHB Bell, SMC Journal Editor 1935-59, and responsible for pioneering many classic routes. © SMC

A bothy in the Western Highlands, location secret. Climber Alastair Walker. © Ken Crocket

Interior view of The Drey c.1976.
© Nicola Campbell

1931 group at Findouran, the home of the Leslie's at Inchrory, Cairngorms. Back: Stephen & JE Cumming, front: John Crofton, Donough O'Brien & David Howarth. © Ian Crofton

CUMC Meet at the CIC Hut, early 1930s. L to R: Stephen Cumming, ?, ?, EJA (Jock) Leslie, Pat Baird. The three named were also JMCS members. © Ian Crofton

Three Creagh Dhu climbers; Hugh Currie (front), Tommy Paul and Mick Noon (right). This club would lead rock climbing standards in Scotland in the 1940s and '50s. © CDMC

Sandy Wedderburn tries and is about to fail on a final tower of Mitre Ridge, taking a 30ft fall on to the rope, remaining unhurt . © Ian Crofton

Climbers on the first ascent of Agag's Groove, Rannoch Wall,
Buachaille Etive Mòr. © SMC

G Graham Macphee (standing)
and Allan McNicol in the CIC Hut
c.1951. Macphee would help
galvanise winter climbing with his
ascent of Glover's Chimney, and
also write a climbers' guide to Ben
Nevis. Photo Tom Weir. © SMC

Alex Small, a teacher by profession, was on the first ascent of Agag's Groove in 1936, and named the route. © SMC

Mira Marko Debelak, an experienced and competent alpinist from Slovenia, who was on the 1st ascent of Slav Route on Ben Nevis.

Hamish Hamilton enjoying a break below the Cobbler. Leader on the 1st ascent of Agag's Groove

January Jigsaw on the Rannoch Wall, Buachaille Etive Mòr, Glen Coe. Climbers unknown.
This classic and popular Severe did receive its first ascent on a January day, in 1940.
© Ken Crocket

Coire an Lochain in the Cairngorms has provided many classic climbs, including the Severe Savage Slit, which unusually delves deep into the crag, allowing a climber a secure feeling. © John Cleare

WH Murray in 1950, while on an Everest Reconnaissance expedition, aged 37. His classic book 'Mountaineering in Scotland', has been an inspiration to countless climbers. © Audrey Scott

A war-time portrait of Sandy Wedderburn, tragically killed in an accident in Italy in 1944. He was on the first ascent of a Mitre Ridge classic in the Cairngorms. © SMC

This well-known photograph is of WH Murray starting the traverse from Heather Ledge on Central Buttress. Probably taken in 1937, photo by AM MacAlpine.

During WWII, several climbers worked on secret anti-submarine research based at Fairlie, just south of Largs. They enjoyed many weekends on Arran, making new routes such as Sou'Wester Slabs, shown here on an early repeat. Photo: Ken Moneypenny. © SMC

Brian Kellett worked on the forestry below Ben Nevis as a conscientious objector. He soloed many routes, some new, and was ironically killed by a fall in 1944 while roped to his companion.

The crux pitch of Eagle Ridge, Severe, on Lochnagar. The crux takes the crack just beyond the climber. Photo: Donald Bennet. © Anne Bennet

One of the illustrations from the Etchachan Club magazine 'Crabs', an Aberdeen based club which never stood on ceremony but otherwise stood on whatever they could use.
© Etchachan Club

The 'S' and 'Y' cracks on the South Ridge Direct, Cir Mhor, Arran. Great positions on superb Arran granite make this route a classic. Photo: Donald Bennet, climber unknown. © Anne Bennet

High up Route II on Nevis, first ascent by Brian Kellett. A Severe with exciting positions and exposure beyond its Severe grade. Photo: Donald Bennet. © Anne Bennet

A Lakes Meet of the Creagh Dhu MC, here at Dungeon Ghyll Bar, Langdale. 1956. Back (L to R): Hugh Currie, Ginger, Sandy Crawford, Bonbon, girl; Front (L to R): Charlie Vigano, Bill Smith, Eric Taylor, John Cunningham, Gordon Macintosh. © CDMC

A classic Cobbler Severe, Punster's Crack was climbed by John Cunningham & Bill Smith (both CDMC). Here, Cunningham is on a later ascent, climbing the last pitch with Jimmy Gardiner belaying. © Anne Bennet

Gordon McIntosh & Bill Smith share a tent at the site of Jacksonville, the CDMC bothy. © CDMC

Creagh Dhu climber Eric Taylor on a 1957 repeat of Gallows Route, Buachaille Etive Mòr. A Cunningham route, serious and requiring a leader with nerves of steel. © CDMC

Grooved Arête on Crowberry Ridge is on superb rock and in a great position. Understandably a popular VS. A 1946 route by Cunningham and Bill Smith. Climber Ken Crocket. © Ken Crocket

Arrow Route on the Cioch Slab is a technically easy climb at Difficult but one requiring a confident leader as protection is difficult without cams. Late 1960s. Climbers unknown.
© Roger Robb

Archer Ridge on the East Face of Aonach Dubh. Climber T Murray. Rough bubbly rhyolite and good positions.
© Roger Robb

Gwen Moffat is a noted lady mountaineer and Britain's first female mountain guide. In 2017 she celebrated her 83rd year. Photo circa 1975. © John Cleare

into the continuation groove of Naismith's Route to join the final slabby rib on Hyphen. Here they had to use a jammed axe in a crack as a belay. Small tried the problem above but had to retreat to the belay. Here he removed his boots again and with some trepidation got halfway up the rib, then eventually to the top of the nose and with freezing hands swept and kicked his way on to the crest of the ridge.

Wood chose the slabby route, coming off twice. Small then forced his feet painfully into his frozen boots before the pair moved together up and down Crowberry Tower to the Gap, where Small very nearly dropped the axe. At 5.45pm they gained the summit in sunshine before descending in another blinding hailstorm.

When MacInnes sent in a note of his ascent in 1953, Small informed Bell, editor of the SMCJ about his 1938 ascent– *'but wee Jim was very canny & said "I'm not going to adjudicate on what are winter conditions." So there you are.'* [23] Small certainly deserves mention for his early winter ascent of the Direct Route's crux. Only circumstances prevented him from making the first complete winter ascent of the summer line. It will be recalled that Murray and Mackenzie also avoided the slabs, when making their ascent of Shelf Route. In 1953, MacInnes also climbed in stocking soles for the crux, while Bonington wore crampons. (See Chapter 10 for more on this.)

❈❈❈

Later in April 1938, two good winter routes were climbed on Ben Nevis. The previous year had seen Bell and his three English friends climb Green Gully. Impressed by what they seen and experienced, two of them, Richard Morsley and Percy Small, joined by F Gardner Stangle, returned to the Ben for another tussle with the ice pitches. Stangle must have learned about the modified slater's pick, as he was carrying one of his own. He also contributed a good note about their climb, published in the Jubilee number of the SMCJ. [24]

Comb Gully (125m IV,4) is a prominent route separating Comb Gully Buttress from The Comb, and Morsley and Small would have had a good look at the route during their approach to Green Gully. March 1938, according to Stangle, had been an exceptionally mild and wet month, and the gully contained much ice and little snow. In fact, across the UK, that March was the second warmest of the century, while Kinlochquoich suffered a massive 252mm of rain on 29 March.

On 11 April the team climbed Gardyloo Gully to prepare themselves for the main course of Comb Gully, which route they tackled the next day. In Comb Gully, some 300ft of moderately hard snow led to where the route narrows to form a chimney, usually icy. The second man cut up to a niche between the ice and the rock, where he used an ice axe belay. Stangle now approached the chimney.

Its left wall had sufficient ice to allow steps to be cut, though the ice was brittle, needing care. Stangle used the pick of his modified slater's hammer, which he referred to as a *piton hammer*. He climbed back-and-toe for 20ft when the gully curled over to the left and the retaining wall receded too far right to be of any use. A short ice bulge was then climbed and after 50ft the bed of the gully was gained.

Easy snow then led to another icy chimney, fortunately with a rock thread belay. Its ice wall was almost vertical, and good hand- and foot-holds were needed, until 50ft up hard snow was reached and a ledge for an axe belay was cut. Above lay the steepest pitch yet, where water ice had formed a solid column 20ft high below a chockstone.

Several episodes of cutting up this, with descents for rest, finally gained the lip, where a thread belay was found after removing some icicles. Above this, 30ft of hard snow led to another cave, entered after digging, to find another thread belay. Stangle now needed a rest, and the second man led a small bulge to finally view the summit ridge above, after which Stangle led through to a good rock belay on top.

The climb had occupied the three climbers for eight-and-a-half hours. They found the three main ice pitches harder than the final icefall in Gardyloo Gully, while Morsley and Small, comparing the route to Green Gully, thought it steeper but safer, as at no time were they without a rock belay. It remains a popular, classic route.

Several days later, Macphee, Williams and eight guests from England used the CIC Hut during the SMC Easter Meet at Fort William. On 15 April, Macphee, along with R Ashley and CH Oates from Liverpool University Mountaineering Club, bagged a good route on Raeburn's Buttress when they climbed Intermediate Gully, which separates Raeburn's Buttress from Baird's Buttress. Given in the current guide as *Raeburn's Buttress* (250m IV,5), this natural winter line provides an excellent and sustained climb. At the time, it must have been one of the technically hardest winter routes on Nevis.

Hodge was present, staying in Fort William, but there is nothing in the meet report about his activity. This seems to have been his *modus operandi*, as an SMC report for the 1952 New Year Meet at Ballachulish remarks that '*The doings of E.W. Hodge, who is allergic to records, remain shrouded in mystery.*'

One hard ascent on an island took place when Ken Barber and Alfred S Pigott visited Arran in 1938. On Easter Monday, 18 April, LS Coxon, GS Bower and Pigott climbed a vegetatious Very Difficult route on Cioch na h' Oighe, linking the second and third ledges. Much better was Barber and Pigott's *Easter Route* (95m HVS), climbed on the East Face of Cir Mhòr's Rosa Pinnacle. This was undergraded and described as a Severe in the SMCJ, while in the SMC's 1958 guide *Rock Climbs in Arran* it was given Hard Severe, positioned on a graded list as fourth out of the five Severes there. A near-forgotten route historically, its current grade of HVS would make it one of the hardest pre-war climbs in Scotland. Like the Mitre Ridge climbs and Raven's Gully in summer, it is not mentioned by Clark and Pyatt.

❀❀❀

April 1939 must have seen a good spell of late winter conditions, as on 7 April Murray and Mackenzie were in Glen Coe making the first winter ascent of *Deep-Cut Chimney* (450m III/IV,4) on Stob Coire nam Beith. This was a climb hatched over a beer in MacAlpine's house in Glasgow, where on Thursday evenings the youthful quartet of MacAlpine, Dunn, Murray and Mackenzie would meet to plan the weekend ahead. Murray was to devote a chapter in *Mountaineering in Scotland* to Deep-Cut Chimney. Inspired by some of the winter climbing innovations which they or others had devised, Mackenzie had a brainwave. As it was in a sense a two-part route, with a lower, harder section and an upper, longer, but easier section, they would not be put off by the short, early winter days but would climb the lower section by daylight and then, if needs must, finish up the easier slopes by torchlight.

The first attempt in January 1939 had seen Dunn, Mackenzie and Murray defeated after five hours of climbing by unfriendly conditions of soft snow and brittle ice. Doubled ropes and combined tactics saw them back on the corrie floor in an hour, when they discovered that their night-time hope, an electric torch, had switched on in the rucksack and was all but exhausted. After that, Murray wrote, they separated the battery from the torch until needed.

The first ascent, on Good Friday, 7 April, was made by Mackenzie and Murray (the other two being unable to join them) in a hard frost under blue skies. It is easy to forgive Murray's writing style of almost eight decades ago, with its attention to detail and almost cinematic drama, for his descriptions ignited a curiosity in many a young head. As an anonymous contributor has it on Wikipedia– *'Though written in an evocative, rather pantheistic, style, somewhat too romantic for modern tastes, they are of significant literary value.'* Or as Colin Wells wrote in an online review of Murray's autobiography: *'Murray's writing style was heavily influenced by a homespun mysticism which lends a mesmerising metaphysical other-worldliness to his accounts of the inter- and post-war climbing scene in the Highlands.'*

Mountaineering in Scotland was Murray's first book, published in 1947 but written twice, first in a prisoner of war camp in Italy, then again, following confiscation, in a German-run camp in Czechoslovakia. It was here, in an atmosphere conducive to much meditation – and emphasised by meeting with and being led along that path by an officer in the Indian Army named Herbert Buck – that Murray's spiritual leanings were firmed up. There are also clues in the posthumous autobiography *The Evidence of Things Not Seen* which provide help in understanding his descriptive style.

In that latter book, Murray describes how he began to write while imprisoned, wondering what had happened to the German officer who had captured him at the end of a tank battle and seeing the winter snow on a distant mountain, both acting as catalysts. Murray states that he was glad he did not have to rely on a diary for his writing; his descriptions were all taken from his memory, which developed with practice. His incarceration would also have intensified his feelings for those distant routes, with their hard-won ice pitches and moonlit walks over glittering summits. It matters little whether his classic accounts do, or do not, impress the modern reader critically; what they did for many was to awaken a sense of curiosity which led to actual action and an introduction to the mountains.

Alastair Cram met Murray as a fellow prisoner of war, in Oflag VIII-F in Czechoslovakia. Cram was obsessed with escape, making 13 attempts in all. There is nothing in Murray's autobiography regarding his own feelings on escape attempts, but it seems that Cram despised those who did not try. Cram's remarkable life itself deserves a biography: a Major during the war and a member of the SAS, an expert linguist, a judge in several African countries after the war, briefly Governor-General in Malawi and an all-round explorer and traveller. While the author was editing the SMCJ, Cram would occasionally send in short but interesting reports on his travels with his wife, and at one point an interesting series of letters were exchanged, in which we each put forward our opinion on how we should address each other. We eventually reached a compromise.

On 7 April 1939, the same day as Murray and Mackenzie were in Deep-Cut Chimney, Macphee was on Ben Nevis with three of his Liverpool University friends – RW Lovel, HR Shepherd and D Edwards – on another winter first ascent, *Good Friday Climb* (150m III), which takes a line at the left end of Indicator Wall.

The climb, which Macphee thought magnificent under the excellent conditions prevailing, was entirely on snow and ice. Two days later, he wrote, it would probably have been impossible– presumably due to end-of-season thawing. It has a lovely finish up a narrow runnel of snow or ice, ending with a dramatic flourish opposite the trig point, from which it is traditional to take a belay, the highest in the country.

Across on Lochnagar, Bell and Murray had laid an ambitious plan. Their idea–almost certainly Bell's–was to walk to the summit, then descend the rocks of Tough-Brown ridge. Assuming that went well, they would attempt to climb Parallel Buttress. Eagle Ridge and Parallel Buttress are the two prominent features which lie between Douglas-Gibson Gully and Parallel Gully B. The narrow crest of Eagle Ridge on the left throws down massive, undercut walls into the Douglas-Gibson Gully, while on its right is Eagle Buttress. Next right, the rocks are incised by Parallel Gullies A and B, between which stands the flat-fronted Parallel Buttress: initially wide, then tapering to a true ridge at the top.

In perfect weather, 28 May 1939 saw the pair on the summit of Lochnagar at noon, peering down the broken rocks at the top of Tough-Brown ridge. They intended to climb unroped, unless forced otherwise, and the first 100ft went easily enough. They then headed straight down, where the original route climbed more easterly, and on ever-steepening ground they dropped down a series of short vertical walls, broken by grassy ledges. As the ground became more difficult they were forced off the crest, until they were looking into Raeburn's Gully. Attempts to descend the crest saw them tiptoeing on nail edges, with no rope or belay and with a 200ft drop waiting for any mistake. The gully it would have to be, and some 100ft of good rock saw them in this, about 100ft above its start.

After a dip in the lochan, Parallel Buttress beckoned. The lower face, between the gullies, defeated them and they finally gained the easy terrace by taking to steep rocks on the left of the terminal waterfall in Gully A. They were now on the original Tough-Brown route of approach, and a rising rightwards traverse saw them crossing Gully A above its lower section, with the traverse reaching a formidable band of slabs girdling Parallel Buttress. They found a weakness on the Gully B face, taking to a thin, vegetated ledge which saw them balancing along a granite wall to a saving incut hold round an edge. A scramble upwards and a long slanting scoop allowed the buttress crest to be gained.

With the rapidly narrowing crest ahead, it quickly became obvious that the choice of route was now set firm; to make matters more dramatic, above could be seen an obvious difficulty in the shape of a tower, shaped like an arrowhead and about 30ft in height. At this point they were 200ft below the top. It was Murray's lead. On either side of the tower the rocks were perpendicular, but a thin crack led up the left side of the initial slab, leading to the left edge of the tower. Murray, then Bell, failed to climb the crack, they had reached an impasse.

Here the two climbers showed their different approach to such a problem. Murray had only recently begun to carry pegs, and those only for winter climbs, when a normal belay could often be hidden and retreats, such as that on Garrick's Shelf, were serious endeavours. The feisty Fifer Bell, on the other hand, was more pragmatic and was almost certainly thinking about the ordeal of a long and difficult retreat. From his rucksack he produced two ring-spikes, pegs with attached rings, the forerunners of pitons with integral eye-holes.

With the pegs and a small hammer Bell climbed the slab until all holds faded, then banged in the first peg until only its ring was visible. He used this as a handhold, then athletically mantelshelfed on to the ring, slowly straightening up. He could now insert his other ring-spike into a crack on the left wall of the tower, again using this as a handhold to gain a small niche where he belayed and brought up Murray – who managed to remove the pegs without needing Bell to keep a constantly tight rope. The belay was good enough to allow Bell to remove his boots, for he could see that the traverse ahead now relied on friction. Stockinged soles could be comforting on slabby ground, and was a technique often employed by Bell and others. Bell described the traverse as being severe, but it led to a good belay. Murray required a tight rope to be kept for the traverse.

The remainder of the ridge was exposed but with good holds, and the climbers continued unroped. Indeed, in his description, Bell remarks that they had climbed unroped except for the crucial tower section, taking a fast time of two hours. As a finale, a beautiful knife-edge of frozen snow led to the plateau. *Parallel Buttress* (280m Severe, VI,6) is described in the current guide as– *'A route with character, history and of course, a fair amount of vegetation. In dry conditions it provides a worthwhile climb.'* Again, as with many a Bell route, it provides an excellent climb in winter.

In his autobiography, Murray looks back at the 1930s and makes many interesting observations. By 1939 he had been climbing with Bell for a year, and was to a fair degree in his thrall; the use of pegs by Bell on Parallel Buttress had given Murray, to use his own word, a qualm, or misgiving, about the action. When it came his turn to second the crux, after removing the pegs he managed to climb it in nails without a pull on the rope. He writes that the pegs were not strictly necessary. As all climbers know, however, there is often quite a difference, especially on a first ascent, between leading a hard section and following it.

Murray's philosophy was that if a climb required pegs then he would rather retreat. Bell, in contrast, had few scruples in this respect. Murray mentions the Bell–Macphee feud in his autobiography, where on Ben Nevis Bell was delighted when Sandy Wedderburn's party used a couple of pegs for belays on Slav Route, as he knew this would infuriate Macphee. In Europe at this time the serial assaults on the north face of the Eiger were ongoing, with German climbers to the fore. The use of pitons for aid was in the ascendant, and other than a few British climbers poking about on scruffy outcrops for fun, it was not popular on the home front. Climbers such as Murray's group had enough criticism from the older generation as it was.

An interesting note appeared in the SMCJ for 1939, entitled *Pitons on the Crowberry*. The author was Wedderburn. [25]

[*Extract from a letter to the Editor by E. A. M. W., who regrets that he cannot divulge the name of the climber in question.*]

"A climber, reputedly of some experience, ascended the Crowberry Ridge by Abraham's Traverse in early June of this year. Not liking the step round, he drove in a piton [ring spike, E. A. M. W.] into a crack which is conspicuous on the well-known photo (' Central Highlands Guide,' facing page 49, also front page of wrapper). The pitch was successfully negotiated by the leader, but the second man was unable to remove this ring spike, try as he would. The party completed the climb and descended Curved Ridge, then reascended to Abraham's Ledge and both together were at last successful in removing the ornament.

❋ ❋ ❋

Other explorations were ongoing in the east, where Richard B Frere and Kenneth A Robertson entered Coire an Lochain in the Northern Cairngorms and climbed, in the late summer of 1939, what they named *Savage Slit* (80m Severe). This is now a classic route, unusual in being a wide crack in a corner into which one may enter, disappearing inside the mountain for some distance.

Explorations was also taking place in Glen Clova, where in July 1938 the first route on the Red Craig was climbed. *Three J Chimney* (13m Very Difficult) on the very accessible south-east buttress was climbed by Jack Scroggie, Jack Scott and John Ferguson, all members of the Corrie Club of Dundee. On 27 August 1939, Bill Ward of the Climbers' Club bumped into Ferguson at a meeting, which led to Ward leading two classic Severes on Red Craig, *Hanging Lum* and *Flake Route.*

Climbing standards in Scotland at this point remained behind those of England, but Scottish socks were about to be pulled up a further notch by the arrival of a new force, meteoric and sadly short-lived. In the summer of 1939, two young climbers en route to the Swiss Alps met on the Paris-Geneva train. One was the 27-year old Esme Speakman (1912-1990), who had been climbing in the Alps since 1934. The daughter of a naval architect, she spoke fluent French and was a fine photographer, professionally trained, with an impressive collection of slides of her travels which made good lectures. She would go on to climb and travel for over four decades.

The other was a Cambridge undergraduate, Henry Iain Ogilvy (1919-1940), adopted son of Sir Herbert Kinnaird Ogilvy and Lady Christina Augusta Bruce. Sir Herbert was a practising Writer to the Signet who succeeded to the title of 12th Baronet Ogilvy, of Inverquharity, Forfarshire in 1914.

Speakman lived at one point in Comrie in Perthshire and had just joined the Ladies' Scottish Climbing Club. The pair got on well and arranged to climb in Scotland. On 5 September 1939, two days after the declaration of war, they were on the Rannoch Wall on the Buachaille, making first ascents a grade harder than anything else on the face. *Red Slab* (80m Very Severe) and *Satan's Slit* (85m Very Severe) both include bold and delicate sections of climbing, and were led by Ogilvy wearing rubbers. In his description of Red Slab, Ogilvy writes–

> The route is slightly artificial in that, at first, it is possible to escape to the left and later to the right; but the centre pitch provides very good climbing of a delicate nature on perfect rock.

The current guide warns, with typical understatement, of the hard middle pitch, which gives the route its name and has small holds, saying that the route finding is not straightforward.

Satan's Slit takes a counter line to Agag's Groove and crosses that classic route below its crux nose. It has a bold and delicate traverse on its second pitch and finishes with an overhanging crucial crack. In one day and with two first ascents, Ogilvy had upped the standard of face climbing on the Buachaille.

There had now been set in motion a series of parallel events, which in combination were to push up standards of climbing in Scotland, both winter and summer. There was the encouragement of Bell, in his sponsorship of young climbers, his refreshment of the SMCJ which saw a new recognition and reporting of new climbs on Scottish hills, and his personal explorations which saw new cliffs opened up for the first time. There was a new boldness of key climbers in winter, with Macphee, Murray, Mackenzie and Bell, along with a new and interesting style of writing up exploits. And there were individual climbers on rock such as Nimlin, Murray, Macphee, Hamilton and Ogilvy, all of whom in their own way showed that there was new ground to explore for those bold enough to grasp the nettle. A new dawn had come.

❈ ❈ ❈

Ogilvy and Speakman were back on the Buachaille in January 1940, and astonishingly they made a first ascent not of a winter climb but of a rock climb. Not only that, it was not on some low level, friendly crag, but on the Rannoch Wall, with snow on the ledges and in poor, misty weather. Speakman gave an interview many years later, which was used as part of a brief article about the Rannoch Wall climbs.[26]

She described Ogilvy climbing in nailed boots, with a double rope tied at his waist, and wearing a blue beret with plus fours and a tweed jacket. There were intermittent, sleety showers, and with a second's task being static and miserable in such conditions, she didn't remember much about the route apart from its disagreeableness. *'It was cold, wet and miserable. Iain took ages to move up and I cried quite often.'*

Ogilvy named the climb January Jigsaw, presumably due to an exposed and improbable crux traverse on the last pitch. *January Jigsaw* (75m Severe) is thought by some climbers to be even better than Agag's Groove, taking a more direct line with interest increasing as height is gained.

Alex Small wrote an article describing the climbs on Crowberry Ridge and Rannoch Wall, where for the first time the name of the face was officially proposed.[26] He tabled the existing routes with their standards and comments, a list that includes the two girdling routes: Helical Route (Severe) and High Level Girdle Traverse (Hard Severe). Helical Route is no longer in the guide.

The other climbs on Rannoch Wall of interest here are given below as in Small's table.

Rannoch Wall Routes

Route Name	Grade	Current Grade	Comments
Agag's Groove	Severe	V.Diff	Severe in exposure; lower chimney and crux technically difficult.
Satan's Slit	Severe	Very Severe	Exposed and delicate.
Red Slab Route	Severe	Very Severe	Exposed and delicate.
Rannoch Wall, Route 1 (original)	Severe	V. Diff	Severe in exposure only; original crux route is technically hard; left variant is easier.
January Jigsaw	V.Diff	Severe	Severe in exposure only; no great technical difficulty.

These climbs are naturally now much cleaner than before, while the Severe grade in earlier years probably covered a wider range of difficulty than now.

Although very few new routes were being recorded by those in the new clubs at this time, there were some exceptions. As well as Nimlin, another member of the Lomond Club, Henry W Grant, made some discoveries. On the Buachaille he recorded four climbs with Peter McGeoch and Miss Drummond on the fast-drying East Face of North Buttress, which is in two tiers and is in effect the right wall of Crowberry Gully. Only two climbs are in the current guide: *North-East Zigzag* (85m Difficult) and *Slanting Groove* (100m Very Difficult). This face had been opened up with the ascent of Shackle Route in 1936, and would become a convenient playground for a new wave of climbers after the war.

Ogilvy returned to Scotland in June 1940 with a trip to Ben Nevis, climbing with fellow CUMC students. Three first ascents were found, all currently graded at Very Difficult: *Evening Wall* on Càrn Dearg Buttress, starting just right of Waterfall Gully; *Compression Crack* on Raeburn's Buttress; and the *Tower Face of The Comb*. These were climbed on 19, 21, and 22 June 1940. All take in less than good rock, with some vegetation thrown in, especially on the last route, and are not recommended in summer.

Of the Tower Face of the Comb route, Ogilvy left the following comment in the CIC climbers' log: *'Owing to the nature of the rock and moss encountered we suggest Quisling Wall as a name.'* The word Quisling comes from the Norwegian war-time leader Vidkun Quisling, who headed a Nazi collaborationist regime during the war. Compression Crack forms many ice smears in winter, and is now V,5. Tower Face of The Comb is a sought-after winter mixed climb at VI,6, of which more later.

Ogilvy's partner was Charles F Rolland, with James R Hewit (1909-1998) joining them on The Comb. Jimmy Hewit was a JMCS member who was to join the SMC in 1947. He was on his honeymoon at the CIC Hut with his wife Elsie, who graciously gave him permission to climb with Ogilvy and Rolland. Living in Edinburgh, Hewit became the local expert on Salisbury Crags, producing a private guide. As Hendry noted in an obituary, *'Local mythology has it that an eponymous route,* 'Hewit's Groove', *required the insertion of an old halfpenny in a crack in order to provide the crucial foothold.'* [28]

Ogilvy also added a variation to the Great Tower on Tower Ridge, climbing up the first groove on the left as one goes along the Eastern Traverse. *Ogilvy's Route* (45m Very Difficult), appeared as a note in the SMCJ, with the comment that it *'is not so difficult as it looks'*. Ogilvy climbed this the same week as the climbs described above, in June 1940, when his partner was Lord Nicholas (Nick) Pelham Piercy (1918-1981). The pair returned to Ben Nevis the following month, and on 25 July made an attempt on Gardyloo Buttress, the steep little buttress at the head of Observatory Gully. Climbing the left edge, Ogilvy made good progress until rain stopped play, necessitating an abseil.

On 18 August, Ogilvy was in the Cairngorms and climbed two routes on the flanks of Sgòran Dubh with his cousin, Charity Lucy Scott-Robson. One route takes in the full height of the Northern Rampart and is recorded in the CUMC Journal. It may well have been the first Very Severe in the Cairngorms, though this is conjecture. In summer its buttresses have generally poor rock, with the guide describing the climbs as ranging from uninspiring to dangerous. The routes climbed by Ogilvy are not described in the current SMC guide.

The two returned to Sgòran Dubh on 22 September, but failing to return a search was made the following day and they were found roped together. It is not known what they were climbing at the time, but they were probably killed in a fall while attempting another line on the Northern Rampart, as their bodies were in the deep cleft known as the Willow Spout.

Bell is likely to have met Ogilvy at some point, perhaps on Ben Nevis, and he would be very much aware of his potential considering his routes on the Buachaille. Bell was probably responsible for the unusual insertion of an SMCJ obituary notice for a non-member, something which had only been done a few times for those who were regarded as special friends of climbers. [29] In part, it read–

> It is unnecessary to refer to the skill and daring of Mr Ogilvy as a climber. The "New Climbs" section of our Journal bears witness to that. He has also done some fine Alpine expeditions and was a most successful President of the Cambridge University Mountaineering Club from 1939 to 1940.

> The sympathy of all Scottish climbers will go out to the relatives of both victims of this distressing accident.

War had been declared on 3 September 1939, two days after the German invasion of Poland. As has been obvious from the climbing described in this chapter, the effects of wartime restrictions on Scottish climbing were not as harsh as in the previous war, although Skye was out of bounds to most, along with the areas north of the Great Glen. There were more service-men stationed in Britain, and the summer of 1940 was blessed with good weather. Ben Nevis in particular was to see fruitful explorations by some familiar names, along with a few new faces.

References

1. *Ben Nevis*. In: SMCJ 7, 39, September 1902, pp.134-176.
2. Murray, W.H. *Review of S.M.C. Guide to the Island of Skye*. In: Alpine Club Journal, 1949, p.115.
3. Murray, W.H. *The Evidence of Things Not Seen – A Mountaineer's Tale*. (London: 2002, Bâton Wicks.)
4. Murray, W.H. *Mountaineering in Scotland*. (London: 1947, J.M. Dent & Sons.)
5. Macphee, G. Graham. *Scottish Mountaineering and its relation to Mountaineering Abroad. II. Remarks on Snow and Ice Conditions*. SMCJ 21, 122. November 1936, pp.85-92.
6. Murray, W.H. *The Evidence of Things Not Seen – A Mountaineer's Tale*. p.44.
7. CIC Hut Log Book, Vol.1. 12 November, 1928 – 5 July, 1949. NLS.
8. Bell, J.H.B. *Recent Climbs in Coire Ardair. III. The Centre Post*. SMCJ 21, 126, November 1938, pp.398-403.
9. Murray, W.H. *The Evidence of Things Not Seen – A Mountaineer's Tale*. p.45.
10. Strange, Greg. *The Cairngorms – 100 Years of Mountaineering*. (SMT, 2010, p.48.)

11. Crocket, Ken and Richardson, Simon. *Ben Nevis - Britain's Highest Mountain.* (Scottish Mountaineering Trust, 2nd edition 2009).

12. Bell, J.H.B. *Personal Log Book. Vol.4.* NLS.

13. Nimlin, John B. *Raven's Gully – Buachaille Etive.* In: New Climbs. SMCJ 21, 125, April 1938, pp.348-350.

14. Nimlin, John B. *Raven's Gully.* The Open Air in Scotland. (1947. Vol.1, No.6, pp.42-45, 53.)

15. MacInnes, Hamish. *Call-Out.* Chapter 8, *Clachaig Gully Rescues,* pp.182-209. (1977. Penguin paperback.)

16. Bell, J.H.B. *The West Face of Observatory Ridge – Ben Nevis.* In: New Climbs. SMCJ 21, 125, April 1938. pp.352-354.

17. Forde, Helen. *The greater Traverse – Remembering the Immortals.* SMCJ 40, 200, 2009. pp.318-326.

18. Charleson, Ian G. *Traverse of the Cuillin Ridge and the Ascent of Blaven and Clach Glas.* SMCJ 22, 128, November 1939, pp.127-132.

19. Hodge, E.W. *Under the Western Horizon.* SMCJ 21, 124, November 1937, pp.255-261.

20. Hodge, E.W. *We Sail Again.* SMCJ 25, 146, May 1955, pp.342-347.

21. *Inner Hebrides & Arran.* Colin Moody and Graham Little. (SMC 2014, ISBN 978-1-907233-17-3.)

22. Small, Alex. *Personal Log Book.* 1938-39, April 3rd, pp.72-73.

23. Small, Alex. *Letter to Rab Anderson,* 6th January, 1981.

24. Stangle, F.G. *Comb Gully, Ben Nevis.* In: New Climbs. SMCJ 22, 127, April 1939, pp.65-66.

25. *Pitons on the Crowberry.* In: Notes and Excursions. SMCJ 22, 128, November 1939, p.151.

26. Thomson, Allan. heraldscotland. 3rd January, 1998. <goo.gl/C7Bn6n> Accessed April, 2016.

27. Small, A.C.D. *A Crowberry Commentary.* SMCJ 22, 129, April 1940, pp.190-196.

28. Shipway, Bill & Hendry, A.H. *James R. Hewit j.1947.* In Memorium. SMCJ 36, 189, 1998, pp.738-739.

29. Anon. *Note announcing the death of Mr Henry Iain Ogilvy.* SMCJ 22, 130, November 1940, p.258.

7

The War Years (1940-1944)

DURING WORLD WAR II, the proportion of servicemen and women in the UK at any one time tended to be higher than during the previous conflict. Mountaineering had meanwhile become more popular. There were difficulties in travelling, golf competitions were cancelled, some hotels and other facilities were used for billeting, while many hotels lost staff through conscription. Rationing of petrol began 22 days after war broke out, and a 'Holidays at Home' scheme was promoted by the government. Train journeys were not banned, but were made more awkward: no extra services at traditional holiday times, and with advertising to discourage their use. People were still determined to travel, however, and often the result was crowded trains and long waits for the next available service.

Soldiers had a generous holiday allowance, initially ten days' leave for every six months if they were on the continent. If stationed in Britain they could have two weeks every six months, or one week every month. [1] By the start of 1940, food rationing had begun, with clothes rationing two years later. Much of the Highlands became regulated; Skye, for example, was basically out of bounds. When Norman Collie died on 1 November 1942, most if not all who lived in the south were unable to attend his funeral. Travel was probably easier for those on leave in the forces, which would account for the two trainee RAF pilots who stayed at the Sligachan Hotel in March 1940 and who provided possibly the very last descriptions of Collie in print. [2] Mountaineering during the second war was therefore curtailed to some extent, though not as severely as during the first.

❋❋❋

The early summer of 1940 was superb throughout Britain, even including Ben Nevis. Jim Bell had been poking around at the great face left of

Zero Gully, and in July 1935 had climbed the Great Slab Rib system left of the central depression on the face known as The Basin. His companion was Violet Roy, a member of the Grampian Club. Bell described not only the route they climbed, but also his other routes on this great face, perhaps the closest Scotland comes to providing climbers with an Alpine atmosphere. [3]

Bell had been interested in this face since 1925, when accompanied by Frank Smythe, but circumstances prevented him from making an attempt until 7 July 1935. His plan was gain the Basin, from where he thought he could continue up the face to eventually gain the crest of the North-East Buttress. The rock structure of the face determined the general line, with the entire face formed by huge ribs, running back leftwards from the vertical at an angle of about 20°. Their target was the rib which ran up on the left of the Basin. Roy was an excellent rock climber according to Bell, well balanced and light. The pair had perfect weather, and plenty of time.

Looked at directly, say from the crest of Observatory Ridge, this face appears to be absolutely vertical, with some overhangs. From the right position on Càrn Mòr Dearg, however, its true angle is much friendlier. Closer inspection would suggest that the great sweeps of slabby ribs may at points be smooth, providing difficulties for nailed boots.

Some 150ft of easy slabs led to the foot of the main rib; Bell had exchanged boots for stockinged soles, allowing friction moves, but Roy was not yet converted to this technique. A pitch of just under 100ft with no protection gained a rock bollard in a grassy recess. Bell considered that a pair of new and therefore soft plimsolls would have been good on the dry rock, but his actual pair had hardened with age and his stockinged soles were better.

An impressive rib now rose up slightly to their right, almost vertical, but with rough, corrugated rock. The slightly overhanging nose at its foot had just enough holds to allow access, using fingers and toes, above which a further 90ft led to a stance. They named this pitch the Great Slab Rib, which is clearly visible in evening sunshine from the CIC Hut. On a later ascent, Bell seconded this pitch in boots, finding no sense of security. Easier climbing up and right now led to the Basin.

After lunch in this pleasant eyrie, they set out to try a continuation of their line upwards. The rib formed the left-hand rampart of the Basin, and Bell took a direct line with some difficult climbing, keeping above Roy so as to better hold her more securely. She found this pitch the hardest of the day, and came on the rope once – presumably, Bell thought, having found a section without holds. Above were splintered rocks, easing access to the crest of the buttress. They had made the first ascent of this great face, and it only now remained for Bell to name both the face and their route.

It was Bell's intention to make a direct ascent of the rib. On 10 June a joint JMCS/SMC group was at the CIC Hut: Bill Murray, Douglas Laidlaw and an English climber W Redman, along with Bell and James Earl MacEwen (1906-1978) from the SMC. Both Laidlaw and Redman, in the RAF, would later be killed in action. Bell and McEwen went up Slav Route and from the high terrace photographed Murray's party. Redman had climbed the Slab Rib by the original route, followed by Murray and Laidlaw, taking in a right traverse at one point. The true direct line therefore still awaited.

Bell returned on 14 June, with John Wilson of the Perth JMCS. Climbing in plimsolls and occasionally socks, they followed Bell's original route to the Basin, then after lunch continued to cross the Basin and climb the crux of the day, a feature known as the Second Slab Rib. Above all difficulties, they gained the crest of North-East Buttress higher than the Mantrap, and so to the top. *The Long Climb* (420m VS) had been climbed.

Both climbers were convinced this was the longest and finest [face] route of sustained difficulty on the Ben. There are routes with better rock on Nevis, but climbed following a dry spell, with the right frame of mind, a grand experience may be had in a big mountain ambience. This climb would later become a focus of attention for a winter ascent.

Bell had several remaining tasks to be performed on this face, the main one of which involved tidying up his original route (thus far known as 'The Basin Route', or 'The Straight Left Route') by avoiding the rightward traverse. This he succeeded in doing on 4 August, accompanied by George Dwyer who had been climbing hard on Clogwyn Du'r arddu in Wales.

As a bonus, Dwyer was also adept at climbing in stockinged soles. One can only guess how tough their feet must have been, compared with the normal softness of a modern rock climber. Their direct line avoided entering the Basin, instead continuing up the crest of the left rim. A few days later they made the direct entry to the Basin from the first platform of Slav Route.

Having completed The Long Climb, it remained to name it. Wilson initially suggested 'The Fall of Paris', as the Nazis were engaged on their blitzkrieg advance through France. Unknown to Bell and Wilson, on that very day, Paris did indeed fall. Later, Bell was on a solitary winter walk on a local hill when the solution came to him. The topography of this face, and the layout of the routes, were suggestive of the great constellation Orion. The ancients described this as the depiction of the mighty hunter, with Sirius, the brightest star seen from Earth, as his dog.

Orion, as seen in the winter sky, has a belt of three bright stars, which on Ben Nevis corresponds to the Basin. From each of those rises one of the upper routes. His right arm (he is facing the observer) is formed by

Betelgeuse, one of the brightest stars in the constellation and known to astronomers as Alpha Orionis, thus giving Alpha Route. With the three stars of the belt being Zeta, Epsilon and Delta, the original route above the Basin is Zeta, in the middle is Epsilon Chimney, and to the right is Delta Route, forming the upper half of The Long Climb and leading to Orion's head.

Descending from Orion's belt a vertical line of stars forms his sword, corresponding to the Great Slab Rib. The bright star Rigel, Orion's left leg, is Beta Orionis, giving Beta Route. Climbers have, through usage, kept The Long Climb as a name. As for the face itself, it is now universally known to mountaineers as the Orion Face, a great name for this magnificent feature. Seen in good winter condition it thrills and inspires, and the narrative will return here in due course.

Bell was not finished with his major explorations on Ben Nevis; if the weather in June 1940 was superb, that of August was a balancing act. Sheltering in the CIC Hut from foul conditions, Bell and Dwyer discussed the possibility of a grand traverse of all the cliffs of Ben Nevis and Càrn Dearg. They knew of a traverse from the left rim of the Basin to the crest of the North-East Buttress, emerging at a conspicuous V notch at the second platform. Bell also knew that they could easily make the traverse from the Basin to Observatory Ridge.

There were, of course, several possible problem sections, but they decided to give it a go, starting from Castle Ridge and making a right-to-left girdle. All went well until in dense cloud they crossed No.5 Gully too low, which led to some confusion crossing the Trident Buttresses. By 3pm, with the cloud even thicker, they halted under the Comb. As they had to return home that evening, they called a halt and finished up Pigott's Route.

With an ever-increasing workload and war conditions, it was not until the autumn of 1941 that Bell was able to make another visit. His companion this time was John D Bruce Wilson (191?-1990). On 21 September they entered Coire Leis and so gained the North-East Buttress. Bell's logic can be seen at work here: he already knew some of the girdle starting from its right end, now he would attack it from the left.

As the pair expected, it went well across the face and Observatory Ridge, until they were about 80 feet short of the *great unclimbed gully*, this being Point Five. Here they were in luck, with a fairly easy crossing between two pitches. They were now above Rubicon Wall, with an easy walk to the base of the Great Tower and a lunch stop.

There was a partial descent of Glover's Chimney, into No.2 Gully, then up Comb Gully to cross the Comb by Hesperides Ledge, with Green Gully then leading to No.3 Gully. At this point, Bell wrote–

Wilson made it quite clear that he hated the very sight of the beautiful plants on Hesperides Ledge and considered that he had done enough for the day. So I rashly agreed to meet him at Achintee at half-past six. [4]

Creag Coire na Ciste was slow, as finding a descent to No.4 Gully was hard, then Bell was speeding across the screes of the Trident Buttresses and across Càrn Dearg Buttress to gain South Castle Gully and so to a finish at the top of Castle Ridge. They had left the hut at 7.30am and Bell finished at 5.22pm, a smidgen under ten hours. At the end of his account, he cheekily wondered who would be first to try the winter girdle.

❄❄❄

Arran had all but been ignored for decades, as the early pioneers in the SMC were seen to have exhausted the potential of the vegetated north-east face of Cir Mhor. The obviously superior rocks of the south face were all but impossible due to equipment and footwear. This was about to change however, with significant ascents made during wartime.

On 9 September 1940, Hamish Hamilton and George S Roger (1907-1983) of the JMCS paid a visit. They succeeded in climbing the ridge but avoided the two difficult pitches, known as the 'S' and 'Y' cracks, by a rightwards traverse leading to a difficult layback pitch. However, this route, now named the Original Route in the current guide, had been climbed in 1935 by James Arthur Ramsay (1909-1988), a lecturer at Cambridge, who did not record his climb in the SMCJ and it thus seems likely that Hamilton was unaware of that ascent. He returned to the route in 1941 with D Paterson and climbed the two pitches directly, and is thus credited with the first ascent of the *South Ridge Direct* (395m Very Severe). The climb is one of Scotland's great classic rock climbs.

Hamilton was not the only climber who, dissatisfied with an ascent, had returned to climb it in better style. Ramsay first approached the route in 1933, when he climbed the original line but used a top rope for the Layback Pitch. His partner on both ascents was unnamed. Hodge and friends were also on Arran in 1933, and made determined attempts to climb the route directly. In 1935, unnamed friends of Hodge bypassed the Layback crux using a corner groove but these ascents and others indicated a rising confidence, and provided a pointer to the future.

The direct crux is the 10m pitch called the 'Y' crack, which is 5a technically and a strenuous and overhanging grunt or two. The author has heard of one unnamed unfortunate who had a foot jammed in a crack here, with a tight schedule for making the ferry back to the mainland. George Roger later went on to join the SMC, and was president in 1970-1972. He was very experienced and came to a sad end during a New Year Meet when he and his dog were walking along the tracks over the Auch viaduct in a blizzard and did not hear an approaching train.

The Ramsay Original Route is also VS, with the rightward traverse under the 'S' crack leading to a difficult overhang and corner, the Layback Crack.

❄❄❄

In July 1940, Henry Ogilvy and Nick Piercy had attempted to climb Gardyloo Buttress on Ben Nevis, but were rained off. The next party to 'have a look' at its attractive left edge – or at least the next known party – was a trio from the Corrie Club of Dundee; Sydney Scroggie, John G Ferguson and Graham S Ritchie. The date was June 1941 and by now Britain was not only at war with Germany, it was being attacked by Germany. The Dundonians were staying in the CIC Hut, and at 2am there was a bombing raid by the Luftwaffe on the Fort William aluminium works. Hearing the drone of an aircraft, the hut residents carried their nightcap mugs of tea outside to watch the action–

> …where the great cliffs of the Ben towered jet-black against a dark sky. No sound came to us save a soft rustle of wind. Yet we lingered expectantly. Then lazily, so lazily, converging streams of red tracer-shells rose from behind Càrn Dearg and mounted the sky. Two great flashes lit the horizon and the hills stood revealed for an instant. But not a sound was heard. It was all rather eerie and exciting, yet peaceful and strangely beautiful. [5]

Later that day the trio approached Gardyloo Buttress via Tower Ridge. They quickly surmised that gaining the central snowy depression high on the buttress was the key, and at 6pm began to climb the left-hand ridge. They soon removed their boots and continued in stockinged soles to gain a ledge below a pair of thin chimneys, topped by some insecure-looking blocks. Time was now short, so deciding that perhaps the best route lay up the wall of Gardyloo Gully on the left, they banged in a peg and roped down. Natural protection had been short thus far, with only two belays found.

Back the following day, Scroggie climbed the gully wall for 40ft, then moved right on to the buttress ridge where 30ft higher he found a good belay and a small ledge. Ritchie settled down while the other two moved up. Time went by, shadows lengthened. A glorious light flooded Gardyloo Gully, painting the rocks purple. Hammering sounds came from above, while the ropes moved up but only in little twitches. Finally two dejected climbers descended to Ritchie's ledge, telling of steep, holdless grooves and ribs, all continuously exposed. They brought with them a deeply rusted karabiner and a weather-faded belay loop, the highest point reached by Ogilvy's attempt.

William Sydney (Syd) Scroggie (1919-2006), born in Nelson, Canada, served as a lieutenant in the Lovat Scouts, then grimly fighting their way up Italy. The Germans were retreating, leaving behind many booby-traps. Two weeks before the end of the war, Scroggie stepped on a Schu anti-personnel mine, losing a leg and his eyesight. This barely slowed the man down, and after recuperating he continued to walk and climb, going on to write a slim but interesting autobiography covering many stories of his walks and bothy experiences in the Cairngorms. [6] (More can be found in an excellent review of his book, which also contains a link to an episode of Weir's Way. [7])

The party decided that the best line was further right. In this they were correct, as shall be seen later, but in the interim a move must be made eastward, where a similar campaign was taking place for another route.

❋❋❋

Bell approached Lochnagar on 7 June 1936, taking with him a friend, David Myles (1895-1968), and also WG McClymont, a visiting climber from New Zealand. Bell was in search of a new route, especially one which could trump the descriptions of wondrous Antipodean mountain days. As they entered the corrie, a great buttress caught the sun's rays, rising just beyond the Douglas-Gibson Gully. The party was not carrying the new edition of the SMC Cairngorms guide, but Bell was certain that such a feature would have been mentioned had it been climbed.

Starting at the lowest rocks, from a patch of snow in the gully, the going went well to the buttress crest some 90ft up. Traversing left above the gully was impossible, and the buttress edge above rose in an almost vertical, smooth wall. They continued rightwards by the western face of the buttress, before returning left above to regain the crest. Above them it appeared steep, exposed and holdless. Another upwards traverse right was made, until they could see steep rocks above what would be named Parallel Gully A, with a corner visible higher up. They succeeded in climbing these rocks and finally gained the buttress summit. It had been the first ascent of Eagle Buttress, if not by the direct line up the crest.

Another party had their eyes on this ridge. Scroggie had volunteered for the army at the start of the war, but as with many others there was a grace period before being called up. So in August 1940, he and Ferguson took this opportunity for a week's holiday. Ferguson, then little more than a schoolboy was, in Scroggie's own words, the brains of the two, with Scroggie the brawn. Ferguson had photographed Lochnagar's north-east corrie and studying an enlargement had seen the possibility of straightening-out Bell's route. They camped in the corrie and climbed Raeburn's Gully, finding its chockstone awkward. At this point in the summer they were fit, having been exploring and climbing in Glen Clova.

The next day, 9 August, the weather broke, with wind and near continuous rain. The mist was down at the tent, but they set off up the buttress –

Mid-day saw John and I well up the new line that John had picked out. Wet through we sat snugly belayed on a little ledge, Douglas Gully on one side, Parallel Gully A on the other, and above our heads, dimly visible in the mist, bulging rock challenging us to find a way, if we could summon up enough nerve.

It meant a long step right to a good hold, then an upward pull round into a scoop. Safeguarded by John I got my right foot on the hold, made a hard move, reached up and found not one hold in the scoop but two. There was no way back. My right foot taking my weight began to shake; I sprang upwards to jam my knees against the enclosing walls. It enabled me to hammer a piton into a crack, slip my rope into it and shout to John to take the strain and let me abseil off. [8]

The 21-year-old Scroggie led throughout the day, with stockinged soles used due to wet rock. It was, as Greg Strange acknowledges in his Cairngorms history, *'an impressive achievement'*. [9] Strange thinks that the two climbed what is now known as the Tower. Some way above this they were forced to divert to the right, before returning back left and so by easy slabs to the top. Four pitons had to be used on the steep 100ft section. Ferguson sent in a brief description, to which was added a generous postscript in the SMCJ–

This is a most meritorious ascent. Perhaps, under better conditions, the use of pitons may be avoided. They are often a sign that not enough time has been or can be spent in pioneering a route. It must be noted that this is still not a direct ascent, but this may prove impossible. [10]

The two had failed at the crux, but Scroggie continued his account by stating that what they had got from that day was what very few experienced– a truly supreme moment, only found elsewhere in the exhilaration of battle in war, when capacity was pushed to its limit and mortal danger threatened.

A direct ascent of the crest of Eagle Buttress still awaited, and would come the following year, when Bell returned in July with Margaret Martha (Nancy) Forsyth, a schoolteacher in Dumfries and a member of several clubs including the LSCC and the Pinnacle Club – and who was, as a friend and fellow member of the LSCC would write – *'a fine climber and a splendid companion on the hills, very tall, with a swinging stride and beautiful balance'.* [11]

Bell was about as determined a climber as Raeburn had been, and this determination was to pay off when, on 24 July 1941, he went back to Eagle Buttress with Forsyth. The weather was perfect as they repeated the initial section, finding a loose piton on a ledge, probably dislodged by frost and sun. Bell tucked this away for possible later emergency use. They soon reached a small cairn, left by Scroggie and Ferguson at the point where they had reached the crest. Above lay a steep section, a narrow wall which steepened to the vertical and necessitated a mantelshelf into a smooth, holdless groove. A crack here held a piton, which Bell could not remove, having no hammer. In the ideal conditions he did not need to use this, but he sympathised with the earlier party and recognised that in very wet conditions it protected the following 40ft of severe climbing with several delicate moves before a hard pull up to a niche and a good belay.

The ridge now narrowed to a knife-edge, leading to a ledge below a smooth wall. A passage on the right led to a corner in front of a vertical wall, with a drop on the left into Douglas-Gibson Gully. The wall was only about ten feet high, with a crack where a piton could be used. Up and left of this was a sloping scoop, with a raised edge on its left side. A small roughening of the rock lay between the crack and the edge. Bell realised this was the crux, and that the key was that left edge– if it provided a good handhold, then there was a chance it could be climbed.

At this point his pragmatism rose to the fore, with the climb promising to become one of the finest of all British ridges as a difficult rock climb, with the wall inescapably a part of the route. He removed his boots and lowered them to Forsyth in a rucksack, then picking up a lump of granite he stretched up the wall and hammered in the piton. With a snap link clipped into the piton ring and his rope through the link, he felt much safer.

His right foot was on a good hold, though not high, while his left foot sloped badly. He reached up his right hand to a higher crack and managed to raise his left foot up to a small toe-crack. Making a delicately balanced move, he reached out with his left hand and grabbed the edge, to his relief finding a perfect hold. His right foot now steadied against the piton while he heaved himself up and hunched up his knees on to the scoop. This only had press and friction holds and he could not afford to pause. Persistent effort, friction and some wriggling gained a perfect handhold and safety.

A belay some 15ft along the ridge allowed Forsyth to come up. With the rope for assurance coming down directly to her she had no problem following. She even managed to remove the piton using another rock and brought it up with her. Bell was still not completely satisfied, however. He came back in April 1948 with his wife Pat and, making the second ascent, again inserted a piton at the crux. This time, with prior knowledge of the holds, he managed to lead the pitch without touching the peg. When Pat followed, she reported that the peg was somewhat loose, as was the crucial left-hand hold. As Bell wrote – *'One cannot be too careful about pulling holds, especially on granite.'* [12]

Above the crux were several difficult, short sections, finally leading to easy slabs and the broad top of the ridge. Bell and Forsyth had enjoyed three-and-a-half hours of the very best of rock climbing, with no halts, for about 700ft of ascent. He was overjoyed with the climb and thought it unique among long, precipitous mountain ridges in Britain. It was very steep and narrow, with a symmetrical curving crest. It had exposure, an uncertain outcome and of course a grand outlook. *Eagle Ridge* (200m Severe) is given the coveted SMC four-star rating.

Bell and Forsyth were not finished on Lochnagar. Prior to Eagle Ridge, they had climbed both Shadow Buttresses, with a direct start to Buttress A and a new line on the steep lower half of Buttress B. They now tackled what Bell felt was his most difficult climb so far on Lochnagar, with a direct start to the original Tough-Brown route. As was seen earlier, Bell and Murray had tried to make a complete direct descent, but were forced into Raeburn's Gully. Bell and Forsyth were determined to tidy up the route and began by leaving their rucksacks at the foot of Raeburn's Gully.

Much of the route is vegetated, with the middle section being the most difficult and cleanest at a grade of VS,4c. Bell used two pegs, the first of which Forsyth could remove and avoid the difficulty by a delicate traverse on the left. For the second peg, on the crux pitch, Bell climbed in socks as all handholds had disappeared. On the right was an edge above a vertical wall, across which the leader had to lean and drive in the peg using a rock. He then had to stand on the peg in order to gain a rounded ledge above. Bell thought this a very severe pitch, and so it has remained. *Tough-Brown Ridge Direct* (250m VS, V,6) is better in winter. The two then used the Bell/Murray descent into Raeburn's Gully to save time.

William Alexander Ewen, who went on to edit the Cairngorms District Guide in 1947, suggested that as Bell had climbed the direct Tough-Brown, the original should be renamed Tough-Brown Traverse. As for the peg used at the crux pitch, in 1942 two Aberdonians, Doug Sutherland and Bill Brooker, climbed both Eagle Ridge and Tough-Brown Direct. They had a difficult time on the crux of the latter, even using the peg, with Brooker, seconding, wondering how Bell had managed to insert it.

Bell and Forsyth now made an attempt to climb the frontal face of the Black Spout Pinnacle, and after an abortive attempt in the left branch, climbing a chimney, they succeeded in climbing a shallow, vegetated gully, *Slab Gully* (80m Difficult).

The stalker at Spittal of Glen Muick told Bell that some climbers had been praising the potential at Creag an Dubh Loch. This impressive front of granite, some three-quarters of a mile long and 700 feet high, rising above the southern shore of the Dubh Loch, had been neglected partly due to its relative inaccessibility, partly due to its fearsome appearance. Bell had looked at the cliff, making a reconnaissance scramble, but from the opposite side of the loch it looked as if finding a complete route up the full height of the cliff was unlikely. Nonetheless, he and Forsyth walked in on 27 July 1941.

The day was sunny and the rocks dry. Forsyth thought she could see a break in the cliffs, just short of the large expanse of lower slabs, beyond which was the scree shoot emerging from Central Gully. They found a splendid rock climb through an inner amphitheatre of the crags, giving several severe pitches but mostly on clean rock. *The Labyrinth* (300m Hard Severe) and variations are now described as winter routes only, but again it was Bell opening up a cliff. This was the end of their fine week of exploration on eastern granite.

❄❄❄

Also in the summer of 1941 two good routes were recorded on the Buachaille by JMCS members Richard Gordon Donaldson and George R McCarter. In 1942, these two became presidents of the Cambridge and Oxford University mountaineering clubs respectively. Donaldson, a medical student during the war, figures several times in Murray's *Mountaineering in Scotland*, either climbing routes or experimenting with high-altitude winter camping.

The routes climbed both tiers of North Buttress, East Face, and are often done as a combination. The lower tier is taken by *Bottleneck Chimney* (40m Hard Severe), which has an interesting bottle-shaped recess, then above the Terrace is *Hangman's Crack* (30m VS 4c). The combination has even been climbed in winter, at VI,7. In Murray's 1949 guide, Hangman's is given a VS grade, climbed in rubbers. Donaldson was back in the summer of 1942, climbing a Severe variation to North Face Route on the Buachaille (North-East Crack Route), which avoided the rightward traverse from Heather Ledge. He does not seem to have been associated with Murray post-war.

One winter route climbed on Church Door Buttress of Bidean nam Bian stood out as an isolated, difficult ascent. *Flake Route* (130m IV,6) followed the original route up the buttress, as taken by the SMC party in 1898 which included Raeburn and John Bell, the former having led the crux. The climbers on the 1942 winter ascent, on 18 March, were GR Scott and FW Cope of the Grampian Club. Little is known of these two. Snow- and ice-covered holds below the arch meant slow progress, while the summer crux chimney above the arch almost defeated the two, with combined tactics used just after this.

Puttrell and the Abraham brothers had climbed this route in May 1900, finding much snow on the lower section but wet rock above, while Jim Bell added to the route record by stating that he was aware of an April ascent *'probably under easier snow conditions'*. The high altitude of the buttress certainly adds to the difficulty of its routes.

❆❆❆

As there was now a war on the go, it was deemed necessary to train troops in the art of mountain warfare. There was a pressing need for mountain-capable soldiers, as the German occupation of Norway had begun on 9 April 1940. While the Allied forces never did invade Norway, its topography being regarded as too mountainous, the Germans were deceived into thinking this might happen, with some 150,000 of their troops being tied down there while the 1944 Normandy invasion took place.

Initially, the west coast of Scotland saw training camps set up, with commandos learning irregular, ruthless warfare based at Lochailort–which provided a blend of rough mountain terrain, sea lochs and of course the often inhospitable weather. The Cairngorms were used to train in mountaineering, skiing, and survival, with a base at Braemar, where Frank Smythe was stationed for some time. Trainers from various walks of life were brought in, as well as Norwegian officers. Mountaineers were used, several of whose names appear in this volume, along with Highland ghillies, polar explorers and anyone who could teach survival techniques in country less than friendly.

And so it was that the Lairig Ghru saw an infantry battalion trek through the mountains with 90 mules carrying 3-inch mortars, ammunition and a 3.7-inch howitzer (disassembled). After 45 miles of this, carrying 60 to 70 pounds of gear, those who lasted the course were the fittest men in the army.

It was a matter of some irony when the 52nd Lowland Division of the Scots Guards, trained for mountain warfare, finally landed in 1944 on Walcheren Island in Holland, below sea level. It was fortuitous that they had been trained well, however, as the weather there was brutal and wet. After advancing across Northern Germany and taking Bremen, the division did enter Norway to assist in the German surrender there.

The commandos moved to Wales in 1943, where the Lovat Scouts were trained as a mountain battalion. An impressive number of JMCS and SMC members were there, including Pat Baird, Norman Easton, Denis Howe, James N Ledingham, Bill Mackenzie, Iain Hamish Ogilvie, Campbell Steven and Sandy Wedderburn. There is an interesting collection of memoirs in the SMCJ headed *Climbing in War-Time*. [13]

Some good things were to emerge from the war, mainly involving advances in equipment. One of these would involve footwear, with the development of the Vibram® sole by the Italian **Vitale Bram**ani. In 1935, Bramani lost six mountaineering friends in the Italian Alps, blamed partly on inadequate boots. He developed a new climbing sole and patented it in 1937 as the *Carramato* (*'tank tread'*) with the financial backing of Pirelli tyres. The material was vulcanized rubber and the design has been in production ever since.

The first production facility opened in Albizzate in 1945. It seems that vulcanized boot soles were firstly issued to the military late 1941 or early 1942, and were used by the commandos for the raid on St Nazaire in March 1942. In addition to the grip, such soles would be much quieter. Itshide® was another company, British in this case, which made similar soles of the 'commando' pattern. There were however some comments by climbers that these were not as good on wet rock as Vibrams.

Initially, the new soles were treated with caution, as they were less effective on wet grass and lichen-coated rocks than nails, and also not as effective on hard snow and ice. Their advantages were gradually seen to win over their disadvantages, in that they did give good grip on dry rock, were lighter, and warmer, and were very low maintenance compared with nails. As they replaced nailed boots, they also forced the development of twelve-point crampons. Many Aberdonian climbers however persisted with nailed boots into the late 1950s.

It would also be in 1935 that another huge leap in climbing technology was made possible, with the American company DuPont Chemical coming up with nylon. Nylon climbing ropes were first manufactured in the US in 1941, with Europe seeing them, at least as retail items, at the end of the 1940s. When the war started, production lines switched from making nylons for ladies to parachute cords for troops. When the commando training moved to Cornwall in the autumn of 1943, one of their tasks was the exhaustive testing of the new nylon ropes. [14]

The early nylon ropes were hawser-laid, with three strands twisted into a larger rope. They had the disadvantages of being somewhat stiff to handle and suffering from abrasion. Advantages included being lighter and crucially, having the ability to stretch – or, in other words, being *dynamic*. This greatly increased safety, as a fall was now much less likely to end with a snapped rope due to it being able to absorb energy.

The new designs also shed water, in contrast to the earlier fibre-made ropes, meaning that they stayed lighter when wet and did not as readily stiffen into solid knots when frozen (when climbers on cold days sometimes had to thaw out ropes in a hut, tent or hotel before they could be unknotted from round their waist).

The availability of all climbing ropes became difficult at the end of the war. Beales of London, who made the fibre ropes normally used, noted in their SMCJ advert for April 1946 that their Alpine Club Rope would be sold when *'yarn is again available'*. Rationing was in effect nationwide, and only essential supplies were being imported. In April 1947, the SMCJ carried an advert for Viking Nylon Climbing Ropes, using a photograph by Major Jimmy Roberts during a mountaineering expedition to the Eastern Karakorum in 1946.

The advert stated that on this expedition nylon climbing ropes were used for the first time in the Himalayas, and they were manufactured in Scotland by British Ropes Limited.

After the war there was a huge amount of military clothing and equipment stockpiled, giving rise to a large number of Army and Navy Stores and similar shops around the UK. Older readers will recall these shops, selling just about everything from socks and sweaters, to rucksacks, dixies and stoves. The family-owned business with the same name still operates.

❋❋❋

James Parker and Henry Alexander had explored the Garbh Choire of Braeriach between 1921 and 1924, and in the last of these years had attempted to climb the lower pinnacle, failing on which they then made the first recorded route there with the easy Pinnacle Gully (see Chapter Two). In September 1941, two brothers from Aberdeen, Sandy (1922-1951) and Sydney Tewnion (1920-2003), along with Sandy McArthur, succeeded in climbing *Pinnacle Buttress* (130m Difficult).

There was a third Tewnion brother, John (1930-1995), a civil engineer who emigrated to Canada in 1950 and became president of the Alpine Club of Canada, (1976-1980). Before the war, the brothers climbed on the pink granite cliffs of Longhaven on the Aberdeenshire coast, south of Peterhead. This is now a wildlife reserve, and in 1980 the North East Mountain Trust was founded to oppose an application for a superquarry there.

In August 1942, a medical student from Aberdeen, Bill Hendry, accompanied by George Lumsden, planned a ten-day climbing holiday to Garbh Choire Mor. They succeeded in recording seven climbs, and joined forces with Sandy Tewnion to climb *West Wall Route* (140m Severe), a steep and exposed route on the Braeriach Pinnacle, still regarded as one of the classic climbs of the Western Cairngorms. There was one section of combined tactics.

It was Sandy Tewnion's last day before being called up for the army. In 1944, he was badly injured in Normandy, with shrapnel embedding in his spine. Although his climbing was over, he eventually continued to walk the hills, studying birds, and became principal teacher of biology at Dollar Academy.

His brother Sydney was wounded twice, fighting as a bombardier, though fate was to provide another end to his life when he was one of four men who died of exhaustion and hypothermia on 30 December 1951. Along with Sydney's wife of four weeks, the sole survivor of what would come to be known as the Corrour Tragedy, the party were walking from Corrour Lodge with the intention of making for Ben Alder Cottage, a distance of seven miles. They were heavily laden and inadequately dressed for bad weather, and had no tent. There are several accounts of what transpired over the following 18 hours, after which Mrs Tewnion staggered into Corrour Lodge where a party of SMC and JMCS climbers were in residence. [15,16]

With Smythe installed in the Fife Arms at Braemar, training commandos in mountain warfare, it was inevitable that a good amount of climbing would be done. This included trips to the Garbh Choire of Beinn a' Bhùird, where several ascents of Mitre Ridge were made. One of the soldiers, Sergeant-Major Geoffrey Douglas Langlands CMG, MBE (1917-), soloed the Direct Route via Ludwig's start, unaware that it had been climbed.

One new route was made by Langlands and David Cox, who descended North-West Gully then climbed the corner to the right of Cumming-Crofton Route. This was the second route on the West Face of Mitre Ridge, and was later named Commando Route by Malcolm 'Mac' Smith. It is possibly VS but very loose in summer, Grade III in winter.

✳✳✳

The commandos moved south to Cornwall in 1943, and the Cairngorms would see no more exploration for the next three years. For new routes in Scotland through the war years, two main centres of activity must be considered, both on the west coast. The first, somewhat unexpectedly, was the Isle of Arran.

Geoffrey Curtis and Gordon Townend were both experienced rock climbers, members of the Fell and Rock. Indeed, Curtis had been interested in rock since at least the age of five, when he was rescued from a spread-eagled position on a remote Cornish tor. In September 1941 he was on the first ascent of *Direct Route* (150m Very Difficult) on South Buttress of Stob Coire nan Lochan in Glen Coe. His companions were Robin Plackett, Miss Carol M Curtis and A Bumstead. Carol, sister to Geoffrey, would later marry Robin Plackett.

Townend was from Liverpool and a naval engineer. For several war years both he and Curtis were stationed at Fairlie, just south of Largs on the mainland opposite Great Cumbrae, working on secret anti-submarine warfare research. With Arran just a short ferry journey across the Firth of Clyde it was convenient for the two, often together and sometimes with friends including Ken Moneypenny and HJ Dunster, to nip over and enjoy a day or two of climbing and exploration on the island's wonderful granite. The ferry in those days was between Brodick on Arran and Fairlie, and by the early sailing it was easy to reach work in good time on a Monday morning.

Moneypenny and Dunster learned to climb on Arran, and were happily press-ganged by Curtis and Townend. Moneypenny had just graduated in physics and was posted by the Admiralty to Fairlie in 1941. The following season Townend arrived. A local boat-building yard meant there was a good supply of manila rope and line, while they also had the nautical equivalent of the karabiner.

Volume One of this history has many accounts of early pioneers scraping their way up some vegetated route on the North-East Face of Cir Mhor, but times and techniques had moved on, with climbing in rubbers and better protection allowing ascents on the vastly superior and cleaner granite found on other peaks and faces, particularly the South Face of Cir Mhor.

Between 1942 and 1947, Curtis, Townend and their friends recorded at least 28 new routes on Arran. This could hardly escape the notice of the SMC publications team, who invited the pair to write a new climbers' guide to Arran. Initially accepting this brief, unfortunately they reneged and the guide was eventually taken up by James M Johnstone, being published in November 1958.

Like other climbers at the beginning of the war, they had no access to nylon ropes, and their routes were done with fibre ropes used for sailing. Despite this, several classic routes were recorded including *Caliban's Creep* (150m VD), *Prospero's Peril* (125m Severe) and *Sou'wester Slabs* (110m VD) on the South Face of Cir Mhor, *Pagoda Ridge* (220m Severe) on A' Chir, and *Midnight Ridge Direct* (85m VS) on Cioch na h-Oighe.

Caliban's Creep, climbed by Townend and Curtis on 25 July 1943, takes a remarkable voyage through interesting scenery, with a seemingly impassable wall tackled by creeping through a narrow rock tunnel. This leads eventually to a great fissure, with escape above. Prospero's Peril (25 July 1943, again by Townend and Curtis) lies further right, on Prospero Buttress which defines the right-hand side of Sub Rosa Gully.

Their best find on the South Face of Cir Mhor was undoubtedly Sou'wester Slabs (3 September 1944, Townend, Curtis, H Hore and MHJ Hawkins). This is described in the current guide as *A classic and much celebrated route on excellent rock* and can hardly fail to please, providing a route on beautiful granite at a uniform grade. Put simply, it is one of the very best climbs at this grade.

In a post-war article including more new climbs on Arran, Curtis and Townend looked back over their four years of climbing on the island, giving a glimpse of their experiences and providing something beyond the bare route descriptions. [17] Their climbing started, as it did for so many, with a traverse of the central ridge; they also met the Old Man of Glen Rosa – a venerable old tree – and little did they guess just how much climbing was to be found, and how often they would return to attempt it.

An account in a small notebook indeed told us of a climb, but not of the great bastion of yellow-white granite that is South Ridge. It could not predict Sunday after Sunday spent on this holdless yet rough, uncompromising yet friendly rock. Since then the notebook has been soaked in Arran rain and squeezed in narrow chimneys: it now holds writing with heather roots where pencil lacked. Yet in retrospect its short stereotyped notes bring alive past days; finding the propitious tunnel on Caliban's Creep; threading the labyrinth of East Wall; crossing the great open sweep of the western slabs of Rosa Pinnacle; climbing the vertical nose on Cioch na-h-Oighe where the granite pardoned our impudence with plentiful holds.

But the notebook tells only a fraction. There is nothing of the wind which inverted our sandwich box before whirling it away, so dumping the contents on our narrow lunching ledge; nothing of the wariness needed to outwit the Rosa bog; nothing of that crafty siren Ben Nuis, whose smiling face lures one on to holdless slabs and perilous grass.

Our season is over: the party scatters. The old man is dead. The gnarled old shape that watched our comings and goings lies broken at the foot of the trunk: only the roots remain.

Curtis was still climbing a few weeks before his sudden death on 5 October 1983, aged 64.

❅❅❅

A grey marble headstone in the Glen Nevis cemetery looks over to the southern flank of Ben Nevis; on it are recorded the names of three Kellett family members: two parents, Lieutenant Richard Pinder Kellett, who died in action commanding HMS Flirt in 1916 in the English Channel and whose body was never found, and his wife Dorothy, who died in 1974, aged 84. The third name is that of their son Brian Pinder Kellett, who died in a climbing accident on Ben Nevis in early September 1944, aged 30. The headstone was erected by Brian Kellett's sister, Lorna.

While most climbers will not be aware of this memorial, many will know of Brian Kellett's other memorials, the first ascents he made of climbs on the shadow side of Ben Nevis. His story may be found in the history of that mountain, where in all he climbed over 100 routes, many solo, with almost one-third of these being first ascents. [18]

Brian Kellett was born on 15 May 1914 in the seaside town of Weymouth in Dorset. At school he was an all-round athlete, possessing a powerful physique. His mind was also good, and he developed into a county-standard chess player for Lancashire, winning that county's championship in 1939. [For the chess-minded curious, Kellett, with black pieces and playing Queen's Gambit Accepted, beat HG Rhodes. [19] This might suggest he preferred open or semi-open positions, fitting in with his climbing.]

After school he trained as an accountant. At some point he became a pacifist and was a conscientious objector when war broke out. For this he served time in prison, then volunteered for the Forestry Commission. His preference was for Skye, but he was sent to Torlundy, just to the north of Fort William, and so began his fateful relationship with Ben Nevis.

By 1942, the war was not going well. The Nazis were securely in overall control of Europe and their submarines and surface ships in the Atlantic were biting deeply into the import of food and other essentials. Kellett made his debut on Ben Nevis, at least as far as first ascents went, with *No. 2 Gully* (120m Scottish VS) on 30 August 1942.

His companion was JA Dunster, and so loose is the gully in summer that while Kellett was climbing the difficult section, Dunster had to move off the belay and shelter from the cascade of rocks. The assessment of 'Scottish VS' indicates that it very probably has never had a repeat summer ascent, and therefore its grade cannot be confidently confirmed.

Before Kellett attempted a serious ascent, he would make considerable efforts to examine the line as thoroughly as possible from various viewpoints, sometimes taking several hours. He was very methodical, perhaps in part due to his training in accountancy, recording the details of his routes in small notebooks, three in total. Into these notebooks, with maroon-coloured covers, entries were made in a neat and concise hand: dark blue for descriptions, red for route names. [20]

Alex Small recalled that if invited into the CIC Hut after climbing, he would gratefully accept a cup of tea and make his notes, *'before disappearing into the dusk down the track'*. His notes were published in the SMC Journals of April 1944, April 1946, and April 1947, the last two being posthumous.[21, 22, 23] Connected to photographs elsewhere in the journals, many route descriptions contained Cartesian coordinates to clearly indicate a route on the corresponding photograph.

In his first full summer on Ben Nevis, 1943, Kellett climbed an astonishing total of 92 routes or variations, 17 of which were first ascents, with 14 of these being solo. There is absolutely no doubt that he would have been the author of the next edition of the SMC Ben Nevis guide, following Macphee's 1936 edition. Macphee, in his introduction to the 1954 edition, stated as much, acknowledging that Kellett would have been the obvious person to write the guide.

Kellett's notes in the 1944 SMCJ included a list of routes classified by difficulty – a graded list. Any route he had not actually climbed was marked by an asterisk, and there were only 14 of these. He had climbed seven out of the eight VS climbs listed, and 16 out of the 20 Severe routes. It was a determined, organised and very deliberate attempt to climb all the rock routes on Ben Nevis, either with a partner or solo if none could be found.

As for his actual climbing, there are the words of one of his occasional partners, William Arnot Watterston Russell (1922-2005), an active president of St Andrews University Mountaineering Club during the war and a master at Trinity College, Glenalmond from 1950. This is a boarding school based near Perth, founded in 1847 by William Ewart Gladstone and now known as Glenalmond College. Russell joined the SMC in 1948. In addition to being a mountaineer, he was a keen skier and determined golfer, nicknamed the 'Galloping Major' for his speed round Crieff golf course.

Russell found Kellett to be a very stable and careful climber, roping up on anything more difficult than a scramble. He climbed solo through circumstance, not choice, and was outwardly self-assured. The two first met on 9 June 1943. Kellett had been high on Càrn Dearg Buttress, looking for a way up the buttress right of Route I. Satisfied that he saw a potential line, he descended to the CIC Hut where a group of St Andrews students were in residence. Russell was probably the best rock climber in the group, and agreed to accompany Kellett.

His plan was an audacious traverse across the top of the slabby area of the 'Great Buttress', as it was then named in the SMC Guide. To access these slabs the pair climbed the lower sections of Route I as far as the top of the third pitch, then began the daring and very exposed traverse across the buttress. It was a cold, dull morning, with low cloud, and vegetation on the buttress was wet and slimy. The students at the hut watched the climbers as they worked their way rightwards from Route I on a rising traverse, switching from boots to stocking soles. From the end of the traverse they finished up the right edge of the buttress.

Route II Direct (235m Severe) is described in the current guide using a direct start, climbed in 1962 by Brian W Robertson and George Chisholm. The guide mentions it as a superb outing, moving through fantastic ground for the grade. It was the second route to be climbed on Càrn Dearg Buttress. The climbers descended by Route I and then, to round off a successful day, climbed the Direct Start to the North Trident Buttress, a Macphee V. Diff. This same summer Russell also climbed Bell's Long Climb with Kellett.

Almost three weeks earlier, on 22 May 1943, Kellett had added a variation to Bayonet Route on the First Platform of North-East Buttress. The Hard Severe variation climbs an overhang directly, which Macphee had bypassed on its first ascent. The rock is perfect and sound, but the boldness and confidence needed to make the moves mark Kellett as someone climbing on a different plane from the average competent climber.

On 2 July, Kellett climbed his hardest route of 1943, a solo ascent of *Route A* on the North Wall of Càrn Dearg. In his graded list it comes top, with an assessment of Very Severe. In Macphee's graded list in his 1954 guide, it is top of the Severes. As Kellett had a fall on a chimney pitch it may be that this coloured his judgment of the grade, though his objectivity was never really in much doubt. This area of Ben Nevis is rarely climbed on in summer as much of the rock is poor with loose, wet sections.

There are at least two reasons why Kellett returned to this face several times, one being that he was determined to clarify the lines of several routes, especially one recorded by Dr Lüscher in 1920. Macphee had failed to identify it to his satisfaction, even after conversing with Lüscher. Route A was the result of a failed attempt by Kellett to pin down Lüscher's ascent. Another reason for his attraction to this face would have been its relative proximity to his workplace, as it could allow him some climbing time at the end of summer work days.

On 24 July he tackled *The Italian Climb* (180m Severe). Its mossy, dank depths in summer are more popular in winter, but he made an intriguing discovery in the cave above the first pitch, where he found a piton and a strong pole studded with nails on either side: a rudimentary ladder, in other words. There had been an attempt to climb the line in 1940, but no one has ever owned up to the ladder. The gully bifurcates higher up, and Kellett thought the left fork would be impossible. Perhaps in summer, though in the distant future and using modern equipment and techniques, it was climbed in the winter of 2006 by Dave MacLeod, at VIII,9.

The following day saw three new routes by Kellett, two at V. Diff., one at Severe – a solo ascent of *1943 Route* on South Trident Buttress. Of the last pitch of this, Macphee in his 1936 guide had written that it was the obvious route, but looked to be impossible. Kellett also made a possible second ascent of Evening Wall, with EM Hanlon and Gordon Scott, then made the first descent of Route II, adding a new groove at the top to provide a separate finish from Evening Wall. As for the green ledge of Route II, visible from the hut, he noted in the logbook that it '...*was carpeted with yellow, white and pink flowers. Those who wish to perfect their turf technique are recommended to visit this airy garden.*' [24]

Kellett's 1943 summer season came to an end on 11 August, which was also very nearly the end of his life as well. He was climbing with Jim Bell and Nancy Forsyth, the Dumfries schoolteacher mentioned earlier. The occasion was the first ascent of *Route B* (30m Severe), on the North Wall of Càrn Dearg. As already described, Bell had climbed with Forsyth on Lochnagar, and it was he who introduced her to Kellett. On the day in question Kellett was leading, and had started up the short chimney of Route A. The following account of the next few minutes is from Bell's personal log.

> K. started off, N.F. belayed round belay near foot of chimney. I was unroped as I was coiling up the 100-ft line which was no longer necessary. A rumble from above & I just caught sight of Kellett flying downward past me. At the

same time I felt a blow on the head, not sharp but dull & my head began to feel all warm - with flowing blood. Nancy shouted to me to grasp & try to stop the rope. It was, of course, utterly impossible. The thing was running down fast & jerking about. Then it stopped, Nancy was drawn up sharp against the belay in a strained position & there was silence. The rope to Kellett was taut. It held.

Looking down the cliff, the rope disappeared about 75 feet down. Then Bell heard Kellett shouting. He was unhurt but had no real handholds, with his hands becoming numb. Bell managed to lower his line and Kellett tied on. Together, Bell and Forsyth helped Kellett climb above the edge, and after a brief rest he gained the ledge. Bell had a scalp wound, while Forsyth had a badly lacerated hand from braking the fall with no gloves. She had done very well to have slowed his fall to some extent. Shaken, the trio slowly began their descent down wet rocks. Here a hold broke off, pitching Kellett downwards a short distance, when he fractured a finger and his left patella.

He insisted he could make the descent unaided, so the others headed for the hut and began to prepare dinner. An hour later, with Kellett still not in sight, Bell went back up and found him descending very slowly. He had been forced to maintain a straight left leg, for which he had arranged a loop of line, the loop under his instep and the rope in his hand.

That night his knee swelled to twice normal size. He was forced to stay in the hut for the next four nights, before being able to hobble down to Fort William using a hut broom as a crutch. With some time required for recovery, summer was over for Kellett. Route B was to be the last first ascent on Ben Nevis for Bell.

As for the cause of the fall, Kellett had been relying on a chockstone placed by him while climbing Route A; on pulling up on this it came out, taking Kellett with it and for all we know hitting Bell on the head for good measure. This was to be the only occasion Bell climbed with Kellett, as the experience had left him in an awkward position. He was now unhappy with Kellett's climbing, but had introduced Forsyth to him. He advised her not to continue climbing with Kellett, though she was to ignore this. With the state of protection on a rock climb still in its infancy, the old adage that *the leader must not* fall remained true.

It should also be mentioned that in January 1943 Kellett soloed Tower Ridge via the Secondary Ridge, and fell at Tower Gap. He cannoned down the entire length of Glover's Chimney, fortunately filled with snow and ice, and shot over the initial ice pitch to land in snow. Somehow he was unhurt, and after descending he pinned a note on the door of the CIC Hut asking for climbers to look out for his ice axe, lost in the fall.

One does need luck from time to time; by the end of 1943 Kellett was coming close to running out of it. Route A is now described as a continuous climb taking in three routes. The following June a *Direct Start to Route B* was climbed by Kellett and Carol Plackett. Combined with *Flake Chimney*, a Moderate which Kellett had soloed the day before Route B, and finishing up Route A, this became *Kellett's North Wall Route* (180m Severe) which forms a logical line up the entire length of the wall.

The war, meanwhile, was becoming increasingly felt, even on Ben Nevis, as it had become a training ground for those soldiers selected for mountain warfare. Over a third of CIC Hut bednights in 1943 went to troops, 131 nights out of a total of 371. SMC members accounted for a mere 31 nights. At least one military party climbed Tower Ridge, with an officer and 14 other ranks in full battle order including rifles. All but the officer wore army boots, and despite wind and rain their five ropes of three climbed the ridge in under six hours.

Murray was by now a prisoner of war, while others less fortunate had been killed. Bell, in his late 40s, spent the latter half of the war working in explosives factories, a reserved occupation. He also experienced the army on Ben Nevis one day when some soldiers were glad to accept the hospitality of the CIC Hut. They began to complain about their commanding officer, calling him a '*bloody mountain goat*'. The goat was Sandy Wedderburn.

In October 1943, Kellett joined the JMCS, easing his access to the CIC Hut. He began his 1944 campaign on 17 June with a variation to Bell's Beta Route, making a direct entry to the Basin and climbing wet and mossy slabs in socks. The weather was set fair, and on 20 June he recorded one of his best climbs on Ben Nevis.

East of the Orion Face, the rocks have a marked tilt to the left and are seamed by three prominent gullies. The steep gully on the left flank of Observatory Ridge had been named by Bell as Zero Gully. The easy gully left of Tower Ridge had originally been No.1 Gully. Between the two stood a steep and fierce unclimbed gully, on the left flank of Observatory Buttress. This, Kellett suggested, should be named Point Five Gully, while the three prominent gullies further left should, by analogy, become Minus One, Minus Two and Minus Three. Consequently, the accompanying buttresses on their left flanks would be the Minus One, Two and Three Buttresses respectively.

On 17 June Kellett had devoted several hours to close inspection of the rocks of the Minus Face, in particular Minus Two Buttress. He felt that Minus One Gully and Buttress looked hard, while Minus Two Gully had potential. Minus Two Buttress, in particular, was promising, and on Sunday 20 June he was joined by Robin and Carol Plackett with that in mind. Slabby rocks with two prominent parallel cracks led to a stance just below and to the right of a large overhanging nose, a marked feature of this buttress. To the left lay a steep, bulging slab, the route's crux.

Each of the three climbers found their own way up this pitch, with Kellett climbing in socks to overcome a wet, slimy crack on the right, Carol taking a bulge in the middle on very small holds, and Robin going up further left. Above, the route took to the left edge of the slab overlooking Minus Three Gully, with continuous rock at Severe standard. *Left-Hand Route* (275m VS 4b) is worthwhile, meriting two stars if the *Left Edge Variation* (80m VS 4c) is taken. This–climbed by Niall and Bob Richardson, and Alastair Walker, on 11 June 1988–climbs the edge of the buttress next to the gully, in keeping with the rest of the original route.

Kellett was now fired up, and the following day with Robin Plackett he made an audacious attempt to climb the major line on Càrn Dearg Buttress, a long, conspicuous chimney near the right-hand edge of the buttress. This is now the route named Sassenach, first climbed by Don Whillans and Joe Brown in 1954 and graded E1 if aid is used to enter the chimney, E3 otherwise. Kellett had been considering this route since the previous year, and planned to traverse in from the left.

To do this, he climbed what is now the first pitch of another great classic, Centurion. Next, he had to gain and traverse a gangway rightwards. A holdless mantelshelf problem forced the pair to follow the corner of Centurion above for 30 feet or so, where they found a spike belay with an old rope sling. Unknown climbers had been there before, presumably intent on climbing what would become Centurion. Kellett and Plackett were daunted by either upward or rightward progress, and retreated. Frustrated, Kellett soloed *Left-Hand Chimney* (215m Difficult) on the Douglas Boulder that same evening.

The weather now regressed to a familiar wetness, but on 1 July Kellett soloed part of Vanishing Gully, these days a popular winter Grade V. He followed this on 8 July by exploring the west face of Observatory Ridge, climbing what is now *West Face, Lower Route* (325m Very Difficult). This was later referred to as Hadrian's Wall, a title now claimed by the direct route further right; both lines would become winter classics.

The last fortnight of July 1944, with better weather, saw Kellett solo seven routes. On Tuesday 20 July he climbed *Right-Hand Route* (275m VS 4b), the companion to his earlier effort on Minus Two Buttress. The route has sections of delicate and exposed climbing, and he probably followed his usual technique and carried a rope where he felt a route might be difficult, though here he noted the lack of good belays.

Perhaps uniquely, this was the only and certainly the first route on Nevis to be climbed trouserless, as his shorts, placed on top of his sack for the walk up, had fallen off somewhere on the track. Rather than embarrass visitors on the summit, he changed plans and climbed the lower line. As for his intended target of the day, that was the line which by now was gaining a reputation, and had already been attempted several times – Gardyloo Buttress.

Kellett had looked closely at the buttress four days earlier, climbing a short, Moderate crack line on the Tower Face of the buttress. Earlier attempts on the main section had been made by Ogilvy in 1940 and Scroggie in 1941. Both had been trying the attractive left edge, but Kellett, with his now highly developed instinct for a line and his experience of Nevis rock, had spotted a line taking the right wall of the left edge. It would be his boldest solo.

Easy-angled rocks led to twin cracks in the steep wall above, then a short traverse under an overhang and another smaller overhang taken direct to gain a tiny stance in a recess. Above lay the crux, a 15ft corner. En route, Kellett had come across a piton with two rope slings. He thought these were probably not from the known earlier attempts, as the rock above was manageable for some distance before becoming unclimbable. For the crux of this route, here are Kellett's own words–

> The 15-foot corner starting on the right of the recess was very strenuous and proved to be the crux of the climb. The left wall is perpendicular, the right wall slightly overhanging; handholds on the left wall, though well placed for climbing straight up it, are not well adapted for preventing the body being pushed off to the left by the overhanging right wall. The key to the pitch is the large spike handhold facing horizontally left; this was used by the left hand and had to take most of the weight of the body, while the mossy holds above were cleaned and tidied with the right hand. The higher holds had to be groped for as they could not be seen from below, and the whole process proved to be very strenuous so that numerous descents had to be made for rests, and this short pitch took nearly an hour to climb.

> Once preparations were completed the right hand was shifted from a flat press hold to a much higher hold (rather unsatisfactory) and then the left hand unwillingly left the beautiful spike for another hold, also much higher. This was really the hardest movement as both feet were on very poor holds and the body was being pushed off left all the time by the overhang. Once both these higher handholds had been reached there was no further difficulty in stepping up on to the large flat hold previously used by the right hand and then climbing the remaining few feet of the corner. [25]

There remained some delicate and strenuous moves before easier ground could be gained. To preserve the central line of the climb, he finished up the gully in the upper funnel, avoiding most of the wet, mossy holds by bridging. It had been the sixth day of a dry spell and the climb had taken him three hours, climbing in rubbers and socks for the gully.

The second ascent in June 1955 was by Bob Downes and Mike O'Hara, in damp conditions due to melt water. They found the crux corner reminiscent of Pigott's Climb on Clogwyn du'r Arddu, though steeper and more exposed. The *'beautiful spike'* of Kellett's ascent was found to be unsound, and due to the wetness they had to use a foot-loop hung delicately from the *'flat press hold'*.

Kellett's Route (140m HVS) was immediately the hardest route on Ben Nevis, a remarkable solo ascent by a bold climber at his best. To stay in command for an hour, while moving strenuously up and down in a very exposed position with no protection and indifferent holds, demands everything a climber can give and more. This, and other routes on the buttress, now provide quality winter climbs when in condition, with Kellett's Route a VI,6 .

As soon as a climber steps on to the buttress, the exposure is immediate, with a long, yawning drop into Observatory Gully. Kellett himself graded it as Very Severe owing to the continuously steep and exposed central section. With Psychedelic Wall across the gully, it is the highest VS in the country.

Kellett would find several more routes in July and August of 1944, including Severes on the lower tier of South Trident Buttress and on the middle tier of the same buttress. On 20 August, he recorded his last route on Ben Nevis, with a direct ascent of Cousins' Buttress at Severe. He referred several times to loose rock here, noting that it required careful treatment.

The first day of September 1944 was the Friday of a holiday weekend, and Nancy Forsyth travelled up from Dumfries for an arranged climbing trip based at the CIC Hut. When Forsyth had not returned south by the Monday evening, her sister contacted the police. On Tuesday afternoon, police sergeant Boa and John Elder, a work colleague of Kellett, went up to the hut. Kellett and Forsyth's belongings were there, but with no indication of where the two climbers might have gone.

The following day a search party of 18 found nothing. Bell was contacted at 9pm that night, and arranged to join Forsyth's sister on Thursday. At Fort William they met Nancy Ridyard, Forsyth's friend in the LSCC, and all three walked up to the hut in heavy rain, reaching it at 7pm. They were joined just after midnight by Archie Hendry's party, which included Geoff Curtis and George Townend.

Bell and Hendry had a good idea of where to search, in Castle Coire, where so much of Kellett's explorations had taken place. Come morning Hendry decided to solo the Castle, with a recall signal prearranged, the beating of an empty oil drum with ice axe shafts. Bell and Ridyard were in No.2 Gully when they heard the doleful booming, and a party of 12 went up to the site of the accident.

The two had suffered severe injuries, particularly Kellett. Forsyth, with the rope coiled over her shoulder, was lower, near the foot of the stepped gully between Cousins' Buttress pinnacle and the base of Raeburn's Buttress. Kellett was around 16 feet higher, in the gully. Both climbers were tied on with waist loops as normal.

Bell thought that the accident had probably happened on the Saturday, 2 September, as Sunday had worse weather and Forsyth had left her oilskin cape in the hut. He also thought that the two had been on easy ground, with Kellett leading. Anything else was conjecture, but loose rock was a likely culprit. That night, Bell and Hendry stayed at the hut in what must have been an unhappy and sleepless atmosphere.

By a grim coincidence, also staying were BP Taylor and JA Dunster – the same Dunster who had seconded Kellett on the first ascent of No.2 Gully. Neither was very competent, according to Hendry. Bell recalled discussing routes with Dunster, and warning that Observatory Buttress was likely to present problems for anyone going off-route. Two days later Taylor was killed on the buttress, both climbers being unroped on the easier, final section.

Bell's thoughts may well have been coloured by his friendship with Forsyth, but he was also a canny observer of other people. He entered a note concerning Kellett in his personal log–

> A brilliant rock climber, he seemed to be devoid of fear on the rocks. Hence, it may be that his margin of safety was really smaller than if he had a touch of fear in his constitution.... I had a sub-conscious feeling since 11/8/43 that K. was not altogether safe. Also, I warned him by mouth & letter later on. On the other hand K. had given up the idea of 2 desperate new climbs which he had formerly contemplated [Sassenach and Point Five Gully]. Also K. was meticulous about his belays. [26]

At the time of his death, Kellett was 30 years of age, and at the height of his game. Alex Small later commented that '...*his appearance and climbs caused little acclaim at the time; there were few climbers about to appreciate his exploits. His fame was very much muted and posthumous.*' [27]

As for Forsyth, we will finish with a few words from her friend and erstwhile climbing partner Nancy Ridyard, who wrote her obituary for the FRCC Journal–

> Nancy was a fine mountaineer at the peak of her strength. She will never know the sadness of failing powers. She will not see the inviting crags and be unable to clasp them, nor look up at the black crest against the blue sky and be unable to reach it. This is the only philosophy for those who are left, but it is poor comfort. Dear, quiet, steady, reliable Nancy. [28]

References

1. *The Scotsman*, Thursday February 29, 1940, p.7.
2. Hillary, Richard. *The Last Enemy*. (London: Macmillan, 1943, 1st edition), pp.40-44.
3. Bell, J.H.B. *A Progress in Mountaineering*. (Edinburgh & London: Oliver & Boyd, 1950, 1st edition).
4. Bell, J.H.B. *A Ben Nevis Constellation of Climbs*. SMCJ 22, 132, November 1941, pp.367-376.
5. Ritchie, Graham S. *Third on the Rope*. SMCJ 25, 144, April 1953, pp.137-142.
6. Scroggie, Sydney. *The Cairngorms Scene and Unseen*. (Scottish Mountaineering Trust, 1989.)
7. Sellen, Jack Robert. Review of Syd Scroggie book. In: *Caught by the River*, 19th August 2014. <goo.gl/aqjqS4> Accessed April 2016.
8. Scroggie, Sydney. *The Cairngorms Scene and Unseen*. pp.115-116.
9. Strange, Greg. *The Cairngorms – 100 Years of Mountaineering*. (SMT, 2010, p.54.)
10. Ferguson, J.G. *Eagle Buttress – Lochnagar*. In: New Climbs. SMCJ 22, 130, November 1940, p.252.
11. Ridyard, Nancy. *N. Forsyth 1935 – 1944*. In Memorium. FRCCJ, 1940-1949. Vol.14, No.2, pp.156-157.
12. Bell, J.H.B. *A Progress in Mountaineering*. p.263.
13. Various authors. *The S.M.C. Abroad – Climbing in War-time*. SMCJ 23, 137, April 1946, pp.356-361.
14. Steven, Campbell. *Climbing – "In the Course of Duty"*. In: (See ref.13.) pp.357-358.
15. Stewart, J. Stanley & Brown, Richard. *The Corrour Tragedy*. SMCJ 25, 143, 1952. pp.53-56.
16. Thomson, Ian. *The Black Cloud: Scottish Mountain Misadventures, 1928-1966*. (Ernest Press: Glasgow. 1993).
17. Curtis, G.C. and Townend, G.H. *Golden Eagles in Arran*. SMCJ 23, 138, pp.415-421.
18. Crocket, Ken and Richardson, Simon. Ben Nevis - Britain's Highest Mountain. (Scottish Mountaineering Trust: 2nd edition 2009).
19. Manchester Chess Association Archives.
20. Kellet, B.P. Personal notebooks – Climbs on Ben Nevis, Vols. 1-3. NLS. <goo.gl/aaAQjR> Nos. 104-106.
21. Kellett, B.P. Recent Rock Climbs on Ben Nevis. SMCJ 23, 135, April 1944, pp.139-152.
22. Kellett, B.P. A Record of Ben Nevis Climbs. SMCJ 23, 137, April 1946, pp.333-340.
23. Kellett, B.P. A Record of Ben Nevis Climbs. SMCJ 23, 138, April 1947, pp.408-414.
24. CIC Hut Log Book. Vol.1. 12th November, 1928 – July 5th, 1949. NLS.
25. Kellett, B.P. A Record of Ben Nevis Climbs. SMCJ 23, 137, April 1946, pp.334-335.

26. Bell, J.H.B. Climbing Log. Vol.6, p.41, September 1944.
27. Smith, Ken. *Two Short Summers: A profile of Brian Kellett*. Published online at Footless Crow, 13th May 2016. (First published in Climber & Rambler. July 1981.) <goo.gl/UeAzVz> Accessed May 2016.
28. Ridyard, N. *In Memorium. N. Forsyth 1935 – 1944*. FRCCJ. No.39, Vol.14, No.2, pp.156-157.

8

Post-War Breakthroughs (1943-1949)

As HIGHLIGHTED in Volume One of this history, from the beginnings of mountaineering in Scotland right up to and indeed past the start of World War I there were no fatalities to a roped party on a Scottish route. There were several accidental deaths to tourists, usually as a result of a fall while scrambling on rocky ground, but the maxim that '*the leader shall not fall*' was rigorously adhered to, as climbers were very aware that a fall could mean severe injury or death not only to the leader but to a climbing partner as well.

The Lake District had seen several such accidents, including the dreadful event on Scafell Pinnacle on 21 September 1903, when four experienced climbers from the Climbers' Club, roped together, fell from the slabs on Pinnacle Face which led directly from Lord's Rake to the cairn. [1] This cairn had been acting like a light to a moth, with many parties having attempted to gain it from below. Three of the climbers died outright, the fourth while being carried down by a rescue party.

Belay methods in 1903 were almost non-existent, basically comprising the second sitting on a ledge, if possible, and holding on to the leader's rope, sometimes passing it over his shoulders. This primitive state of belaying only very slowly improved, as did the equipment and techniques involved in using it, and this undoubtedly delayed a rise in standards. With time, and as the number of climbers increased, standards rose and the potential of a serious fall increased somewhat. There was a balance between how far an experienced climber would push their limits, and how much of a safety factor was desired. Obviously an experienced and sensible climber would not deliberately exceed their limit, but the unforeseen was always hovering around any ascent and circumstances such as weather, fitness and the state of equipment could be variable factors.

There was also one of the most common causes of an accident: the simple slip while descending. Everyone has experienced this, perhaps due to loose or wet rock, combined with tiredness or a temporary lapse in concentration. With certain rock types a hold can appear to be sound yet snap off when used, even after testing.

The number of accidents on Scottish hills, as elsewhere, quickly rose with time. This placed a considerable burden on the rescuers, who were often locals such as stalkers, ghillies and shepherds. As communication improved and the telephone network spread, the custom was for members of mountaineering clubs to phone round and organise a party to search, or to aid in a rescue. These people would be raised from the main cities such as Glasgow and Edinburgh, so it would be hours or even days before help could arrive in the form of experienced and equipped climbers. The preceding chapter include just such an example, with the search on Ben Nevis for Kellett and Forsyth.

A picture of the difficulties facing an accident victim on a Scottish mountain was given by Alfred Ian Lennox Maitland (190?-1989), an SMC member who worked as a surgeon at the Western Infirmary in Glasgow. He was, as Bill Murray wrote honestly in his obituary–

> …a positively bad rock-climber. When we both joined the SMC in 1945, he had something more positive than most of us to contribute to mountaineering. He gave himself to mountain rescue. His arrival on that scene coincided with its greatest need.

> Before the second war, Scotland's rescue service had been primitive. In 1936, the SMC had set up a First Aid Committee and provided four rescue posts (stretchers only). Two more were contributed by the Grampian Club and the Ski Club. And that was all. The few rescue teams needed were rustled up locally or summoned by telephone from the Lowland clubs.

> In 1946 climbers faced a different mountain game. The ASCC [Association of Scottish Climbing Clubs, forerunner to the Mountaineering Council of Scotland, now named Mountaineering Scotland] was formed and one of its first duties was to take aboard mountain rescue problems. Ian Maitland was appointed convenor of a new First Aid Committee to take urgent action: lay down basic principles, site rescue posts, prevent accidents, and draft rescue teams. During the next decade he worked hard to develop the service. All was not sweetness and light. His task needed infinite patience and tact in dealing with relations between the Ministry of Health, Police, RAF, MRC England, SCPR [Scottish Council for Physical Recreation], etc., plus many opinionated members of the clubs. Helped most of all by Donald Duff and Ben Humble, Ian set up the new Scottish rescue service that evolved over the years into the comprehensive service we know today. [2]

Ian Maitland died in a car accident in 1989. He had been honoured by the SMC in 1958 with a vice-presidency. In a 1955 SMCJ article he described a typical scenario.

> An accident is an unfortunate event which takes place outwith one's foresight or expectation. It can happen to anyone at any place at any time, but when it occurs in the mountains the special circumstances surrounding such an occurrence add great difficulties which may be illustrated by the following comparison. A young man trotting down his office stairs slips, falls and breaks his leg. In an hour he can be in hospital, X-rayed and under treatment for his fracture in ideal circumstances. If, however, the young man sustains the same injury on the upper slopes of Ben Macdhui in the Cairngorms it will almost certainly be twenty-four hours before he is in a place where the same facilities are available, and these intervening twenty-four hours will have been packed, if not with incident, at least with unremitting arduous toil for approximately a dozen people. The first case would only require a telephone call, a short stretcher journey; a few yards, and a ride of possibly a mile in an ambulance. In contrast, the second case would involve a 9-mile walk to give news of the accident, a similar walk for the rescue party bearing the stretcher and other equipment and lastly the traverse of the same 8 or 9 miles of difficult country by the party with a loaded stretcher before the ambulance was reached. This illustration will perhaps provide the background to the difficulties of mountain rescue and stress the need for prevention of accidents on the hills. [3]

In addition to Maitland's efforts, mountain rescue in Scotland received a boost due to World War II. With the huge war effort, the numbers of aircraft flying over UK airspace increased dramatically. Many were bombers returning from raids in Europe, perhaps damaged and certainly with aircrews stressed and fatigued. There were training flights, often with inexperienced pilots, and long flights across the Atlantic delivering new aircraft. In 1943 alone, there were 242 crashes in mountainous and upland areas of the UK, and over 570 aircrew lost their lives. Rescue units were set up by RAF Flying Training Command, initially at four stations, and from this evolved the RAF Mountain Rescue Service.

As the number of climbers grew and more of these lived in mountainous areas, so began a growth in civilian rescue teams comprising local mountaineers. This organic growth eventually led to a number of strategically placed, autonomous teams. Then, as now, the police have a statutory responsibility for any accident, including in mountainous areas, although of course they can contact a civilian team or call for military assistance, including the use of helicopters.

Currently, Scotland is covered by two police mountain rescue teams (MRTs), two RAF MRTs, 23 civilian MRTs, one search and rescue unit, two Search and Rescue Dogs Association (SARDA) teams and one Cave

Rescue Organisation. Add to this the Scottish Avalanche Information Service <www.sais.gov.uk> and the Mountain Weather Information Service <www.mwis.org.uk>, along with the quality climbing guides published by the SMC and others, and the hill user has never been better served for information making mountain excursions safer. We can add mobile phones and GPS units as aids to safety.

The civilian teams consist of volunteer mountaineers, usually with some local police members. The Mountain Rescue Committee of Scotland, also known as Scottish Mountain Rescue, is the governing organisation, and the use of trained dogs is a valuable part of mountain rescue. The Bristow Group won a ten-year contract to run the airborne side of the service from 2015, a £1.6 billion deal that brought to an end 70 years of search and rescue from the RAF and Royal Navy.

Those interested in further reading about this period of mountain rescue can do no better than find a copy of the book by Hamish MacInnes, the pioneer and activist in mountain rescue. The narrative will return to him later. [4]

❄❄❄

Despite the blanket ban on travel to Skye during the second war, some climbing did take place on the island. Sorley MacLean (1911-1996), born on the neighbouring island of Raasay, wrote his poem *An Cuilithionn* (The Cuillin) around this period, and managed a few solo trips on the hills.

> In those days I could not get very few people to go with me, practically nobody in those days, and I used to wander about alone on them, ridge-wandering and doing some rock-climbing to avoid detours and being there in all kinds of conditions... I remember an evening being on Sgùrr Alasdair, a summer evening, and seeing glitter – the glitter of the sun, west of Barra. And another day, for instance, being on the Cuillins, with swirling mist on the narrow top of Sgùrr a' Ghreadaidh, and the mist suddenly clearing and there was a glint of the sun on the wings of a golden eagle standing on a ledge about twenty feet below me. [5]

One climbing highlight came on Sròn na Cìche. As Stuart Pedlar put it, *'the most important event of the war years was a brilliant new route made by Ian Allan in 1944 on the seemingly smooth Cìoch Slab'*. This great feature to the left of the Cìoch appeared so bereft of holds or protection that some doubted the ascent.

Allan duly returned and climbed the route again, this time scratching arrows with a rock as he climbed, hence its name. *Arrow Route* (60m Difficult) is now a classic, though often avoided even by those who can climb at a harder standard. The current guide notes that camming devices offer protection, but it still demands a confident lead. Also, many climbers in the lower grades might not usually use camming devices.

As recently as the late 1960s it was possible to spot some of Allan's original arrows, while the 1969 SMC Climbers' Guide stated baldly that '... *although technically not very hard, Arrow Route is a serious climb, having inadequate belays and no protection*'.[6] The route made it into the pages of *Classic Rock*, while Cliff Lawther described it as a '...*delicate solo job, with the footwear toeing weather pockets, and fingers flat against the warm rough gabbro*'.[7]

Skye guide and SMC member Mike Lates spotted however that Arrow Route had in fact been climbed earlier, in 1928 by the Lake District professional guide Jerry Wright. He had named the Cioch Slab route *Central Climb*, giving it a length of 200 feet and a grade of Severe–

An exhilarating climb in rubbers; more so in boots. Solo work is recommended owing to absence of belays. Perfect conditions (rubbers) – solo. In boots – 45 minutes. 200 feet of line used. [8]

On 25 July 1945, members of the Climbers' Club were on Skye including Robin and Carol Plackett, Geoffrey Curtis and Gordon Townend, all of whom featured in the preceding chapter. Along with EJW Morrison, they made two first ascents on the western face of Sgùrr na h' Uamha, the fine peak guarding the entrance to Harta Corrie. These routes are on the same face as *Murray's Climb* (240m Difficult), the sole contribution to Skye by Murray, climbed with JKW Dunn on 26 June 1937. The Climbers' Club routes are not described in the current guide but were graded Severe and 3A, the latter from the old grading system used in the SMC Guide to Skye and equating to about Difficult. (More information on grades is given in Chapter 4.)

❊❊❊

The war aroused democratic ideas in many minds, as people had fought and died to free populations and countries from oppression and dictatorship. There was a feeling, around which lay an atmosphere of hopeful equality, where land would not be bounded by barbed-wire fencing, and where landowners would not automatically bar access to climbing or walking areas. Historically, some of the established mountaineering clubs, especially the SMC, have tended to tread delicately (like Agag, perhaps) when it comes to access.

This was in small part due to the connections some members of the SMC had with the land, whether as landowners themselves, or through landowning friends. In Aberdeen, the Cairngorm Club tended more towards championing the independent and perhaps occasionally abrasive 'stravaiger', the '*breed of walkers who professed a healthy disregard for the trifling of autocratic landowners*'.[9] The SMC preferred to negotiate by diplomacy. It might take longer, but it usually resulted in agreement.

This democratic process was a continuation of that which had become prominent in the late 1920s and 1930s, and was then interrupted by war.

The story of early access struggles – and in particular the efforts of James Bryce – is outlined in Volume One. Two highly recommended books covering land ownership in Scotland are those by the Dundonian, Andy Wightman, who was elected as a member of the Scottish Parliament for the Scottish Green Party in 2016. [10]

There was a certain irony, considering the early history of the SMC, that in 1935 it was three of the club's members, one of whom was also a member of the National Trust for Scotland, who reacted positively when Lord Strathcona put the Glen Coe hunting estate up for sale. Arthur Walker Russell (1873-1967, one of three Russell brothers in the club), Percy John Henry Unna (1878-1950), and NTS activist Logan Aikman (1902-2002) set about raising funds, in which they were successful. SMC member James Wordie and others were also involved in this very worthy cause, and two years later they added the neighbouring Dalness estate.

These acquisitions, handed over to the NTS, were in part inspired by the earlier purchase of Kintail by the NTS through the generosity of an anonymous donor. Aikman, a Glaswegian, was SMC secretary at the time and during the war years; he died in his 101st year.

One of the conditions of the gift was that it should be administered in accordance with general principles expressed by SMC members at the time that Dalness was acquired. These general guidelines have gone down in history as the *'Unna Principles'*, and were written in a letter from Unna to the NTS, dated 23 November 1937. [11,12]

As with many other sets of rules or principles, through time changes in circumstance have brought pressures to bear. It would have been a remarkable soothsayer who could have predicted the numbers who would stream out of the cities and enjoy the mountains, and in Glen Coe, bridges were built and paths tinkered with. The use of the land for hunting would cease, however, with unrestricted access to the public. It is a debate which continues.

❄❄❄

The end of the war naturally saw an increase in climbing and walking: slowly initially, then with ever-increasing speed. One group in particular sprang into life and not only began climbing, but also put up new, hard climbs. They were members of the Creagh Dhu Mountaineering Club, mostly from Glasgow and mainly from the shipyards on the Clyde.

Andy Sanders had formed the Creagh Dhu in 1930, and while climbing was certainly a part of club life, so was hunting, fishing and shooting, usually without the knowledge of the landowner. Employment was scarce in the 1930s, so it was a logical response to the availability of free time and the scarcity of food.

Working life in the shipyards – of which there were 30 to 40 at that time–was for the most part hard outdoor work in all and any conditions. It was often dangerous work too, requiring good co-operation – not that much different in some respects from hard climbing. Scottish guidebooks include many classic lines first climbed by Creagh Dhu members, and the club's name became synonymous with interesting, difficult routes. The happy hunting grounds were concentrated around Arrochar and Glen Coe, but the club moved wherever good times were to be found, whether on rock, ice or in a remote bothy.

For many climbers in the west of Scotland at that time, a day or week-end could begin by bus from Glasgow heading north towards Drymen. Loch Lomond would be a little further, while en route was Carbeth, with the nearby Craigallian fire mentioned in Chapter Three. Just up the road was Queen's View, with a path contouring round Auchineden Hill to the Whangie, an unusual rock feature facing Loch Lomond and the Arrochar Alps beyond. On its dubious rock many a climber could develop skills and finger strength. Eventually the Creagh Dhu established its own ad hoc bothy, Jacksonville, below the Buachaille, on the site of an old sheep fank.

Edinburgh climber Jimmy Marshall recalled his own introduction to the Creagh Dhu in a brief but informative SMCJ article. [13] Jacksonville, named after Jimmy Jackson, an early member, grew organically on the west bank of the River Coupall, just down from the stepping stones. Various rag-tag climbers, including the author, feel honoured to have been a guest under its roof, and Marshall tells how he and his friend Olly had the temerity to shelter there when the weather broke.

> Therafter [sic], we festered twenty four hours in the pits, till a darkening doss indicated arrival of owner representation, fortunately in the form of big Smith. 'Aye lads, what are you doin' here, hardly your style, is it?' he queried, casually staking a place in the mire. However, our luck was in, Wullie was the most tolerant member of that eclectic group, kind hearted for bye and it wasn't long before we enjoyed the fruits of his seemingly bottomless bag, all conjured with effortless bludging.

That night Smith casually dropped in the suggestion that Raven's Gully was a good route for a wet day. This stuck in the youths' minds, and the next morning they headed up the hill towards that dark slot, to find Smith behind them. Marshall failed on the crux, allowing Smith to demonstrate with seeming effortless style the way to climb it.

> Nonchalant, he latched onto the wall, big boots sticking to the rock like magic: then with an imperious doff of the cadie and 'Haud this, Jimmy' he disappeared over the roof like smoke. Christ, that put us in our place and like to disappear into our boots we followed up on taut rope and nerve to join a tactful Wullie, promising the rest of the climb would be great.

Other such saving interpolations by Smith followed, until they emerged happy and very impressed:

> In retrospect, I know we'd been 'taken' by Wullie, I've often done the same to others since, we didn't know it then but we could not have picked a better man for the initiation.

> However, at the time, I didn't give a damn, what a fantastic climb it had been. I resolved I'd get back into the gully again but now it was great to be out of that hole! Off we went into the drizzle and down, burning off the adrenalin with delighted release. In the doss our elation dissipated under increasing pressure from the multiple owners, in an introduction to unimagined depths of ribald coexistence, far beyond the wildest dreams of our hitherto protected environment.

> Twenty four hours on, deep in wet and windblown contemplative escape from the harsh reality of a lift by open lorry, and still pondering on the power and grace of these same men on the rocks of Buachaille Etive, it came to me that we had partaken of the height and depth of experience, but more significantly, had been shown the way and the light by Glasgow's Ullysean [sic] crew, to a new and vital life style waiting to be enjoyed in our Scottish mountains.

Bill Smith (1924-2012) was born in Glasgow, and could perhaps stand as a model for a new breed who eventually lived and worked in the mountains. He left school at 14, and two years later was fortunate to gain an apprenticeship with Rolls-Royce at Hillington, where he met some in the climbing world. Apprenticeship over, two years in the Paras followed. The late 1940s were not easy, and like many a young Scot Smith paid the £7 fare and sailed to New Zealand. Two years later, back in Scotland, he joined other Creagh Dhu members in the resurgence of skiing, with Meall a' Bhùiridh just south of Glen Coe the new playground. Here, the combination of an experience of harsh outdoor winter conditions and mechanical engineering provided work in developing the new tow, along with the Scottish Ski Club.

The first prototype tow was installed in the early 1950s, with a Breco tow added in 1955. In 1957, Smith skied a total of 34,000 feet in one day. After seven years' working at that, along with other Creagh Dhu members he headed off to work with the British Antarctic Survey (BAS). Smith was on the first ascent of Mount Andrew Jackson, at 3184m the highest peak in BAS territory. Home again, and with skiing now using commercial models, Smith and his colleagues became involved as winter sports engineers in the east of Scotland, at Glenshee and Cairngorm. All this activity took care of the winter months; in the summers much rock climbing was carried out, as will shortly be seen.

❄❄❄

The end of the war did not automatically lead to a surge of first ascents, or even to much climbing. Not all servicemen and women were demobilised immediately, employment might have to be looked for, and of course various other life-changing events would have received priority. What seems to have been the situation for the first post-war year or so was a tentative revisiting of the hills, with a slow realisation that there was new ground to be explored.

One immediate and obvious benefit of the war was the availability of a huge amount of cheap clothing and equipment. Photographs of the period often show climbers in army kit, carrying army rucksacks and probably wearing army boots, socks, gloves and using cooking utensils built to last. One item, made for the US Army in 1942 and still in production, is the famous P38 can opener. This brilliant invention, a mere 38mm or so in length was reputedly named after the usual 38 or so punctures which were taken to open a can of C-rations. There is a larger brother opener, the P51. The first post-war advertisements for climbing equipment occasionally listed manila ropes, but nylon ropes would soon be available.

Climbing hardware also came on the market, at a price, while slings were soon to appear and could be bought already spliced for the best strength. Karabiners were also on the market, though prices sometimes forced climbers to manufacture their own. The original climbers' 'karabiner' was a hook with a sprung closure, used to assist in carrying a gun, but from around the year 1900 climbers saw the advantage of using a suitable device for attaching to the eye of a piton, easily allowing running a rope through the karabiner. Early models were of steel, and accordingly very heavy.

It was not until until post-war years that alloy karabiners would become available, with commercial manufacturers in the US beginning to market designs in the late 1950s. In rock climbing footwear, Pierre Allain redesigned his soft-soled boots for hard rock in 1948. Hard routes before then would often have been climbed wearing sandshoes or rubbers, as with several instances described earlier. It would take until the mid to late 1950s before the French-designed rock boots became widespread.

Some exploration was taking place on the Hebrides, for instance in July and August 1947 when J Gordon Parish, a GP based in Edinburgh, stayed on Rum for almost a month with his wife. A group of EUMC students also visited for a week, during which 15 new routes were climbed. Some of the students were shortly to join the SMC, giving rise to a lengthy period when an Edinburgh clique dominated that club.

What were to become the usual suspects included Charles George Malcolm Slesser (1926-2007), Iain Hugh Murray Smart (1928-2017), Donald John Bennet (1928-2013) and Geoffrey J Fraser Dutton (1924-2010), with

William Wallace MBE (1932-2006), Hamish Nicol (1929-1997) and J Gordon Parish aiding and abetting. The Rum routes recorded were mainly in the lower grades, up to Hard Severe. A guide was written to the island (using the Victorian spelling of Rhum) by the Junior Mountaineering Club of Yorkshire, formed in 1941 and renamed the Yorkshire Mountaineering Club in 1952, probably due to confusion with the various branches of the JMCS. In September of the same year, Harris was explored by ECW Rudge, author of the 1941 book *Mountain Days Near Home* and a FRCC member.

Parish was also one of the climbers exploring the gullies on the Glen Nevis flank of Ben Nevis. Along with J Murray, on 23 March 1946 he recorded *Five-funnel Gully*, the infamous trap now known as Five Finger Gully, down into which many an errant climber or walker has been lured in the dark or in bad weather. By August 1947 six other gullies were partially or totally climbed by various parties, whose members included DG Duff, J Ness, R Murphie, DH Haworth, G Ritchie, Slesser and others. The gullies are for the curious or the cognoscenti, or those looking for lost climbers, walkers or gear.

Climbers were returning to Skye, where on 21 May 1947 Derek Holden Haworth (1924-2008) and Ian ap G Hughes climbed the *Crack of Double Doom* (120m VS 4b) on the wall between Crack of Doom and Central Gully Arete. Close by is also their *Doom Flake* (90m Severe). Haworth was born in Blackpool and graduated in medicine from Edinburgh University. He emigrated to Canada in 1953, by when he had climbed some alpine routes and made various other ascents, including *Steeplejack Staircase* (E2) on Edinburgh's Salisbury Crags.

As if the Crack of Double Doom was not enough, in 1949 the same pair returned to snatch what has become one of the Cuillin's most popular climbs with *Integrity* (75m VS). Haworth and Hughes had good eyes for a line, and with Integrity, climbed on 11 July 1949, they struck a rich lode. It tackles the steep wall above the Cìoch Slab, first breaking through an intimidating bulge. At this point a glance downwards will take in the massive exposure. Above, the line continues straight up on superb rock.

In the 1949 SMCJ, Haworth received a paper slap on the wrist for reporting a winter ascent of Clachaig Gully in February 1948. [14] His claim, for the first complete winter ascent with Parish, included the latter sliding into a watersplash before the last pitch, then having to make a rapid escape by the side wall on account of his sodden state. The SMCJ included the following comment–

First Winter Ascents.—The Editor of the 'Glencoe' Guide has noticed that winter ascents are being claimed when the rocks are free from snow and ice. The fact that a climb has been made during the six winter months does not of itself qualify the climb as "an ascent under winter conditions" for Guide Book purposes. Such a claim merely misleads other climbers. The Editor has therefore disallowed the claim to a first winter ascent of Clachaig Gully published in the last issue of the Journal. The rocks were free of snow. Similar ascents have been disallowed for the Chasm, Church Door Buttress and Rannoch Wall. [15]

The editor of the Glen Coe guide was Murray–who, as noted above, had enough on his plate without having to adjudicate on such matters. His comment seemed to work however, with winter claims settling down.

❄❄❄

Jock Nimlin was working in the Clyde shipyards as a crane-driver with Harland and Wolff; he would be with that company for the next 30 years, a job which suited him admirably. He made several radio broadcasts following the war, either describing his job and what he could see from his eagle's eye point of view high on his crane, or expressing opinions as to where society could or should be heading after the war, based on his socialist leanings.

He made two first ascents on the Cobbler in May 1940, one of which was *Sesame Groove* (30m Very Difficult) with Jennie Dryden, his girlfriend and later his wife, and R Peel. This grassy corner and groove led to the start of *North Wall Traverse* (55m Difficult), which they then followed to its finish. While not a great route, it opened up this steep face and would be used to access harder climbs in the near future. It is now part of a winter climb which incorporates Sesame Groove and North Wall Traverse and is referred to in the current guide as *North Wall Traverse* (140m IV,5).

The steep face above saw a visit by the Creagh Dhu in the form of Bill Smith, climbing with C Wilson in August 1945. The pair climbed *North Wall Groove* (55m Severe), a vegetated line in summer but transformed into a superb winter route at V,6 when it was first climbed on 16 February 1977 by Norrie Muir and Arthur Paul. One of the more widely known members of the Creagh Dhu was John Crabbe Cunningham (1927-1980), due in part to his first ascents and also to the publication in 1999 of a biography. [16] In some ways Cunningham's experience mirrored that of Smith and others in the club, with Cunningham diverting into outdoor education in later life, eventually becoming an instructor at Glenmore Lodge.

Moving from the Whangie to the Cobbler, skills learned at the lower crag were easily and profitably transferred to the higher, with such classics as *Chimney Arete* (25m VS 4b), Cunningham and Ian Dingwall in 1947; *Ardgartan Arete* (55m VS), Cunningham, June 1948 (solo); *S Crack* (40m VS 4c), Cunningham and Smith, June 1948; *Gladiator's Groove* (65m VS), Smith and MacInnes, August 1951, with *Gladiator's Groove Direct Start* (E1) added by Smith and R Hope, June 1952 (and climbed in rubbers).

MacInnes popped up here, demonstrating enthusiastically the use of pitons for protection and direct aid. For some time he was nicknamed 'MacPiton'. The Cobbler sustained its usefulness for Glasgow-based climbers due to its proximity and also the convenient accommodation in the Glen Loin caves and high dosses in the corrie. As time allowed and transport problems eased, the Creagh Dhu stretched their muscles in other venues, especially Glen Coe.

✻✻✻

Back from the prisoner-of-war camp and climbing again, Murray was given the task of researching and writing the SMC Glen Coe guide. His introduction gives much insight into how he wrote, and what criteria he used in describing the routes–

> The supreme delight of rock-climbing is that of exploration. Therefore, it is the Editor's conviction that the ideal rock-guide is one that gives at most an indication of a climb's existence, a clue to its whereabouts, and a vague description of what the mountaineer may expect to encounter. Beyond these bare essentials, every elaboration of detail denies to the climber a chance to exercise initiative.

He modified this somewhat Spartan outlook by admitting that factors such as weather, experience and unknown ground, along with a majority of climbers preferring to follow nail-marked rock, prevented the ideal guide from being published. The ideal guide, in Murray's mind, would follow the edicts given in the preceding quote. There was also reference to SMC policies which had been followed for 60 years–

> ...to honour the mountaineer rather than the specialist, to encourage exploratory rock-work and the art of route-selection, especially under winter conditions, rather than the ascent of short VSs in rubbers. These latter give excellent sport and practice, but they are usually artificial and are not of first mountaineering importance.

As noted earlier, Murray's writing was an inspiration for many and, as Robin N Campbell pointed out in his obituary in the Alpine Journal, led hundreds of climbers in the 1950s on to the crags:

> His first book and its sequel *Undiscovered Scotland* (Dent, 1951) are inspirational writings – the Iliad and Odyssey of Scottish mountain writing. It is impossible for any young person to read them without experiencing strong exploratory urges.

The Creagh Dhu attitude to Murray was a mixture of respect for his obvious love of the mountains, as expressed in his classic books, and disdain for some of the writing itself, described by John Cullen and others as being *'right over the top'*. [17] Murray's writing was also too spiritual for the hard-nosed and hard-living men of the shipyards, for whom daily work had more of its fair share of dirt and death. Murray also, in their consideration, wrote up some routes out of all proportion to their actual difficulty, including Rubicon Wall on Ben Nevis and Clachaig Gully in Glen Coe.

The Creagh Dhu certainly had promise, but for a year or two following the war they had signally failed to break out of their 1930s attitude of classic outdoor pleasures, walking and howffing, with the odd bit of poaching thrown in for food and fun. As Jeff Connor comments in *Creagh Dhu Climber*, they had failed to move the standards on from that era, with Murray and his JMCS friends leaving them standing, especially when it came to winter pioneering. With the partnership of Smith and Cunningham in particular, however, and the stimulus of Murray's guide, that was about to change.

A significant date was June 1946, when Cunningham led Pete McGonigle up two new routes on the East Face of North Buttress on the Buachaille. On Sunday 23 June he began with *Shattered Crack* (45m VS 4c), then followed this on the Monday with *Crow's Nest Crack* (80m VS), a fine sustained route just right of the first climb. Descriptions did not appear in the relevant SMCJ, but in *Creagh Dhu Climber* it states that Cunningham was, as expected at this point, wearing sandshoes, while on Crow's Nest Crack he asked McGonigle to untie and move up behind him when he ran out of rope. He was, in essence, soloing the climb.

Chris Lyon, then president of the Creagh Dhu, was looking on and had gone to the climb's finish with a rope, in case it was needed. When Cunningham reached the top he was met, not with congratulations, but with a severe talking to from a furious Lyon for stupidly endangering himself and the less proficient McGonigle. Murray's guide has Crow's Nest Crack graded as Severe and Shattered Crack as VS, both in rubbers.

In October 1946, Smith and Cunningham teamed up on the Buachaille and in one weekend made first ascents of *Autumn Slab* (25m VS), which is now pitch one of *Whortleberry Wall* (115m HVS), *Curving Groove* (80m VS) and *Grooved Arete* (90m VS), all on Rannoch Wall. Each of these climbs required bold leads, and it is easy now to overlook the lack of protection a leader would have experienced. Curving Groove and Autumn Slab were again climbed in rubbers. Cunningham had joined the Creagh Dhu when aged 17; he was now 18, Smith 20. Britain did not completely demobilise in 1945 as conscription continued after the war, and Smith, then in the Parachute Regiment, was on leave from Palestine.

This was a busy time for the Creagh Dhu, with Kenny Copland and Lyon climbing *Juniper Groove* (45m Hard Severe), while Copland and Smith climbed *Fracture Route* (65m VS). Over on Great Gully Buttress, facing Slime Wall, Sam Smith and Ian Dingwall climbed *Direct Route* (45m Hard

Severe), another bold lead in rubbers with poor protection and the first climb on this buttress of excellent rock. In the same timeframe, Murray, RV Waterhouse and Hector Cameron were putting up *Waterslide Wall* (60m Severe) on the South Face of Central Buttress. Also on Central Buttress, this time its North Face, two members of the Alpine Club, John Poole and Richard Brooke, were climbing *The Gangway* (90m Hard Severe), with its nerve-tingling traverse on the second pitch.

This grand outburst of climbing, most of which was on excellent, rough rhyolite, indicated a new confidence. Protection still had not moved forward much, and it is a mark of how proficient the good climbers were that despite long, bold runouts there were very few falls or serious injuries during this period.

Smith still had time to serve in the armed forces, and returned to Palestine. Cunningham therefore joined forces with Dingwall, and in June 1947 the pair recorded a climb on the Buachaille which remains a test piece. *Gallows Route* (25m E2 5b) may be short, but it packs in much climbing. Protection is practically absent until after the crux, but Cunningham led it in sandshoes with no protection.

When it was first recorded, the top grade in Scotland was still VS, a situation which naturally produced quite a few epics for those not fully aware of its difficulty. Don Whillans led the route in 1951 and is later reputed to have asked Cunningham where he found '...*these bleedin' chop routes*'. [18] It was certainly the hardest route in Scotland for some time. Eric Taylor, a Creagh Dhu member for several years, also made an early ascent, his rope held by Bill Smith who declined to follow.

Murray's *Mountaineering in Scotland* was published in 1947 to near-universal approval. He had chosen to send the manuscript to JM Dent in London, knowing that their literary director was in the Alpine Club. Their reply came back two months later, after the manuscript had been read by Graham Irving – who had introduced Mallory to climbing and had been on an early climbing holiday to Ben Nevis with Mallory (see Volume One).

The Dent publishing house then seems to have been stuffed with mountaineers, as Ernest Bozman was an editorial director there. He had co-authored a book with Bell, as well as writing various articles himself, and would be working with Murray on *Mountaineering in Scotland*. [19] Irving wished to cut down the spiritual content, but this was vetoed by Murray, who got his way. Murray's timing was also good: the country was ready for something to take minds off the prevailing austerity, while many climbers returning to civilian life were ripe for inspiration. It made Murray's reputation as a writer and remains in print.

Murray extended this productive period in Glen Coe to a cliff which had been staring many a climber in the face: the East Face of Aonach Dubh.

It was not so much the discovery of the cliff itself, but it being found to consist of excellent rough and sound rhyolite. The trade route up to the cliffs of Stob Coire nan Lochan lie opposite this face, on the other side of the burn issuing from Coire nan Lochan. As Murray wrote in *Undiscovered Scotland*, during the winter of 1946-47 he and Donald McIntyre passed this lengthy cliff half a dozen times, en route to something icy.

Donald Bertram McIntyre (1923-2009) was a geologist, with academic posts at Edinburgh University and, from 1954 to 1989, at Pomona College in California. As he wrote in a personal contribution for the Perth MC Millennium Journal, it was love for mountains which led him to geology.[20] Work reduced his climbing, then when his son Ewen was born with cerebral palsy, climbing stopped entirely. As for his geology, McIntyre was most proud of his paper written in 1945 with CA Beevers, when both worked at the Dewar Crystallographic Laboratory in Edinburgh.[21]

On a sunny evening in May 1947, Murray and McIntyre boulder-hopped the River Coe and walked up the steep-sided glen between Gearr Aonach and Aonach Dubh. This was before the NTS made its controversial decision to build a footbridge across the river, and there is an anecdote which Bob Aitken tells in his obituary for Murray–

> I cherish a memory from one of an apparently endless and inconclusive series of meetings in Glen Coe with the Trust in the Seventies and Eighties to discuss Those Bridges, when (the rest of the group having dwindled, distantly debating, into the Hidden Valley) Bill and I rested companionably on a knoll above the Coire Gabhail gorge. In reminiscent vein Bill described how in the thirties he and JMCS friends would cross the river below Coire nan Lochan, boulder-hopping under heavy packs. 'I was good at it,' he said; 'the others quite often fell in.' This with his most endearing wry grin, abashed at his own small vanity. With Bill you had to wait patiently for such moments, but you waited willingly. [22]

The two climbers stopped at their chosen bivouac site, a small hollow in the rocky eastern wall of the glen, where an overhang provided some protection from the elements. From there they could step across the burn and in a few minutes gain their planned explorations the following morning. They made first ascents of four routes: *The Bowstring* (150m Difficult), which was McIntyre's first new route; *Archer Ridge* (70m Severe); *Quiver Rib* (65m Difficult); and *Rowan Tree Wall* (75m Very Difficult).

These were climbed on the same day, with another four climbed later. They had not been the first climbers on this pleasant face, however, as the lower part of *The Bow* had been climbed in April 1946 by J Neill and AH Henson. (Neill was probably John Neill, one-time editor of the Climbers' Club Journal and co-author of the guide to Snowdon South with CT Jones in 1960. Harold Henson was a Rucksack Club member who died in 2002.)

Over the years, the East Face of Aonach Dubh would be extensively explored and climbed, with excellent routes at most grades being added. Murray expressed much surprise at the amount of good, sound rock he found. [23] Some of the climbs have rhyolite at its rough, bubbly best, including Archer Ridge, where the first pitch in particular is a palpable delight. Add in its low altitude, proximity to the road, south-eastern outlook and good climbs ranging from Moderate to E6, and the cliff is understandably popular. The real surprise, as Murray himself confessed, was how long it took to be discovered.

Murray graded Archer Ridge at Mild Severe in his 1949 guide; it is currently Severe, with the first two pitches given a technical grade of 4a. On the first ascent Murray attempted to follow the ridge, but was forced on to the wall on its right. A Direct Variation was climbed in May 1954 by Len Lovat (1926-1996), Ian McNicol and A Way and is graded Severe. The author, having backed off a few times, suspects it is a pretty formidable Severe.

On Ben Nevis, little had been done since the death of Kellett in 1944. There was however one ascent which stands out as something of an anomaly, when on 16 June 1946 H Arnold Carsten of the Climbers' Club and Tommy McGuinness (1928-) of the Lomond Mountaineering Club climbed *The Crack* (250m HVS) on Raeburn's Buttress. The line, as the name implies, takes a conspicuous split in the front face of the buttress, and is described in the guide as daunting and atmospheric. It sees few summer ascents, but has been resurrected as a hard winter climb at VIII,8 . The Ben Nevis history provides more detail of this hair-raising route, climbed in the rain, which ten years after its first ascent would see a certain Robin Smith become benighted.

❊❊❊

The intensity of winter climbing in Scotland had increased, with Murray, Mackenzie and their friends setting much of the pace. The interruption of war had forced a pause on many climbers in the services, not just due to their absence from the hills but also due to their experiences. Some would return to climbing with a more cautious or relaxed outlook, while some carried on as before. For those with employment which kept them at home, it was still possible to climb much as before, albeit with some geographic restrictions and belt-tightening due to food and fuel rationing.

Rock climbing standards were soon on the rise, and on his return to civilian life Bill Smith resumed climbing with John Cunningham. In June of 1948 they made their way up Great Gully on Buachaille Etive Mor, aware that there was much unclimbed, if very steep, rock on both sides of the amphitheatre below Cuneiform Buttress.

On Saturday 12 June they climbed *June Crack* (60m VS) on Great Gully Buttress on the west flank of the gully. The first route here had been *Direct*

Route (45m Hard Severe), climbed by Sam Smith and Ian Dingwall in October 1946 (though earlier top-roped by another party). June Crack is one of a trilogy of early good climbs here all named after their month of ascent–June, July and August–with the latter two both at Hard VS. As Smith later recalled, he was 'allowed' to lead the route, probably, he thought, as it was his birthday.

The following day saw a taste of things to come, as Cunningham and Smith succeeded in climbing Slime Wall on the eastern, shady side of the amphitheatre. This superb wall of excellent, grey rhyolite had been named earlier, possibly due to some of its shallow corners and grooves holding moss watered by weeps, slow to dry. Its name is a misnomer, however, as after two or three dry days the rocks are good to go, if in some places short of ideal protection.

This time Cunningham took the lead, probably with the intention of climbing the very prominent hanging groove high above the foot of Raven's Gully. In *Creagh Dhu Climber*, Smith provides some details of that day. They had aimed at the large cave which dominates the top of the face, but moisture forced them off line and they eventually trended rightwards and up. They found protection poor, and borrowed a second rope. All this time they had an audience, as many of the club had turned up for the weekend.

Cunningham carried one peg, one karabiner and one sling. He tried to use the peg at halfway, but without a hammer it was hopeless. On the second pitch he had to run out 140ft of rope with no runners. The new guidebook would describe this as two pitches, but a note from a Creagh Dhu party pointed out that no intermediate belay existed. [24] They ended up in the curving groove/ramp which runs above Raven's Gully, and which in its unclimbed state was slimy. As Cunningham himself stated, Gallows Route was harder, but far less serious.

Another Creagh Dhu climber, Tommy Paul, was watching from a good vantage point on Cuneiform Buttress, on the right of Raven's. While there were dissenting voices from the audience, who thought the climb was pushing it too much, Paul knew that to descend would have been even harder and they were right to continue. It was a struggle for the pair, climbing steep, hard rock in less than perfect conditions and needing to keep their nerve, but eventually they succeeded. They named the climb *Guerdon Grooves* (180m HVS), a guerdon being a reward or recompense. As for the route they had originally aimed to climb, it later would be recorded as Shibboleth, of which more later.

The SMCJ for May 1949 noted that–

As the new Glencoe and Ardgour rock-climbing Guide will be published very shortly, it is not intended to reprint any new climbs which are to be included in it. Of recent discoveries this covers (on Buachaille Etive Mor) the direct start to McKenzie [sic] slanting shelf route on Central Buttress, June Crack, Guerdon Grooves and Raven's Gully, direct route and on Aonach Dubh a route by Nicol on B. Buttress. [25]

The new guide did come out later that year, including these routes, with Guerdon Grooves listed as VS in rubbers. It is difficult to know what Murray thought of these routes: he still had the advantage in winter climbing, but had now been surpassed in summer. After the war, and having just bought a house on Loch Goil, he had the Glen Coe guide to finish. As mentioned in his autobiography, he was kept busy by a wave of new routes, as climbers by now were aware of the guide in preparation. [26] Most of the new routes came from Creagh Dhu members, who were beginning to be noticed by raising the standards. Murray confessed to feeling exasperated by the pressure, enjoyable though the new climbs were. It is unlikely that he climbed either June Crack or Guerdon Grooves, and certainly not Gallows Route, but he would surely be aware of their seriousness.

As the new climbs kept coming in, Bell, as editor of the SMCJ, seemingly became somewhat bemused. There was a generational gap here, and it became evident over the simple issue of naming routes. According to Bill Smith, when the Creagh Dhu made a first ascent they would send in the description to the SMC in the standard way, but–

> …this bloke called Bell wouldn't have it, he was always objecting to the names of the routes or something like that. It got so you wouldn't even bother sending them in. I think there's a lot more routes in the Coe that we never did got [sic] recorded. [27]

❄❄❄

In 1946 and 1947, Bell enjoyed two summer holidays in Scotland with his wife Pat. They explored the Northern Highlands and made several first ascents of climbs in the Very Difficult and Severe grades. Not only that, they were the first to climb on some crags, while on others they were the first visitors for several decades. On 9 August 1946 they discovered and climbed *Route 1* (Cracks Route, 15m Very Difficult) and *Route 2* (Red Slab Route, 15m Severe 4a) on the enjoyable gneiss of Gruinard Jetty Buttress, which they had named. Considering the eventual number of routes climbed on the collection of crags in this area, perhaps they deserve more recognition.

The couple were also on Waterfall Buttress of Beinn a' Mhuinidh, recording *West Climb, Bell's Variation* (90m Very Difficult), and they went to Beinn Dearg in Ross-shire, climbing a 500ft Severe on the Ghrandda Slabs and revisiting the Bonaidh Dhonn on Beinn a' Mhuinidh, the previous visit having been that by William Inglis Clark in 1910. Here the Bells climbed *Route II* (120m Very Difficult), while on Liathach they found *Bell's Buttress* (150m Severe) in Coire na Caime. Perhaps the apostrophe should be moved to rename it Bells' Buttress, as Pat Bell was a competent climber in her own right.

Murray, too, was doing some exploratory climbing in Scotland. By 1948 he had recovered from an accident in the Alps the previous year, when with Michael Phelps Ward (1925-2005) and John Edward Quintus Barford (1914-1947) all three were swept into a bergschrund by an avalanche. Barford was killed outright and Ward trapped. Both Murray and Ward had fractured skulls, but Murray somehow succeeded in pulling out Ward.

Barford was perhaps best known for his book *Climbing in Britain*, published in 1946, and for being the first secretary of the British Mountaineering Council (BMC), founded in 1944. His book sold over 10,000 copies, at one shilling as a Pelican paperback. He also tried to resurrect numerical gradings for climbs, but much as with the earlier SMC attempt this proved too radical for the times. Ward wrote several textbooks on high-altitude medicine.

Murray and Ward enjoyed some success on Rum, making several first ascents including *Archangel Route* (120m Very Difficult) and *Bloodstone Crack* (30m VS) in May 1948. Oddly, although the current SMC guide (2014) describes Archangel Route as *'A route of great character with splendid positions – a Rum classic'*, it receives no stars. In fact most of the Rum routes described in that guide are not starred; a lack of feedback from climbers may be the reason, as many of the routes appear to be worth climbing. There is also the guide to Rum by Hamish Brown (Cicerone Press, 1988, out of print); used copies can be found via the internet.

Bloodstone Crack was named after the mineral found at the foot of the crack, bloodstone being a variety of jasper also known as heliotrope, usually green jasper (chalcedony) with red inclusions of hematite that are supposed to resemble spots of blood, hence the name.

In 1948, Garbh Bheinn of Ardgour was under investigation by a party from the Moray Mountaineering Club. No precise descriptions were made, but right of the Great Ridge they climbed two prominent slabs at a grade of Very Difficult. They also queried whether *'anyone has tried a face climb on the wonderful south wall of the Great Ridge'*. The answer to this was… not at this juncture, though its superb, grey-striped gneiss would later yield excellent climbs. Other areas on the western seaboard and in the Hebrides were by now receiving attention, including Lewis and Harris, the latter seeing several easy climbs recorded on Sròn Ulladale by two members of the London JMCS, M de V Wills and RG Folkard.

Bell recorded his last new route in the Cairngorms on 8 May 1948, when along with his wife and William S Thomson (Lochaber JMCS) he climbed *The Hanging Garden* (300m Very Difficult) on Creag an Dubh Loch. A botanical route, as the name would suggest, it now provides a good winter climb at V,4. Bell was slowly winding down his exploratory climbing, but Cairngorms climbers had reason to be grateful to him for his championing of the good granite he had found along the way.

❊❊❊

On the Cobbler, two routes climbed in summer 1948 just missed the deadline for the Southern Highlands guide. This was not a rock climbing guide, rather one of the series of district guides; it was eventually published in 1951, edited by John D Bruce Wilson.

The routes were both on the South Peak: *Dead Man's Groove* (90m VS 4c), climbed by the Creagh Dhu team of Cunningham, Bill Smith and Sam Smith on 23 May, and *The S Crack Route* (40m VS 4c), by Cunningham and Bill Smith on 20 June. The names as given here are from the original record in the SMCJ; both were subsequently changed, to Deadman's Groove, and S-Crack. The grade of S-Crack has also morphed, from its original Severe in rubbers. Both climbs have received winter ascents, Deadman's at VII,7 , S-Crack at V,7 .

While on the subject of changing grades, one of the most glaring examples of undergrading has to be the very short route, more of a problem, on the North Peak of the Cobbler, *Overhanging Recess* (10m Severe). This had been climbed in 1948 by Kenny Copland, regarded then by Cunningham as one of the best balance climbers. He did not record many routes, but with this short exercise, just below the bealach under the North Peak, he left an intriguing problem. As the current guide has it–

> "The route is probably technically Severe, but it started out as a Difficult in the 1954 guide and the authors would feel really humbled if it were upgraded again." The current authors apparently felt similarly, but the editor has no such scruple. One suggestion for this edition was 5a!

In the 1954 guide, by Ben Humble and Jock Nimlin, not only does this route have a grade of Difficult, but in the graded list it sits in the middle of the Difficults. The route is deceptive, appearing like it would go with a bit of a heave off the ground, with the result that many experienced climbers cannot be bothered to rope up for such a short effort; but as soon as you leave the horizontal, the exposure taps you on the shoulder, the angle is steeper than at first evident and the result of a fall becomes obvious. Possibly a classic Creagh Dhu tease.

Another of this type might be *Club Crack* (40m E2 5c), climbed by Pat Walsh after many attempts by the club. It became symbolic, as rumour has it that you could not join the Creagh Dhu unless you had led the route. Strenuous, awkward and serious, it remains a touchstone.

❊❊❊

Climbers were beginning to visit Skye again, and in July 1946, Allan Allsop and Richard G Morsley were based at Glen Brittle House. Allsop was a Peak District climber, responsible for the third guidebook on gritstone climbs. [28] Dick Morsley was from Capel Curig and had been on the first winter ascent of Comb Gully on Ben Nevis in 1938, as well as the second winter ascent of Green Gully with Bell and others in 1937.

On 19 July, Allsop and Morsley climbed *Diamond Slab* (180m VS) on the Western Buttress of Sròn na Cìche, just right of Central Gully. In the logbook, Allsop provided a detailed description, giving the climb a standard of 4 with the third pitch hard at this grade. The English classification was Severe, with the third pitch probably Mild VS in rubbers. The crux took in the sustained, steep slab on large sloping holds with few positive handholds. On the same day, J Wilkinson, DW Jackson (both FRCC) and H Ironfield, climbed *Apex Route* (240m Severe), left of Western Gully.

All these climbers were relying on the 1923 SMC guide to Skye, edited by Harry MacRobert. With the guidebook over two decades old, the proliferation of new routes and the scale and complexity of Skye was becoming a source of confusion and frustration. This was especially a problem on Sròn na Cìche, where there was a basic reprint in 1948 of the 1923 guide, with an appendix listing climbs done since the first edition, collated by Mackenzie and Dunn. Mackenzie was then given the poisoned chalice of producing a new guide, devoted to climbing routes, which he began in 1948. It would not be published until 1958.

Britain's first female professional climbing guide was Gwen Mary Moffat, *née* Goddard (1924-). Her first autobiography was published in 1961.[29] She was an early, hippy-style climber, sleeping rough, hitching rides to any climbing ground and preferring to climb in bare feet. She also wrote about her experiences with the RAF Mountain Rescue, from 1945-55.[30] In the summer of 1947 she stayed at the Glen Brittle youth hostel and climbed with David Thomas. Between swimming and sunbathing they climbed Waterpipe Gully and found a new route on the south face of Sgùrr Dearg, *Lagan Route* (90m VS 4b). Later she wrote crime fiction books, featuring a heroine named Melinda Pink, a middle-aged magistrate and climber.

Although Skye lies open to the Atlantic weather systems with its sudden thaws and generally moist air, it can from time to time exhibit all the winter glory of an Alpine habitat. In early March 1948, Tom Weir (1914-2006) met Arthur MacPherson at Kyle of Lochalsh. They were intent on climbing Pinnacle Ridge on Sgùrr nan Gillean in winter condition. Two days later the weather improved and they found to their delight that the pinnacles were coated in iron-hard snow, the very best of material, allowing hand- and foot-holds to be cut with ice axes.

The last pinnacle, the Sgùrr proper, was the demon. The whole face was plastered, giving them a delightful problem, with long runouts of delicate climbing and necessitating careful route-finding. At last they stepped out on to the sunshine and scrambled on to the summit. Around them, slow coils of mist drifted in spectacular fashion, with the ridge curving away in a fierce southward sweep.

Leaving the top we traversed the Western Ridge, treating the Gendarme with care, and climbed on to Am Basteir for a view of the sunset. The Outer Islands were clear, dark against a coppery sky. On the sea itself bars of gold were being drawn as the low sun strengthened its light against the screening clouds. A look at the Tooth was sufficient to put it out of the question for to-night.

Now for the joys of descent. We anticipated a fine glissade and we got it. Balancing on our feet, we slid effortlessly downward to the floor of the corrie above the Bhasteir Gorge, nearly a thousand feet of undiluted joy, the perfect finish to a mountain day. [31]

The West Buttress of Sgùrr Mhiccoinnich long had a reputation for loose rock, but on 24 May 1948 an SMC/LSCC party confounded this by finding an excellent climb. *Jeffrey's Dyke* (300m Difficult) follows the most continuous trap dyke on the left of the long West Buttress, above Lochan Coire Lagan. Two parties enjoyed the ascent: Robert Jeffrey and his wife Mabel, and Jim and Pat Bell with Colin Allan. Pat Bell wrote up the day for the LSCC Journal.

On 20 September 1949 Hamish Gordon Nicol and Allan S Parker found themselves at the top of a gully on the North Face of Sgùrr a' Mhadaidh. Nicol, born in Hong Kong, was an outstanding alpinist following the war. Living in Edinburgh, he attended Fettes College, which he disliked. He then studied medicine at Oxford, and made guideless first British ascents in the Alps with Tom Bourdillon.

Nicol was less lucky on Ben Nevis. Attempting a first winter ascent of Zero Gully with Anthony Rawlinson he fell off and pulled the ice pegs, resulting in a 600-foot fall which both survived. He would have been on the 1953 Everest Expedition but for an unfortunate accident in the Alps (not of his making). He was president of the Climbers' Club in 1972 and died following a climbing accident in Cornwall.

Deep Gash Gully (240m HVS 5a) is described in the current guide as being the Cuillin version of Glen Coe's Raven's Gully. In other words, it is frequently wet and requires strength and determination. Nicol wrote two articles describing their ascent: one for the SMCJ and another for the Alpine Club Journal. [32,33]

They had been glancing up at the gully several times while walking below the corrie, but so deep and shadowy were its confines they could see no details within. Climbing in tricouni nailed boots, their first obstacle was an overhanging mass of chockstones, both side walls running with slime and water. The 15ft overhang was overcome by Parker, swinging outwards from underneath the overhang on a sling and lunging upwards to grasp a hold. This pretty much set the scene for the rest of the route. Parker also led the next section, repeating on a larger scale the first pitch. Above were more overhangs, some pouring with water.

In all they found three cruxes, before being able to flop down in the sun above, where steam rising from their clothing mingled with the shimmering heat haze over the rocks. Naismith and Gibbs had tried the route in 1898, and Murray and Ward in May 1948, but both parties were defeated. The gully received its first winter ascent on 2 February 1991, by Mick Fowler and J Lincoln. Unaware of this ascent, it was climbed a second time two weeks later by Martin Moran and M Welsh.

Skye was not alone in showing a rise in activity; in the Cairngorms, summer and winter explorations showed a marked increase from about 1948 onwards. Greg Strange notes that immediately post-war the standard of winter climbing in the Cairngorms was not as advanced as it was in the west, perhaps due to a belief that ice did not form in the east. [34] This theory seems somewhat specious, as icefalls are generally quite prominent, and an alternative reason could be simply the long approaches required for access in the Cairngorms were a disadvantage during the short winter daylight.

In addition to this, the Cairngorms climbing community was for the most part very close-knit, the existing SMC guidebook was well out of date, and there was as yet little information in circulation which could entice climbers from outwith the area. Whatever the cause, or causes, the next decade would see east-of-Scotland climbers rapidly catching up with their contemporaries in the west.

References

1. Abraham, Ashley P. *The Scawfell Accident.* Climbers' Club Journal 1903, No. 21, pp.42-51.
2. Murray, W.H. *In Memorium.* A. Ian L. Maitland, FRCS. SMCJ 34, 181, 1990. P.543.
3. Maitland, A.I.L., F.R.C.S. (Ed.). *First Aid and Mountain Rescue.* SMCJ 25, 146, May 1955, pp.327-334.
4. MacInnes, Hamish. *Call-Out.* (London, Hodder & Stoughton, 1973; also Penguin paperback, 1977.)
5. MacDonald, Donald Archie. *Some Aspects of Family and Local Background: An Interview with Sorley MacLean.* In: Sorley MacLean, Critical Essays. (Edinburgh Scottish Academic Press, 1986, pages 218-220.)
6. Simpson, J.W. *Cuillin of Skye, Vol.1.* (Scottish Mountaineering Club, 1969.)
7. Lawther, Cliff. *The Cioch of Skye.* Climber & Rambler, November 1978, p.32.
8. Wright, J.E.B. *Mountain Days in the Isle of Skye.* (The Moray Press, 1934, Page 234.)
9. Lorimer, Hayden. *'Your wee bit hill and glen': the cultural politics of the Scottish Highlands, c. 1918-1945.* Doctoral thesis, Loughborough University, 1997.

10. Wightman, Andy. *Who Owns Scotland* (Canongate, 1996); *The Poor Had No Lawyers* (Birlinn Books, 2013).

11. Unna, P.J.H. *Preservation of Scottish Mountain Land for the Nation.* SMCJ 23, 136, April 1945, pp.261-262.

12. The National Trust for Scotland – *Wild Land Policy.* 2002, pp.10-11. <goo.gl/FdmigL> (Accessed May 2016.)

13. Marshall, J.R. *The Initiation.* SMCJ 33, 175, 1984, pp.1-3.

14. Haworth, D.H. *Sgor na h' Ulaidh and Clachaig Gully.* In Notes: SMCJ 24, 140, p.77.

15. Murray, W.H. *First Winter Ascents.* In: Notes. SMCJ 24, 140, May 1949, p.163.

16. Connor, Jeff. *Creagh Dhu Climber – The Life and Times of John Cunningham.* (Glasgow, Ernest Press, 1999.)

17. Cullen, John. Ibid., p.65.

18. Perrin, Jim. *The Villain – The Life of Don Whillans.* (London, Arrow Books, 2006, p.80).

19. Bell, J.H.B., Bozman, E.F., and Fairfax-Blakeborough, J. *British Hills and Mountains.* (B.T. Batsford, London, 1940.)

20. McIntyre, Donald B. *Magical Land of Hills.* (Contribution from Donald B. McIntyre as Honorary President for the *Millennium Journal* of the Perth Mountaineering Club, March 2000.) <https://goo.gl/yHdhwM>

21. Beevers, C.A. and McIntyre, D.B. *The atomic structure of fluor-apatite and its relation to that of tooth and bone material.*

22. Aitken, Robert. *Bill Murray's work in mountain conservation.* SMCJ 36, 187, 1996, pp.155-158.

23. Murray, W.H. *The Forgotten Cliff of Aonach Dubh.* In: Undiscovered Scotland, Chapter IX. (London, Dent. 1951, 1st Edition.) Also in twin book format by Diadem Books, London 1979.

24. *Buachaille Etive, Guerdon Grooves.* In: Short Notes. SMCJ 25, 144, April 1953, p.191.

25. *Glencoe and Ardgour.* In: New Climbs, SMCJ 24, 140, May 1949, p.139.

26. Murray, W.H. *The Evidence of Things Not Seen* – A Mountaineer's Tale. (London, Bâton Wicks, 2002.)

27. Connor, Jeff. *Creagh Dhu Climber* (Glasgow, Ernest Press, 1999, p.78)

28. Allsopp, Allan. *Some Gritstone Climbs, Volume 3: Kinder, Roches and Northern Areas.* (Birkenhead, 1951, Willmer Brothers.

29. Moffat, Gwen. *Space Below my Feet.* (London, 1961. Hodder & Stoughton. 1st Edn.)

30. Moffat, Gwen. *Two Star Red.* (London, 1964. Hodder & Stoughton.)

31. Weir, Tom. *Snow on the Cuillin.* SMCJ 24, 141, April 1950, pp.181-185.

32. Nicol, Hamish G. *Deep Gash Gully.* SMCJ 24, 141, April 1950, pp.199-201.

33. Nicol, Hamish. *Deep Gash Gully, Sgùrr a' Mhadaidh, Skye.* Alpine Journal, Vol. LVII, November 1950, No.281, pp.542-544.

34. Strange, Greg. *The Cairngorms – 100 Years of Mountaineering.* (SMT. 2010, p.64.)

9

Aberdonian Revolution (1949-1953)

William Dixon Brooker (1931-2011) was born in Calcutta, where his father was working as an engineer. After six pleasant years under the hot Indian sun, he returned home to Aberdeen to begin his schooling—a schooling that would continue throughout his life, including in the bothies of the Cairngorms, where ex-servicemen such as Mac Smith were respected leaders and learned professors of orology.

Entering the teaching profession, Bill Brooker would eventually be tutor-organiser in extra-mural studies at Aberdeen University. He was president of the SMC (1972-1974) and an honorary member of the Cairngorm Club. He would edit the SMCJ from 1975 to 1986. In 1990 he was diagnosed with motor neurone disease, to which he finally succumbed in 2011.

The bothy atmosphere was wittily painted by another who was a young climber at that time: Tom Patey. In a classic article in the SMCJ, Patey describes the Cairngorms climbing scene in the late 1940s and 1950s, including a New Year spent in Bob Scott's bothy at Luibeg. [1] As a Robert Gordon's College schoolboy, Patey had been sent to sleep in the stick shed, with minor snow drifts inside and a thermometer registering 40 degrees of frost (-22°C).

> Next door in the bothy, which was reserved for the hierarchy and where the heat from a blazing log fire drove one back to the farthermost corners, were two very celebrated mountaineers—Bill Brooker and Mac Smith. We soon guessed their identity by the excited buzz of conversation that signalled their return from a climb, the sudden hush as they entered the bothy, and the easy grace with which they accepted the seats of honour nearest the fire.

> The bothy armchair, which has only recently been vacated and converted into firewood, was Mac's prerogative—a rustic throne. Bill Brooker, 'the

young Lochinvar,' cut a more dashing figure, the complete counterpart to Mac's slightly reserved manner. To all outward appearances he was merely another pimply-faced schoolboy like ourselves, full of wild talk. But then who could forget that this was the same young heretic who had but recently burst into the climbing arena with a series of routes which had defied the best efforts of preceding generations? With such a wealth of mountaineering experience behind him, you could overlook the lad's extravaganzas.

Bob Scott was the keeper at Luibeg from 1947, and soon established good relations with local climbers who, depending on the pecking order, stayed in the adjoining bothy which had a good fire, or in the over-ventilated stick shed.

With trainee architect Johnny Morgan and young engineer Doug Sutherland, Brooker burst on to the climbing scene with, in 1949-50, over a dozen routes. These included *Shadow Buttress A* (300m IV,5, 1949), *Giant's Head Chimney* (220m IV,4 , 1950) and the third ascent of Eagle Ridge (free from aid) on Lochnagar.

By 1948, Alexander's 1931 guide to the Cairngorms was beginning to show its age and weaknesses. In May, two of the Tewnion brothers, Sandy and John, with Sandy Russell, returned to Coire Sputan Dearg of Ben Macdui for a look. In 1941, Sydney and Sandy Tewnion, along with Peter Marr, had attempted a line on the largest buttress, composed like its neighbours of rough, clean granite. They had failed, but were determined to return. They climbed the far left buttress, naming it Pinnacle Buttress. The climbing had been easy on clean, sound granite, which was in startling contrast to Alexander's comments that the rock was '...*not suited for climbing, being rounded and devoid of holds*'.

Word spread rapidly, and in September Bob Still and Elizabeth Lawrence climbed and named *Crystal Ridge* (120m Difficult), which became an instant, popular classic. It received its first winter ascent by Brooker and Mac Smith on 5 January 1949, at IV,4. Brooker had turned 17 the previous month, and had spent Hogmanay at Luibeg. Smith was interested in a climb, so both set out for the Sputan, finding hard snow on the ledges with occasional ice-covered rock holds. Three hours later the first winter ascent was complete.

Four days later, Lochnagar saw the winter ascent of *Black Spout Buttress* (250m III,5) by Sutherland, John Tewnion, Charlie Hutcheon and Kenny Winram. The slightly unusual grading indicates a well-protected climb with technically difficult sections, in this instance a 15ft wall with holds obscured by hard snow.

The summer of 1949 saw an astonishing amount of exploration in the Cairngorms, with over 30 rock climbs, most achieved by Aberdeen-based climbers. One of the non-Aberdonian routes was significant, however, as it was the first route on a major crag which had thus far been ignored despite its attractive appearance and its relative accessibility. Creagan a' Choire Etchachan was dismissed in Alexander's guide as having rocks which were '...*rather fragmentary*', thereby delaying its exploration by decades.

The visitors were from that wellspring of good climbers, Cambridge University Mountaineering Club. Its members Alan Parker and John Young roamed the Cairngorms at Easter 1949, putting up six new routes including a winter climb right of Crystal Ridge on the Sputan. Their most significant line was *Cambridge Route* (180m+ Severe) on the far left of Creagan a' Choire Etchachan, which thus became the last but one major Cairngorms cliff to be explored. Young later moved to Australia, and in 1955, with two others on a Melbourne University Mountaineering Club meet, he disappeared on Mount Cook in New Zealand.

Two days after their Cambridge Route, the pair returned to the Sputan and in unusual late March conditions found sufficient dry rock to climb the large buttress on the right of Crystal Ridge. This resulted in *Hanging Dyke* (120m Very Difficult); snow at its foot meant they began a little further right and joined a rock dyke further up. In June the same year the Aberdeen party of Brooker, Sutherland and Hutcheon unknowingly climbed this route, beginning more directly as the snow had gone. The buttress was later named by Mac Smith as Grey Man's Crag, after *Ferlas Mor*, the Big Grey Man of Ben Macdui. [2] On the same day they recorded *Snake Ridge* (130m Hard Severe), climbing the long ridge on the next buttress to the right.

In August that same year Brooker and Sutherland climbed the Black Spout Pinnacle by *Route* 1 (180m Severe), the last of the great Lochnagar buttresses to fall and now a V,6 winter climb. As Brooker wrote, Route 1 was not all smooth sailing. [3] The Pinnacle has a very steep, slabby face rising about 600ft, its right half being a sheer wall and the left half more broken, with the lower 200ft or so being a smooth wall of slabs culminating in a green ledge, which the climbers named the 'Springboard'. Above this were three fault-lines, the central one leading to a great overhang. Boldly, they chose this as it was the most direct.

The climbing became more and more difficult, until a vertical crack petered out on a smooth, convex slab which swept up to the great jutting overhang. Starting from Brooker's shoulder, Sutherland gained the crack, and using a piton climbed it as far as the slab. Here he decided that life was too sweet, and descended to the belay ledge. They roped down another 60ft, from where they could traverse to the left-hand fault, determined now to make up for lost time and effort.

Brooker made the traverse and climbed 60ft to a large pointed block below a 12ft wall, on which he placed a belay loop to bring up Sutherland. Standing on the tip of the block, Sutherland put his foot on its mossy back and slipped off, sending him downwards and accidentally removing the belay loop in the passing. Somehow his hands caught on the sharp edge, saving both men from a fall and certain death. Further excavation behind the block found a good belay, from where more climbing led to the crest of the pinnacle and so to the top, after just over six hours of climbing.

One peg had been used for aid on what had been a committing climb, but Brooker thought it would be unnecessary under dry conditions. The central fault with its overhang would be climbed in 1976 at HVS, as a variation to a later, harder climb. Route 1 was not only a bold ascent: it set an example for other young climbers in the North East and would lead eventually to a good number of hard rock climbs on the buttress.

The Aberdeen sea cliffs, meanwhile, were being put to good use by some of the local climbers, again including Brooker and Sutherland. At the end of May 1949, fit from their coastal exertions, in one weekend they climbed the Jim Bell triptych of Eagle Ridge, Parallel Buttress and Tough-Brown Ridge Direct on Lochnagar, the latter two being the first known second ascents, and Eagle Ridge the third (and the first not to have featured Bell). With this, Brooker had sealed his reputation.

The cliffs of Coire Sputan Dearg continued to act as a sweetie shop for local climbers, and in the summer of 1949 a further six routes were recorded here. The final route was the result of a return visit by Sandy and Sydney Tewnion, who in 1941 had attempted a line on Grey Man's Crag. Sandy was unable to climb, due to war wounds, but was happy to watch the action with Sydney's girlfriend Anne, as his brother, along with John and Ernie Smith, battled up the groove. *Pilgrim's Groove* (120m Hard Severe) would be the hardest route of 1949 in this corrie, with a grade of VS. As mentioned in Chapter 7, Sydney Tewnion would die in the 1951 Corrour tragedy along with three others, with his wife of four months Anne being the only survivor.

❈❈❈

By the end of 1949 the JMCS could boast of a membership of over 400– although, as the secretary J Stanley Stewart reported to the club's AGM, there were misgivings at the high proportion of those who appeared to be little more than nominal members. Glasgow had almost 200 members, Edinburgh 85, Perth 27, Lochaber nearly 40 and London 54, while there were hopes that the Inverness section could be revived.

Brand new, ex-War Department ice axes could be bought for 15s 9d (79p), complete with a sliding ring and sling, while ex-WD snow shoes were also available at 3s 6d (18p). The winter of 1947-48 had been severe, and most young climbers would have been wearing ex-WD trousers and jackets. Murray's SMC guide to Glencoe and Ardgour was retailing at 7s 6d (38p, roughly equivalent to £12 now).

In 1949-50, the average annual male earnings in Scotland was £352.[4] Clement Atlee was Prime Minister, George Orwell's *Nineteen Eighty-Four* was published, EDSAC, the first practical stored-program computer ran its first program at Cambridge University, and the gas industry was nationalised. More relevantly, the average central England temperature of 10.6°C for 1949 was a new record for the warmest year, to remain unequalled until 1990, and this might well have been a factor in the quality of the climbing summer.

❄❄❄

Christopher Michael Dixon (1931-2004) was a Climbers' Club member from Leeds and an internationally known photographer of antiquities. Soloing many routes on gritstone as a schoolboy in nailed boots gave him a formidably high standard, particularly in 1949, when in training for a trip to Skye he would climb between 50 and 100 routes in a day. [5] Evidently a believer in preparation, he had his eye on climbing Mallory's Slab and Groove, and with the long pitch of this in mind he purchased 130 feet of quarter-weight line (5mm diameter).

Reaching Skye in 1949 was a slow business, and Dixon and his climbing partner Neville Drasdo spent four days hitching there. The two then wasted no time in climbing Crack of Doom, the hardest route in their 1923 SMC guide. Dixon, still a schoolboy, stayed on after Drasdo left and continued to climb and walk, often solo and also completing a traverse of the Cuillin ridge with Donald Wooler. During this visit he spotted the cliffs of the Coireachan Ruadh face of Sgurr MhicChoinnich.

In 1949 Brooker had also been on Skye, and with a companion climbed a short way on these cliffs before being forced to abandon the line when a traverse under an overhang petered out. In 1950 Brooker and Dixon met fortuitously in Glen Brittle, both looking for a climbing partner. They immediately teamed up with the Coireachan Ruadh face in mind.

This north face had been virtually ignored since two 1912 ascents by the Irishmen Ernest L Julian and Edward CM O'Brien. On their first visit on 24 July 1950, Dixon and Brooker found *North-East Buttress* (120m Very Difficult), originally graded Difficult. It was a consolation route as they had arrived at the huge main buttress after 3pm, too late for an attempt at a serious climb. They soloed the buttress until a steep wall induced them to rope up and finish the climb on the summit ridge of MhicChoinnich.

Next day they left Glen Brittle at 1pm, and climbing directly up easy rocks just right of the An Stac scree made '...*another nightmare descent of Rotten Gully*' to stand under the main buttress at 3pm. They had decided to climb the same route attempted by Brooker in 1949. A small rib led to the same traverse as before, moving right under the overhang for 50ft where it gave out. Here Dixon belayed and brought Brooker up. Dixon then led on and after throwing down some loose blocks found good holds. A pull, a sidestep, a heave and a final delicate upward move saw the overhang overcome.

The main defence lay 100ft above, where the whole front of the buttress reared up in further overhangs. The buttress was split into three projecting fins by three steep cracks: these were impossible, while the two outside cracks overhung too much. The central crack had only one short overhanging section, and this they decided to attempt. Dixon wrote –

> A chill drizzle was just beginning as I attacked the overhanging section and I dangled in the crack, trying to layback up with fingers numb and slimy, my boot-nails slipping away on the smooth rock. Three times I tried, each time reaching the top of the crack, but never had the confidence nor the wherewithal to climb the final bulge into the groove. I came down, exhausted, and we realised that we must descend if we were to get off the buttress at all. [6]

Some down-climbing, a few free abseils–'...*rather too sensational for our state of mind at the time*'–and they were back at the terrace at 8.30pm, with the first 200ft of climbing having taken over five hours. They then scuttled back to Glen Brittle.

A rest day followed, followed by a spell in a rescue party and some foul weather, so it was 1 August before they returned to the fray, taking a new approach which permitted a first view of the huge wall bounding the main buttress on the south-east.

> A terrific crack curved up the wall and soared into the mist, an awe-inspiring sight. A name at once sprang to my mind—"The Crack of Dawn"—and I was filled with a desire to climb it. But Bill took one look at its repellent angle and dragged me away to the original problem.

It took them a full hour to reach the foot of the fluted overhangs, which they decided to try to break past on their extreme right edge, using a shelf seen on the previous visit but initially considered too difficult. Dixon brought up Brooker then moved out on to the wall on the right, moving delicately up and right on small shaky holds. At last he pulled over on to easier rocks. Above lay slabs, and as they had intended to follow the easiest line up the buttress, these they climbed to gain the main ridge above.

Although it was a relief to be off the buttress, which had imposed upon them a strain greater than technical difficulty alone, they now felt they had not faced the challenge of the final tower, surely a more satisfying finish. A few hours of daylight remained, so they hurried back down the slabs and looked for a line up the tower itself.

A rib of clean rock was found, and they climbed this to a ledge below the last cliffs of the tower. Rain, which had threatened all day, now began to fall, chill and drenching. They tried to the left, along the ledge, but what they saw sent them *'scuttering back to the right'*.

Bill led while I sat shivering below a dripping overhang with a far from adequate stance and belay. Bill seemed slow in moving across a slab, then disappeared into a groove on the right and halted. Eventually he made a few quick moves. Suddenly I heard his boots grinding on the rock and a huge block whizzed out of the groove, narrowly missed the rope and zoomed off into the mist below. I shouted to Bill, but he did not answer immediately. When he reached a stance he told me that the groove was greasy and holdless. Near the top he was forced to swing to the left on a large spike which he had already tested—his only positive hold. The block came away and Bill slipped, but his tricounis caught in a tiny hold and held him till he regained his holds and could continue. When I came up the pitch I was glad of a gentle hint from the rope, as the groove was treacherously greasy and my fingers were numb. I saw the scratches on the rock where Bill had slipped and the minute incut that had saved him—it seemed a miracle — from plunging out of the groove.

The two final pitches were easy after what had gone before, and took them up a delightful series of ledges and right-angled corners to the crest of the main ridge. After five hours of continuously hard climbing they had an accomplished route, *Fluted Buttress* (210m HVS 4c). As the current guide states—*'This classic route tackles the broad buttress left of North-East Gully. It is bold and gives the full mountain route experience.'*

Brooker now had to leave Skye, but Dixon spent a day on the other side of the ridge, climbing *Hourglass Crack* (150m VS 4b) with Tom Shaw. Before leaving, Dixon revisited Fluted Buttress and the North-East Buttress, finding the former as exacting as before.

Dixon and Brooker met up again in 1951 and headed up into Coireachan Ruadha on 6 August, intent on climbing North-East Gully. But a chance view of the Crack of Dawn seduced them into attempting it, and three hours later the deed was done. It seemed like an omen when, halfway up, they saw three eagles soaring over Coruisk, a rare sight even in the Cuillin.

Crack of Dawn (180m HVS) was climbed in rubbers, with Dixon stating in his route report that *'The climb is probably the hardest route in Skye at present, even among the newer routes of the past few years.'* Along with his first ascent details, Dixon included known later ascents of his climbs on this face.

The route received a second ascent on 23 August, by N Coulson and PG White, with a third ascent following on 19 September by P Vaughan and Dan Stewart, the latter being a Helensburgh man who joined the SMC in 1967. A few days later, Brooker was attracted by a gigantic clean-cut groove on the Coireachan Ruadha face, directly below the summit cairn, and he and Dixon climbed this fine route, *Forgotten Groove* (75m Very Difficult). Another attempt to climb North-East Gully was met by wet weather, but though Brooker had to leave, Dixon spent one more day in the corrie with Stewart, first tackling O'Brien and Julian's Route on Sgurr Dearg, a thoroughly enjoyable climb. They then approached the gully, scrambling up its lower section.

> At the steep part we roped up and, with Dan leading, climbed it throughout. We agreed that the climb was at least Hard Severe, instead of the Severe given in the Guide, and seriously wondered whether the gully had ever been climbed since its first ascent in 1912. I have since seen Conor O'Brien's own account of the first ascent, and saw that we followed his line exactly. He considered that the gully was probably the hardest route in Skye at the time, and I think this is true. Yet the Gully has missed the popularity it deserves...
>
> And the finish of each climb gave great delight, for we would pull up, steep rock and space below, and suddenly, surprisingly, burst out into the sun, with the view of Coire Lagan and Glenbrittle, the sea and the Western Isles poised like gems upon the haze. What cliff could give more completely the spirit of the Cuillin than this crag rising from the Coireachan Ruadha, the forgotten cliff of Sgùrr Mhic-Coinnich?

Ian McNaught-Davis and GH Francis recorded *Cioch Grooves* (150m HVS) on 21 September 1951. Close to Cioch Direct, the description mentions two pitches as being '*...long and exacting. On both a piton is used.*'

Having tasted the wine that was in this corrie, climbers were disposed to return for more, and in August 1953 Brooker returned with Patey to climb *Thunderbolt Shelf* (150m Severe) on Bealach Buttress. The climbers' grapevine would soon be humming with the rumours of routes awaiting, and Dixon returned in June 1954 to be rewarded by five days of glorious weather, using this to record five new climbs on Bealach Buttress including *Pinnacle Face* (135m Hard Severe), *Gemini* (155m VS) and *The Bow* (165m VS). These were climbed with either John E Monk or W Roger Cra'ster of the Climbers' Club.

❃❃❃

The expansion of post-war exploratory climbing in Scotland was not just confined to Skye. The Northern Highlands were being investigated after– in some areas–a long period of neglect. Frank F Cunningham, latterly a professor of geography and author of a substantial book on the glaciologist James David Forbes, had joined the SMC in 1947. Cunningham taught at Inverness Royal Academy, which conveniently allowed exploration of the northern hills, and he wrote a review of rock climbing in that area which appeared in SMCJ for April 1951. [7] Had Cunningham stayed in Scotland, he would have been a shoo-in as the editor of a Northern Highlands climbing guide, but he went off to Canada in 1965 and was still publishing articles on glaciology in the 1990s.

Cunningham's review paper worked through what was known about the various areas in the north, with the comment that there were evidently no new routes made in the whole of the 1920s. (He was not aware of Alf Pigott and Morley Wood, who climbed a Severe on the Central Buttress of Beinn Eighe in 1922. In mitigation, however, Pigott did not report his climb to the SMC.) The overall picture, Cunningham continued,

'...is a neglect of splendid opportunities, largely due to misapprehension. For this north-western area probably includes more rock than any comparable extent of Britain, *and much of it is far better than is frequently given out.*'

Cunningham's stated intent was to add more recent climbs to the 1936 SMC edition of the *Northern Highlands Guide,* the second edition of the district guide, by Willie Ling and John Rooke Corbett. In the Applecross group, Cunningham could include several climbs, for instance the A' Poite spur of Beinn Bhan, with two steep arêtes first climbed by A Parker in July 1949, and the North Buttress of A' Chioch, climbed in July 1950 by S Paterson and Donald Bennet at Mild Severe.

Later that year, Bennet broke a leg while on Rum with the Edinburgh University Mountaineering Club. A highly competent and efficient mountaineer (if not, at least on the surface, imbued with the warmest of natures), he joined the SMC in 1955 and served as president 1986-1988. Deeply involved in various conservation bodies, including the Scottish Rights of Way Society (now ScotWays), Bennet received an OBE in 2001. He was also an energetic author, with several of the SMC District Guides to his credit. He suffered a serious and incapacitating stroke in the summer of 2001, and never recovered.

In the Achnashellach area, Cunningham's cadre from the Inverness Royal Academy climbing group found a Very Difficult in June 1948 in the form of Academy Ridge on Sgorr Ruadh. The Torridon hills were popular destinations for any climber who saw them, either on the ground or in photographs. Liathach had several routes, though it is not a mountain particularly suited to rock climbing due to its vegetated nature. In winter, however, it provides one of the best arenas in Scotland, especially in its northern corries. Pigott continued to spread his usual confusion with a possible Difficult on the most easterly peak, while Jim and Pat Bell climbed *Bell's Buttress* (150m Severe) on 30 June 1947, thus opening up this cliff in Coire na Caime for later winter routes.

The queen of mountains in Torridon is Beinn Eighe, with most of the climbing being found in Coire Mhic Fhearchair on the Triple Buttresses. Cunningham's review included a fine sketch of this corrie, indicating some of the known routes and variations. He referred to the East Buttress, where the sandstone lower tier *'has almost been variationed out of existence'.* His final comment on the buttresses is that they *'literally reek with unaccepted opportunities for magnificent climbs, whether judged by length, difficulty or scenery'.* He was prescient in noting that the area of cliff east of East Buttress (now known as the Eastern Ramparts) is exceedingly steep and would repay further investigation.

The routes recorded by Cunningham were mostly at easy grades and not especially outstanding; as one example he and his brother found *Zigzag Gully* (45m Difficult) on Beinn a' Mhuinidh, near Kinlochewe, but his article must have been a source of interest to exploratory climbers, mentioning as it did areas of untouched rock with potential. Perhaps the best example of this is Beinn Lair which was still, as he wrote, *terra incognita.* In the same year his review was published, 1951, three separate parties visited Beinn Lair in June and in August and enjoyed productive climbing.

The climbers in early June were Glasgow University MC members. They explored the Fionn cliffs, at the north-west end of Beinn Lair. This long face has a north-north-west to north-east outlook, with the greatest escarpment of hornblende schist in the country. The rock has a faintly greenish colour, with sharp holds. Although greasy when wet, with protection difficult to arrange, it has interesting climbs in the lower grades.

This first party named buttresses Molar, Angel and Wisdom (perhaps one of the climbers was a dental student). The party comprised Angela Hood, J Stewart Orr (also JMCS), DC Hutchinson, BS Smith and J Smith. Orr was the son of SMC member John Neil Orr (1887-1953), and although he did not follow his father into the club, he was responsible for communicating route descriptions. The second party, in mid-August, was the pairing of Frank Adams and Edward (Ted) Addison Wrangham (1922-2010), both CUMC members. They were unaware of the earlier climbers, so some duplication of routes was inevitable.

As editor of the SMCJ, Bell had to sort out the ensuing confusion. Obviously the first climbers on the scene who named the features had priority with nomenclature. As Bell wrote: *'This procedure, the only possible one, must, of course, tend to belittle the achievements of the later party.'* As a matter of historical curiosity, the CUMC party named the three buttresses 'Pear', 'Overhang' and 'Cigar'.

Sorting out the actual routes was more difficult, and Orr could not differentiate between most of them, as one would expect, given natural lines on the buttresses which the separate parties would tend to follow. But the GUMC party certainly, and deservedly, climbed the best routes, with *Wisdom Buttress* (220m Severe) being the outstanding one (climbed by Smith, Hood and Orr). Exposed, sustained and low in its grade, this is the most popular route. Orr's party inserted a piton for protection, where one pitch demanded a long runout. For a later account of climbing Wisdom Buttress, see the *footless crow* blog for 7 July 2012. [8]

Two other parties were on the Beinn Lair cliffs in July 1951. Slesser, Geoff Dutton and J Wight climbed a Very Difficult further right of the above routes, while *Marathon Ridge* (400m Difficult) was climbed near the centre of the cliffs by Brooker, S McPherson, Johnny W Morgan and Stewart.

Also on the central area of Beinn Lair, JD Foster and D Leaver climbed several worthwhile routes, including *Falstaff* (120m VS), *Sesame Buttress* (140m Severe) and *Rainbow Wall* (105m Severe). Wrangham may have been disappointed in being beaten to the classic routes on the left, but he evidently like the cliffs so much that he was back in March 1952 and 1953, climbing two Difficults and a Very Difficult.

Wrangham added another route on 24 March 1952, one which opened the door to one of Britain's finest crags, when with Arthur Clegg he climbed *Diagonal Route* (250m Severe) on Càrnmore Crag, with its superb, steep, southward-facing gneiss. It was to be, as the current guide states, the start of a long association between Càrnmore and Cambridge University, with the major line of Càrnmore Corner as the lure.

❀❀❀

The superb south wall of Garbh Bheinn in Ardgour was eventually breached on 13 April 1952 by Donald Norman Mill (1931-1981) and Daniel (Dan) Stewart, who recorded three routes including *Scimitar* (105m VS). Mill, from Edinburgh, was killed in 1981 when attempting to cross the Allt Coire na Ciche above Loch Nevis. Like many a Highland burn, innocent-looking when low, this can be a killer when in spate. Mill's friend Stewart was a climbing instructor for the RAF Mountain Rescue teams.

It was not long before Jimmy Marshall was attracted to the hill, with three routes in 1956: *Razor Slash* (75m Severe) was climbed with Lovat and Hendry, and the superb *Butterknife* (105m VS) with Hendry, Ritchie and Iain D Haig. Upping the grades again, Marshall led *The Clasp* (60m E1) in April 1960, with no second recorded, a bold lead on the faultless wall on the upper tier. Robin Smith recorded his very first new route on Pinnacle Ridge here, in 1957 with *Blockhead* (60m E1) and returned in June 1961 with Moriarty to climb *The Peeler* (45m HVS) at the left end of the upper tier.

❀❀❀

As mentioned earlier, Brooker was not the only new climbing star to emerge from Aberdeen in the late 1940s and early 1950s. Thomas Walton Patey (1932-1970) was a son of the manse born in Ellon, Aberdeenshire, and became one of the group of schoolboys from Robert Gordon's College known locally as the *Horrible Heelanders*, due to the kilt worn by some of them. He went to Aberdeen University in 1949, by which time he had been learning to climb—in what must have been an accelerated course, as his first major climb, and a new route at that, was the winter ascent of the much-attempted *Douglas-Gibson Gully* (200m V,4) on Lochnagar, on 28 December 1950, with Gordon (Goggs) B Leslie. Both were second-year medical students.

Several days after another party from Aberdeen had just failed to climb the gully in poor conditions, Patey and Leslie cut steps in good time to reach the upper wall. Conditions were much improved, with firm snow-ice allowing the cutting of good steps for hand- and foot-holds. A runout of 90ft saw the pair in a rocky cave out of which sprang a chimney. They failed to climb this and moved left, climbing to the foot of a 15ft wall of vertical snow. Above was the cornice, with a snow cave below. The vertical wall was one of the most difficult sections of the day, and at one point Patey emulated the great Harold Raeburn during his first ascent of Green Gully on Ben Nevis by standing on an ice axe driven horizontally into the snow.

Patey brought up Leslie, who belayed at the back of the snow cave. Above them, the huge cornice overhung by some 25 feet. They were now committed, with no safe way to retreat. After much hard work, with an ice axe used as an inefficient shovel, the leader tunnelled through the cornice and safety was gained with a dramatic release on to the plateau. The final 200ft of the gully had taken the climbers over six hours, with continuously difficult and exposed climbing. At the finish they were shaken but triumphant, and were now 'made men'.

In *Cairngorm Commentary*, Tom Patey made an honest confession–

> It was also our first *première* and earned grudging recognition from our more talented contemporaries together with admission into the select conclave that gathered in the Fife Arms, Braemar, on a Saturday night. We did not broadcast the principal factor in our surprise *coup*—that having climbed well beyond the point where we could have safely withdrawn and finding no belays for an abseil we had little option but to continue climbing. In the long run we both profited from this good fortune, and learned several important lessons. I cannot recall ever again suffering such agonies of apprehension on a climb.

Douglas-Gibson Gully is widely recognised as having been the first Grade V winter route in Scotland, and as Patey wrote '*...thereby ushering in a new era of winter expeditions on routes which had hitherto been regarded as solely within the provinces of the rock specialist*'. Indeed, in the current guide, the route description states: '*When free from winter's grip, the gully is a death trap. The upper wall is totally rotten, wet and ungradeable.*' This death trap was, as will be recalled, first climbed in September 1933 by Charlie Ludwig, solo, wearing gym shoes.

Patey and Leslie were members of Aberdeen University's Lairig Club, then entering the height of its influence. Patey was wittily scathing on some of the Aberdeen clubs' reputations at this time. The Etchachan Club

was a splinter from the Cairngorm Club, the latter seeming to be somewhat moribund, most of its members being hill walkers and with very few
rock climbers in evidence.

> Even the club circular had an archaic quality, describing club meets as
> 'motor coach excursions' and ending with the solemn injunction 'Members
> are requested not to ring the Meets Secretary at his residence.' We later
> found that the wording of the circular could be adapted with only minor
> alterations to a West Indian Calypso tune, and the song enjoyed a fair
> measure of popularity among the nonconformists.

It was not until 1954 that a new SMC guide to the Cairngorms was
planned, with the strong triumvirate of Mac Smith, Mike Taylor and Patey
as editors. Others in the Etchachan Club assisted, but in the main it would
be Smith who after six hard years of work produced Volume 1 in 1961,
covering the Northern District. Reviews included one from the Yorkshire
Ramblers Club by a JGB, who remarked on the useful change from the
older, larger guides, to the new, smaller climbers' versions –

> …since the last large guide to the Cairngorms was published in 1950, two
> hundred new rock routes have been discovered and in fact there are now
> more than 400 major rock courses recorded.

> This rather disposes of the accepted notion (in England at any rate) of the
> Cairngorms as essentially walking country in summer and skiing ground in
> winter. It also clears away the unsound rock illusion by pointing out that,
> apart from some of the gullies, the rock on buttresses, walls and ridges is
> of sound honest granite. Furthermore the rock climber can still find in the
> Cairngorms some measure of isolation and will not have to queue up to start
> a climb as in some other rock-climbing areas.

> Snow and ice climbing is also covered but the Editor, Malcolm Smith,
> wisely recognises that snow and ice climbs, unlike rock, cannot be accu-
> rately graded owing to changing conditions. Tricounis are recommended in
> preference to crampons. [9]

The reference to tricounis was telling, as outwith the Cairngorms many,
if not most, climbers had by the mid to late 1950s switched to wearing
crampons for winter climbs. Earlier models of crampons were helpful if
walking on glaciers and easy snow slopes, but not dramatically useful for
climbs, where nailed boots could be placed on even small rock holds and
holds cut on hard snow or ice. As with other innovations in climbing technology, the spread of new ideas and equipment moved slowly from west to
east in Scotland, aided by increasing forays by some of the leading climbers
from outside Aberdeenshire.

In his history of Cairngorms mountaineering, Greg Strange in the chapter on the early 1960s writes–

> Although some Scottish climbers were now using crampons, most Aberdonians still wore nailed boots for winter climbing, often walking up to the bothy in vibrams then donning their nailed boots for the day's climbing–adding considerably to the weight of the winter weekend sack. [10]

This disinclination to pick up on recent trends can only in part be put down to a natural conservatism by those in the North East. Until good, clean rock began to be climbed on the granite hills in that area, nailed boots were probably safer, in summer biting through slimy moss and vegetation to find any holds underneath, while in winter a good climber could work wonders even on ice. It was seen earlier that Bill Murray had little use for crampons in the 1930s, but this was due to the fact that for the climbing Murray was doing, current models of crampon, with ten points, were not of much use.

There is confirmation in a 1953 review by Brooker, where he puts forward the idea that the Cairngorms saw a slow development of difficult mountaineering because most summits in the region consisted of bleak, level plateaux, with no sharp peaks of narrow ridges such as attract mountaineers from the west. [11] Discussing the rocks of the Cairngorms, Brooker admitted that lichen prevailed, becoming rather slippery when wet–this was why Vibrams were not much used. Most pitches, he continued, were more difficult than they first appeared, and route finding was often difficult due to the rock structure. In winter, hazards included long approaches in deep snow, blizzards, and low temperatures not normally found elsewhere in the country.

In Europe of the 1930s, the top climbers were in a seemingly different world. This is perhaps most dramatically illustrated in the 1959 classic book by Heinrich Harrer, *The White Spider*, when he records that on the first ascent of the North Face of the Eiger in July 1938 the German pair Anderl Heckmair and Ludwig Vörg, using 12-point crampons, swiftly overtook Harrer and Fritz Kasparek of Austria, who were flat-footing it in hobnailed boots and ten-point crampons respectively. The four teamed up for the rest of the ascent. As Harrer wrote: '*I looked back, down our endless ladder of steps. Up it, I saw the New Era coming at express speed; there were two men running — I mean running, not climbing — up*'. This was on the Nordwand's second icefield.

The change from ten-point to 12-point crampons was a seminal shift in design, and had occurred in 1929 when Laurent Grivel, son of the Grivel company founder Henry, added two inclined front points, thus enabling climbers to tackle steep ice. Henry Grivel had been the local blacksmith in Courmayeur, Italy, when the English climber Oscar Johannes Ludwig

Eckenstein (1859-1921), a talented engineer and mountaineer, designed a better crampon around 1908 and took it to Grivel for production. Apparently it was an immediate hit with local guides and porters, though Grivel could not patent the design as mice had eaten the original drawings. [12]

❀❀❀

More good climbs were appearing in the early 1950s, particularly on Lochnagar, which saw much development. On New Year's Day 1952, *Gargoyle Chimney* (120m IV,4) was climbed by Brooker and Taylor in six hours. In the years before front-pointing, where steps were cut with an ice axe, ascent times were often quoted for first ascents as they were an indication of difficulty. This was of even more importance as there was as yet no grading system in place for winter routes. Brooker and Taylor found perfect conditions, with the chimney pitch full of ice, and on the same day Patey and Donald Aitken succeeded in the first winter ascent of *Tough-Brown Traverse* (300m IV,3), climbing it in five hours. This grand mountaineering route may not be technically difficult, but care is needed with route finding and the climbers required combined tactics to escape from the Great Terrace.

The last unclimbed gully on Lochnagar now received the undivided attention of North East climbers. Parallel Gully B is divided by the traverse line of Tough-Brown, with a 250ft chimney cutting steeply through slabs in the lower section and a more open section above. At the end of May 1952, Ian Brooker and Sandy Lyall failed to climb the lower section, then attacked the upper section, approaching via Tough-Brown. They succeeded after some time, finding particular difficulty at a holdless crack at VS standard, thereby causing even more attention to be focused on the lower section.

Two weeks later, on 8 June, a beautiful summer day, a Lairig Club meet saw eight climbers swarm up to the foot of the gully. The pair in front of the charge were Patey and Taylor, in tricounis, and they soon climbed the lower section. Patey was very competitive, and while the others were discussing who should start, he quickly slipped into the lead along with Taylor (probably to the relief of most of the remainder). Patey supplied details in an SMCJ article, and *Parallel Gully B* (260m VS) was climbed in a friendly if competitive atmosphere, with much banter and even a cine camera wielded by John Henderson.

Gathering on the scoop above the lower section, four climbers decided to finish via the traverse, leaving Patey, Taylor, Bill Brooker and Dixon determined to climb the entire route by continuing with the upper section. Spotting a piton left by Ian Brooker and Lyall from two weeks earlier, they firmed up their resolve and completed the climb, avoiding a final, easy stretch up a loose and wet pitch by moving on to the rocks of the Tough-Brown Traverse, finishing up this unroped in a familiar Lochnagar drizzle.

For some reason, although four of the climbers had not done the entire route, their names are included in the first ascent record: Aitken, Henderson, Mike Philip and Charlie Morrison. In October, Patey, Bill Brooker and Taylor returned to Lochnagar and climbed *The Stack* (150m Hard Severe), the steep, squat buttress in the angle between the branches of the Black Spout. This climb rapidly gained in popularity, with good pitches on relatively clean rock.

As Strange remarks, the winter of 1952-53 was to be seen as one of the most significant, with ice starting to form in early November. The pace of exploration had increased to the extent that some summer routes were receiving winter ascents within a year or so, and occasionally in the winter following the summer ascent. Such a climb was *Shadow Chimney* (225m IV,5) on Lochnagar, a *'good old-fashioned struggle'* as the guidebook has it, with more than a passing nod to the first winter ascent on 22 November 1952 by Freddy Malcolm and Dave Ritchie which took seven hours including a fall from the upper chimney by Malcolm. He was saved by having threaded the rope behind a chockstone for a runner.

A chockstone–or chokestone, as it tends to be known in the North East–is a pebble, stone or rock wedged in a crack. In the early years of climbing these were sometimes placed deliberately by a climber, with the rope threaded behind so that in the event of a fall it could act as a running belay. Probably first used in such a way by leading climbers in Wales and the Lakes, the technique would eventually lead to manufactured chockstones, referred to as *nuts*.

While this method of using a running belay often worked adequately, assuming the climber checked that the rope was running without jamming in a crack or other constriction, there were serious safety issues connected to its use. One fatal accident occurred in the summer of 1953, when the young Aberdonian climber Bill Stewart fell from the upper section of Parallel Gully B on Lochnagar. His fall from a difficult traverse was short, but he had run the rope behind a rock spike which cut through the rope. With the use of a rope sling and karabiner, both of which were by now available, this situation could usually be averted. Stewart's death strongly affected his contemporaries.

Another climb which rapidly received a winter ascent was The Stack, just 53 days after its summer ascent. On 29 November 1952, Mike Taylor, Goggs Leslie and Leslie Fallowfield entered the Lochnagar corrie. It was too early for much ice to have formed in the gullies, so a buttress route was preferred–and with a crown of golden sunlight playing on The Stack, that route was chosen. It gave the climbers a hard ascent, mostly on snow with some verglas-coated rocks, a thin glaze of ice which can cause many problems as it obscures small holds. The three climbers started up the route at midday, with combined tactics needed at one point. Evening had arrived by the time they reached the upper crux, but luckily the full moon was only two days away.

At this crux, a chimney had to be left, stepping out on to a sloping ledge, now with its rock holds buried in ice. Taylor, as the only one of the party who had been on the summer ascent, was leading, and had to use a piton here. Lower down the route, Taylor had used an ice axe shaft in a crack as a hold, presaging a future technique on hard winter moves. (See *The Early Years*, p.195 for another early reference to this technique.)

The climbers were well satisfied with their ascent of *The Stack* (150m V,6). The use of tricounis had been justified in their eyes, with these boot nails finding small holds even if buried under snow or thin ice. Technically the route was ahead of its time (possibly the first to have a technical grade of 6), and must have given a boost in confidence at such an early stage of the winter. There was more to come.

The following month, Taylor and Patey were joined at Derry Lodge by Graeme Nicol and Ken Grassick, another pair who would figure large in the Cairngorms climbing landscape. They were from the same ex-grammar school group which had by now morphed into the Corrour Club (also known as the Boor Boys). As Patey wrote in an article later reproduced in his autobiographical book–

> I had done a route with them the previous week-end, and by dint of climbing well beyond my limits of safety and using more than a little "climbsmanship", had managed to earn their temporary respect. Whether we could maintain this relationship was less certain. [13]

Their target was the 700ft face of Càrn Etchachan, above the Shelter Stone and, according to Patey, dismissed by Mac Smith (probably, Patey suggested, because he was waiting for an opportunity to return himself and bag some good routes). Snow and ice continued to be plentiful and the weather was frosty, with crisp snow underfoot. When they gained the view of the crag after a four-hour approach, they saw a multitude of cracks and chimneys, all in fine condition. There were, they estimated, about 20 lines waiting to be climbed.

This pointed crag has two distinct faces: the Main Face, looking north over Loch Avon, and the Gully Face, soaring over Castlegates Gully, the huge fault between Càrn Etchachan and the Shelter Stone Crag. The chosen line began near the boundary between the faces and finished up a huge, square-shaped fault. The climbing was initially complicated by competition within the party, but order was restored to a degree when Patey reached a deep crack diving straight into the mountain, up which he squirmed like a Victorian chimney sweep.

After three hours' climbing they were not quite halfway up the face, with progress more difficult than their initial estimate. Patey, disorganised in all things personal, had forgotten his gloves. He suffered from Raynaud's Disease, a condition in which cold or emotional distress cause the blood vessels in fingers or toes to contract, impeding bloodflow and becoming visible when affected digits turn white. He confessed to being quite proud of this, and found it useful for avoiding disagreeable pitches. Above the deep crack he climbed a slightly overhanging wall, taking an hour for the first 30ft. It had good holds but these were hidden under snow and ice.

Eventually the climbing eased off slightly, and they came to a stretch of broken ground below the final obstacle, a 250ft vertical rampart, clearly not climbable on the day. To the right, a steep, rocky gully curved round an edge and out of sight. '*There is the route,*' Patey assured his friends–but no, two tiers of overhanging rocks, coated with verglas, blocked the gully. It would have to be the overhangs.

Patey had by now accepted Nicol's offer of his gloves, which suited Nicol anyway, as he had a somewhat Teutonic outlook in life and was, for example, quite indifferent towards an involuntary bivouac. A 'hard man', he would later join the SAS. Somehow Patey struggled up the pitch, with additional adhesion from the gloves on the verglas. A desperate swing out right on a finger-hold was the key to a frozen turf hold and the stance was reached. A fixed rope on this traverse allowed the rest to follow–Grassick fell off at the top but luckily landed in deep snow.

The leading pair continued edging along a tiny ledge, until 50ft further on the moonlight revealed an easy snow slope leading to the top. Below, Taylor was leading up the groove, his headtorch showing the way while he sang the old Scots tune '*The Four Marys*'. This lament, as Patey remarked, had been taught to generations of primary school children and seemed to gain additional pathos from the melancholy surroundings. After the second pair accepted a rope for the last section, all four were reunited at the top, seven hours from the start and with strengthened bonds.

Sometime after their ascent, Patey suggested it be called Scorpion, after its '*sting in the tail*'; he also fancied that from a photograph of the crag he could see the outline of a scorpion, the upper gully being the tail. *Scorpion* (240m V,5) is now a popular classic line, the first on this face.

On 24 January 1953, following a thaw which stripped away all the unstable snow before a period of cold, calm weather settled in, Grassick and Hamish SM Bates made the first winter ascent of *Polyphemus Gully* (200m V,5) on Lochnagar–described in the current guide as the finest gully climb on the mountain. In good conditions, such as experienced by Grassick and Bates, it is not hard for its grade, with good rock belays. There may be a cornice problem, but even this can often be circumvented. Six hours of enjoyable climbing saw the two on the summit.

As with most winter gullies, difficulties can vary; in the 2011 winter Polyphemus received close to 20 ascents, with many climbers stating that they found it an easy Grade IV. Its name is from Greek mythology, after the giant with one central eye who was encountered in his cave by Odysseus. The gully has a cave, high up the route, so perhaps this suggested its name.[14]

The following day, the iron triumvirate of Patey, Taylor and Brooker climbed *Eagle Ridge* (VI,6). Conditions were perfect: snow-ice on the slabs and ledges, ice in the chimneys and grooves. Combined tactics were used on the tower and summer crux, with brittle ice in the groove above the old piton at the tower proving the most difficult section. At this time, it was one of the hardest winter climbs in Scotland.

The Aberdonians were certainly enjoying a fantastic spell of weather and winter conditions, but they would not have it all their own way. In February, the Edinburgh JMCS held a meet in Glen Clova, where a sketch of Corrie Fee in the Cairngorms district guide indicated four gullies on the main face, with A, B and D appearing straightforward, but C apparently unclimbed. This was pointed out by Charles Logan Donaldson (193?-2002), who was the Edinburgh JMCS secretary in 1949, joining the SMC in 1950. He was in the Civil Service, dispensing–or dispensing with–benefits. [15]

Donaldson suggested that another JMCS member, James (Jimmy) R Marshall (1929-), who was to join the SMC in 1955, should have a look at the route, so on 15 February 1953, Donaldson and the 24 year-old Marshall stuck their noses into Gully C. By now warmer weather had begun to strip ice off the hills, but the prominent groove was filled with white ice. Water was singing its way down behind the ice, but when struck with an axe it proved to be firm, at least until it collapsed and the pair climbed the rocks on the right. Higher up, Marshall led an ice curtain by an upward traverse. *Look C Gully* (200m IV,4) became the classic ice route of Glen Clova, readily accessible to those living in Edinburgh and Dundee. Marshall would go on to record many other classic routes, and we will see more of him.

There was one more great winter ascent to be snatched in the Cairngorms before the end of this superb season, when on 12 April Bill Brooker and Patey climbed *Mitre Ridge* (220m V,6) in Beinn a' Bhùird's Garbh Choire, described in the guide as one of the finest winter expeditions in the area. Brooker was to write an article reminiscing about this in the 2001 SMCJ. [16]

Easter Sunday in 1953 fell on 5 April, too early for ambitious rock plans on Ben Nevis; this however did not deter Patey, Brooker and Taylor, who were in the CIC Hut at the end of March, hoping for the big line on Càrn Dearg Buttress–the prominent chimney now known as Sassenach. With poor weather they moved north, finding a good buttress route on No.1

Buttress of Sgurr a' Chaorachain in Applecross on 28 March with *Jupiter* (300m Severe).

With increasingly poor weather the students retreated to the Cairngorms, where there were snowstorms. By 12th April better weather and good snow conditions arrived, and with more daylight and the start of the university term looming they decided to try a winter ascent of Mitre Ridge, the classic summer Hard Severe. Taylor was unable to go, so it was Brooker and Patey who set out.

Conditions were excellent, cold with little wind, abundant snow on every ledge and recess, steep rock faces showing bare granite. Patey had climbed the route in summer a couple of years earlier, and on recalling the initial groove they moved right and took to the easier alternative start. The first two pitches went well, then it was Patey's turn, with the third pitch involving a traverse right above the head of an open chimney, choked with snow. The crucial hold was a rounded ear of rock, about the size of a large plate. Brooker described what happened:

> I watched from about 10ft. away as Tom reached out, tested it carefully and swung on it. There was a crack as it snapped off and I braced the rope round my waist as he fell downward. I crouched awaiting the shock but it came merely as a gentle tug. He had plunged into the soft snow packing the little gully beneath and had only fallen about 15ft. Remarkably, he still had his ice axe.

Brooker used the word *'remarkably'* as Patey did not use his axe with a sling, unlike Brooker who had a sliding wrist attachment. Both men had by now followed the leading climbers in the west in having their axes shortened. This was not yet a universal practice, and a photograph of Taylor on the ascent of North-West Gully on Creag an Dubh Loch in December 1952 indicates a longer axe in use, forcing him to cut steps with both hands. [17] The picks remained straight, and of little use for anything other than cutting ice, clearing cracks or breaking into sardine cans. Using a sling meant that should the axe be dropped it would not go far, but changing hands for cutting steps was a nuisance. The author, reading about Jimmy Marshall's slingless habit, followed suit, though this was a method which required confidence and was certainly not one recommended for the accident-prone.

Brooker commented that in the early 1950s leader falls were very rare, but usually had serious consequences. He could easily have extended this observation back to the beginnings of roped climbing. Patey was unhurt but somewhat shaken, and passed the lead to his colleague. The next problem soon confronted Brooker: a deep-cut, narrow chimney 40ft high and smothered with snow. Underlying the snow was ice, and with the chimney out of sight of the belay Brooker began to feel isolated and lonely as he failed to make upward movement. Clearing snow on the right revealed holds and he was finally able to move up to the next stance.

Above a short vertical wall they could see the three towers on the crest. An awkward right traverse was attempted, but disliking this they decided to try another way:

> In Aberdeen we were still very traditional, even old fashioned, in our rock climbing style and were quite ready to use combined tactics in the manner of distinguished predecessors like Raeburn and Ling. Like them we still climbed in nailed boots which made this technique reasonably acceptable to the winter climber being trodden underfoot, even though the tricounis we used were harsher than the clinkers of yesteryear.

To ensure their safety, Brooker banged in a piton as a main belay and called Patey to climb over him and so gain the ledge above:

> I braced myself and he stepped from knee to shoulder to the nape of my neck and with his scrabbling boot getting a final steady from my up stretched hand he was up the short wall. Another 60ft. or so of still steep but easier climbing led to a ledge at the foot of an inset vertical corner where he planted another piton belay.

The first tower was now above, and Brooker found gaining the wide ledge below it the hardest lead of the climb. He traversed a slab leftwards to reach a shallow chimney, at least 20ft high and very steep, but by clearing away snow and ice he found small rocky flakes and pockets of frozen turf which allowed progress.

> It [...] demanded concentration to the point where the entire outside world was shut off from my consciousness. There was only me, this steep iced rock, the need for precise and careful placing of tricouni nail edges whenever a move was made, and the dry throat which I always developed in such situations. Gradually, I rose to the top and in one final move I was on the big ledge, feeling jubilant about our prospects.

When they had climbed to above the first tower it was now after 4pm, but the day had brightened and it looked as if they had time enough. Ahead was the second tower, with three ways of climbing it–but they did not like the look of any of these and found another way, making an exhilarating traverse across a plastered slab until corners led to the crest of the tower. As Brooker called on Patey to climb, the day was fine, the sun was shining on the upper flank of Ben Avon above the outer Garbh Choire and the climb was in the bag.

Mitre Ridge in winter would not be climbed direct and free until 1984, by J Anderson and Andy Nisbet. Brooker and Patey's access had been eased by use of Brooker's motorbike (a BSA Sloper) on the estate road, reducing the 14-mile walk-in to just eight.

The early 1950s had seen the emergence of Cairngorms mountaineering as a distinct and serious entity. The number of young climbers living in and around Aberdeen who formed coherent and supportive groups was one factor. Their energy and spirit was another. The grades of climbs being recorded rose significantly, and particularly in winter matched anything being done in the west–and this with virtually no influence from outwith the area. Their equipment and climbing style matched the rocks in summer and the mountains in winter. Similar advances were happening elsewhere at this time, and for these a move back westwards must be made.

References

1 Patey, Tom. *Cairngorm Commentary*. SMCJ 27,153, May 1962. pp.207-220.
2 Gray, Affleck. *The Big Grey Man of Ben Macdhui*. (Edinburgh. 1994. Birlinn Books.)
3 Brooker, William D. *The Black Spout Pinnacle*. SMCJ 24, 141, April 1950. pp.202-205.
4 Cairncross, Alec. *The Scottish Economy: A Statistical Account of Scottish Life by Members of the Staff of Glasgow University*. (Cambridge University Press. 1954. p.152.)
5 Drasdo, Neville. *Christopher Michael Dixon (1931-2004) Member 1955-2004*. Obituary In: CCJ, 2008-10, pp.132-133.
6 Dixon, C.M. *The Forgotten Corrie*. SMCJ 25, 143, 1952. pp.2-13.
7 Cunningham, Frank. *Rock Climbing in the Northern Highlands. A Review*. SMCJ 24, 142, April 1951, pp.295-308.
8 Gifford, Terry. *Wisdom* Buttress. <goo.gl/rzub6H>
9 J.G.B. *Review of Climbers' Guide to the Cairngorms Area*. In: YRCJ, Vol.9, No.31, 1962.
10 Strange, Greg. *The Cairngorms–100 Years of Mountaineering*. (2010, SMT.) p.134.
11 Brooker, William D. *Winter Climbing on Lochnagar and the Cairngorms*. SMCJ 25, 14, April 1953, pp.101-114.
12 <http://www.grivel.com/company/product_history> (click on *Read More*. Accessed July 2016.)
13 Patey, Tom. *One Man's Mountains*. (London: 1971. Victor Gollancz. pp.22-27.
14 Richardson, Simon. *New Look Parallel B*. <goo.gl/o85HIa>
15 G.J.F.D. [Geoff Dutton]. *Charles Logan Donaldson j.1950*. In Memorium. SMCJ 38, 193, 2002. pp.258-259.
16 Brooker, Bill. *Mitre Ridge in Winter*. SMCJ 37, 192, pp.555-559.
17 Ibid. 10. p.93.

10

Splinter Groups (1953-1956)

IN THE GLEN COE AREA, as in the Cairngorms and on Deeside, the early 1950s saw a marked rise in activity. The Creagh Dhu was prominent here, while the Rannoch Wall on Buachaille Etive Mòr and the east face of Aonach Dubh saw much of the action.

Dr Hamish MacInnes, OBE, BEM looms large in the Scottish mountaineering pantheon. Born in 1930 in Gatehouse of Fleet, his father was from Fort William and his mother from Skye. After World War II the family moved to Greenock, from where he was taught to climb by a neighbour, Bill Hargreaves. This was on the Cobbler, and in beginning his climbing here MacInnes followed in the footsteps of many others from the west of Scotland. He must have possessed an innate practical nature, as he built a car when he was aged 16, the finished product being fully MOT'd and licensed. [1]

National Service in the army was in Austria, where climbing continued, and it was there that his early love of pitons began. More importantly, MacInnes climbed with the Munich set (including two ex-SS members), picking up their advanced use of equipment such as 12-point crampons which allowed front-pointing and speedier ascents. This was some years before climbers used them in the UK.

Back home, he would found the Greenock Climbing Club and eventually meet and climb with members of the Creagh Dhu–although that club would be quick to point out that he was never a member. MacInnes is similarly quick to confirm this, being averse to having any sort of definition placed upon him. He is certainly a man who has always ploughed his own furrow. The Creagh Dhu did polish his climbing, however.

He moved to Glen Coe–where he lives still–in 1959. There he created the Glencoe Mountain Rescue Team in 1961, leading it until retirement 30 years later. He set up the Search and Rescue Dog Association (SARDA) in 1965, and with Eric Langmuir the Scottish Avalanche Information Service (SAIS) was established in 1993. He has written numerous books, including two on his mountain rescue experiences while based in Glen Coe, and also a standard mountain rescue handbook. [2,3] He started the Glencoe School of Mountaineering, employing some of the best climbers in Scotland, with Ian Clough as a partner. A long list of first ascents would be made by pupils and teachers from the school.

If that were not enough for one man, his mechanical bent was employed to great use with various mountain-associated inventions. These include the MacInnes stretcher, now using recently developed, lightweight composite materials and including folding versions. Models are widely used in many rescue situations worldwide. His metal ice axe designs will be discussed later, while his two-man expedition to the Himalayas, with John Cunningham and financed with £40 of capital, is embedded in Scottish mountaineering legend. The two set off in 1953, planning for Everest and using equipment and food left by a Swiss expedition. Perhaps fortunately, they were beaten to the first ascent by the team led by John Hunt.

In May 1952, with Bill Smith of the Creagh Dhu, MacInnes climbed *Shattered Wall* (55m Severe) on the Rannoch Wall. In July 1953, the pair upped the difficulty with the bold *Wappenshaw Wall* (70m VS), originally described as a Hard Severe. (A *wappenshaw*–from the Old Norse *vápn* meaning weapon and *schaw* meaning show–was a muster of men in a particular area of Scotland, as a demonstration that they were properly armed.) The same month saw *Peasant's Passage* (70m HVS), climbed in rubbers with Willie Rowney of the Creagh Dhu. '*An interesting and improbable line on good rock with impressive situations*', as the guide has it.

Other routes were recorded in Glen Coe during the early 1950s, with the Creagh Dhu responsible for many of them. For the most part these were on the easily accessible rocks of the Buachaille and the East Face of Aonach Dubh. There were several very interesting winter routes, beginning in March 1951 with a first winter ascent on the West Face of Aonach Dubh. *No. 6 Gully* (240m IV,4) is a popular climb, in condition most winters and prominent from the road below. The climbers were Peter Drummond Smith and David Henry Munro, both of whom were killed in an avalanche on Ben Nevis on 1 April 1953, descending having climbed South Castle Gully in bad weather. The Glasgow JMCS Coruisk Memorial Hut on Skye, is named in their memory.

The early part of 1953 saw a staggering series of winter ascents by MacInnes. These at least matched for technical difficulty the winter routes being climbed in the Cairngorms, but took in shorter and steeper rock climbs as opposed to gullies or buttress routes with mixed climbing. On

Sunday 8 February, five climbers made their way through gently falling snow and soloed Curved Ridge to gain the foot of the Rannoch Wall. Chris Bonington, then aged 18, had come to Scotland to meet John Hammond and gain experience in winter climbing. Both were promising climbers and very good on rock. MacInnes was wearing his Austrian 12-point crampons, Bonington his 10-pointers.

MacInnes, whom they had just met in the Lagangarbh hut below the Buachaille, had his eyes on a winter ascent of Agag's Groove, the classic Very Difficult on the Rannoch Wall. Hammond asked if he and his companion could string along, which was acceptable to MacInnes so long as they also climbed with the Creagh Dhu *gnomie*, or apprentice, Gordon McIntosh. MacInnes, meanwhile, would climb with Creagh Dhu member Kerr McPhail. As Bonington confessed in his autobiography, they were happy to attach themselves to MacInnes's coat-tails, as with their lack of knowledge of the local mountains and conditions they would feel safer that way. [4]

The rocks were plastered with snow with some ice thrown in. MacInnes and McPhail climbed steadily, with two peg runners used for protection, taking just over two hours. The second rope, having three climbers and with less experience, needed four-and-a half-hours for the ascent. Bonington admitted that they were glad to have the Scots to guide them on to and off the mountain, but he complained at the slowness of the *gnomie*. Considering the difficulty of the route, both times were nonetheless impressive.

Agag's Groove (105m VII,6) remains a hard and respected climb in winter, with the difficulty linked to the amount of snow present. With the introduction of front-pointing, it now normally sees a few repeat ascents each winter. The second edition of the SMC Climbers' Guide to Glencoe and Ardgour, authored by Len Lovat and published in two volumes in 1959 (Buachaille Etive Mòr) and 1965 (Glencoe, Beinn Trilleachan and Garbh Bheinn), remarks that the standard was severe and that the crux was the summer crux, the short open 80ft corner. The current guide gives the winter crux as being the nose on pitch three.

The climb received a winter ascent in the 1980s by Murray Hamilton and John (Spider) Mackenzie, who found it very hard in conditions of heavy snow. This was using very different equipment from the 1953 visit, when each of the climbers wielded a single wooden-shafted axe. MacInnes made another ascent later, with a pupil from the Glencoe School of Mountaineering.

Bonington and Hammond climbed other routes in the following days, much less taxing than Agag's Groove but in unconsolidated powder snow which made the approaches hard work. Hammond had also spent a productive week on Skye in 1951 with R Morden, climbing classics such as Cìoch

Direct, Direct Finish to Crack of Doom, and Mallory's Slab and Groove. On 16 May they climbed a new route on Theàrlaich-Dubh Buttress, *Quiver* (80m Severe). Mike Lates, author of the current Skye guide, together with Stuart Pedlar, has clarified much of the confusion caused by earlier guides and has restored Quiver to its rightful history. Its name comes from quivering leg muscles on the first ascent, and it is almost certainly undergraded, taking in a very steep wall with small holds on the right of the Grand Diedre.

The 'three Johns' – Young, Vidulich, and Hammond, all experienced mountaineers–disappeared on the Hooker Glacier of Mount Cook in 1955 when MacInnes was in New Zealand and had arranged to meet Hammond. The bodies were never found, and the Three Johns Hut above the Mueller Glacier was built as a memorial. As a measure of the extreme weather potential in the Mount Cook area, the hut was itself blown into the Dobson Valley in 1977, killing four New Zealand mountaineers.

On 13 February 1953, Bonington joined MacInnes for another audacious climb, a winter ascent of Crowberry Ridge Direct. This had been first climbed in summer by George and Ashley Abraham, Jim Puttrell and Ernest Baker in May 1900. There was still too much unconsolidated snow for safe climbing in the gullies, so MacInnes decided to attempt the steep buttress route. The pair soloed to the belay ledge at the start of the famous Abraham Traverse, but MacInnes had great trouble climbing this difficult section and after 30 minutes returned to the stance.

The sloping holds were icy, and Bonington wrote that the leader's nails were not holding. (There is an inconsistency here: in his autobiography, published 13 years after the ascent, Bonington twice mentions MacInnes's nails, but MacInnes states that both men were wearing crampons. [5] This could be backed up by Bonington later stating that both climbers used crampons for their next route the following day.)

With no obvious good crack at the crux into which a protection peg could be inserted, this was a serious obstacle for MacInnes. His solution was to remove his boots and climb in socks, which could at least become 'sticky' on the icy holds and provide some security. Another hour saw him up the pitch. The steeply sloping slabby section following the traverse which had given the leader so much difficulty had been protected by a peg driven half an inch into a thin crack. This provided a tenuous handhold, allowing a long stretch upwards for a decent hold, MacInnes's socks meanwhile sliding slowly downwards. The remainder of the climb went comparatively easily.

What MacInnes and Bonington would not have known then was that the crux of the Direct Route had been first climbed in the winter of 1938 by Alex Small, a member of the Tricouni MC, the JMCS, and later the

SMC (see Chapter 6). On these 1953 winter ascents, MacInnes was wearing crampons, apart from the sections climbed in socks.

MacInnes and Bonington were not quite finished; the day after climbing Crowberry Ridge Direct they entered Great Gully, again on the Buachaille, intent on making the first winter ascent of Raven's Gully. This is a fierce gully in summer conditions, at HVS, with several chockstones to be negotiated. It had almost become the property of the Creagh Dhu, often climbed by them in less than ideal conditions. From the ascent of Crowberry Ridge Direct, MacInnes had realised that conditions were better than originally thought.

He had been on several earlier winter attempts on Raven's Gully, with the most recent, the previous month, leaving him stuck in an ice-lined chimney for over eight hours. He was climbing on a 200ft-length of nylon, about 9cm circumference, non-stretchy and made to order. When this jammed about 100ft up the pitch, he was forced to untie and solo onwards until reaching a crevice not far below the finish, with the climbing now impossible. Here he stopped, jamming himself with his back on one wall and his feet on the other, balancing on his front points and dressed only in jeans and a tartan shirt, with his spare clothing in a rucksack lower down.

His companions were Charlie Vigano and John Cullen, both in the Creagh Dhu. Luckily for MacInnes, their torches were spotted by other members and a rope was eventually lowered just before 3am. Once out of the gully, they managed to descend by traversing right above Cuneiform Buttress to gain access to the Lagangarbh corrie. Great Gully is a known danger area, very prone to avalanche.

MacInnes attributes his survival in such conditions and with inadequate clothing to having studied yoga as a youth. When he was eight, his father had given him some books, one of which was *Magic and Mystery in Tibet* (1929) by Alexandra David-Néel (1868-1969), a Belgian-French explorer. In 1912 David-Néel was living in a monastery in India, close to the border with Tibet. Here, in her anchorite cave, she practised Tibetan yoga which included the technique of *tummo*, mobilising internal energy to produce heat. MacInnes was influenced by these stories, and certainly managed to survive his ordeal with no obvious injuries. There was no frostbite, but he had been badly exposed and spent the next day in bed.

On the first winter ascent of Raven's Gully both MacInnes and Bonington climbed in crampons, although MacInnes again removed his boots and climbed in socks for one hard pitch. It may well have been freezing, but water was coming down and winter climbing was rapidly losing its appeal for Bonington. The crux chockstone occupied MacInnes for about an hour-and-a-half, with some pegs required, while higher up another chockstone was lassoed to save time and effort.

Raven's Gully (135m V,5) will always provide difficulties, and even modern technology will fail to remove its tremendous atmosphere. The crux chockstone, winter or summer, is a trial requiring cunning, strength and stamina, and has defeated numerous leaders over the decades–including, according to MacInnes, John Cunningham. MacInnes later considered that the difficulties of the three routes, in descending order, were: Crowberry Direct, Agag's, and Raven's Gully.

Other faces in Glen Coe were being explored at this time, including the continuation of new climbs on the east faces of both Aonach Dubh and Gearr Aonach. The routes were, for the most part, at an easy standard, particularly on the latter face which looks out over the tranquillity of the Lost Valley. This ambience persists to this day, and for climbers looking to enjoy routes in the low and middle grades there is much to entertain here.

Two climbs introduced a new rock face, the Lower North-East Nose of Aonach Dubh. Its prominent wall would have to wait a little longer, but in August 1955 Cunningham and Noon climbed the two corners at its left, with *Boomerang* (75m HVS) and *Little Boomerang* (65m VS 4c). The former has one 5b move at the crux, which is slow to dry.

Several climbs were recorded in 1954 on the East Face of Gearr Aonach by parties from Glasgow University MC. J Stanley Stewart was a prominent member, and later joined both the JMCS and the SMC. J Stewart Orr, son of SMC member J Neil Orr, was also a participant. The climbers found some easy climbs here and pondering on their naming decided to follow the concoction of strange names invented by Lewis Carroll in his nonsense poem *Jabberwocky*–hence *Mome Rath Route* (135m Very Difficult) and *The Wabe* (135m Very Difficult), both climbed in May 1954.

❃❃❃

The summer of 1954 would see Ben Nevis in the limelight, with ascents of two major lines on Càrn Dearg Buttress. Both routes had a history of attempts, and both attracted leading climbers of the day before being successfully climbed. The first line to fall was *Sassenach* (270m E1), but before assessing the climb there should be clarification of the word itself. It derives from the Scottish Gaelic *Sasunnoch*, in turn from Latin *Saxones*, or 'Saxons'. In other words, the Sassenach was someone who did not speak Gaelic and was usually from the Lowlands of Scotland or from England. Throw in some modern tribalism and it is sometimes used in a humorous way.

It was certainly the latter when, seeing the first ascenders Don Whillans and Joe Brown descending via No.5 Gully, SMC member George Ritchie, soloing nearby, shouted *'English bastards'*. Ritchie, an unsubtle character on occasion, was being direct but also in a sense expressing the dismay of

Scottish climbers, several of whom had being making attempts. The first ascenders duly named their route Sassenach.

Donald (Don) Desbrow Whillans (1933-1985) and Joseph (Joe) Brown (1930-) were working class climbers from Salford and Ardwick in Manchester respectively. Brown was a jobbing builder, Whillans a plumber. Both were self-trained as regards climbing, and owed much of their high standard to climbing on gritstone. Their upbringing and work was similar to the Creagh Dhu climbers in Scotland, which explains their toughness and physical fitness. Both would go on to make outstanding climbs in the greater ranges. Brown would also establish a network of outdoor equipment stores in Wales, while Whillans would design a climbing harness and a high-altitude box tent.

Sassenach is described in the current guide as a *'magnificent old fashioned classic'*. It takes the prominent chimney line towards the right-hand end of the front face of the buttress, and the grade of E1 assumes that a direct start is taken using slings for aid, otherwise it will be E3. Those known to have attempted it included Kellett and Plackett in June 1944, Jimmy Marshall (first with Charles Donaldson, then George Ritchie) in September 1953, and probably one or two unknown climbers, as Kellett had come across a sling in the huge 'book corner' further left of the Sassenach chimney.

Bill Smith of the Creagh Dhu managed the first 100ft, being stopped by the roof below the chimney. Brooker, Taylor and Patey tried in October 1953. Kellett and Plackett attempted to gain the foot of the chimney, which lies above very steep ground, by traversing from the left, while the Aberdonians traversed in from the right by a variation now known as the Patey Traverse.

It was on an Easter visit to Nevis in 1954 that the Rock and Ice team of Brown, Whillans, Nat Allen and Ron Moseley struck gold. The previous summer, Brown and Whillans had been in the Alps, where they had met Marshall and Patey. One of these, or both, had innocently mentioned the unclimbed chimney. Easter 1954 fell in the middle of April, but Moseley and Brown were hoping to climb Point Five Gully. While they were trying to avoid the avalanches in that gully, Whillans and Allen spent two days probing the chimney's defences, trying to make a direct approach via the very steep rock beneath, where there is often a damp section.

On the third day, Brown gave in to the avalanches and came down to join the pair under the chimney. He used two slings and almost reached the chimney before darkness fell. The next day, the fourth of the attempt and with Brown still tired after his efforts, Whillans took over and succeeded in gaining the foot of the chimney, where they had agreed he would belay. Feeling fit, however, with Brown's agreement he carried on; the chimney was climbed and the climb completed. Both men were wearing soft shoes known as *pumps*, plimsolls with canvas uppers and rubber soles. It would be fair to say that the climbers probably balanced this weakness in their equipment with superior finger and arm strength.

It is easy when looking back at significant routes to forget that they were often achieved by young climbers at the peak of fitness, and it is no different in this case. Brown was 23 years of age, Whillans 21. Jim Perrin tells the story of this ascent, and of a fatal accident on Tower Ridge that same night, in his highly recommended biography of Whillans. [6] Another source is the Ormerod biography of Whillans, and finally there is the Ben Nevis history. [7,8]

Once again, the superior training of gritstone climbers had made an impact on Scottish climbing. The Minus Face climbs of Kellett in 1944 had been pointing the way to the future of rock routes on this grand mountain and with Sassenach the future had arrived. From then on, any sound, steep rock on Nevis was considered fair game.

The second ascent of Sassenach introduced two names to Ben Nevis: Bob Downes and Mike O'Hara of the Cambridge University MC. Robert O Downes had started climbing in the early 1950s and soon proved to be a natural, moving quickly up the grades. He met Michael John O'Hara (1933-2014) at Cambridge University. O'Hara studied geology and would become an eminent petrologist and professor at Aberystwyth University. Downes would die of high altitude pulmonary oedema on Masherbrum in 1957. He was 25 and would doubtless have made many other quality climbs.

The two teamed up for a trip to Ben Nevis in June 1955, camping for five perfect days of weather. They made the second ascent of Kellett's Route on Gardyloo Buttress, 11 years after the first, and also climbed Kellett's Right Hand Route on the Minus Face. Downes remarked that the crux of Kellett's Route reminded him of Pigott's Climb on Cloggy, though steeper and more exposed. On a visit the previous year, he had also noted the potential further right, on Minus One Buttress, one of the longest and finest pieces of rock architecture on the Ben.

Their ascent of this buttress, over two separate days, began on 17 June and was completed four days later, by which time they had been joined by Eric Langmuir. It was also indirect, due to a band of overhangs about one-third height, forcing them to cross Minus Two Gully, following its left edge for a distance before regaining Minus One Buttress by a rightward traverse and continuing up to finish *North Eastern Grooves* (295m VS), the first route on the buttress. They used one peg for aid.

There were some good explanations as to why Scots climbers seemed to be quiet at this point, one being that Ben Nevis was an awkward distance away from the major conurbations. As many were working class, they had no car. There was as yet no bridge at Ballachulish and the ferry ceased operation before dark, adding extra distance and time via Kinlochleven. Even a club bus was inconvenient, as travelling south it would have to leave Fort William by 5pm to allow those who did not live near a city centre to catch a service bus home. Some used motorbikes–but, as Glen Coe was well-endowed with huts and bothies, many were content to stop there. Most impecunious Scottish climbers travelled by hitching lifts.

There was a visitation from the Creagh Dhu in August 1955, when two landmark gullies received their first summer ascents. On 27 August, Bill Smith, Gordon McIntosh and Mick Noon climbed *Zero Gully* (300m Hard Severe) in three-and-a-half hours, wearing Vibrams. Rarely dry and poorly protected, this does not see much summer traffic. The following day it was the turn of *Point Five Gully* (325m Scottish VS). Always wet and not recommended, it was climbed in nails with 11 pitches. Marshall probably made the second summer ascent of Point Five, implausibly rating it as a good and worthwhile climb, if slightly loose.

❄❄❄

Even better climbs were to emerge during the summer of 1956, again led by members of the CUMC post-exams. First, however, a brief note on the early history of rock climbing shoes is in order. Climbers who began after the mid-1950s would in all probability have been wearing French designed and manufactured rock boots, blue and white uppers of canvas and suede with hard rubber one-piece soles. They were referred to as either PAs or EBs. Before then, the choice was nailed boots, and latterly Vibram boots, or plimsolls (also known as sandshoes or pumps).

On wet rock, socks might be worn over plimsolls or without any other footwear at all. The increase in standards post-war had a brake applied by the lack of suitable footwear, both when it came to climbing slabby rock using mainly friction, and also on steeper rock with smaller, rounded holds requiring the edge of a boot with some friction.

In 1947, the French climber Pierre Allain (1904-2000) began to experiment with lightweight boots known as *Kletterschuhe*. Conveniently, he was active on the Fontainebleau forest boulders near Paris, and two years later he joined forces with another climber, Emile Bourdonneau, a member of a shoe-making family–hence the common names given to their early models of rock boots, PAs and EBs.

Their first commercial model of rock boot was produced in 1950 and had the appearance of a high-topped basketball shoe, with lacing extending down close to the toes. The uppers were of blue-coloured canvas with white suede reinforcement, while the soles were smooth and fully randed. A sewn-in circular inner ankle pad had the initials PA stamped on it. British climbers began to use these from the mid-1950s.

Sometime later the two climbers split, with Bourdonneau retaining the rights to produce the original shoe, branding it EB, while Allain moved to the French mountain boot company Galibier, which produced the PA with black canvas and red suede leather. Climbers seemed to find the original technically superior, particularly on tiny rock edges, and the name EB Super Gratton appeared, *gratton* being a French word for a fine rock edge hold, one so tiny that it almost has to be rubbed with a hard boot edge to become visible.

From the mid-1970s, other makes appeared, with the Spanish brand Boreal producing the Firé in 1984, its rubber soles sourced from recovered aircraft tyres and 'sticky' compared to older models.

It is salutary for younger climbers to bear in mind the achievements of their predecessors, putting up hard routes with comparatively primitive equipment, particularly footwear. On the downside, the design of modern rock shoes has often made them less than comfortable.

❄❄❄

As noted above, Downes and O'Hara made the second ascent of Sassenach during their June 1956 visit to Ben Nevis. Both were wearing newly acquired PAs. Even so, and partly due to climbing through a prolonged hailstorm, they were very impressed by the route, which occupied them for a marathon of 11 hours. The crux second pitch in particular took four hours, as there was loose rock present which had to be handled with care, with the climbers encased by the chimney. O'Hara later told a friend that he found it *'desperate'*.

> The chimney itself is very strenuous, characterised by loose chocks and green slime. The security itself is sufficient, but owing to the width of the chimney it is a mistake to carry a rucksack [...] The pitches above are not easy [...] it's difficult to think of a route which has the character of Sassenach, or its *grande envergure. Although the hard pitch is only half the length of Cenotaph Corner, to this party at least, it seemed more tiring, more precarious, certainly more baffling than that climb. [9]

> *grande envergure (fr.) Largeness of scale.

This second ascent was on 13 June, but a few days earlier they enjoyed some success at straightening-out their line on Minus One Buttress. Downes, O'Hara and Mike Prestige were camping on the mountain, and on 10 June they headed for Minus One Buttress with a score to settle. They followed the first three pitches of North Eastern Grooves, eliminating the aid point on the second pitch. Downes led the fourth pitch, which turned out to be the crux; several committing moves were required, using one peg, albeit on beautiful rock. Confidence and perfect balance are prerequisites with this type of climbing, as most cracks are blind and handholds scant.

The pitch following the original crux makes a regrettable diversion, starting up a wide crack then moving right into the summer looseness of Minus One Gully. Higher up, they traversed left across a loose wall to regain the upper part of the arête. A variation was made in 1967, by Squirrels Ian Rowe and Peter MacDonald who, climbing without a guidebook and with the intention of climbing the buttress, followed the first three pitches of the original route then continued leftward as for North Eastern Grooves. Realising they were moving off the buttress proper, they made a rising traverse back right above the crux, to regain the original line below the wide crack, so making the *Plinth Variation*.

A later pair of climbers inadvertently made another variation, again climbing without guidebook. In August 1972, the author and Ian Fulton approached the buttress. Even in late summer there was a large patch of snow at its foot–and here they found the remains of a copy of the most recent guidebook (published in 1969). This had most likely been dropped by someone the previous winter, but the two climbers preferred to find their own route up the buttress, discarding the tattered guide and following what they felt was a logical line.

They climbed through the original crux pitch which led to the foot of the obvious wide crack. Here they realised it led into a section of Minus One Gully, diverting them from the crest of the buttress. Instead, they moved left and up, crossing a slabby wall then continuing up again, keeping on the buttress, to eventually gain the final arête and the North East Buttress. It was only on a later ascent in 1976, climbing with Alastair Walker and this time following the guidebook description of the original route, that the author realised his 1972 ascent with Fulton had accidentally made a variation, one which improved the line. The variation name was fairly obvious, and so it became the *Serendipity Finish* (155m HVS).

Fulton is one of a select group of climbers whose technique on rock was honed on the boulders and steep faces beneath Dumbarton Castle. Others were Rab Carrington, Ian Nicolson, John Jackson, Neil Macniven, Brian Shields and Michael Connolly.

Another good variation was made in August 1983, when local climber Noel Williams, with Stevie Abbott, climbed the *Arete Variation* (80m 5b) using one tension move. Williams returned the following year with Willie Jeffrey to make a free ascent.

Whichever variation is taken, the climb provides a tremendous experience courtesy of a great line through superb rock scenery. *Minus One Direct* (295m E1) will not disappoint. It is widely regarded as one of the best mid-grade mountain routes in the country.

As if Scottish mountaineers in 1956 had not had enough of a wake-up call, a major ascent on Ben Nevis would now shake them out of any complacency. On 30 August 1956 the formidable rope of Whillans and Downes appeared. The latter had made several good alpine ascents in 1955 despite poor weather, plus the second ascent of Sassenach, and he was certainly making a name for himself. The two met in Chamonix and decided to do some routes together. More poor weather in the Alps, however, persuaded them to return to the UK.

Whillans by now had a motorbike with a sidecar, and when he arrived in Cambridge to pick up Downes, O'Hara was offered a place. His research work was being badly impeded by too much climbing however, and to his lasting regret he declined the offer. Keen climbers will sympathise.

The line on which Whillans and Downes had their eyes was the prominent corner on the front face of Càrn Dearg Buttress, now known as *Centurion* (190m HVS) and the scene of several failed attempts. In the current SMC guide, like Minus One Direct it is given the sought after but infrequently awarded four-star rating.

The climb has two difficult pitches, the second and the seventh, both graded 5a. Whillans led all pitches bar the seventh, technically probably the hardest with a subtle route finding puzzle built in. Here Downes weaved a masterly line through the overhangs.

It seems that the climb was named from the likeness of the overlapping slabs to the protective body armour on a Roman centurion. Even after this, Downes and Whillans were not quite finished with their disgruntling of Scots climbers, as on the last day of August they made the first ascent of another climb on the buttress, *The Shield* (215m HVS). This takes the line of chimneys on the huge wall above Waterfall Gully, on the right flank of the buttress, and the pioneers had trouble with wet conditions. It now also provides an excellent winter climb at VII,7.

Zero Gully had been climbed in 1955 at Hard Severe, but all eyes were on a winter ascent, as indeed they were with Point Five Gully. Both routes had been attempted several times, with unfriendly conditions–spindrift and minor avalanches–forcing retreats.

One attempt, in 1951, saw two Oxford University MC climbers, Hamish Nicol and Anthony Rawlinson, ejected from the gully when the leader came off, and both were very lucky to survive a 120m fall. Nicol later admitted that it was inter-university rivalry with Cambridge which had pushed them on.

By the start of 1956 only two new winter ascents had been made on Ben Nevis in the previous 17 years. The war had badly affected exploration in Scotland, but this was still a remarkable statistic. Winter activity then came fully to life in February 1957, with no fewer than five routes being made in very good snow and ice conditions. So good, in fact, that prominent climbers were drawn to the mountain from all parts of Scotland, with Creagh

Dhu, JMCS, SMC and Etchachan Club members stuffing the CIC Hut to near bursting-point.

There was enthusiasm for one route in particular, with Zero Gully apparently in near-perfect condition, assuming that the spindrift abated. The tale of its final ascent is well known, littered along the way with epic failures, sometimes multiple by certain climbers, especially MacInnes. He had made six previous attempts, most recently in January 1957 when with Bob Hope of the Creagh Dhu he had climbed most of the hard pitches only to be defeated by spindrift avalanches.

On Saturday 16 February 1957 a strong south-west wind was affecting the major gullies, shifting snow down into them. Following an earlier Bill Murray tip, Len Lovat, Tom Patey and Graeme Nicol visited Coire Leis, adjacent to the eastern section of the Càrn Mòr Dearg arête and better protected from the wind. Here they climbed *Cresta* (275m III), a popular route with much character which readily builds ice. It received a second ascent two days later, by Norman Tennent and Malcolm Slesser, who finished slightly more directly. On the same day, another popular, easy classic was climbed by Lovat and Donald Bennet, recording *Number Three Gully Buttress* (150m III).

Leonard (Len) Scott Lovat (1926-1996) served as Sheriff Principal of South Strathclyde, Dumfries and Galloway at Hamilton from 1978 to 1993. He was the author of the two-volume SMC Climbers' Guide to Glencoe and Ardgour (1959, 1965) and an experienced alpinist. Malcolm Slesser (1926-2007) was a professor of energy, or something allied to that nebulous specialty. He certainly had plenty of personal energy, usually employed in achieving some goal no matter who or what was in the way. Exploration was his main joy, and Greenland figured large.

Slesser was a keen, yacht-owning sailor, and the author was once at the helm of his boat in the Sound of Mull when he was commanded to continue along a heading which just happened to be a collision course with the Mull ferry. Fortunately the ferry gave way. It is well known that sailing craft, at least in theory, have right of way, but very few would wish to test this. Or was Slesser perhaps testing the helmsman? He was also the author of the 1970 edition of the SMC Skye District Guide. A splendid obituary by Iain Smart, another member of this Edinburgh clique, will be found in the SMCJ, containing many similar stories. [10]

The main event on Ben Nevis that season was the first winter ascent of Zero Gully on Monday 18 February 1957, the events of which were chronicled in a long and entertaining article by Patey. [11] With various partners, Patey had been on Ben Nevis six times in recent winters with the then unclimbed Point Five Gully as a target, but conditions had always prevented a serious attempt. This time, Patey and Nicol had been lucky in finding lifts and thus arrived a day earlier than planned. According to Patey, there was mutual agreement between the various climbing teams chasing the two winter prizes.

The following day, Cunningham and Noon from the Creagh Dhu turned up, followed by the dramatic arrival of MacInnes, who had been instructing, based at the Steall Hut in Glen Nevis.

> It was impossible to remain indifferent towards such a man: his appearance alone invited controversy. A great rent extending the whole length of one trouser leg had been repaired unsuccessfully with string. In his hand was the famous all-steel hammer-pick, named affectionately by the club "The Message."

> Cunningham challenged him gruffly, "Just where do you think you're goin'?"
> "Zero Gully, of course."
> "Solo?"
> "I suppose I might allow you two along as well."
> "That's very generous considerin' we're goin' anyway."

> So the composition of the party was settled to the chagrin of the rest of the company, who had not allowed for such formidable competition. We reflected sulkily that there was always Point Five.

The two Creagh Dhu climbers had already staked their claim for Zero, so MacInnes, who through his multi-attempts was a virtual part-owner, was not entirely welcome. However the party had now been decided. According to MacInnes, he had ripped his trouser leg descending from the Càrn Mòr Dearg arête. This was before there were any abseil posts set up to facilitate descent.

The following day, Patey and Nicol climbed Comb Gully with spindrift providing discomfort and excitement in equal proportion. Cunningham, Noon and MacInnes meanwhile had been turned back by avalanches thundering down Zero. That evening, the Creagh Dhu men had to return to Glasgow on Noon's sidecar motorbike, so the scene was now set, with MacInnes, Patey and Nicol as the ascent party.

As for the other climbers in the hut, Lovat declined due to an absolute requirement to be in Glasgow the following afternoon, while the remaining quartet–Bennet, Slesser, Tennent and Douglas Scott–had been battling heavy ice on the North-East Buttress, returning to the hut at midnight, and had an understandable reluctance to face a serious and uncertain climb the next day.

The A-team was up at 6am to find a clear sky and hard frost. MacInnes laid out the plan of attack, with Patey leading the first 400ft as MacInnes had done that in a previous attempt. MacInnes was the only member of the party wearing 12-point crampons; Patey had 10-point crampons, while Nicol persisted with nailed boots. In Patey's article, he refers to MacInnes supporting himself by the angled spikes on the front of his crampons, allowing some level of support without cut footholds.

Zero Gully was in perfect condition, consisting of snow-ice, hard snow which has consolidated with a series of thaws followed by freezes until hard enough to support climbers while allowing holds to be cut easily. Patey's first pitch ended at 120ft, where the loop of an ice axe protruded from the snow. The axe belonged to Bob Hope, left on an earlier attempt with MacInnes, and had been used to protect their descent. It came in useful when Nicol dropped his own axe from the top of the same pitch.

The next pitch started up a fair-sized overhang, on which Patey used ice pitons for support while cutting steps. His technique was to place a piton as high as possible, then take tension on this while cutting handholds. The next move was to insert a higher piton while hanging on with one hand, then remove the lower piton and begin all over again.

This technique was obviously not without danger, as these pitons would not have held a fall in most cases, and could easily come out if pulled in the wrong direction. A slight fumble at any time could lead to a lost piton. It was a difficult section of around 20ft for the leader, who ended up crouched in a cramped stance above the overhang. Somewhere below the snow surface was one of MacInnes's earlier ice pitons, but Patey hammered in an ice-axe shaft using 'The Message'.

These ice pitons were much less sophisticated than the array of ice screws available to modern mountaineers, and usually consisted of a straight length of metal, longer than a normal rock piton. The Czech climber Milan Doubek would not make his slimmer carbon-steel, pound-in, screw-out ice pitons until the mid-1960s.

These 'drive-ins' would then lead to an improved design manufactured by Salewa in the mid-1970s, named the Warthog and much loved by mountaineers, especially in Scotland, where they worked well not only on ice and hard snow but also on frozen turf. There is a brief history of ice pegs in the *Alpinist* magazine. [12]

So far, 300ft up the gully, the trio had taken only one-and-a-half hours, mainly due to the usual climbing technique of Patey–lacking in any style, but fast. The route now went rightward, along a narrow strip of steep snow between two overhangs, before running up easier angled snow for 80ft to below a huge ice pitch. This, Patey decided, would be for MacInnes.

The party was belayed on two ice axes and three ice pitons as MacInnes set off up this last difficult pitch, using ice pitons for protection and cutting a bucket hold every six feet which allowed for rests. It was at this point that his two companions decided to encourage him musically, Nicol choosing a New Orleans funeral song, *'Oh, didn't he ramble'*, (written by Bob Cole and J Rosamond Johnson in 1902.) It has the chorus–

And didn't he ramble, ramble,
He rambled all around, in and out of town,
And didn't he ramble, ramble,
He rambled till the butcher cut him down.

Despite, or perhaps because of this morbid serenade, MacInnes finished the pitch. Patey and Nicol found it as hard as any below, all at a standard of Very Severe. The current grade of Zero, for reasonable conditions, is V,4 (300m). The three pioneers now unroped and moved together until, some five hours after the start, they collapsed in a happy heap on the summit plateau. As with any long climb, conditions on the day should be carefully judged, and even though the upper stretches are technically easy, care is needed all the way.

Hard ice in lean conditions would markedly increase the difficulty. Zero Gully was the first Grade V to be climbed on Ben Nevis, and is, as the current guidebook states, an all-time classic, a must-do route.

❀❀❀

Glen Coe and Skye saw some good climbing in the mid-1950s, with the Creagh Dhu prominent. One of their members was Pat Walsh, the son of a Clydebank docker. A powerful, compactly built man, his short-sightedness gave rise to stories that some of his bold leads were due to not seeing all of the difficulties ahead, with his superior strength keeping him on the rock, but this surely denigrates his abilities.

There was, however, the occasion when he was climbing on Clogwyn Du'r Arddu in Wales and wished to climb the Sheaf (VS), but mistakenly climbed *Walsh's Groove* (E3 5b) so perhaps there is some truth in the myopia legend. Alternatively, it was a classic Creagh Dhu 'wind-up'.

Walsh's Groove is now the third pitch of West Buttress Eliminate (E3 5c), climbed by Ingle and Crew in 1962 and described as an amazing pitch requiring sustained back-and-foot technique. He was friendly with his clubmate Cunningham, ten years his senior, though this did not mean that competition was lacking between the two.

Between September 1952 and June 1956, Walsh made a series of new rock climbs on Slime Wall on the Buachaille. The first of these was *Bludger's Route* (48m HVS), with MacInnes and Tommy Laurie.[13] It took the left-most of two prominent grooves towards the left-hand side of the main face. In June 1956 Walsh was back with Vigano to climb *Revelation* (88m HVS), taking the upper tier of the face.

The two routes were connected in July 1957 by Jimmy Marshall, J Griffin, G Adams and Marshall's brother Ronnie by a direct finish to Bludger's, the *Link Pitch* (15m 5a), providing a superb combination climb that was logically named *Bludger's Revelation* (141m HVS) in the author's 1980 SMC guide to Glen Coe and Glen Etive.

Charlie Vigano (1928-1998) was on the second ascent of the combination route. Born in Paris to an English mother and an Italian father, his early years were spent in Milan, fleeing in 1943 when the Nazis came close. Moving to Scotland, as did so many Italian families at this time, he began training as a chef in the Central Hotel in Glasgow. Once he started to climb with the Creagh Dhu, however, he was regarded as their worst cook. He met John Cullen on the Cobbler in 1948, and both became members of the club three years later. [14] He died in Spain in a climbing accident, to date the only Creagh Dhu member to die this way.

Bludger's Revelation is one of the best routes in Glen Coe at this grade, and provides a splendid introduction to Slime Wall. This face probably received its name not due to any marked problem with vegetation, but because after heavy rain it needs a couple of days to dry out as it receives very little sun. The bubbly, rough rhyolite provides less protection than other faces with this rock, but compensates for this in every other way.

In June 1956, Walsh and Vigano also climbed *Doom Arete* (45m E1), an exposed and poorly protected route often combined with the Link Pitch, while Walsh along with J Crawford climbed *Bloody Crack* (40m E1 5b) on the far left of the top tier. At the time, Walsh considered this route the hardest in the Glen Coe area. Given the name and his comment on its difficulty, there may be more to the ascent than we know. Gallows Route for example, climbed in 1947 by Cunningham, is harder, graded E2 5b.

The following month Walsh climbed with Mick Noon to produce the enigmatic *Nightmare Traverse* (75m E2 ✠). The cross symbol indicates insufficient information to pin down this route's difficulty; although it has had some ascents, and is generally agreed to be about E2, the precise line is uncertain. It starts 4m below the slab corner at the top of pitch three of Bludger's Revelation, includes a downwards tension, a section of the route Apocalypse,and finishes up Guerdon Grooves.

On Skye, Walsh teamed up with Harry MacKay on 16 July 1956 to climb *Trophy Crack* (80m E1) on Cìoch Upper Buttress, just right of Integrity (VS). Walsh had freed this route, and the descent peg left by MacInnes after an earlier attempt was immediately confiscated by the Creagh Dhu and became the trophy after which the route was named. [15]

On the same day, Cunningham, J Allan and Bill Smith put up another hard route *Bastinado* (115m E1) on the Cìoch Lower Buttress, just to the right of Little Gully. [16] With a remarkable show of energy, the two parties then made second ascents of each other's routes, also on the same day. Bastinado used a peg and sling at the crux but with better protection the route is now free. Walsh died in 2017.

In 1958, Bill Mackenzie's Climbers' Guide to Skye was finally published. Oddly, Trophy Crack was not included, though Bastinado was.

❊❊❊

1954 saw a wonderful new climbing playground opened up in Scotland. It has been estimated at some six acres (2.4ha) in area, is set in spectacular scenery, and is composed of almost faultless rock. The Trilleachan Slabs are gained by a twisting drive along the passing-place road down to the head of Loch Etive, from where a short if squelchy walk leads to the foot of the slabs and a prominent rock gloomily named the Coffinstone due to its shape.

The slabs are inclined at about 40°, which sounds like a comfortable stroll in the park until one finds that the Starav granite which composes them feels almost glass-like underfoot. It would not do to be a myopic leader here, as you must constantly read the slabs and look for the faint ribs which stand out slightly above the surface as they are slightly harder–these can be life-savers. The scrambly descent is not pleasant and demands care.

The Slabs came to the attention of Eric Langmuir through his father, an enthusiastic fisherman. Mike O'Hara was a friend of Langmuir, and he had also spotted them, in the spring of 1952 during a camping trek along the south shore of Loch Etive. The pair decided to investigate, and the summer of 1954 saw several visits, culminating in first ascents of two routes: the best-forgotten *Sickle* (190m VS) on 13 June (Langmuir, O'Hara, A John Mallinson and Miss JM Tester), and *Spartan Slab* (190m VS) the following day (Langmuir, O'Hara and Mallinson).

Spartan Slab is now a classic, probably one of the most popular routes in Scotland and without doubt the most climbed route on the slabs. It has an infamous crux move on pitch three, well-protected but awkward unless you are tall. When the climbers first saw the slabs their impressions were that they were larger than expected, and that they looked easy enough. In the last they were of course deceived, as they found they were close to the limit of friction.

Regarding footwear, Langmuir had gym shoes, while the other two wore vibrams. Langmuir had spotted the potential route and O'Hara led the first three pitches, including the short but awkwardly strenuous overhang of the third pitch. Above this he was baffled by a slabby pitch seemingly without holds. When several attempts proved fruitless, Langmuir took over, climbing a difficult and exposed pitch, and eventually leading the rest of the route.

Describing their ascent in his obituary for Langmuir, Mallinson regarded the climbing as a bold and brilliant lead for the time. [17] What should also be taken into account is that the pioneers would have encountered some vegetation, undoubtedly obscuring some holds and adding to the difficulty. The current guide prefaces the description with the terse warning that the third pitch often draws blood.

Agony (155m E2) was climbed in April 1957 by the Creagh Dhu team of Cunningham, Noon and Bill Smith, and there are now over 50 climbs on these slabs, with five gaining the SMC's highest accolade of four stars. Most climbs on the slabs used some aid initially, due to a lack of handholds or good cracks, but these have been whittled down over the years as peg placements began to provide finger holds and any vegetation in the cracks was removed.

The Creagh Dhu dominated exploration here over the next decade, with Cunningham and Noon prominent. Later, other good climbers from Edinburgh and Glasgow would pick up the challenges of the blank spaces. The Cambridge team was back later in 1954 along with Downes, and attempted the line now known as Hammer. Low down, the route has an infamous section known as the Scoop, due to its slight hollow which presents a steeper series of moves than on the surrounding slabs.

The party tried to ascend the Scoop with a circus-like three-man pyramid, Langmuir on the shoulders of Downes who was in turn on the shoulders of O'Hara. As O'Hara wrote in his obituary for Langmuir—

> We had the wrong technique, it was a deceptively easy angled slab but a steep learning curve; faith and friction or 'nutless guts for gutless nuts'. (R. Campbell) are required. [18]

Sadly, Downes, one of the best 1950s climbers in the CUMC, was to die of oedema at Camp VI on Masherbrum.

Eric Duncan Grant Langmuir (1931-2005) was born in Glasgow and educated at Glasgow Academy and later Fettes College. His Cambridge degree in 1955 was in the natural sciences, and as he was already heavily involved in outdoor sports his membership of the CUMC was a given, followed by the Cairngorm Club and the SMC. He would eventually move into various posts in outdoor education, including as principal at Glenmore Lodge (1964-1970), ending as assistant director of the Recreation and Leisure Planning Department of Lothian Regional Council.

More pertinently, Langmuir was heavily involved in mountain rescue, avalanche research and the advancement of a national park system. His book, *Mountain Leadership*, published in 1969, is now in its fourth edition as *Mountaincraft and Leadership*. It was for his role in avalanche prognosis and contribution to outdoor education that Langmuir was elected to the Royal Society of Edinburgh (1978), and he was awarded an MBE in 1986 for similar contributions to mountain safety and training. He eventually settled in Aviemore.

As an aside, Beinn Trilleachan is probably named after a common wader, the oystercatcher (*Haematopus ostralegus*)– its call being an unmistakeable peeping. The sandpiper is another candidate. For anyone wishing to hear the Gaelic pronunciation of Trilleachan, there is a sound file on the Walk-highlands website. [19]

The Creagh Dhu climber Noon was on first ascents of five Trilleachan Slabs routes in 1957, including the classics *Hammer* (150m HVS) and *Swastika* (200m E2), and one more in 1958, *The Long Wait* (255m E2). The slabs are popular with some climbers, though they require a very cool approach and careful footwork. As an example, one hard piece of 'slab padding' is required on the crux of *The Band of Hope* (210m E3), first climbed in 1971 when the leader, the late John Newsome, maintained one fingernail longer than the rest for a crucial hold. The author can attest to this, having been a well-protected passenger for most of the climb.

The later introduction of 'sticky' rock boots with increased friction on rock might imply that all became easier, but these could also lead the inexperienced leader into more difficult situations. The new boots have certainly made the harder slab climbs that bit easier, but they make no difference to the amount of protection available, and a bold approach remains a useful attribute on the harder climbs here.

❄❄❄

Several new faces were to appear at the Trilleachan Slabs and would loom large over the Scottish mountaineering landscape, putting up climbs which would be instant and long-lasting classics. Some would even go on to make their names in the greater ranges. By now the number of climbers was increasing and commensurate with this was the number of new climbs being recorded. With improvements in equipment, such as rock boots and nylon slings, it was becoming that bit easier and safer to climb, though there were several caveats.

There was a number of accidents, some fatal, when leaders had fallen and an under-strength nylon sling had been used as a belay. An SMCJ note from 1959 summarised a circular published by the BMC and the Association of Scottish Climbing Clubs, presenting the facts from a fatal accident near Llanberis. Two young but experienced climbers were on Main West Wall Climb on Cyrn Las, using a 1¼-inch circumference nylon rope– which was later found intact.

They had belayed at the foot of the third pitch, using a loop of inch circumference nylon and a karabiner attached to a waist loop. The leader fell, and it is probable that the second was pulled from his stance. The loop broke at the belay. Both climbers were killed.

The belay loop, when new, had a breaking strain of 2,000lb (900kg) under perfect conditions. The load falling on a second when the leader falls may rise to over 3,000lb. The circular recommended that belay loops should be of the same quality and size as the main climbing rope. Note that the nylon rope as used in this accident would have been of the hawser-laid construction, as this accident pre-dated kernmantle ropes which have a sheath-and-core construction. As the full-size loops would not fit into smaller cracks, climbers continued to use thinner sizes, especially for running belays, and there would be more accidents before the message was clearly received.

The older, more conservative mountaineering clubs were in the main not the drivers of exploratory climbing in Scotland at this time. The JMCS was generally the club to which most young climbers were attracted, and many would of course remain in that club. It provided a good introduction, with advice, meets and often weekly transport, and made it easier to use huts. The SMC began to maintain and use Lagangarbh at the upper end of Glen Coe in 1946, leasing it from the NTS.

The main thrust of exploration would come from individual climbers, including several outstanding individuals such as Brian Kellett. He was, however, an anomaly, climbing during the war years, often midweek and after working hours. Even Kellett sought out other climbers when the chance arose, such as when he dropped into the CIC Hut and teamed up with Arnot Russell to climb Route II on Càrn Dearg Buttress. In the main though, climbing works best as a small group, from two climbers upwards.

There were several such splinter groups active in the 1950s in Scotland, leading the charge in repeating existing routes and finding new challenges in summer and winter. Some were visiting groups, such as the successive waves of Cambridge students who often made their mark. The Rock and Ice was another group. Some of these groups were Scottish, with three factions in particular making significant impact. The first was the Aberdeen group, with prominent figures such as Mac Smith, Patey, Brooker, Nicol and Grassick. Their locus was obviously the Cairngorms in the main, although good conditions and the prospect of ripe plums could see their vanguard head for Ben Nevis and Skye.

Next up was the Creagh Dhu, based mainly in Glasgow and the Clydeside, active on the Cobbler and latterly in Glen Coe and Glen Etive. As far as any training and/or getting fit was concerned, the Creagh Dhu was often to be found at the geological curiosity of The Whangie. Although Creagh Dhu climbers would range over Scotland, with their background and geographical locus they would be most active in the west of Scotland.

The third group came from Edinburgh. Just outside the modern bypass is the village of Currie, on the city's south-western margin. The Pentland hills back it to the south, and the surrounding rural countryside offered many distractions for energetic, mischievous boys. It was here that three friends grew up and stretched their muscles along with many an adult's patience. Duncan (Dougal) Curdy McSporran Haston (1940-1977) was the son of a journeyman baker, and at school had two staunch friends, James Moriarty (1940-2005), later widely known as Elly, and James Stenhouse (1940-). Moriarty was one day younger than Haston, and Stenhouse slightly older than the other two. Moriarty's nickname–a shortening of 'elegant'–was a compliment, as he was not only a good climber but possessed a graceful climbing style despite possessing a large frame. It had several spelling variations; Eli, Eley, or the Elly used here.

As was common in these days, the boys spent every hour they could outdoors, in all weather, giving them an enviable fitness. The trick of course was to hope that mischievous behaviour could be channelled into worthwhile and innocent pastimes. Some help came from a Currie youth club founded in 1954 by Alick Buchanan-Smith (1932-1991), who farmed at nearby Balerno and later became a Conservative MP, serving as a minister under Margaret Thatcher. He became, as Jeff Connor noted, the first and unlikeliest mentor in Haston's climbing life. His family owned an old cottage near Crianlarich, and this became a useful base for exploring the higher hills.

It was a friend of Buchanan-Smith who took the trio up their first route, Curved Ridge on the Buachaille, in late 1954. This is a good introduction to bigger things, and it must have provided inspiration as they began to train, firstly in the school gym, then at their own outdoor crag, albeit a man-made one. This was composed of two retaining walls, one above the local railway line, the other adjacent to the Water of Leith, into which waste water from the local tannery flowed. These walls were not of smooth, well-jointed and mortared brick walls, but had been built using sandstone with rough outer surfaces which over time, and once cleaned of vegetation and slime, could provide a good training ground for rock climbing.

The teenagers evidently enjoyed their discovery of these walls, and with the climbing bug now well instilled took to them with great enthusiasm, their fingers and arms growing stronger with every outing. Mistakes could be punished by a 'dooking' in the filthy Water of Leith, but the Currie Wa's, though only 15ft in height, became the equivalent of a gritstone crag. Long traverses provided not only strength but stamina, while soloing added a useful mental attitude. As Moriarty would later relate to Connor, they did not realise for some time just how good at climbing they had become–until, that is, they visited mountain crags and tried established routes.

In 1967, the climber and gear-shop owner Graham J Tiso (1935-1992) funded a guidebook. *Creag Dubh and the Eastern Outcrops* described the various railway walls, and included a section on the Currie Wa's compiled by Haston. He used a continental grading system for the routes, from I to VI, with all first ascents ascribed to Haston, Moriarty and Stenhouse.

About then, Glasgow climbers would find and use their own equivalent, with the Finnieston railway walls, a marathon 3,000ft in length and now to be seen adjoining a stretch of fast road parallel to the Clyde and leading to the Kingston Bridge. There are other such walls, superb for developing strong fingers and stamina. Indoor climbing walls have now, sadly, all but replaced such pioneering urban venues, but for an interesting article on the Glasgow walls see the article by John Mackenzie. [20] Aberdeen climbers of course have their natural sea cliffs, with a guidebook published in 2003 including the cliffs of the east coast. [21]

It was in late 1956 in Glen Coe that Haston met Ronnie Marshall, an experienced climber and member of the JMCS. Brother of Jimmy Marshall, Ronnie was less ambitious with his climbing but unselfish enough to introduce Haston's group to roped routes. These included Agag's Groove, the sight of which only one year earlier had impressed the boys as they scrambled up Curved Ridge. Two days later Haston was leading Stenhouse up Crowberry Ridge, following one of the easier variations, Greig's Ledge, a Difficult. From then on the group would follow the classic curve taken by most young climbers, moving up through the grades, learning from mistakes and developing their own styles.

Jimmy Marshall meanwhile continued to stretch his wings, and on 12 February 1956 was on the first ascent of *Scabbard Chimney* (170m V,6) with Len Lovat and Archie Hendry. Lovat had made the first summer ascent of this route on Summit Buttress, Stob Coire nan Lochan, 30 May 1954, with Ian D McNicol and A Way at Severe, and was obviously aware of its potential for a winter climb. Combined tactics and two pegs were needed to overcome an overhang; it is a route which does not hold much ice, and it usually provides a testing ascent.

Ronnie Marshall persuaded the three Currie boys to join the JMCS– where, despite being reluctant to join anything which they saw as part of the establishment, they realised that the transport which the club organised was a boost to their climbing, as was information that could be gleaned from other members. This group of four would shortly grow into a gang of six, whose combined efforts over the next decade or so would take mountaineering in Scotland to new heights.

References

1. Interview with Hamish MacInnes, 24th August 2016.
2. MacInnes, Hamish. *International Mountain Rescue Handbook.* (1972.)
3. MacInnes, Hamish. *Call-Out.* (London, 1973. Hodder & Stoughton).
4. Bonington, Chris. *I Chose to Climb.* (London, 1966, Victor Gollancz). Chapter 2, Winter in Scotland.
5. MacInnes, Hamish. *Personal communication.* July 2016.

6. Perrin, Jim. *The Villain–The Life of Don Whillans.* (London, 2005, Hutchinson.)

7. Crocket, Ken and Richardson, Simon. *Ben Nevis - Britain's Highest Mountain.* (Scottish Mountaineering Trust, 2nd edition 2009).

8. Whillans, Don and Ormerod, Alick. *Don Whillans: Portrait of a Mountaineer.* (London: Heinemann, 1971).

9. Downes, R.O. and O'Hara, M.J. *Scotland 1956.* In: Cambridge Mountaineering, 1957.

10. Smart, Iain. *In Memorium. Malcolm Slesser j.1948.* SMCJ 40, 199, 2008, pp.234-238.

11. Patey, Tom. *The Zero Gully Affair.* SMCJ 26, 149, May 1958, pp.205-216.

12. <http://www.alpinist.com/doc/ALP47/27-tool-user-wart-hog>

13. A Bludger was originally the British name for a pimp who robbed his prostitutes' clients; it later morphed into the Australian/NZ name for an idle or lazy person, who would rather scrounge than work.

14. Mason, John. *Charlie Vigano. 1928 (1967)–1998.* In: Climbers' Club Journal, Obituary. 1998, pp.156-159.

15. Lates, Mike. History Section, The SMC Guide to *Skye–The Cuillin*, 2011, p.14.

16. Bastinado. A form of torture involving beating or caning the soles of ones feet.

17. Mallinson, John. *Eric Langmuir.* Obituary in CCJ, 2004-05, p.142. <http://climbers-club.co.uk/journal/original/2004-05-Journal-p131-156.pdf>

18. O'Hara, Michael J. *Obituary notice for Eric Duncan Grant Langmuir.* Royal Society of Edinburgh. <http://bit.ly/2e2TQw6> (Accessed August 2016).

19. Pronunciation of Trilleachan. <http://www.walkhighlands.co.uk/corbetts/beinn-trilleachan>

20. Mackenzie, John. *Beanntan Glaschu.* SMCJ 30, 164, 1973, pp.115-121.

21. Morrison, Neil (Ed.) *The North East Outcrops.* 2003, SMT.

11

A Mess of Mediocrity (1956-1959)

WINTER CLIMBING in the east of Scotland began slowly in 1956, finally seeing better conditions by 4 March when *Parallel Buttress* (280m VI,6) on Lochnagar received its first winter ascent from Patey, Brooker and Jeremy (Jerry) Smith. Eyed by many parties, and with several attempts having failed due to icy conditions, it lies between Parallel Gullies A and B and provides continuously interesting climbing.

In some quarters this ascent was regarded as imperfect: the lower third had been bypassed by climbing the start of Parallel Gully A, a difficult 100ft section in the middle had also been bypassed, and four pegs for aid had been used –in addition to which the crux tower had been climbed with the aid of an étrier, or short ladder. The first free ascent was that by Douglas (Doug) F Lang and Neil Quinn in January 1969. To be fair on the 1956 party, however, conditions were sub-optimum, with loose snow and high winds.

The ascent of Parallel Buttress highlighted the competitive nature of Patey who, despite an agreement by all to share leads, hogged much of the route. He displayed another unattractive habit by climbing with inadequate clothing; in modern terminology this might be regarded as 'macho', but probably Patey simply did not care. There is a classic photograph taken by Brooker on this route showing Patey with no headgear. Most of his clothing was borrowed, and in an article in the Climbers' Club Journal Jerry Smith described him as '...*looking cold, his hair matted with snow. His face, where visible, shades of mauve and green.*'[1] Sadly, Jerry Smith was to die in an abseiling accident in the Alps in 1958.

In the mid-1950s, Mac Smith and Patey were working on the new Cairngorms guide. With increasingly difficult climbs being put up in winter, the use of adjectival rock grades was becoming inadequate. A new system of winter grading was thus devised, based on that used in the Alps, with the easiest grade being 1 and the hardest, at that time, 6. This explains the title of Jerry Smith's article *Sestogradists in Scotland*, with sestogradist being Italian for a sixth-grade climber. Later, this system would be enlarged and improved by the addition of technical grades; the first grade, now using Roman numerals, indicates the overall seriousness of a climb, and this is followed by Arabic numerals giving the hardest technical grade to be encountered, such as Parallel Buttress at VI,6.

There remained one major Lochnagar buttress still to be climbed in winter, and as conditions improved in March 1956 Brooker returned to make the most of it. The loose powder which had hindered the ascent of Parallel Buttress had now turned to perfect hard snow, and Brooker, Jerry Smith and Dick Barclay duly gathered at the foot of the Black Spout Pinnacle. Chapter 9 described Brooker's summer ascent, and now he was after the winter experience. Barclay watched as Smith cut his way up the first pitch of Route 1, reaching with difficulty the overhung recess from where a peg above allowed him to swing on to the upper slabs. Watching this, and suffering from a hangover, Barclay decided not to join the fray.

Above, using another peg, Smith climbed a bulging nose of rock to gain easier ground and a belay. Previous attempts on this line had failed on the first pitch, and success on it provided an extra boost in confidence. There were more hard sections above, one requiring what Brooker referred to as a *Knubel* move. [2] This was a reference to the Swiss guide Joseph Knubel (1881-1961) who, on the first ascent of the east face of the Grépon, had jammed his axe pick in a crack and pulled over an overhang. After five hours of sustained climbing, the Pinnacle had been climbed.

Route 1 (200m V,6) was given the grade of 5 when reported in the SMCJ, even before the new guide was published with an explanation of the revised winter grading system. Until then, summer grades had been universally applied. Climbers would also rely heavily on an awareness of who had made the first ascent, so that if a summer climb had been graded simply as VS it was of more use to know that if it was, for example, a Jimmy Marshall route, then it was probably fairly hard and worth climbing. Of course talking to anyone who had climbed the route was usually better still. Ascent times were often provided for a winter ascent, but these could vary widely depending on snow and ice conditions. A route's difficulty remained a guessing game until further improvements in grading, including technical difficulty, were implemented.

The Black Spout Pinnacle was one of Brooker's favourite bits of rock, and he was back on 16 June with Ken Grassick (1935-1989), one of the 'Boor Boys' (officially the Corrour Club). Grassick joined the SMC in 1955 and was working as a GP in Newcastle before succumbing to acute leukaemia. On Lochnagar the pair made the third ascent of Route 1 – then, seeing that the wind had dried the rocks, Brooker suggested a line he had considered for some time, taking the right-hand fault above the Springboard. This resulted in the first ascent of *The Link* (180m VS,4c), so named as it connects Routes 1 and 2. From Strange's Cairngorms history, it seems that this was regarded as being the hardest rock climb on Lochnagar for ten years.

Brooker and Grassick were back in action on 24 June, exploring Creagan a' Choire Etchachan. They were attracted to the clean-cut edge at the left of the crag, forming the right edge of the buttress named the Bastion. This resulted in one of the most popular climbs in the Cairngorms, *The Talisman* (100m Hard Severe). On the first ascent, combined tactics were used on the crux pitch, with the actual crux move á memorable one, rounded, indifferent handholds allowing an uncertain move on to an exposed arête. The climb was named after a piece of aluminium alloy which Brooker carried and which provided the belay peg for the crux pitch.

Chapter 9 mentioned the discovery of this crag, which disproved the negative comments in Parker's early Cairngorms guide. Exploration would continue for several decades, particularly on the expanse of reddish granite on the right of the crag, the Crimson Slabs. These were climbed on 4 September 1955 by Patey and John Yeaman Leslie Hay (1938-), another who had been a pupil at Aberdeen Grammar School. Hay joined the SMC in 1956, and his other clubs include the Cairngorm and the Etchachan.

Patey and Hay climbed *The Dagger* (130m VS), the right-hand of the two major corners on the slabs. Unfortunately, four pegs for aid were used; the route was probably freed in the early 1960s. Hay returned on 22 July 1956 with fellow Etchachan Club members Ronnie Wiseman and Allan Cowie to make an ascent of *Djibangi* (140m VS), the left-hand corner on the Crimson Slabs. The route used two aid pegs originally but is another quality line.

As for its exotic-sounding name, Strange's history gives two possibilities; the first was supplied by Alan Will, who thought it referred to an empty oil drum which George Adams carried to the foot of the climb, while Hay stated that it was the name of an Australian duck. As no such listing for the latter can be found, the first option seems more likely.

Càrn Etchachan received some interest from Patey the following winter. On 10 February 1957, he and Mac Smith walked in from Derry Lodge and found hard snow and ice on the rocks. Starting from the foot of Castlegates Gully, they worked out a very fine mountaineering route up the buttress, taking in ramps and grooves and linking with a groove system on the upper cliff. *Route Major* (285m IV,5) has complex route-finding, a mountaineer's delight.

❅ ❅ ❅

The great crag known as Càrnmore, in the beautiful and remote heart of the Fisherfield Forest, remained all but unknown to climbers until 1952, when Clegg and Wrangham recorded Diagonal Route (250m Severe). In 1954 an RAF party, including a certain CJS Bonington, recorded a poor line with *Poacher's Route* (210m Very Difficult).

All then stayed quiet until the stone-walled barn beneath the cliff hosted four climbers on a walking trip at New Year 1955. They included Mike O'Hara and Bob Downes, and all were impressed by the potential lines on the great crag above.

O'Hara returned the following Easter with Marjorie Langmuir (Eric Langmuir's sister) and George J Fraser, and three climbs were found including *Original Route* (200m VS). O'Hara was back again in June with Bob Kendell to climb *Red Scar Entry* (150m VS).

Dissatisfied with Original Route, which has some vegetation in its lower part, he returned in late March 1957 with SGM Clark, Marjorie Langmuir and William (Bill) D Blackwood, climbing the superior *Fionn Buttress* (240m VS) with the latter. The climb provides a good long-day introduction to the crag, while the crux may give some VS leaders pause for thought.

> The third pitch is probably the technical crux of the route, a superb piece of climbing on perfect Lewisian gneiss. The first ascent of this wall must have been as bold a lead as any seen at Càrnmore, as protection would have been impossible. From the belay step on to the slab, gain a ledge and go up and left, back right a few moves then straight up passing a peculiar cavity in the rock. After rain this is full of water. Ignore the obvious shallow groove on the right. The crux follows, as one heads straight up for an overhung ledge, climbing a steepening wall on diminishing holds. Don't bother looking for protection – there isn't any and you'll just get tired. With relief gain the ledge and a runner, move left to cross a corner and belay on blocks. [3]

The author can state in all honesty that four of the routes he has climbed on this crag remain four of the best rock climbs he has climbed in Scotland. They are *Fionn Buttress*, along with *Dragon* (95m HVS), by Fraser and O'Hara, 22 April 1957; *Gob* (110m HVS), by Robin Smith and Dougal Haston, April 1960; and *Balaton* (105m HVS), by Willie Gorman and Con Higgins (Creagh Dhu), May 1966. Other climbers will have their favourites, but most would be happy to climb the above.

Many climbers (including O'Hara retrospectively) have felt that Dragon deserves a grading of E1 5a, and certainly one needs to be climbing well. The line had been examined top and bottom before the first ascent, with the easy first pitch already climbed and the upper section investigated from above the previous year, with Bob Kendell. On the day, O'Hara led the crucial third pitch, gaining a tiny perch under the overhang and traversing left under the great roof.

The exposure here is terrifying, and a fall by a second would see them hanging in space, so O'Hara protected Fraser as best he could, firstly inserting a leaf piton in the roof above. This demanded a delicate operation as his right arm was keeping him in place by friction on a slanting shelf, while the peg had to be inserted with his left hand and he could not afford to drop the peg, nor himself fall. As O'Hara wrote in an article co-written with Fraser, *'It took a long, long time.'* [4]

The next step was to rig a belay which would adequately protect Fraser. A second peg under the roof and several slings allowed O'Hara to move off his tiny footholds and belay his second very close to the crucial traverse. Fraser now felt secure and a short traverse left, with the void sucking at his heels, allowed the final rocks to be climbed with release on to soft, flat turf above.

The rock is Lewisian gneiss, and the author once made a mistake by asking O'Hara what had caused the wonderful pockets found on sections of the crag. O'Hara was by then a distinguished petrologist, and his chemistry-rich explanations were about as high above the author's head as was the crux of Dragon. Indeed, Professor O'Hara FRS, FRSE was a principal investigator in experimental petrology for all six Apollo missions which had been successful in bringing back rock samples from the surface of the moon.

Where Fionn Buttress follows the prominent buttress standing out at the left of the crag, Dragon takes a crack system on the upper wall, right of a prominent corner, leading steeply to a huge jutting roof, turned on the left. Its name comes from O'Hara's partner George Fraser, who solved the final section and thus slayed the dragon. [5] Two years later, Fraser disappeared while attempting the first ascent of the 6812m Nepalese peak Ama Dablam. Together with Mike Harris, they were last seen 300m from the summit before clouds and snow obscured them.

April 1960 saw two men who were to be among the outstanding climbers of the 1960s team up to record Gob, on the upper wall at Càrnmore. In March 1962, Robin Smith and Ted Wrangham attended a meeting of climbers bound for an expedition to the Pamirs in Russia. Wrangham recalled an earlier conversation with Smith, when they talked about two climbs in Scotland on which Wrangham had failed but where Smith was to succeed: Thunder Rib on Skye, and Gob.

Thunder Rib (240m E1 5a) was climbed in April 1960 by Smith and G Milnes, another Edinburgh student. It seems to have a reputation. Smith's description was a recipe, if not for disaster, then at least frustration– *'The fine rib on the left of Deep Gash Gully. Follow line of least resistance.'* Fortunately for those intent on safe navigation on Skye, Peter F Macdonald, who made another very early ascent, perhaps the second, sent in fuller details. He summed up the route, on Sgùrr a' Mhadaidh, as having two hard pitches, then a delightful V.Diff continuation. Another later ascender noted that the hard traverse on the second pitch, though devious, is the natural line of weakness. It can be surmised that Smith felt his description adequate, but then he was capable of climbing out of, as well as into, difficulties.

Regarding *Gob* (110m HVS), presumably his first conversation with Wrangham had led Smith to team up with Haston for this spectacular route, which climbs to an overhanging headwall, then makes a daunting traverse to find a breakout above. The traverse crosses an out-thrust shield of rock, the 'Swallow's Nest', and continues to belay at a 'pulpit' just before the pedestal of Dragon.

As the current guide remarks in the introduction to the crag–

> The most popular routes are Fionn Buttress, Dragon, and Gob, and it is worth bearing in mind that all three contain very exposed traverses and are not recommended for inexperienced seconds.

As for the name, the SMCJ editor explained that Gob was Gaelic for the beak of a bird, though some cynics might make a connection to Haston's early years in Currie, where local urchins would hang over the top of the railway walls to gob or spit at Haston and his friends climbing below. [6]

Two good routes were found on either side of Dragon, with *Abomination* (100m HVS), John McLean, A Currey and John Cunningham, 22 July 1966, climbed by the Creagh Dhu and apparently not as desperate as it appears, taking the obvious plummeting groove starting left of the top of the first pitch of Dragon. Another natural line is *The Sword* (80m E3), Richard (Dick) J Isherwood (1943-2013) and Eddie Birch, June 1967, starting right of the top pitch of the Dragon slab and taking the big groove above the cave. This Cambridge team used about three aid points, and some poor rock on the first pitch lowers the quality slightly. The route crosses Gob next to the 'Swallow's Nest' to break through the roof. It was the third first ascent of the day by Isherwood and Birch, who had already climbed *Penny Lane* (70m HVS) and *The Cracks* (40m Scottish VS).

Isherwood was born in Lancashire and read zoology at Cambridge. He was a leading rock climber in the late 1960s. Birch was a member of the Black and Tans, a Manchester-based club.

O'Hara would return to this magical area and find routes on other crags for the next decade or so, including *Hieroglyphics* (130m VS), 19 April 1957 with JDC Peacock and Fraser on the adjacent crag of Torr na h-Iolaire. Other climbs include *Ecstasy* (95m Severe), 20 August 1955 with Kendell and *Dishonour* (115m Very Difficult), 10 April 1955 with Marjorie Langmuir on Maiden Buttress.

Mike O'Hara was a modest man who gained much respect from Scottish climbers. His routes for the most part were climbed in plimsolls, and pre-dated commercially manufactured nuts. His climbing legacy, at least in Scotland, included the opening-up of the Trilleachan Slabs and Càrnmore Crag, both resulting in a profitable surge of quality climbs, many of which remain classics.

It would be remiss not to mention the role which successive landowners played in this area. The difficult times included the reign of Colonel Whitbread, he of the brewery, who brooked no generous access to the hills on his estate, basically the area with Loch Maree as its south boundary. Climbing had to be carried out sneakily, walking in with heart in mouth and preferably at night, with Whitbread's keeper hopefully asleep.

When the Colonel became too old to hunt and fish, the estate went on the market and was purchased by a Dutch businessman, Paul Fentener van Vlissingen (1941-2006). He had good memories of Highland trips with his mother in the late 1940s and could hardly have failed to fall in love with the country around this area. There are articles online which provide more detail on van Vlissingen, but in essence he was a good landowner, maintaining a healthy relationship with the local inhabitants and an enlightened involvement in the access debate. [7,8,9]

This debate led to the 'Letterewe Accord' in 1993, with walkers, climbers and others, in which van Vlissingen offered unlimited public access in exchange for a pledge of responsible conduct. In turn, this would help to lead to the establishment of the National Access Forum in Scotland, and subsequent access legislation. He had the barn under the crag, often shared with a pony, made more habitable for climbers and walkers. He died of pancreatic cancer, leaving his partner Caroline Tisdall, the writer and art historian.

❋ ❋ ❋

The doldrums into which Scottish mountaineering fell after the war, and which had so far only seen signs of life courtesy of the Creagh Dhu in the west, had by the mid-1950s been swept away by the splinter groups mentioned in Chapter 10. The newest of these, based in Edinburgh, was now poised to resurrect climbing yet further, raising standards and entering Scottish mountaineering like a blast of spindrift to the face. There were several advance notices of this in 1957, as new climbers appeared and partnerships were forged.

On a Sunday morning in May 1957, the 'terrible trio' from Currie were exploring some of the loose rock problems of Caerketton, the hill a couple of miles east of Currie where the ski centre was later built. There, presumably by chance, Jimmy Marshall was also enjoying some fresh air. He was now 28, and an architect. Dougal Haston and Jim 'Elly' Moriarty were 17, James Stenhouse 18. They were climbing fit, stronger than they realised, and unknowingly poised for some leadership in the right direction. Marshall was about to become their metaphysical architect.

Marshall worked through the Caerketton problems with the trio, and perhaps to his surprise they succeeded in climbing the hardest. He recognised that this collection of individuals could, with some help, be guided into something better. It is doubtful whether they too were thinking along these lines, but they did know that they wanted to climb better things – and, as better things were still outside their ken, some guidance would be of help.

Writing in his autobiography 15 years later, Haston commented on the poor state of Scottish climbing at that time. [10] Other than the Creagh Dhu, it was a *'mess of mediocrity and pettiness, full of mountaineers who considered their average talents to be exceptional'*. Considering the level of winter climbs being recorded by Aberdeen climbers at this time, and the individualistic nature of the climbers there, this was too broad a brush. Yes, the Cairngorm Club was mostly into walking, while the SMC was not yet leading any charge towards higher standards, being content in general to improve the infrastructure with guidebooks and climbing huts. Haston may well have had issues with one or two of the older and stuffier members – and before taking his leave of Scotland he would certainly test their patience with some outrageously antisocial behaviour.

His criticism might have been harsh, but there was a kernel of truth in it. On the weekend Zero Gully succumbed there was an obvious hierarchy present at the CIC Hut, with several A-teams and more B-teams. All were competent climbers, but the Creagh Dhu and several Aberdeen climbers stood out above the others. There was nothing wrong or out of the ordinary with that, with some good climbs being recorded by both groups, but in general Marshall, Haston and a few others were beginning to strain at the leash.

Marshall admitted that he joined the SMC in 1955 partly to give them a wake-up call. He wrote in 1978, as contributor to a tribute to Haston–

> Generalizations can be misleading but it is probably safe to state that Scottish Mountaineering wallowed in mediocrity, from the demise of Harold Raeburn into the 1950s, the dynamic Creag [sic] Dhu MC being a notable exception. [11]

Marshall somehow bridged both worlds, climbing and consorting with the Creagh Dhu and his own coterie, and doing some good work within the SMC, such as his guidebook for Ben Nevis and helping with Len Lovat's Glen Coe guides. He was also involved with the CIC Hut. He would resign from the SMC in 1970, apparently in protest at MacInnes becoming an honorary member, and also at what he felt was overt plagiarism by MacInnes of SMC guidebooks for his twin-volume photograph-based guides to Scottish climbs, published in 1971. [12]

The three Currie boys, along with the Marshall brothers, were about to have a sixth climber added to the bubbling pot. In August 1957, Stenhouse and Haston were festering on a wet day in their tent in Glen Coe, on a patch of grass adjacent to the River Coupall and not far from Jacksonville, the Creagh Dhu bothy. A face appeared at the tent door and introduced himself as Robin Smith. Wearing an oilskin jacket, sou'wester hat and wellington boots, he asked whether they wanted to go climbing, and suggested Revelation on the Buachaille's Slime Wall.

The Currie boys' hesitation was partly due to them not having climbed a VS as yet, and also only having gym shoes and welly boots of their own. Smith dismissed these minor problems, saying they could leave their boots at the foot of North Buttress and wear socks over their gym shoes for the climbing. The challenge was taken up. The rocks were running with water as Smith started out on the first pitch, a traverse across a steep wall. Revelation, now the upper section of Bludger's Revelation, is graded Hard Very Severe. Smith, climbing as he often did in a pair of tattered walking boots, slipped a few times, while his gear was as basic and shabby as that of the two seconds; four old slings, ex-War Department steel karabiners and a scarred nylon rope, only 80ft in length.

The trio finished the climb and splashed their way back to the tent, delighted at a successful outing. It had been the first VS for the Currie boys. If Haston had been expecting any compliments, however, he records being disappointed at the reaction from his contemporaries.

Robin Clark Smith (1938-1962) was born in Calcutta (now Kolkata), where his father was a naval architect. The war delayed his normal education for two years, but in 1946 he and his older brother moved to Scotland to begin their formal education at Morrison's Academy in Crieff. After four years, Smith moved to George Watson's College in Edinburgh, one of Scotland's top schools. Bow-legged, thick-set and of medium height, Smith would, in an all-too short climbing career, extend the envelope of Scottish mountaineering. His mother, a keen hillwalker, was a significant factor in his introduction to the Scottish hills, and he walked up Ben Nevis with a school friend when he was 16.

For those who wish to know much more about the man, his first rock climbing partner and school friend Jimmy Cruickshank wrote an in-depth and near exhaustive biography. [13] For a succinct description of Smith's climbing by a fellow climber who was a partner on several hard and outstanding ascents, there is no better source than Jimmy Marshall.

Whilst others (e.g. the Creagh Dhu) were climbing at least equal in difficulty to Smith, it was the consistent aesthetic of line in which he surpassed and from 1957 till his death in the Pamirs, he more or less at will plucked some of the finest rock and ice lines in the country, e.g. Shibboleth, winter

Orion Face, Yo Yo, The Bat, Big Top etc. Remarkably, he had no consistent climbing partner but chose anyone available from contemporary, talented associates. Furthermore he rarely exhibited much concern as to footwear, frequently making serious ascents in battered old walking boots. His fairly short thickset physique, coupled with a finely developed sense of balance, seemed to enable him to hang about on difficult sections for hours, e.g. three hours on the entry pitch of Shibboleth, and four hours on the Barrier Pitch of the Aonach Dubh Girdle.

These aspects were expressions of an awareness to the corrosive nature of protection, aid, and gear, and wherever possible he would maintain a minimal use, 'to give the mountain a chance', as he was wont to say. [14]

In addition to creating many fine routes, Smith also wrote articles on some of these, including The Bat on Ben Nevis, first climbed by Smith and Haston in 1959. His writing style has been described as 'beat', after the group of authors whose work explored and influenced American culture in the post-war period. One such author was Jack Kerouac, and it is likely that Smith would have read *On the Road*. It is fashionable now to comment that Smith's articles have become dated, but several of them, especially *The Bat and the Wicked* remain popular and much admired. [15,16]

Those who are overly critical may be missing the point; the SMCJ–which first published much of Smith's (and Marshall's) prose–is a club journal. It has a duty to its members, and also to the climbing public, in that it attempts to chronicle the doings on Scottish hills and to a lesser extent elsewhere which its editor deems worthy of being recorded. Writing styles inevitably evolve, but readers can enjoy, and even admire, some of the 19th-century tales of vertical explorations by those betweeded and bewhiskered pioneers.

Smith was a teenager when his first articles appeared; he obviously matured, and his writing style would have continued to evolve and improve with time. Writing of an epic ascent on Ben Nevis, in September 1956, just before he entered Edinburgh University to study philosophy, he described how he managed to find two inexperienced JMCS members, Ted Wise and Ian Douglas, and together they charged up the mountain.

As their second route there, having climbed Route 1 on Càrn Dearg Buttress, they chose The Crack (250m HVS) on Raeburn's Buttress, between Càrn Dearg and The Castle. This ended with Smith spending the night alone, above the crux and trying to climb an overhanging chimney in the dark. It was a typical Smith experience. In the dawn light he found an escape route to easier ground, just avoiding rescue. (His companions would later die in separate mountaineering accidents.)

From this came an article, published in the EUMC Journal and praised by that club's vice-president, the experienced alpinist Thomas Graham Brown (1882-1965), a Scot and a physiologist. [17] He had spotted a new voice in climbing literature and advised the 18-year-old that he had a natural style which exactly suited the subject.

Smith's rock climbing had begun in 1954, with Salisbury Crags above Edinburgh and routes on the Buachaille and elsewhere in the Glen Coe area. He had as a mentor Archie Hendry, a language teacher at Watson's and member of the SMC. This was an incredible stroke of luck, as Hendry was experienced and patient enough to introduce Smith to the rock climbing playground that is Glen Coe. At Lagangarbh, he would meet Marshall and others, see them climbing, and join the competitive search for lines.

Smith's first recorded new climb was on the gneiss of Garbh Bheinn of Ardgour, a short hop over the ferry on Loch Linnhe. On an earlier visit with his school friend Cruickshank he had spotted and attempted a crack-line on a face on Pinnacle Ridge. He returned in March 1957 with EUMC novice Victor Burton and succeeded in climbing *Blockhead* (60m E1,5b). In June 1961 he visited the pride of Garbh Bheinn, the South Wall, where with Moriarty he recorded *The Peeler* (45m HVS) on the top tier. The name would suggest a fall but there is no evidence of this. Perhaps it was raining.

In June 1957 Smith recorded a climb on the South Peak of the Cobbler, *Glueless Groove* (45m E2,5b). There is a mystery here, as no second climber was recorded, and even Cruickshank has no first ascent details for this route. The author climbed it in April 1974 in two pitches. The first was easy and enjoyable, on steep, clean rock with big holds. The crux second pitch was a steep wall with tiny quartz holds which had to be revealed by brushing off moss. There was no protection on this stretch and it was a serious and bold lead, particularly for an 18-year old Smith with just a sling or two round his neck.

As John Inglis noted in his posthumous article in the SMCJ, *'From the beginning, Smith produced routes of a high technical standard, often with little secure protection.'* [18] It is quite possible that Smith, who in his formative years as a climber would on occasion set out for the rocks with no partner, hoping to find someone who could hold his rope, had chanced on such a person on the Cobbler. The standard would have defeated most seconds from following. There is no suggestion that the climb was soloed, but this is not impossible.

In the summer of 1957 Smith ran rampant through classic routes in Wales, significantly increasing both his experience and his equipment, courtesy of abandoned gear found on the rocks. He also climbed many of the established Glen Coe VS routes. His alpine climbing was initiated this summer, with JMCS member Jim Clarkson (1927-1968) and JF Gunn Clark (1937-1970). His winter climbing was slower in advancing than his rock work, but in December he climbed with JMCS member Derek Leaver FRSE (1929-1990) and made the first winter ascent of *The Long*

Chimney – Ordinary Route combination (135m IV) on Cuneiform Buttress on the Buachaille.

On the same day, Jimmy Marshall, Donald Mill and George Ritchie climbed the Ordinary Route in its entirety at the same grade, whereas Smith and Leaver moved right high up that route to finish up The Long Chimney. Leaver was from Lancashire and a lecturer in chemistry at Edinburgh University at this time. He joined the SMC the following year and his name appears on many excellent routes including, on Scafell, Chartreuse E1 5b, climbed on-sight with Smith in May 1957. On that same day, Smith also climbed Leverage E1,5b, but Leaver's name is absent, so perhaps it was another occasion where the second could not follow.

In early 1958 Smith made an early winter ascent of Crowberry Ridge Direct, and almost succeeded in finishing Eagle Ridge on Lochnagar. He was staying at Loch End Bothy at Loch Muick with an Edinburgh party and set out with Doug Dingwall. With no prior summer knowledge of the route and no working torches, the pair ground to a halt just below the crux. A slow climbing descent and a return to the bothy at midnight ensued. It would have been the first non-Aberdonian winter ascent.

At Easter 1958 Smith teamed up with Haston and made his second visit to Wales, the pair storming through many classic routes culminating with an early ascent of Joe Brown's classic Cenotaph Corner (E1,5c). At this point, as Cruickshank writes, Haston and his Currie friends had survived their baptism of fire with Smith. They would climb again, with the occasional shaky moment, but Haston was now confident enough to follow his own path. It would be one suffused with much drinking, hell-raising and petty thievery, with some hard climbing along the way.

The 'gang of six', a label used by Robin Campbell, was now formed. The three Currie boys, the two Marshall brothers and Smith would come in and out of focus for the next few years, with no fixed partners, content to climb with whoever was available. They would raise the profile of climbers from Edinburgh, and add to the catalogue of routes not only in Scotland, but internationally.

❊❊❊

As Strange's history noted, by 1958 mountaineers in the east of Scotland had enjoyed an almost free run of their area for nearly a decade. Climbers in other areas were not short of new rock to explore and on the whole access to climbing was easier in the west, particularly Glen Coe, where many of the crags were within an hour or so from the main road.

In April 1957, Marshall had given a slideshow to the Etchachan Club, followed next day by an outing to Lochnagar with Patey. As usual, the latter hogged all the leads, excepting Polyphemus Gully which they soloed. After climbing Route 2, they made the first ascent of *Shylock's Chimney* (50m VS).

During this visit Marshall could hardly have missed seeing Parallel Gully B, still unclimbed in winter. Surely it was now that the germ of an idea entered his consciousness– he should try for a winter ascent. After all, the Aberdonians, along with that maverick MacInnes, had pinched the winter ascent of Zero Gully.

And so it came about that in February 1958 a raiding party from Edinburgh left the Allt-na-giubhsaich bothy in Glen Muick: the two Marshall brothers, Jim Stenhouse and Graham Tiso. The latter was a Birmingham man who decided he liked Scotland so much that he would live there. Working for Cadbury's as a salesman meant that he was always good for chocolates; he even had a car, which made him a magnet for the impecunious 'gang of six'. As an Englishman, he would suffer much verbal abuse, taking this in good humour.

It was hearing of the expense and difficulty of buying such items as boots that persuaded Tiso to set up a business importing and selling climbing and walking equipment. At first he sold from the back of a sailing shop run by a friend, but business was so good that he and his partner Maude, a Scots lass from Eigg, opened a shop in Rodney Street, thus starting the Tiso empire. It is indicative of the state of outdoor retailing at this time that climbers from Glasgow and other parts of Scotland felt the need to trek to Edinburgh to purchase rock boots and hardware.

Conditions on Lochnagar on the morning of Saturday 22 February 1958 were excellent, and Jimmy Marshall and Tiso headed straight for Parallel Gully B. The lower chimney was lean, with ice in the back only, while above were two steep ice bulges. Marshall led the first short pitch over awkward, iced rocks before Tiso, at the time a novice, led the next pitch, taking in the first steep ice wall and leading to the main chimney.

Higher up, the second ice bulge loomed overhead, with the chimney diving more deeply into ice. Difficult climbing led to the overhang, where Marshall stood in a sling from a peg, cutting holds above the bulge. The scoop above the chimneys was gained after four and a half hours of climbing, and the rest of the route followed until the final steep wall. This being bare, they followed a groove up and right to finish.

Marshall considered that *Parallel Gully B* (260m IV,5) was the both the finest and the hardest winter climb he had done in Scotland to date. Patey was furious, and from England wrote a letter to Nicol asking why his route had been stolen by a party from Edinburgh. Aberdonian climbers had been caught napping.

Sadly, two huge rockfalls in 1995 and 2000 significantly altered the route, extending from the right edge of the gully leftwards across the Tough-Brown Face. The classic back-and-foot lower chimney is now a smooth right-facing corner, requiring exceptionally icy conditions to be climbable, and it is unlikely that the gully has been climbed in summer since 1995, hence the removal of star grades.

Haston had a temporary setback in May 1958 when an old motorbike that Moriarty had bought and rehabbed crashed at speed, resulting in a dislocated break of his right arm. It meant a summer bringing the arm back to strength, but a testing weekend on the Buachaille three months later saw him back in action, and in September he was strong enough for a visit to Wales with Smith, climbing Cemetery Gates and Hangover, both E1.

❋❋❋

Doubtless to Haston's frustration, the summer of 1958 in Scotland saw many plum climbs carved out in Glen Coe. Smith in particular was working on a project, one which would see the best line on Slime Wall achieved and further boost the climbing reputation of Edinburgh. His partner for the most part on this project was a medical student from Edinburgh, Andrew Fraser. The weather improved in June and the pair made first ascents on the Buachaille of *Dwindle Wall* (45m E1 5a), on Creag na Tulaich near the entrance to Lagangarbh Coire, and *July Crack* (50m HVS 5a). This they apparently climbed thinking it was the adjoining route August Crack (50m HVS), almost certainly so that the pair could scope out the proposed line on Slime Wall across the gully.

Then came the weekend of the attempt on what was to become the line of *Shibboleth* (167m E2). The first pitch is shared with Guerdon Grooves, above which is a series of cracks and grooves, leading thinly up the huge steep wall. The second pitch, and the first new one, is the crux, and contains a weep. Here Smith clung to the rock for hours, vainly trying to dry it using a towel. He eventually threw in the towel and, as his second man wrote, continued up with simple levitation. The next pitch went, but much time had been lost and eventually dusk and increasing difficulty prompted a retreat from the fourth pitch, the pair moving left and climbing the flake of Revelation.

They returned the next day and approaching by Revelation recommenced their attempt on pitch four. With resolve weakening somewhat, they decided that the fine flake pitch of Revelation was the way to continue, and so they finished on the hillside above. Doubt had now re-entered their minds however, and on descending a chimney on Cuneiform Buttress which gave them a clear view of Slime Wall, they admitted that the direct line was still to be climbed.

Back the following weekend, Smith led the first two pitches again, fixing a peg runner at the crux. When Fraser followed, the peg resisted removal, tiring him severely. Smith finally allowed him to continue, but on giving the peg an extra thump it suddenly released, and Fraser swung out into space. He managed to regain the crux, holding himself in with a fingertip in the vacated crack, but he was now exhausted. With a tight rope and extra help from rope loops he gained the belay.

The third and fourth pitches were climbed, leaving the final two, which they had climbed the week before. It had been agreed that Fraser would lead the fifth pitch, determined as being the easiest (at 5a). The difficult section was a 15ft-long and shallow overhanging corner. This turned out to be a mistake, as seven-and-a-half hours spent struggling up steep, difficult rock had drained him of upper arm and hand strength. Fraser had worked out what the next move needed as he was in semi-layback position, but his strength was fading fast so he had no option other than to make the move. His fingers refused to tighten on the hold and again he was off.

He fell about 30ft and finished about level with Smith but off to one side. Things would have been all right, as Smith and the belay peg had held the fall, but unluckily Fraser had broken a leg. There was a small ledge just below and Smith lowered him until he could sit here, all 12 inches wide and 18 inches long of it. Fraser had recalled that the previous week Smith's runner on this section had fallen off as he moved up, so with his peg hammer he had chipped out a crack and pushed in a single strand of baby nylon. This had held Fraser's fall, shortening it considerably and possibly saving their lives.

The time was now 7.30pm. Fraser set about examining his leg and determined that both bones were broken about halfway up the shin. Any movement was painful. The climbers were about 300ft above the foot of the wall and had 200ft of steep rock above. They shouted for help, and two hours later a rescue party was on its way. This was of course before the official rescue teams were set up, but the two stranded climbers could not have been in better hands.

Creagh Dhu, JMCS and SMC climbers made up the party, and before long the cliff was a hive of industry, with ropes lowered from the top and tied together, while other ropes came in from the North Buttress flank. Splints were also lowered. Eventually, with Smith supporting Fraser on his arms, the pair were pulled over to a platform on North Buttress. Five ropes in all were handling this operation, three from above and two from the side. These were designed for climbing and were therefore stretchy, which would have added to the difficulty. Finally Fraser was on the platform, to be met with the stretcher and a drink of hot chocolate, courtesy of Tiso.

The stretcher was then hauled up the mountain until screes allowed it to be contoured across and down to the top of Lagangarbh corrie, with five ropes pulling and one man guiding from the stretcher. As can be imagined, there was a festive atmosphere despite the trials of the rescuers, with Edinburgh and Glasgow patois bouncing off the rocks and each other. Some of the Creagh Dhu thought that the fall had been the just and awful retribution of the gods, as it was obviously their cliff. [19] Fraser recovered and eventually returned to his studies and to climbing. The second ascent was by Jimmy Marshall and Moriarty.

Smith was still discontented with his line, and in June 1959 returned to climb a direct finish with John MacLean. As for the name of the climb, Smith thought long and hard even before climbing the route, and had come up with Shibboleth, a biblical word used by one tribe to differentiate people from another who could not pronounce it in the right way with a strong aspirate, and who were then to be taken away and killed. It was a type of linguistic password, and as a route has remained a great classic.

As John Inglis noted–

> This characteristic tendency to edit and improve was a hallmark of Smith's attitude to his climbing, and he clearly valued the long-term aesthetic impact of his best lines as well as the transient pleasure of their execution. [20]

The new guidebook was in the very last stages of production, and Shibboleth made it into its pages. What also made it with days to spare was the ascent of *Carnivore* (160m E2) on 9 August 1958 by the Creagh Dhu team of Cunningham and Noon. Aid was used on two pitches, but it was the first route to break out onto the central wall of this very steep crag, taking in several long traverses. The route had a history, as Marshall attempted it but did not find the key, while Whillans also tried in 1955. Then, at the end of May 1958, Whillans came north on his honeymoon, along with Charlie Vigano and his wife. Whillans persuaded Vigano to look at the route, and this time Whillans found the entry pitch, climbing a faint pillar at the left end of the face, then making a long and partly descending traverse right to gain the centre of the crag.

At this juncture they were being impeded by the justifiable complaints of a peregrine, which ultimately helped in the naming of the route. Whillans drove to Fort William and purchased a catapult, which sorted that problem. The other issue was Vigano being unhappy at seconding the traverse, which in those days would have meant a serious fall as protection was minimal. The day was saved when Cunningham turned up, and the route was continued for some way but not finished.

On their descent, Cunningham had noticed a direct finish and, partly annoyed by Whillans' habit of using Cunningham's gear whenever it looked as if it might be difficult to retrieve it, he returned two weeks later with Noon and completed the route by continuing the rightward traverse. Whillans in turn was annoyed, but was not quite finished, and in June 1962 he returned with Derek Walker to climb Carnivore by the Direct Finish, now graced with the name Villain's Finish. This would be his last new route in Britain. The route by the *Villain's Finish* is E2 , and E3 if the original finish traversing right is taken.

Good finds continued to be made in Glen Coe. In September 1958, Jimmy Marshall and Derek Leaver climbed *Trapeze* (150m E1) on Aonach Dubh's West Face E Buttress, while Haston and Stenhouse found the short but sustained *Dingle* (30m HVS) next to Fracture Route on Crowberry Ridge. Smith meanwhile was doing good routes in the Alps, and in October 1958 was admitted to the SMC along with Leaver, Ronnie Marshall, Ronnie Sellars and Graeme Nicol, the last two from Aberdeen.

Other hard climbs in the late 1950s included *Pontoon* (100m E1) on the South Face of Central Buttress on the Buachaille, by the Marshall brothers and Moriarty in April 1959. Jimmy Marshall and George Ritchie had opened up this steep wall in September 1957 with *Pegleg* (90m HVS). In August 1958 Cunningham and Frith Finlayson (1929-2009) had climbed the short but serious *Bluebell Grooves* (40m E4,6a) with some aid pegs. Finlayson was a Glasgow man who pioneered skiing in the Scotland and set up what would become the British Association of Snowsport Instructors.

Ian Nicolson made the second ascent with two points of aid, as did Ed Grindley and Alan Austin on the third ascent. In 1978, an astonishing 20 years after its first ascent, Willie Todd and Dave (Cubby) Cuthbertson reduced aid to one point. Books since the 1980 SMC guide to Glen Coe and Glen Etive have indicated that the Todd-Cuthbertson effort was the first free ascent, but in a 2000 blog Cubby states that they used one point of aid. [21]

On Slime Wall, Haston and Jimmy Marshall climbed *Lecher's Route* in June 1959, taking the groove parallel and right of Bludger's with two pegs. It was later combined with a direct start and *Superstition* (Davie Todd and Willie Gordon, May 1962) to provide *Lecher's Superstition* (110m E2). Marshall and MacLean teamed up in September 1959 to find the bold *Apparition* (160m E1). On the North Face of Aonach Dubh, April 1959 saw an uncharacteristic poor line from Smith and Haston in May 1959, with *Stook* (120m VS,4c), climbing above Pleasant Terrace.

In May 1958 Smith had started to explore a great line in Glen Coe: a corner on the North Face of Aonach Dubh which, not content with being simply overhanging, actually overhung in two planes. The author has had a small taste of what Smith and his companion, David Hughes, an engineering student from Edinburgh, must have felt as they scrambled up the terrace and rounded a corner to suddenly see the line before them. The line is so commanding and direct that it simply shouts 'Climb Me!' It would be named *Yo-Yo* (90m E1).

In 1958 there were still no harnesses or nuts, karabiners were of heavy steel, and slings were an unvarying dull or dirty white like the rope – which was probably a hawser-laid 'Viking'. The only real advance in equipment was rock boots, if the climber could afford a pair, which Hughes could not. Smith probably had a tatty pair of walking boots, or may have had rock boots – we don't know.

Hughes wrote an interesting account of this route which was included in the Cruickshank biography. [22] A visit in May 1958 saw the first pitch, the crux, climbed. The rock was reasonably dry and Hughes makes the interesting point that stories of Smith hanging about for a long time on this pitch, drying the rock with a towel, as given in Ken Wilson's *Hard Rock,* just don't fit. Much more likely is that the author of that entry was confusing this tactic with Shibboleth, where Smith certainly did try to dry wet rock using a towel.

At the foot of the first pitch the ground slopes down very steeply, so that a climber only has to move up a few holds to find that the fall potential has grown exponentially. The start is quite bouldery with holds, but on a line which is initially devious. Higher up, the corner provides a fine layback. Smith came across a peg from which hung a Stubai peg hammer – this had been left by Whillans who had attempted the route in very wet conditions. As they had spent some time trying to arrange protection, with jammed knots, by the time Hughes seconded the pitch (and very much enjoying the layback) darkness had started to fall. So they abandoned the route and climbed off up a rising ramp on the left, leading to the sarcastically named Pleasant Terrace.

Smith naturally wanted to finish the climb, so he wrote it up and called it *Halfway,* thereby staking a claim. Along with Hughes he returned in May 1959; the ropes – they used two as on the first run – were the same, but Smith now had a pair of rock boots. With their previous knowledge they were soon at the top of what is now the first pitch (on the 1958 attempt Smith had split this into two pitches). As in 1958, Hughes was wearing rigid boots.

The next five hours saw Hughes hiding under the hood of his anorak as Smith threw down plenty of rubbish from the second pitch, until the light began to go and thunderclouds swelled. When lightning started to appear *below* the level of the cliff it was definitely time to leave, so Smith down-climbed the second pitch, removing gear as he went. With the ropes tied together, an abseil led to the approach route.

It rained the next day, a Sunday, but on Monday they were back and Smith climbed the second pitch with its rattling chockstones, arms grasping them for security with nothing below but empty space. The third and final pitch went smoothly and the route was climbed. Its name, Smith and Hughes decided, was fairly obvious, what with all the uppings and downings required. It was a typical Smith line: striking, obvious, and another Glen Coe classic.

Smith soon exercised his SMC membership and began using the CIC Hut legally. One of the less salubrious sides of a few of the new groups of climbers was their predilection for breaking into huts. One can sympathise

Celebrated Scots mountaineer Hamish MacInnes in action on a new ice route on Buachaille Etive Mòr, possibly the Grade V Route 1 on the Rannoch Wall. February 1972. He's wearing Salewa 12-point crampons and wielding an early model of his Terrordactyl hammer. Partner unknown. © John Cleare

Dr. Tom Patey - recce at the Black Rock Gorge of Novar, Sutherland. February 1967. © John Cleare

Creagh Dhu climbers Norrie Muir (leading) and John McLean on Wappenshaw Wall (VS) on the Rannoch Wall, Buachaille Etive Mòr. © Ken Crocket

The infamous scoop of Hammer (HVS) on the Trilleachan Slabs, first ascent Mick Noon and John Cunningham in 1957. To use a cautious approach here will probably fail. Climber Colin Stead. © Ken Crocket

August Crack on Great Gully Buttress, Buachaille Etive Mòr. A HVS climbed in 1955 by Bill Smith & John Cunningham. Climbers here unknown. © JR Marshall

John Cunningham on Grooved Arête, a 1946 VS by Cunningham and Bill Smith on Crowberry Ridge, Buachaille Etive Mòr. © SMC

A Creagh Dhu group before their bothy Jacksonville in Glen Coe. © CDMC

Bob Richardson gains a good hold above the crux wall on Fionn Buttress (VS) on Carnmore crag. © Ken Crocket

Dougal Haston (1940-1977) - celebrated Scottish alpinist and high altitude mountaineer. Hoy July 1977.
© John Cleare

Pat Walsh on the 2nd ascent of Bastinado (E1) in July 1956.
© CDMC

Ian Fulton above it all on the exciting traverse of the Carnmore route
Gob (HVS) first ascent Smith & Haston in 1960. © Ken Crocket

The short but white-knuckled traverse on p2 of Balaton (HVS) on the lower tier of Carnmore. Climber: Colin Grant.
© Ken Crocket

Ken Crocket on p1 Carnivore (E2/3) Glen Coe. Sought after by the best climbers of the day.
© Ken Crocket

Three of the 'splinter group'; Dougal Haston, James Stenhouse, and its chief architect, Jimmy Marshall. © JR Marshall

Alastair Walker on p1 June Crack (VS) Great Gully Buttress, Buachaille Etive Mòr. The first VS on this crag, a John Cunningham – Bill Smith route. © Ken Crocket

Squirrels MC climber John Porteous step cutting the first pitch of Smith's Gully (V,5) on Creag Meagaidh. Route named by first ascender JR Marshall as Robin Smith had been defeated by poor conditions on an earlier attempt.
© Ken Spence

Robin Smith in Glen Coe. *'...short, stocky and amazingly loose-jointed; bandy legs; very long arms, with huge hands like bunches of bananas; a large head; and a lot of charm.'* © JR Marshall

Robin Campbell, poor conditions on Pinnacle Ridge (IV,4), Sgurr nan Gillean, Skye. Photo: Malcolm Slesser. © SMC

Tom Patey in action on Aladdin's Buttress Direct (IV,4), Coire an t' Sneachda. February 1967. © John Cleare

Archie Hendry and Robin Smith. Hendry (1919-2013) was an early climbing mentor to Smith, and a language teacher at George Watson's Boys' College in Edinburgh. © SMC

JR Marshall on the first ascent of The Bullroar (HVS) May 1961. This climb takes in several exposed traverse pitches across the huge slabs of Càrn Dearg Buttress, Ben Nevis. © SMC

Robin Smith on the Barrier Pitch of the North Face of Aonach Dubh Girdle, May 1962. © SMC

The beautiful Torridonian sandstone of Sword of Gideon (VS) South Face of Sgùrr a' Chaorachain, Applecross. Climber: Colin Grant. © Ken Crocket

Bob Richardson and his Austin A40 in Glen Coe. The car made it to the Dolomites and back. Mainstay of the Greenock MC. c.1962. © SMC

The Cioch Nose (Severe), Applecross. Iain Macleod on the 2nd pitch. © Anne Bennet

Rab Carrington on p2 of Titan's Wall (E3), Càrn Dearg Buttress, Ben Nevis. © Ian Fulton

Sgùrr Dearg and the Inaccessible Pinnacle from the top of the Sgùrr Alasdair stone chute. © Roger Robb

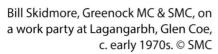

Bill Skidmore, Greenock MC & SMC, on a work party at Lagangarbh, Glen Coe, c. early 1970s. © SMC

Alastair 'Bugs' McKeith at play, referring to a guidebook. © SMC

Rab Carrington, p1 Torro (E2) Càrn Dearg Buttress,
Ben Nevis. 2nd ascent, and first free ascent, 1970.
© Ian Fulton

First ascent of The Giant (E3)
1963, Creag an Dubh Loch
© SMC

Nigel Tranter. © Peter Macdonald

First ascent of Am Buachaille sea-stack, Sandwood Bay, Sutherland. July 23.1967. Tom Patey in action, Ian Clough belaying. *".the rock was weathered into horizontal dinner plates with the fragility of digestive biscuits..."* © John Cleare

Crux pitch of Point Five Gully (V,5) Ben
Nevis. 1st front-pointed ascent, 16 March
1971. Climber: Mike Geddes.
© John Higham.

Mike Geddes in Snell's Field, Chamonix,
1972. © Harold Gillespie

1st winter ascent Astronomy (VI,5), Ben Nevis, March 1971. Allen Fyffe,
Hamish MacInnes & Ken Spence. © Allen Fyffe

Panorama of North-East Face of Ben Nevis. © Alex Gillespie

King Rat (E1) Creag an Dubh Loch. Colin Grant on p3 . © Ken Crocket

Apollyon Ledge (II) Creag Meagaidh. Climber Dennis Gray © Diana Djknaak

Hamish MacInnes, Scottish mountaineer, inventor and mountain-rescue leader, at work in the ice-axe factory at his Glen Coe cottage. An early metal axe. April 1968. © John Cleare

when in bad weather a hut is found empty and locked, and with there being no opportunity to gain access via normal channels. There even exists a short video showing a member of a well-known mountaineering club climbing into a roof window of Lagangarbh. The CIC Hut was another popular destination for the instant-access mob, and Jimmy Marshall wrote amusingly of the stooped-over posture that such climbers had, brought about by frequent wriggling through one of the windows at that hut. It was not a good time to be a hut custodian.

❄ ❄ ❄

Smith put the convenience of the CIC Hut to use at New Year 1959, staying there with EUMC member Richard (Dick) K Holt. Smith's visit was typically audacious, and on Ne'erday the pair climbed *Tower Face of the Comb* (250m VI,6). Noted in the current guide as being one of the best mixed routes on the mountain, it climbs the steep face starting just above the start of Comb Gully. Knowing full well the limited amount of daylight, and given the obvious difficulties facing them, it was inevitable that there would be a night-time finish. Additionally, there was no moon.

The climb engaged the two for over ten hours, as even the easier-angled ground higher up the buttress was difficult in deep snow and high wind. As a mark both of Smith's reputation and of the route, it would be 28 years before a second ascent was made, by Stephen Venables and Victor Saunders. Many an able climber had stood below the route but walked away. It was the first grade VI to be climbed on the mountain.

Winter climbing in Scotland is not solely about climbing ice and snow; a mixed route can and will throw in rock, frozen turf, icy patches and snow. In contrast to pure snow and ice routes, it is often easier to find protection on mixed ground, though even here iced-up cracks can be awkward. A good mixed climb is often sought out by the knowledgeable, being one which should present a multitude of problems to be thought out and chewed on. Such routes can be hard on gloves, however, with much clearing of snow to find holds and protection.

In Scotland, leading mountaineers were now actively seeking big lines, routes which were of a good length and, perhaps more important, followed strong features such as cracks, chimneys and of course gullies. Not the gullies favoured by the Victorians, with convenient ledges for belays, jammed rocks to throw a rope over and lush vegetation. This might be an exaggeration, but on the whole the rise in climbing standards was allowing ever-steeper rock and ice to be climbed. Smith, as one example, was a master at finding and climbing the best lines on a crag.

On Ben Nevis, by the end of 1958 only a few major gullies still awaited a winter ascent, with the three Minus Gullies and Point Five being prominent. Zero Gully had led the way, and it was obvious that the focus would now shift to Point Five. Several known attempts had been made– by Joe Brown's party in 1956, by Patey and also the Creagh Dhu in 1957, and by MacInnes and Clough in 1958.

Other than snow conditions, with spindrift avalanches often forcing retreats, one major problem was the lack of good protection. Ice pegs were simply longer rock pegs and were of dubious use for belaying, as were ice axe shafts. It was having come across two broken wooden axe shafts–and three bodies–below Zero Gully that had prompted MacInnes to begin work on metal axes. The party in question had no ice pegs and the leader had fallen from the third pitch in less than ideal conditions.

The ethos of British mountaineering was to minimise the use of artificial aid. There were many examples during exploratory climbing when combined tactics were used, perhaps standing on a partner's shoulders as the holds above were out of normal reach. Standing in a sling became another tactic, allowing an overhang to be climbed, and of course an occasional peg was used, sometimes as a runner, sometimes for direct aid. Although standards were on the rise, protection equipment was not as yet keeping pace.

In winter climbing, at the end of the 1950s moves up a difficult ice pitch might have been protected by a pair of ice pegs, as for example on the first ascent of Zero Gully (see Chapter 10). At Easter 1958, MacInnes had inserted a bolt for a belay, leaving a rope and descending, to return the following day when he climbed back up the fixed rope.

The use of artificial aid was about to be taken to its limit and beyond, however, when Point Five Gully was subject to siege tactics. On 7-8 January 1959, Ian Stewart Clough (1937-1970) and four friends made the first ascent of *Waterfall Gully* (300m IV,4) on the right flank of Càrn Dearg Buttress. The only difficult pitch on this is the first, and it is hard to accept a two-day ascent, leaving a fixed rope. The author and Colin Stead climbed the same route in the last days of step-cutting, taking three hours for the entire climb in icy conditions. This, though, as it turned out, was just a warm-up for Clough's next deed.

Clough was a gritstone-trained Yorkshireman who made many good alpine ascents, including the first ascent of the Central Pillar of Frêney in 1961 with Bonington, Whillans and Jan Duglosz, and the first British ascent of the Eiger's North Face with Bonington in 1962. He was to become an instructor at MacInnes' Glencoe School of Mountaineering and died on an expedition to Annapurna when a sérac collapsed.

By all accounts an excellent climber and instructor, Clough was a member of the RAF's Kinloss Mountain Rescue Team; as his colleague Ray Sefton recalled, its members were mainly National Servicemen who disliked the

RAF but lived for the team. In the mid-1950s, the team's climbing standards were in general low, though personal fitness was high. Clough was posted in from RAF West Freugh in Wigtownshire in early 1957. He wandered into the billet, and the team stared at him as he unpacked his kit and hung his slings and pitons on a locker. Someone shouted *'What are we going to call him?'*, and up came the suggestion *'Dangle'*, and so that was his nickname from then on.

Clough and three others–John Alexander, Don Pipes (both ex-Kinloss MRT members) and Robin Shaw (GUMC)–began their siege on Monday 12 January. There are more details in the Ben Nevis history, but basically it was a case of climbing on a pitch until tired, retreating to the foot of the climb, allowing another to take a turn, fixing pegs where possible, using étriers, and so on. Deciding that pegs were not always possible, the group made a trip down the hill and had bolts and hangers made.

Overall, their ascent took 29 hours of actual upward climbing, with 40 hours in total in the gully spread over six days. Clough was not, as Marshall had commented on Robin Smith, *'giving the mountain a chance'*. In his autobiography, Haston wrote that in later years he would become friendly with Clough and do some good climbing with him, but at that time he and his contemporaries were suspicious of any Englishman who thought he could climb ice. [23] As will be seen shortly, the gully had its first one-day ascent the following year.

Another climb was made on the Ben soon after this by Smith, again with Holt. The mighty Orion Face, with its complex tracery of rock climbs named by Jim Bell according to astronomical mythology, was an obvious if daunting target for a winter ascent. On 25 January 1959 Smith and Holt left the CIC Hut at 4.30am, pressured by what they thought was competition from Clough's party who were also in residence. Smith had an ascent of The Long Climb in mind, but the climbing turned out to be more difficult than expected and some hard times were found on the lower pitches.[24]

The third pitch was the crux of the day, Smith leading up parallel cracks in the wall of the Slab Rib, no protection and with crampons bridging widely. They reached the Basin at 3.20pm with light fading, and decided to head for the North-East Buttress. Gaining this by some line, perhaps Epsilon Chimney, they found themselves below the dreaded Mantrap, the short but bulgy wall impeding progress up the ridge. Smith tried standing on Holt's shoulders, but fell off. They found another way up, finishing the last steepness as the constellation of Orion shone down on them. The climb, rarely repeated now, is named the *Smith-Holt Route* (420m V,5) and was the first winter climb to breach this face.

The next weekend, on 31 January, Marshall was on the Ben with Patey, the two climbing *The Winter Girdle* (1500m IV,4). This grand traverse goes from right to left from Observatory Gully to the Càrn Mor Dearg arête, following natural features. Marshall wore crampons, Patey nails. The following day, it was Brooker, Patey and Marshall on *West Face Lower Route* (325m IV,5), originally known as Hadrian's Wall.

January 1959 was a cold but mainly sunny month, with several heavy falls of snow particularly in the north. This built up the ice on Creag Meagaidh, where on 8 February Marshall and Tiso picked a plum line with *Smith's Gully* (180m V,5), the name being a dig at Smith who had failed here in 1957 due to poor conditions. Haston and Stenhouse made up a foursome, and travelling in Tiso's beat-up Ford with no heating they dossed in a barn near the approach path. En route, a primus stove placed between the front passenger's feet helped stave off hypothermia.

Despite Marshall's frequent disclaimers, he was clearly not only a qualified architect but also the architect for this gang of six, carefully advancing their climbing, pointing out routes which had not yet been climbed, generally advising and tolerating their excesses with the air of a benign uncle. Haston, in his autobiography, mentions that although he did not know Marshall's mind at this point, he could see he was plotting.

On Creag Meagaidh he '*dragged a protesting Tiso*' up Smith's Gully, harder than anything yet climbed there, while pointing Haston and Stenhouse at the Centre Post, the long gully which was awaiting a direct ascent of its dominating ice pitch. This was not climbed until 1964, and if included on an ascent it raises the grade from III to V. It was Haston's first route wearing crampons, if only ten-pointers, and he sensibly took the easier option.

The next day Tiso, who could only manage the weekend, left, and the remaining three enjoyed a long mixed climb on Pinnacle Buttress, climbing *1959 Face Route* (450m V,4). Haston remarked how he had been finding it harder to advance his ice climbing compared to rock (which paralleled Smith's experience), but was confident that he could manage Marshall's next planned ascent, Minus Two Gully on Ben Nevis. Climbing rock was natural, but snow and ice was a changeable and fickle medium for which experience was a desirable quality.

Tiso and transport having left for Edinburgh, Marshall, Haston and Stenhouse hitched to Fort William, reaching the CIC Hut on the evening of 10 February 1959. Next day they headed up to the Minus Face. If Haston thought he was ready for the gully, he was about to be disillusioned, as Marshall demonstrated how to cut steps with maximum efficiency, moving up the initial ice pitch.

The plan had been to share leads, which with two fairly matched leaders would have been ideal, as a rest can be gained while belaying, but Haston and Stenhouse were relegated after following Marshall up the first pitch.

For Stenhouse and me it was both a stunner and a mind-awakener [...] after we had followed Jimmy over the bulge it became apparent that his experience and ability were still beyond ours. We were taking as long to second as he was to lead. [25]

They finished the climb in the traditional manner–in the dark, aided by a four-day crescent moon, stars and the aurora. The hut was regained at 2am, no doubt disturbing Clough and his RAF rescue comrades. As for Haston being relegated, ten-point crampons would be a handicap on *Minus Two Gully* (275m V,5), particularly if leading a pitch, as steps would need to be cut more deeply so as to provide a sound footing. It is a superb gully climb, the best that Nevis can offer, fully deserving its accolades. The cognoscenti know that on gaining North-East Buttress in bad weather, a couple of abseils will reach the First Platform followed by a traverse left into Coire Leis, thus avoiding the hard sections above and the summit plateau. Experienced and wizened climbers often do this anyway, if only to avoid the dreaded Mantrap.

References

1. Smith, Jeremy. *Sestogradists in Scotland.* Climbers' Club Journal, Vol. XII, No. 1, No. 82, 1957, pp.51-58.
2. Brooker, W.D. *The Pinnacle Again.* SMCJ 26, 149, May 1958, pp.229-234.
3. Crocket, Ken. *Unpublished MS.*
4. O'Hara, M.J. and Fraser, G. *Highland Dragon.* Climbers' Club Journal 1958, pp.140-147.
5. Atkinson, Dave. *The Dragon of Carnmore.* Climbers' Club Journal, 2011, pp.42-47.
6. Haston, Dougal. *Creag Dubh and The Eastern Outcrops.* (Graham Tiso, Edinburgh, 1967.) p.82.
7. *Dutch Master of all he surveys.* Heraldscotland. 21 Feb 1996.
8. *Paul Van Vlissingen.* Independent. 25 August 2006.
9. *A Decade of Freedom.* March 2013. <goo.gl/IQoUOv>. Accessed October 2016).
10. Haston, Dougal. *In High Places.* (Edinburgh, 1972, Canongate.) p.14.
11. Marshall, J., Bonington, C.J.S., and Scott, D. *Dougal Haston – a tribute.* Alpine Journal 1978, pp.132-139
12. MacInnes, Hamish. *Scottish Climbs – Vols. 1 and 2.* (London, 1971, Constable.)
13. Cruickshank, Jimmy. *High Endeavours – The Life and Legend of Robin Smith.* (Edinburgh, 2005, Canongate.)
14. Marshall, J.R. *Personal Communication.* 7 February, 2001.
15. Smith, Robin. *The Bat and the Wicked.* SMCJ 27, 151, May 1960, pp.12-20.
16. *The Bat and the Wicked.* Footless Crow, 15 October 2010. <http://bit.ly/2erMSEc> (Accessed October 2016).
17. Smith, Robin. *Twenty-four Hours.* EUMCJ 1956-57.

18. Inglis, John. *Smith's Routes – A Short History*. SMCJ 38, 193, 2002, pp.1-14.
19. Fraser, Andrew. *Shibboleth*. EUMC Journal, 1958-59.
20. Inglis, John. *op.cit., p.9*.
21. Scotland Online – Outdoors. *The Cubby Column*. 01/12/2000. <goo.gl/gL7QlS> Accessed November 2016.
22. Cruickshank, Jimmy. *High Endeavours – The Life and Legend of Robin Smith*. (Edinburgh, 2005, Canongate.) pp.94-97.
23. Haston, Dougal. *op.cit.,* p.25.
24. Holt, R.K. *The Orion Face of Ben Nevis*. EUMC Journal, 1958-1959, pp.7-10.
25. Haston, Dougal. *op.cit.,* p.26.

12

Greeks on Skye (1959-1962)

IAN CLOUGH and a variety of partners were active on Ben Nevis, recording at least 27 first ascents, summer and winter, during 1958 and 1959. Most routes were in the lower grades, and perhaps the best effort came on 11 February 1959, with *Nordwand* (430m IV,3) on the north face of Castle Ridge, the large, sprawling face which dominates the approach path from Lochan Meall an t-Suidhe. The climb is described in the current guide as being a serious mixed route with a genuine North Wall atmosphere. The face has other climbs, but being lower than the rest of the Ben Nevis climbing areas means it is less often in condition.

The last winter route recorded on Ben Nevis in 1959 was *Platform Rib* (130m IV,5) on 8 March, by Clough, MacInnes, Terry Sullivan and M White. Taking the rib left of Minus Three Gully (then unclimbed), several pegs were used.

'Dangle' was joined by 'MacPiton' on 19 April to make an aid route on the impressive vertical wall on the right side of Càrn Dearg Buttress. Clough and MacInnes, to give them their real names, aided cracks which were the only lines of weakness on this wall, taking around 12 hours. The cracks had most likely been eyed-up for several years by leading climbers, but with the poor protection gear then in existence, and the level of ability at the time, they were regarded as routes for the future. The line was then attempted by several of Scotland's best climbers in the late 1960s and early 1970s, including Rab Carrington and Con Higgins, finally being freed in 1977 by the English rope of Mick Fowler and Phil Thomas. *Titan's Wall* (245m E3) is a brilliant route with two outstanding pitches.

Clough applied to join the SMC later in October 1959, sponsored by Tom Patey and seconded by Jim Bell, but was rejected. One possible reason for this was that his ascents of Point Five Gully and Titan's Wall were regarded by the committee as being serious erosions of climbing ethics–specifically that pegs should neither replace skill nor supplement a lack of skill. One vote on the committee would have been that of Robin Smith, who was certainly obsessive about bringing Scottish rock climbing standards up to the levels found in England.

A letter from Clough to Patey dated 2 October 1962 reveals more. Clough had been asked by an SMC member if he would join if re-invited. Clough admitted to Patey that although he was '...*bloody annoyed at being "black-balled" by Wheech*', he was '...*not a proud man...and would still like to get into the S.M.C.*'. He went on to write that he did not take personally Smith's attempt to black-ball him, as he saw Smith as being intensely nationalistic. His death in the Pamirs came as a great shock to Clough. Another reason put forward for Clough's initial rejection was that he was at that point a mountaineering instructor. [1]

We have to assume that the SMC committee in 1959 contained some members who were not disposed to admit Clough as a member. Clough revealed that his rejection letter contained the comment that—'...*it was also observed that you did not appear to have any obvious connection with Scotland giving you a reason for wishing to join this Club in particular.*' The Secretary at this time was Ross Higgins, finishing a decade of service. He would demit office with a few comments which appeared in the SMCJ– '

> ...it would be wise to pause and consider whether we were tending to lose the Club atmosphere, so notably preserved during the past 70 years...There was also a tendency to stick rigidly to high climbing standards, regardless of personal knowledge of the candidate.' [2]

There were at this juncture, patently a few '*preserved*' SMC members who were unaware of or unwilling to recognise the winds of change taking place in Scottish mountaineering. These winds would eventually help shift some of the entrenched attitudes then existent. The twelve successful candidates from this 1959 committee meeting included Graham Tiso, Dougal Haston, and James Moriarty, while Jimmy Marshall was on the committee. Bell would be handing over the SMC Journal Editor's chair to Geoff Dutton, and within a short time changes would be afoot. Clough reapplied successfully in 1962, again sponsored by Patey, and would become a welcome face in Scottish mountaineering.

With friends and pupils from the Glencoe School of Mountaineering, he would make many first ascents in the glen and on Ben Nevis, particularly during the winter of 1969 which brought excellent conditions and provided a number of leading climbers with useful employment at the school. A slim paperback guide to winter climbs was published in 1969, written by Clough and available for seven shillings. [3] With useful diagrams by R Brian Evans it filled a need, as the SMC guides to these areas were either already outdated or soon would be. Len Lovat's two guides to Glen Coe had appeared in 1959 (Buachaille Etive Mor) and 1965 (Glencoe and Ardgour), while the Macphee guide to Ben Nevis dated from 1954. Clough had written to JR Marshall in 1962, offering assistance with the Ben Nevis guide, but received no answer. Perhaps this rebuff prompted Clough to write the Cicerone Press guide.

As the pace of exploration had speeded up, and with the annual crop of new route descriptions in the SMCJ not being accessible to many, there was a gap which Clough's guide filled. It was immediately successful and was reprinted the following month. In its 51 pages of route descriptions a phrase cropped up several times, especially in the Ben Nevis section: *'Formidable and unrepeated.'* For some climbers, this was a challenge; for others, a warning.

The description for Point Five contained the following— *'The controversial first ascent was made when the climb was "out of condition"' (i.e. continued hard ice').* [4] Mention will shortly be made of several of these formidable routes, some of which were about to be repeated.

❄❄❄

MacInnes and Clough enjoyed good summer seasons on Skye in 1957 and 1958, climbing 22 new routes in all. MacInnes was still over-enthusiastic in his use of pegs, but his legacy nonetheless was the finding of a good number of fine lines, with any original aid usually eliminated by those who came later. In both years MacInnes was working as an instructor for the Mountaineering Association.

In 1957 the pair's outstanding routes included *Creagh Dhu Grooves* (95m E3 5c) on the eastern Buttress of Sròn na Cìche, and *Prokroustes* (120m HVS 4c) on the North Buttress of Sgùrr Sgumain, both with John M Alexander, a Kinloss MRT member who had been on the siege of Point Five Gully. Creagh Dhu Grooves was originally graded HVS, and the climbers used aid, with a bolt and pegs on the third pitch. Pedlar's Skye manuscript notes that in 1977 the magazine Crags reported that–

> ...raiders Gabriel [Reagan] and his mentor Richard McHardy [...] pulled off what may have been the first free ascent of [...] Creagh Dhu Grooves. They report that the difficulty was not excessive.'

Prokroustes was another MacInnes route which took its name from Greek mythology. As to his use of aid, nowadays regarded as excessive, MacInnes has absolutely no regrets. [5] Also being interested in mechanics, he perhaps named the route after the robber (also known as Procrustes) who put travellers up for the night but adjusted their limbs to their beds by stretching or amputation. MacInnes in turn adjusted Prokroustes by the use of a bolt on the first pitch.

The Greek theme continued in 1958, with MacInnes and Clough aiding a route immediately to the left of Integrity on the Cìoch Upper Buttress. *Atropos* (100m E1), climbed on 29 May, was originally graded Very Severe (A3), with the description stating *'Belays, pitons, bolts, tension traverse involved.'* It was freed in 1977 by Fowler and Thomas who are now credited with the first ascent, the route having suffered a massive rockfall. It is still free and direct, though with some loose rock.

Two members of the Lomond MC, D Gregory and R Hutchison, recorded a fine route on 27 July 1958, with *Crembo Cracks* (190m HVS) taking the steep slabs and wall to the right of Cìoch Direct. As the guidebook has it, *'A superb but serious climb'*, and many retreat from the 5a third pitch. The first ascent used two pegs. On 22 August, Bill Brooker was back on his favourite crag, the Coireachan Ruadha face of Sgùrr Mhic Choinnich, with Dick Barclay, climbing *Dawn Grooves* (175m HVS) on the Upper Face, just right of the central cleft. The upper section of a groove avoided by Brooker, though recommended for future parties, was climbed in the mid-1970s–*Mongoose Direct* (195m E1).

Vulcan Wall (70m HVS) takes the fine wall left of Creagh Dhu Grooves and was climbed by MacInnes, Clough and John Temple on 30 May 1958. Temple had earlier looked at the line but became frightened by the lack of protection and what would have been a brutal ground fall. He was climbing at the low end of VS, and was way out of his comfort zone. [6] The climb used aid and was originally graded at VS (A2).

Not surprisingly, MacInnes came in for some criticism, and Temple himself was dismayed at the use of aid to force the route up the wall. In 1971 John Cunningham was interviewed for the magazine *Mountain*. He felt that routes climbed with a lot of aid, and subsequently freed, should be credited to the climber who used far less aid.

On reading this, Temple sent a note to Brooker (who was president of the SMC 1972-1974, and SMCJ editor 1975-1986), explaining that the first ascents of both the first and third pitches were free climbed onsight. [7] The full story is told delightfully by Temple in an SMCJ article. [8]

In 1957 Temple had led the first pitch, climbing with a girl who was a novice. Wearing ex-army gym shoes, with a short length of half-weight, hawser-laid rope, two line slings and two heavy steel karabiners, he found himself in trouble on a steep wall, unable to reverse and with a ledge 40ft higher. He struggled on, amazed and relieved to gain the ledge. Sensibly, the pair abseiled from here, leaving a sling and a karabiner. Temple returned next day after having calmed down, but circumstances repeated themselves and all they gained was the karabiner, this time abseiling down from the sling.

And so to Easter 1958. Temple was camping on Ben Nevis when a voice outside the tent enquired whether he had seen three English lads.

The speaker was tall and lean, hard-eyed, unsmiling, his face as sparse as his words but conveying all the information you needed to know. His companion was smaller, chubbier and, but for the Woodbine in his mouth, would have flashed a grin. My first contact with MacInnes and Clough. Pat and I had been up Gardyloo the day before but had seen no one else. Hamish and Ian headed off briskly but were soon back with the bad news. Alfie Beanland and party had fallen out of Zero.

This was the triple fatality mentioned earlier. Beanland, an experienced climber, had been climbing with two Birmingham friends and was leading when the ice avalanched and brought down rock. All three were swept down and killed and the ice axe belays snapped. Temple was soon helping to carry down the bodies. Then on Skye at Whitsun he would have been climbing with Mike Dixon but the latter broke his collarbone before the trip. MacInnes and Clough were meanwhile running their Mountaineering Association course and invited Temple to join them on an attempt at Vulcan Wall. The name was suggested by MacInnes, who was proud of his heavy hammer, The Message, which had been made for him by a welder and coated with stellite® for hardness. [9]

> Ian, a.k.a. 'Dangle', led off and set what was to be the rather low tone of the day by aiding the initial corner, belaying at its top and handing the lead over to Hamish. I was bemused rather than aghast that he then murdered the pitch. Should I have protested? Perhaps, but I did not have the moral fibre to do so, the more so as I would have been obliged to attempt the pitch again. 'Thanks, but no thanks.' I got to lead the third pitch.

> Years later in an article in Mountain, Cunningham used our ascent as an example of how not to do it. Who, I wonder, was the first to do it right?

More climbs appeared from the MacInnes/Clough stable, with several of the lower-grade routes proving popular, including *Aesculapius* (70m Hard Severe) climbed on 24 June 1958 and taking a line on the North-West Buttress of Sgùrr Dearg on Skye. MacInnes was climbing with three women on this, one of whom, Catherine, he later married. The climb missed inclusion in the 1969 SMC Climbers' Guide by Jim Simpson (who also served as a custodian of the Glen Brittle Memorial Hut) due to a note in that hut's logbook which stated erroneously that it had been climbed earlier by G Barlow and party.

Robin Smith had been to Skye in 1955, climbing with Jimmy Cruickshank. Smith, then aged 16, was working his way up the grades. The pair made ascents of Cìoch Direct (the crux led by Cruickshank), Cìoch West and, for dessert, Mallory's Slab and Groove in mist and rain. They were back in 1956, when Smith had an arm in plaster, having broken his wrist at school. This did not prevent an ascent of the Crack of Doom. Cruickshank made one hard lead on this, after which he stopped climbing completely. Latterly he had been slipstreaming Smith, but it was now clear that the steady rise through the grades was becoming too stressful—and also that Smith was better unleashed.

In September 1957 Smith returned to Skye with Hugh Kindness, and made the first ascent of *Left Edge* (90m E1), to the left of The Chasm of Sgùrr nan Eag, described in the guidebook as *'Fine climbing with only just adequate protection.'* It may be assumed that this was another bold lead by Smith with virtually no protection. Further left, he recorded *Ladders* (110m VS 4c), no second listed and given in the guide as *'good, sustained and pleasant'*.

The early summer of 1959 saw the official opening of the Coruisk Memorial Hut, built in memory of Peter Drummond Smith and David Munro who had died on Ben Nevis on 1 April 1953. The SMC and Glasgow JMCS had been active in seeing this project through, and the latter club took over the running of the hut, situated in an idyllic spot. It was visited in the spring of 1960 by Russian and English climbers, entertained by the SMC. Robin Smith wrote the brief report:

> Of an evening we four put an end to the Crack of Dawn to lend that route some matter and form. The Russians tight-roped the razor Ridge, they cut their feet to ribbons. 'At home we haff not such feats' they said, dismayed.

The four were George Ritchie, Elly Moriarty, Jimmy Marshall and Smith himself.

❄❄❄

In 1959, before going to the Alps, Smith went to Ben Nevis with Dick Holt to investigate a line he had spotted on the Great Buttress of Càrn Dearg: a steep corner lying between Centurion and Sassenach. The initial barrier of steep rock which had delayed ascents of the latter route gave a similar problem on the new line, which Smith and Holt overcame with a clever traverse rightwards from the Centurion second pitch corner. Night fell, but they had found the door to the main line. The next day it rained, so they left, with Smith going off to the Alps where with the English climber Gunn Clark he made the first British ascent of the Walker Spur, then one of the hardest and finest Alpine routes. Several other ascents were made, before it was back home for the unfinished business on Càrn Dearg Buttress.

The 'unfinished business' was to be the ascent of a route to be named *The Bat* (270m E2), climbed in September 1959 with Haston over two separate days. There would be falls by both men, jammed pebbles, several pegs and a wedge, and the climb would became immortalised by the Smith article in the SMCJ which followed. [10] This is reproduced in full in the Cruickshank biography, in Ken Wilson's anthology, and in a Footless Crow blog. [11,12] The SMCJ editor was Geoffrey J Fraser Dutton (1924-2010), a professor of biochemistry at Dundee University and a writer in his own right with several commended poetry collections and a series of humorous mountain-related stories about a quasi-fictional 'Doctor'. Dutton was also a piper, gardener, snorkeler and regrettably a committed practitioner of the dismal art of pouring a minimal dram.

The SMC was twice blessed in 1960– it had a new journal editor in Dutton, who replaced the long-serving and now tiring Jim Bell in a *'gentle, bloodless coup'*, and it also had the Smith article. [13] Very probably, the column inches written about this exceed the actual length of the climb. No extra eulogy will be added here other than to say that in the 1960s there seems to have been one of those periods in time where events and people collide to form something even better. As for critics of the 'beat' style of writing—as Smith noted in the Bat article, *'You got to go with the times.'*

In Cruickshank's biography, the article is followed by what Dutton thought about Smith and his writing style, taken from correspondence from editor to writer. Dutton found Smith's writing objective, with meticulously crafted contributions and no need for tiresomely unnecessary expletives. His contributions, Dutton added, were the antithesis of other brilliant climbing writers such as Patey who sent in chaotic and barely legible script—hilarious and uncomplicated prose, but in need of much editorial input.

The climb was named after the monster fall Haston had on the first visit, when as night fell his black and bat-like shape came hurtling over the roof above the belay. The route's successful ascent went a long way towards addressing the shame of seeing Centurion and Sassenach pinched from under Scottish noses. In 1978, the climber, author and cameraman Jim Curran made a film based on the ascent, with Rab Carrington and Brian Hall playing Smith and Haston respectively.

It is worth remembering that rock climbing in 1959 still had no manufactured nuts, no harnesses and no helmets. Smith wore a borrowed pair of *kletterschue* for the initial bout with Haston, as his pair had been stolen at Harrison's Rocks. They shared Haston's PAs, before Smith acquired another pair for the successful ascent.

Later that September, Cunningham and Robin Smith were on the Trilleachan Slabs, completing an ascent of *The Long Wait* (225m E2), a route with input from several climbers over a period of time, including Cunningham, Noon and Whillans.

❈❈❈

The winter of 1960 was to see another of those occasions when a sport rises to its best and produces an almost magical result. In February of that year there was the conjunction of ideal conditions and a formidable partnership of two mountaineers primed for their best climbing—Marshall and Smith, who climbed seven winter routes together during a week on Ben Nevis.

Limited space precludes a detailed telling, but fortunately for posterity both men wrote articles about their activities. There is also a long piece in the history of Ben Nevis. [14] The climbers were on form, as was the mountain. With new technology and current training practices, a modern winter climber can look at the routes climbed that week as being fairly straightforward, given good conditions. However, any attempt to climb them on sequential days, with a single axe and cutting steps, will radically shift the perspective. A 'rest' day was taken after five days of consecutive climbing, when the pair awoke in the CIC Hut to mist and wind.

This 'rest' took the form of crossing the Càrn Mòr Dearg arête, climbing Aonach Beag and traversing the Grey Corries to Stob Choire Claurigh. They then descended to Spean Bridge, found refreshments in a pub, caught a bus to Fort William, found more refreshment in a pub, then had a lift to the police station where they explained how a set of draughts had found its way into Marshall's rucksack (it seems Smith had hidden it there). After release it was back up the hill to the CIC, ready for another two days of climbing.

As for the routes, they began on Saturday 6 February with *The Great Chimney* (65m IV,5) on the east flank of Tower Ridge. Some consider this is V,6. Sunday was *Minus Three Gully* (150m IV,5), one of the best Grade IV gullies on Nevis, but not often in condition. Monday saw them on a gripping ascent of *Smith's Route* (125m V,5), a steep ice climb on Gardyloo Buttress at the head of Observatory Gully. It would be 11 years before a second ascent was made, by Michael (Mike) George Geddes and Nigel Rayner, who climbing it by front pointing.

Tuesday 9 February saw Smith and Marshall climb *Observatory Buttress* (340m V,4). This was not recorded initially, as they thought that it had been first climbed in winter by Harold Raeburn–understandable, as Raeburn had attempted it with three companions in 1901. It is another classic buttress climb, following a good line up a drainage groove which ices up well in most winters. It was also climbed by the Squirrels team of MacEacheran and Renny, who recorded it as The Liquidator in 1965, unaware that they were in fact making the second ascent. Wednesday was reserved for the second ascent of Point Five Gully (325m V,5), with seven hours of step-cutting, returning some sense of dignity to this classic line following its siege ascent by Clough's party the previous year.

Thursday was the 'rest' day, then on the Friday they resumed climbing with *Pigott's Route* (250m V,6) on The Comb, described in the guide as a *'fickle climb which is not often in condition'*. It would not have a second winter ascent until 1986.

On their last day, Smith and Marshall climbed what would become one of the most popular winter routes on the mountain with *Orion Direct* (400m V,5), realistically described in the guide as '*One of the finest winter climbs in Scotland, with all the atmosphere of a major alpine face.*' Let no one be under any illusions regarding this week in February 1960–physically and mentally it was punishing. Cutting steps up any hard winter climb took a fair amount of strength and certainly demanded stamina and a strong mental attitude. Doing this on the first ascents of six difficult routes plus the second ascent of Point Five Gully demanded a huge physical effort. Additionally, to have sustained this level of climbing over the week, with the rudimentary equipment of the period and the notoriously poor protection available on Ben Nevis, would have been mentally taxing.

Both men produced fine articles based on this week. Marshall, as a bonus to an article on Scottish winter climbing, described the ascents of the Orion Face and Gardyloo Buttress. [15] Smith wrote an article for the EUMC Journal. In his biography of Smith, Cruickshank revealed that the title for this should have read *The Old Man and the Mountain*, not Mountains plural, as used in error by the Editor. It was reprinted in the magazine *Mountaineering*, and also in the SMCJ after Smith's death, with both publications perpetuating the error. [16] Smith would of course have been aware of the classic short novel by Ernest Hemingway, *The Old Man and the Sea*.

Marshall has confessed several times that one of the stimuli for this week was that he was getting married a month later, so in a sense he regarded it as a 'final fling' before settling down. And Smith, of course, was just being Smith. The latter did complain that Marshall was hogging the cruxes throughout the week, Smith's Route being one obvious exception as he led the crux pitch, which explains its name.

Haston and his fellow Edinburgh University student Andrew (Andy) Wightman were on Ben Nevis towards the end of March 1960, and a late wander up the hill to Zero Gully resulted in one pitch. The gully was awaiting its second ascent, but the pair had no ice pegs and less enthusiasm. That changed when Smith turned up in the evening, however. He mentioned the option of a new route on Gardyloo Buttress (probably Kellett's Route, later climbed at VI,6 and lying to the left of Smith's Route), but then decided that as there were existing steps for the first pitch of Zero that would do instead.

The next day the trio had a late start, and with a 'borrowed' rope from the hut (where an Oxford party was also in residence) they were at the foot of the gully at 2pm. There were five hours of daylight left, and difficult, icy conditions. Inevitably they finished in the dark, having found unexpected difficulties on the upper slopes where rocks were showing through. In his autobiography Haston mentions Smith cutting steps like a precision machine. At least they had some protection, as they had also borrowed the hut poker, suitable for banging into hard snow or ice. Its value, however, was probably mainly psychological.

Smith also paid a visit to Ben Nevis in May 1960, when with J Hawkshaw he climbed *Central Route* (275m HVS) on Minus Two Buttress. It was to be his last new rock climb on the mountain. Towards the end of May a party of Russian mountaineers paid a visit to Britain as a cultural exchange, the invitation having come from the Alpine Club. The Russians went to Glen Coe, where they met Smith, Moriarty and a few others. After showing the visitors around, Smith and George Ritchie headed for Gearr Aonach.

Here they recorded *Marshall's Wall* (80m E2) on the North-East Face, a wall of smooth, reddish rhyolite looking down to the entrance of the Lost Valley. The name was good-natured payback for Marshall naming Smith's Gully on Creag Meagaidh, on which Smith had failed, as Marshall had looked at the Glen Coe route but not succeeded. The author and Dave Jenkins, both then students at Glasgow University, made what may have been the second ascent in September 1969, leading through and finding, as the current guide remarks, some bold climbing. The route had recently seen off several hard teams. The author's log records that *'the first pitch had a hard traverse, and the second pitch a strenuous bulge. A good route.'*

❄❄❄

Tom Patey meanwhile had left Aberdeen and was practising as a GP in Ullapool. The other doctor there was a keen fisherman, so when the water was up he went off fishing, and when the rocks were dry Patey went off climbing. Or so the story goes. Patients who had interactions with him recall him fondly, if difficult to find on occasions. The move certainly opened up more of Scotland for Patey to explore, with the lack of easily found climbing partners proving no bar to his climbing urges.

Patey had made several climbs in the north-west in the early 1950s, which probably instilled a love for the area. In the summer of 1960 he arranged a climbing holiday with Bonington, leading to an article for the Etchachan Club journal which would later be reprinted in his posthumous collection of writings. [17] The pair began in Torridon, moved to Applecross and finished on Skye.

In 1959, Patey had found an easy line up the East Buttress of Coire Mhic Fhearchair on Beinn Eighe with *Gnome Wall* (150m Hard Severe 4a). On 11 August 1960, he and Bonington made a grand traverse of the mountain, following an obvious geological feature from left to right, cutting across the Eastern Ramparts and Central Buttress to gain West Central Gully. They completed their day with a new variation at the top of the West Buttress.

The Upper Girdle (750m Severe) provides tremendous situations, with unrelenting vertical rock on the first section. Bonington, meanwhile, was eyeing-up the potential lines on the Eastern Ramparts. These now provide a superb choice of hard climbs with, in the current guide, a total of 33 routes, 15 of which are E1 or harder.

The next stop was Applecross, where an Aberdonian gang including Patey had explored and climbed several easy routes on the buttresses of Sgùrr a' Chaorachain in 1952 and 1953. On 12 August 1960 Patey and Bonington found one of the most popular routes in the north-west with *Cìoch Nose* (125m Severe), climbed on rough Torridonian sandstone. The upper section provides tremendous exposure, leading to the A' Chìoch ridge. Patey would also have seen the potential of the South Face of Sgùrr a' Chaorachain, the crag overlooking the Bealach na Bà road. On 11 October 1961 he returned alone to record there *Sword of Gideon* (100m VS).

Four days earlier, he had soloed *The Nose Direct* (140m VS) on the Lower South-East Nose of Fuar Tholl, a climb which must have provided some interesting moments. His comment on the route was– '*The climb is very exposed and although holds are plentiful many are masked in vegetation and of doubtful security. Climbing is continuously severe. There are no escapes.*'

When considering Patey—and especially his articles—a certain amount of hyperbole must be expected. This route is exposed in part, with a fair amount of clean rock, though dry weather is recommended. What is generally agreed on is that Patey was not the most stylish climber, more of a heave, clutch, thrutch, grunt adherent. He made up for this by climbing at a fast pace.

❄ ❄ ❄

Patey and Bonington reached Skye on 13 August 1960. Here they spent a week, and their first target was the Coireachan Ruadha face of Mhic Coinnich, where they hoped to straighten out Brooker's Dawn Grooves. Bonington, however, had spotted a completely new possibility further left. There was more than one line, and several false starts were made before Bonington settled below an obvious diedre. When Patey climbed up this he came across old gear: a piton and some nylon string. He moved right and entered a harder-looking diedre, where he belayed. Bonington led through and reached a cluster of overhangs. Two overhangs later and the hard climbing was over.

Having done the route there remained the pleasant task of naming it. Existing names included 'Crack of Dawn', after one of Brooker's infrequent early morning starts, so they thought of 'It Dawned', but this was rejected as being too flippant for such a wonderful cliff. Patey came up with 'Alligator Crawl', as the route was smooth and in a groove–but not all climbers would know of or appreciate the jazz connection. They settled for King

Cobra, due to the way the cliff reared above their heads, especially when viewed from the east. *King Cobra* (210m E1), Bonington later recalled, '... *was the best new route we did that summer and certainly the best route I've ever done*'. [18] King Cobra is a good route, but not *that* good.

On Sgùrr a' Mhadaidh they found *Whispering Wall* (160m Severe) on the other side of Deep Gash Gully from Thunder Rib. It was originally recorded as Very Difficult, but subsequent ascents have it as Severe and not well protected. It suffered a rockfall in 2008, and the penultimate pitch up a chimney is perhaps best avoided.

Next, the intrepid duo headed for the tottery pinnacles of the Storr Rocks, where Patey decided to avoid the Whillans route of 1955 and instead tried a new pinnacle, 200 metres north of the Old Man. The rock, as elsewhere here, was so bad that to descend they had to run the ropes in a pulley system over the top, then abseil the rest.

❈❈❈

The summer of 1958 saw several breakthroughs in the east of Scotland, where leading climbers were jousting with unclimbed steep rock on major faces. One of these was Creag an Dubh Loch, a huge expanse of excellent granite lying to the west of Loch Muick, from which it is most often approached.

The first route was put up in 1928 by Symmers and Bruce with *South-East Gully*, a 200m stretch of continuous crumbling rock at Difficult. Recommended climbs would not arrive until the mid- to late-1960s, with better equipment and protection, although Jim Bell recorded Labyrinth Route with Nancy Forsyth in 1941 at Hard Severe. Several ropes attempted lines on the crag during 1957 and 1958, with varying degrees of success.

Central Gully Wall, to the right of Central Gully, was a prime example of virgin rock until it was climbed on 26 August 1958 by Barclay and Brooker, just back from their successful trip to Skye the previous week. The pair had still not graduated to PAs, with Brooker in *kletterschuhe* and Barclay in baseball boots. Some exciting climbing on continuously steep, clean rock was found on the upper part of the wall, gained via a sloping grassy terrace known as the Caterpillar. Two pegs and combined tactics were required. *Waterkelpie Wall* (260m E1) is an updated combination of the original route while a direct start was added in 1964.

Further north, Coire an Lochain and Coire an t-Sneachda were other places with much potential, particularly in winter. February 1959 was to provide superb conditions in the Cairngorms, with a spate of new winter routes ensuing. [19] Patey, who was ski-training with the Royal Marines, found himself conveniently based at Glenmore and on 3 February was in Coire an Lochain with Vivian Stevenson, climbing *Ewen Buttress* (90m

III). The next day saw a solo ascent of *Spiral Gully* (150m II), followed on 5 February by *Patey's Route* (120m IV,5) in Coire an t-Sneachda, solo. On the following day he was again in Coire an Lochain for a solo of *Western Route* (120m IV,6), a good, sustained route climbed in 45 minutes.

On Sunday 8 February, Ronnie Sellers, Jerry Smith and George Annand decided to visit Creag an Dubh Loch and look at the Labyrinth. In nailed boots they made a good five-hour ascent, avoiding the bottom ice pitch and with Sellers and Smith alternating leads. The Labyrinth in the current guide (*Hanging Garden Route*, 300m V,4) is one of the early routes in condition and has variations, with *Labyrinth Direct* (300m VII,6) climbed in 1972 being outstanding.

On Creagan a' Choire Etchachan that same day, John Hay and Ross Ibbotson climbed *Red Chimney* (150m V,5), a route on the left of the Crimson Slabs which is a natural funnel, icing up readily. Hay had been defeated the previous year and was keen for a rematch. In the event he followed the summer line, moving right at the top to finish up a rib. This avoids the impressive upper icefall, climbed in January 1967 by Ian Paterson and Stuart Hepburn, with the current guidebook listing the latter rope as first ascenders.

Brooker was never one to miss a good chance, and on 10 February, with a relative novice Douglas Duncan, he set out for Creag an Dubh Loch where he found *Labyrinth Edge* (300m IV,5) in excellent condition. The crux was the exit of a chimney on the upper buttress, and the route was finished in the dark.

Patey had a second week's 'ski-training' still to go, and visited Hell's Lum Crag on 12 February to make a winter ascent of *Kiwi Slabs* (150m IV,3) with Stevenson. The early part of February had supplied great winter conditions, but these turned out to be short-lived, with a thaw setting in midway through the month. Patey and Stevenson were racing the thaw as they completed a semi-winter ascent of The Slash on Sgòr Gaoith (finally climbed in full winter conditions in 1987 at Grade V).

On the same day Patey was on The Slash, Sellers and Annand walked in to the remote Garbh Choire of Beinn a' Bhùird, where winter's teeth was still set and they enjoyed the first winter ascent of a highly-prized *South-East Gully* (200m V,4).

The thaw which had begun at lower altitude now started to reveal the Jock's Road tragedy, in which five men from the Glasgow-based Universal Hiking Club had attempted to walk from Braemar to Glen Doll on New Year's Day 1959, a Thursday. They would have encountered grim conditions on leaving Coire Breac for higher ground, with Force 11 winds, driving snow and a probable windchill of -25°C. They were reasonably well-equipped, though none had waterproof trousers.

The storm lasted over two days with the Glen Clova road blocked with snow. It was Saturday before police were alerted, with a search starting the next day. Despite blizzard conditions rescuers found the first body above the head of Glen Doll. With a temperature of -19°C recorded that night in Strathdon and icy conditions on the hills, the search nonetheless continued on the Monday and Tuesday, with no results.

It was not until 1 March that the second victim was discovered, while the fifth and last was found in a metre of snow as late as 19 April. All five had died of hypothermia, spread out along a two-mile stretch of the White Water. They had attended mass at Braemar, which meant a delayed start at about 11.15am, while a set plan to meet other members of the club at Glen Doll hostel probably pressured them to continue their walk.

Bad news continued when North-East climbers were shaken by the news that Ronnie Sellers had been killed on Lochnagar on 10 May. His plan had been an ascent of The Link, climbing with Jerry Smith. In the afternoon, abseiling from the Springboard, a huge block used as an anchor became dislodged while Sellers was on the rope. In a double blow to Aberdeen climbers, later that summer Jerry Smith was also killed abseiling in the Alps, on the Aiguille de Peuterey. From England, and a quiet man, he fitted in with the Etchachan Club where he was given the name 'Sluefoot Smith' due to his battered pair of rope-soled climbing boots. [20]

Sellers had been secretary of the Etchachan Club, despite having been a member for less than a year, and some of his crag drawings were earmarked for the new Cairngorms guide, attesting to his talent as an architectural draughtsman. He was aged just 26. [21]

A late route in the 1959 season was *The Mousetrap* (180m VS), climbed in November. The rope was Jimmy and Ronnie Marshall, with Ronnie Anderson. Not content with his masterly acquisition of the winter ascent of Parallel B Gully in February 1958, Jimmy Marshall had sensed that something was afoot on Creag an Dubh Loch. He had seen reports of Waterkelpie Wall with its mention of aid pegs, and decided to have a look. They were one step ahead of the Aberdonians in that they were now wearing PAs; according to Strange, this would have been the first use of these rock boots for a new climb in the Cairngorms.

The climb has several pitches at a technical grade of 4c, and is the easiest climb which takes in the entire height of the cliff. In his report in the SMCJ, Marshall was at pains to write that all pegs were used for belays only; he had been interested to see why so many of the existing climbs had used pegs for aid–and, if possible, he was determined to make an ascent without recourse to aid.

Mac Smith was finalising the new Cairngorms guide and was able to include the route. He was generous in adding a note stating that it would appear to be 'one of the hardest and most outstanding routes of recent years on granite'. As for its name, on the way north, the party's car had almost run over a field mouse, darting between headlamp beams in the pouring rain.

The only other late-1950s climb to match Marshall's came in August 1958, when Sellers and Annand succeeded in breaching the Shelter Stone by a direct line. They had attempted it earlier but had been unable to climb a bulging corner. This time Sellers used two aid pegs to overcome the obstacle. Higher up, a spectacular hand-traverse allowed the leader to gain a vertical crack system. This was taken using a wedge and further on an étrier, before easier ground could be gained.

Their line was named *The Citadel* (270m VS), with the current grade as given, following a free ascent in 1966 by McArtney and Lawrie. It was beginning to look like the use of aid for these big Cairngorms routes was partly psychological; it was early days still in the east, with PAs slowly being accepted and awe of the big walls being overcome. Certainly, to stand under the Shelter Stone and look up at its leaning headwall would prompt a shudder from many a young climber.

Allen Fyffe remarked that there was peer pressure amongst Aberdeen climbers against the introduction of anything which was new and purported to make climbing easier, including PAs. This innate conservatism held back advances which were happening elsewhere. [22]

Two events at the start of the 1960s had an impact on mountaineering in the Cairngorms. The first was the building of an access road to the foot of Coire Cas, with a car park at its end at a height of over 600m. This came about through pressure from the skiing enthusiasts and local hoteliers, but it also benefited climbers, allowing much easier access to the Northern Corries and to Cairn Gorm summit. The Loch Avon basin, too, became closer.

It was Patey, at the end of a lengthy article in the SMCJ, who voiced a critical point felt by some. [23] While admitting that Coire Cas had been changed from a characterless and dreich corrie into something more colourful, he noted that 'Nevertheless the danger in the Coire Cas scheme is that it may be the forerunner of others which would threaten the finer and more remote fastnesses of the Cairngorms.'

The second event was the publication, in 1961 and 1962, of the SMC guides to the Cairngorms area–the first covering the area north of the Dee, the second covering Lochnagar, Creag an Dubh Loch and Glen Clova. Both were mainly the work of Mac Smith who, as was the custom at the time, received no payment. Pocket-sized, with stippled red covers, they followed the fashion of Macphee's Ben Nevis 1954 guide and Lovat's Glencoe 1959 guide.

As happens from time to time in mountaineering, in the North-East the end of the 1950s saw a local and temporary lower level of activity. Some activists had moved to other areas or had taken up new pursuits; others had been killed or ceased to climb through injury or illness. Patey left the Royal Marines in 1960, and after a few locums in 1962 took up his GP post in Ullapool, from where he could stravaig over the North-West Highlands.

❀❀❀

In Jimmy Marshall's SMCJ article of 1961 he prefaced his descriptions of the Orion Face and Gardyloo Buttress ascents with a general summary of winter climbing and techniques. It may be assumed that this was how those at the sharp end at the start of the decade climbed in winter. Marshall's summary began with some commonsense advice, such as the value of acquiring experience over several seasons due to the fickle nature of conditions. Fitness was also a necessity, gained by hillwalking in all weathers, providing stamina and what Marshall called *general mountaineering sense*. Hillwalking, he continued, *may appear tedious, but it is of considerable value, as will be appreciated when a hard climb finishes in deteriorating weather and darkness, and there's still a long way home*.

In Scotland, many climbers used the spell between summer and winter to go for long walks, often over a weekend. Poor weather was accepted, and often unavoidable. A mountain or more could be included, either en route to a bothy or campsite or climbed from some such base.

As for winter equipment and technique, Marshall recommended 12-point crampons, with the Grivel make then being the best choice. Crampons, he wrote, had been made necessary by vibram-soled boots, though nails still had a place depending on the route. The axe remained a problem in that these continued to be manufactured in long lengths. Along with many others, in the late 1960s the author took his first ice axe to the Greaves sports shop in Glasgow to be shortened. Those with the tools and the necessary skills would of course do this themselves.

There was one design quirk with the Grivel crampons: the two front points were not joined at their base with a transverse section, which meant that while climbing, if a move ended with one of these points only making contact with hard ice or rock, the force could cause it to bend to some extent, like a tuning fork. Some climbers duly joined their front points together using bailing wire.

Grivel crampons were superseded for many by the Salewa brand, consisting of two sections, heel and sole, connected by an adjusting bar. They were lighter and quite functional especially on mixed routes, with rock, snow and ice all underfoot. This also made them suitable for hillwalking in icy conditions, or descending following a climb. A peg hammer was commonly carried, as pegs were in common use as the best protection and belay item. Marshall boldly recommended that the axe should not have an attached wrist loop, but this was a method which few adopted, as to drop the axe could mean losing it, leaving the climber stranded. The major advantage however was that one could easily switch hands when cutting holds without the loop becoming fankled.

As seen on the first ascent of Zero Gully, elite climbers on a hard ice climb sometimes resorted to using a pair of long ice pegs on the steepest sections. One peg would be hammered in as high as possible to take one's weight, allowing steps to be cut and moves upward made until the second peg could be inserted and the lower one taken out. This demanded good conditions with hard snow or amenable ice, plus a cool head, as such pegs could not be relied on totally.

Dachstein woollen mitts were used almost universally. These came from Austria and were made over-large then shrunk by boiling, so as to provide a thick and highly functional glove. Even when wet they provided some insulation and warmth. When conditions were very cold, they developed a frozen outer shell which provided further insulation by making them more windproof. Mixed climbs were tough on Dachsteins however, as the almost constant brushing of snow from hidden holds would eventually see them wear through at the fingers. They are still made and have the advantage of being cheaper than the high-tech, fingered gloves now available.

If there was one item which continued to cause frustration throughout this decade, it was the headtorch, or rather the lack of a model which worked reliably. For several years climbers made their own, using a standard small tungsten filament bulb at the head end and a bell battery at the other end, wrapped in a plastic bag. There were a few early commercial models in existence, but their design was appalling and they were usually heavy, given the size of the batteries in use at the time, and using a metal battery case.

Many a wet walk back down a dark glen was made even more tedious by a failing headtorch. Things became so bad at one stage that for two winters the author chose to make the Friday night squelch up the Allt a' Mhuilinn bogs on Ben Nevis with no torch, relying on night vision and a bit of luck. A good moon was a luxury, seldom encountered.

❄❄❄

In Scotland, there was felt to be a pause following the Marshall-Smith week on the Ben. Some might have said it was more of a stunned silence, though Alex Small, a long-time and enthusiastic mountaineer in his own right, commented that it was due more to there being few climbers around who could fully appreciate this *tour de force*. Poor winter conditions could also have been a reason why exploratory climbing in Scotland dipped for a while in the early 1960s, and there are several comments that back this up.

There were of course noteworthy exceptions, one being a fine ascent on Ben Nevis by Graham Tiso and Ronnie Marshall on 15 January 1961, with *Vanishing Gully* (200m V,5). Tiso led the crux pitch, usually a vertical or bulging wall of ice taking an obvious line on Secondary Tower Ridge. There is also an interesting entry in the CIC hut logbook for 21 January 1961 – *'Attempting new stuff on Carn Dearg Buttress. Got gripped & came down after 200ft. A. Wightman & D. Haston.'* In fact Wightman had taken a leader fall of over 30m on to a poor belay. Haston must have been keen on this line, as he was up the next day with Robin Smith. Both attempts failed, and *Route II Direct* was eventually climbed in winter in February 1978 at VI,6 , being described as one of the finest mixed routes on Ben Nevis. The attempts are mentioned in the Cruickshank biography. [24]

The major ascent in the summer of 1961, at least in the west of the country, was *The Bullroar* (285m HVS) on Ben Nevis, from the hand of the master, Jimmy Marshall, aided by James Stenhouse. This great rock climb, making an exhilarating traverse across the slabs of Càrn Dearg Buttress, has come to be regarded as Marshall's finest summer addition to Ben Nevis, if not to Scotland as a whole. The outstanding move comes on a descending traverse of a slab above the lip of an overhang. Those keen on good protection might advise their second to use a back rope, otherwise they risk emulating the late Doug Lang who fell here, swinging across the slab and hanging down the overlap below.

The name is taken from the *bullroarer*, the ancient ritual musical instrument, examples of which have been found in many parts of the world including Scotland. Basically it is a rectangular thin slat of wood attached to a cord. The cord is given a slight twist and the *roarer* is swung in a large circle, vertical or horizontal. When the cord unwinds it will begin alternating its twisting, and the roarer will make its characteristic vibrato sound. It has been used for long-distance communication, made possible by the low-frequency component of its sound, and has also been a popular toy.

Exceptionally dry conditions at the end of May 1961 brought not only Marshall to the Ben; Ian Clough and Keith Sutcliffe were also tempted, and the day after The Bullroar they worked out a long and devious girdle of Càrn Dearg Buttress. *The Orgy* (670m HVS) went from left to right, starting up the subsidiary buttress of Route I. En route, it descends sections of the classic routes Centurion and Sassenach (the chimney), then finishes up Shield Direct.

Not content with this, the following day Clough and Sutcliffe went to the left flank of the buttress and found the large slab on the right of Number Five Gully dry, giving them *Mourning Slab* (100m VS). In winter, this slab forms the highly popular climb *The Curtain* (110m IV,5), climbed in 1965. Clough and Sutcliffe continued their sideways predilection the same day by adding *The High Girdle* (400m Severe) on Càrn Dearg Buttress, based on Route II.

Robin Smith was by now showing increased interest in the Alps, and in a season later regarded as poor he succeeded with Haston in making the first Scottish ascent of the Swiss *direttissima* on the North Face of the Cima Ovest di Lavaredo in the Dolomites, a route almost continuously overhanging, with roofs added for more interest.

On his return to Scotland, at the end of August 1961 and also in poor weather, Smith managed another Glen Coe classic, *The Big Top* (160m E1). He had met the Creagh Dhu climber Jimmy Gardiner at Jacksonville, where Gardiner, then a student in Glasgow, was relaxing after everyone else had left for home. On the Monday the rain relented slightly in the afternoon and to Gardiner's surprise they managed to climb the first two pitches of Carnivore before retreating. It rained the next day, but on the Wednesday it ceased and Smith announced that he had '*a wee line*'.

This turned out to be on the West Face of Aonach Dubh, on E Buttress. Gardiner guessed that Smith had attempted the line before, as he offered the first pitch to him. This is in fact the easiest pitch on the four-pitch climb, which goes 4c, 5a, 5a, 5a. There is a difficult move near the top of the second pitch, leading to an exposed arête on the edge of everything. The next two pitches are impressively exposed, the last taking in a '*monster flake*' with a traverse right above an open groove. A good leader ensures this traverse is protected–there have been fatal falls here–before an easier groove leads to the top. The situations on this climb are memorable.

Older climbers may recall watching a live televised ascent of this route in June 1970, where Chris Bonington was teamed with Joe Brown. On the last pitch, Bonington was visibly in trouble and looked as though he was about to fall, but somehow managed to cling on and complete the route. Comments from other climbers indicate that many consider the route to be 5b, while the fourth pitch can also present route-finding difficulties.

Two more new climbs from Smith followed in September and October 1961, including *The Clean Sweep* (185m VS) on Hell's Lum Crag, at the head of the Loch Avon basin. Smith was climbing with Tiso and the pair graded the route as Severe when they sent its description to the SMC. It is one of the best lines on the crag, well-protected and on excellent rock, all of which increases its undoubted popularity.

In October Smith was in the west, and with Wightman made the first frontal ascent of the Eastern Ramparts on Beinn Eighe. *Boggle* (110m E1) is described in the guide as being a devious line. It starts at the same point as a newer three-starred E2 following an obvious dièdre, and one has to wonder if this was Smith's intended route but either conditions were not ideal, or he came up against something he did not like. Patey had earlier found a Severe further right, at the end of the ramparts.

Smith's intentions for the higher ranges were possibly influenced by his choice of London for further study. He went out to Chamonix in January 1962, one of the vanguard of British climbers who began winter climbing in the Alps. In February he accepted the offer from University College London to read for a PhD degree in philosophy.

In 1960, Smith had begun a project on the North Face of Aonach Dubh in Glen Coe. This was no less than an attempt to create a girdle traverse of the face, starting at the wall on the right of Ossian's Cave. With Haston he succeeded in the first section, exiting via Fingal's Chimney. Later that year, he added the next part with Wightman, where a turfy section in a downward direction, followed by a traverse across a steep loose wall, led to an exit via Pleasant Terrace.

The following year, Smith and Haston added two more pitches before grinding to a halt at what they christened the Barrier, a huge bulge which stretched the entire height of the cliff. As Robin Campbell wrote in his article describing the route, *'It looked like pegs and Smith didn't like pegs.'* [25] Smith moved on to other climbs, allowing the project to stew in his mind. The pot was stirred again in May 1962, after the brothers Marshall had a good go at the girdle before likewise halting at the Barrier.

This was on a Saturday, and brought Smith out of his meditation, and when the brothers descended to Lagangarbh they met Smith, who had just arrived from Edinburgh. The next day he went up the face again with Ronnie Marshall and succeeded in climbing the Barrier pitch, using slings on spikes and three pegs.

On the Monday, a foursome left the hut for the north face: Smith and Haston, along with Neil Macniven and Robin Campbell. These last two were additions to what had become a splinter group, based at Edinburgh University. Campbell has confessed to attending the university (studying psychology) because Smith was there, and Marshall too was climbing out of that city.

Neil H Macniven (1942-1963) had decided on Edinburgh University for the same reasons as Campbell, and it was inevitable that they would do some climbing together. Macniven was a good climber, though several successive poor winters in the early 1960s slowed his progress. On an Alpine holiday in 1963, he suffered a skull fracture when a French climber accidentally dislodged a rock on the West Face of the Blaitière. Despite a brilliant rescue in bad conditions, he died in hospital. It was his third Alpine season and he was 21.

On the North Face of Aonach Dubh, Haston and Macniven were first on the hill. Smith was his usual chaotic self and discovered he had no PAs.

Haston and Macniven meanwhile had cheated and missed out the first section of the route having found a short cut on to the start of the Barrier, *'leaving the first 500 feet of Ancient History to us, since somebody had to do it'*, as Campbell put it. He then described the situation:

> The Barrier is the right-hand wall of the big corner to the left of Yo-Yo. Two monstrous overhangs with a lesser one in between about sums it up. You go swinging across the lesser one in slings or étriers, from peg to spike to peg to spike to peg, then make a last big reach to a last big spike and after that it's only desperate to a belay right out on the edge of everything.'

When the rearguard arrived Haston was at the belay and Macniven was just leaving the last peg. On the Sunday, as Smith had used up all the daylight crossing the Barrier, Ronnie Marshall had not fancied removing the gear, so the pitch was, as Campbell described it, *'a magpie's dream of glittering metal and shining white nylon. So we had to go and do the route, if only to get Wheech's gear back.'*

When it came to the Barrier pitch, as last man Campbell had the unenviable job of removing the gear, including that which he was dependant on. This meant fixing prusik loops so that when the last aid point was removed and Campbell was hanging on the rope, his weight could be taken by using these loops, one for each of the two ropes they were using. This last point is interesting, as up until then most climbs had been done with one rope between climbers. Perhaps the necessity of using aid had suggested two ropes on this climb. Or the possibility of long abseils.

In any event, Campbell had to throw himself into space, whereupon the twisted ropes caused almost endless gyrations.

> Everything merged into a dizzy swirl. Wheech's horrid prune-face, the mountain, the sky and the Glen chased each other round the rope like some sort of hellish kaleidoscope, and all the while fiendish laughter echoed from above, across, and below. Raucous bellows from Wheech, horse-laughs and screams from Macniven, and, away to the right, graveside chuckles from Haston every five seconds, when he could just see the tips of my P.A.'s on the way round.

Eventually, after a titanic struggle with the ropes and against gravity, Campbell fought his way up to the belay. Further along, Haston was trying to find a way across Yo-Yo, which he did. The teams split for the final section, Campbell claiming the better finish right across to the bottom end of Pleasant Terrace.

> We ran away down the rubbish in the dark and back to Lagangarbh, where we wrote it all up in the Book, and lo and behold, when the pitches were all added together they came to 1000 feet exactly, which made everyone very happy and we all went to bed.

Good sleep or not, the next day Smith and Macniven had a go at Carnivore. The North Face girdle rarely sees any takers from the modern crop of climbers: it is on a mountain, it has stretches of turf and poor rock, particularly at the beginning, and it is a girdle, which means it really doesn't go anywhere; across rather than up. There was a fashion for girdles in the 1960s, probably stemming from visits to the Alps.

On 8 June, 1962, Robin Smith recorded his last new climb in Scotland. It was, and remains, a brilliant line, and it was not on the dark andesite of Ben Nevis, nor on the banded rhyolite of Glen Coe, but instead soared up the pristine grey granite of the Shelter Stone Crag in the Cairngorms. Smith could hardly have failed to have seen the line from the other side of the glen the previous September, when he was climbing with Tiso on Hell's Lum Crag. They may even have crossed to the crag to peer into its potential treasures. Smith certainly studied photographs, working out a possible line, and there was textual bait in the 1961 Cairngorms guide with its mention of the *'manifestly impossible [...] great vertical bastion'.*

The genesis of this climb is interesting. The Marshall brothers had made a foray in late May 1962, climbing the lower slabs by the initial pitches of Steeple but ending up too far left. [26] The first week of June had excellent weather, and Smith was due to leave at the end of the month for the joint expedition with the Russians in the Pamirs. The pressure was on to bag what looked to be a superb line.

Smith had no one immediately at hand to climb with, so unannounced he arrived on the doorstep of Davey Agnew in Clydebank. Agnew was in the Creagh Dhu, a shipyard apprentice. A strong wrestler, he was probably one of the few matches for John Cunningham in that sport. The climb needed little selling by Smith, and the pair travelled by bus to Perth. A lift then took them to Aviemore and a comfortable night in their sleeping bags behind a dyke.

The journey continued smoothly the next day, when another Creagh Dhu member, Tommy Paul, gave them a lift up the ski road. Better still, he worked in the ski centre, so after tea and doughnuts in the middle station they benefited from the chairlift up the White Lady, arriving at the Shelter Stone by 10am, probably a record early start for Smith.

The main feature of *The Needle* (260m E1) is the imposing final corner, seemingly heeling over everything below. As the guide has it, the route is *'A brilliant classic: long, varied, extremely good and continuously interesting.'* The author climbed this route with Ian Fulton in September 1971, describing it in his personal log as *'a fantabulous route'.* It has three standout cruxes: the 'bulging crack', the 'crack for thin fingers' and the 'needle chimney.' The last of these is certainly one of the best pitches the author has climbed, and even the finish of the route, with its sudden, cathartic release on to the horizontal plateau, adds something to the emotions of the day.

The Needle received a second ascent in 1967, by Mike Forbes and Mike Rennie. They were members of a newly formed small club, the Aberdeen Spiders, named after an Italian group and perhaps intended as a counter-blast to the Edinburgh-based Squirrels.

A few weeks after his Needle ascent, on 24 July, Smith was killed on descent from Pik Garmo (6595m) in the Pamirs. The climber he was roped to at the time, Cuthbert Wilfrid Frank Noyce (1917-1962), was aged 45, Smith 23. Wilfrid Noyce may well have been, as one of his climbing friends stated, 'A brilliant Alpinist', but he was also, it would appear, accident-prone.

One member of the expedition, Derek Bull, witnessed what happened. Noyce was in front and almost a rope's length ahead before Smith could tie on. Noyce then ran across a gully, with the ensuing tug on the almost taut rope pulling both off the mountain and down the 1200m face. [27]

Only six participants on the expedition were privy to this description, and when Smith's sister and sister-in-law heard of the circumstances they decided that the details should not be made public while Noyce's widow was alive. Even Malcolm Slesser, the team's deputy leader, remained unaware of the facts.

On the same day that Davie Agnew heard the news on the radio, he received a postcard sent by Smith. The expedition had been beset with problems from the start, including early discussions about the make-up of the UK side between the SMC and the Alpine Club, both of which had received invitations.

The story of the expedition is described in a book by Slesser. [28] Details also appear in the Cruickshank biography of Smith and Joe Brown's auto-biography. [29] The expedition had not been a particularly happy one, though Smith seemed at ease with the Russians. The bodies were left in a deep crevasse close to where they were found. Inevitably, thoughts go to what Smith could have become in terms of his mountaineering. The Eiger North Face was one immediate goal, to be attempted with Haston after Smith's return from the Pamirs. Instead, all that remains are his writings and his climbs, for which we are the richer.

References

1. Extract from letter by Ian Clough to Tom Patey, enclosed with 1962 Application Form, and submitted by Patey without Clough's knowledge as support-ing evidence.
2. SMC Annual General Meeting —Secretary's Report. SMCJ 27, 27, 151, May 1960, p.89.
3. Clough, Ian. *Ben Nevis and Glencoe.* (March 1969. Cicerone Press).
4. Clough, Ian. op.cit., p.13.
5. Crocket, Ken. *Interview with Hamish MacInnes,* 24th August 2016.

6. Pedlar, Stuart. *Letter from John Temple, 25th February, 2009.*
7. Pedlar, Stuart. *Ibid.*
8. Temple, John. *Failing on Vulcan Wall.* SMCJ 41, 201, 2010,pp.9-12.
9. Stellite alloys is a range of cobalt-chromium alloys designed for wear resistance.
10. Smith, Robin. *The Bat and the Wicked.* SMCJ 27, 151, May 1960, pp.12-20.
11. Wilson, Ken (Ed.) *The Games Climbers Play.* (London, 1978, Diadem.)
12. <http://footlesscrow.blogspot.co.uk/2010/10/bat-and-wicked.html>
13. IHMS [Iain Smart] and Campbell, Robin N. *In Memoriam. Geoffrey Dutton j.1954.* SMCJ, 41, 201, 2010, pp.280-285.
14. Crocket, Ken & Richardson, Simon. *Ben Nevis–Britain's Highest Mountain.* (Scottish Mountaineering Trust. 2nd Edn. 2009.)
15. Marshall, James R. *Modern Scottish Winter Climbing.* SMCJ 27, 152, May 1961, pp.107-117.
16. Smith, Robin. *The Old Man And The Mountains.* SMCJ 28, 155, May 1964, pp.28-32.
17. Patey, Tom. *Over the Sea to Skye.* In:*One Man's Mountains.* Pp.51-65. (Gollancz. London. 1971.)
18. Bonington Chris. *Desert Island Climbs.* Crags magazine, No. 30, April/May 1981, page 25.)
19. For this, and other difficult pronunciations, <http://www.cnag.org/en/mountain-names> (Accessed November 2016).
20. Patey, Tom. *In Memoriam–Jeremy Smith.* Climbers' Club Journal 1960, pp.117-118.
21. Brooker, W.D. *In Memoriam–R.H. Sellers.* SMCJ 27, 151, May 1960. P.87.
22. Fyffe, Allen. *Personal communication.* February 2017.
23. Patey, Tom. *Cairngorm Commentary.* SMCJ 27,153, May 1962. pp.208-220.
24. Cruickshank, Jimmy. *High Endeavours–The Life and Legend of Robin Smith.* (Edinburgh, 2005, Canongate.) pp.182-183.
25. Campbell, Robin. *The Ugly Sister* and *North Face Girdle.* SMCJ 28, 155, May 1964. pp. 13-15, 16-18.
26. Cruickshank, op. cit., p.226.
27. Cruickshank, Jimmy. *They Also Said of Robin Smith.* SMCJ 43, 206, 2015. pp.410-415.
28. Slesser, Malcolm. *Red Peak: A Personal Account of the British Soviet Expedition 1962.* (London: Hodder & Stoughton, 1964.)
29. Brown, Joe. *The Hard Years.* (London. Victor Gollancz. 1967.)

13

The Squirrels (1962-1967)

NEW FACES WERE BEGINNING to appear on the Scottish mountains in the early 1960s; many were from Edinburgh, which would initially boost the Edinburgh JMCS and later lead to new splinter groups and clubs, notably the Squirrels Mountaineering Club. A few would even join the SMC. Jimmy Marshall was still very much active and producing new routes, some with the Currie Boys.

The new faces in the east included Dave Bathgate, James R Brumfitt, Robin Neil Campbell (1942-), Neil Macniven, Arthur W Ewing, Fred Harper (1938-2000), Jonnie (Jock) Knight, Ian MacEacheran (the foregoing pair being from Dundee), Alasdair 'Bugs' McKeith (1945-1978), Brian W Robertson, James Renny, Ken Spence and William (Bill) Sproul. There were of course young climbers appearing in the west as well, for instance the Dumbarton Boys mentioned in Chapter 10. Also in the west, the Creagh Dhu remained active and would soon have new, younger members.

The Squirrels club was named after an earlier and similarly minded bunch of climbers in Italy. The Scottish Squirrels had a liking for red articles of clothing, particularly socks, the wearing of which in the 1960s was regarded as a bit *outré*. They were not only active in Scotland; most also climbed in the higher ranges including the Alps, making first ascents in addition to repeating many classic routes. Several members would emigrate, for instance McKeith (nicknamed 'Bugs' due to his prominent teeth) to Canada, where he would make many good climbs and become a popular and highly influential member of the climbing community. Indeed, for many Canadian climbers he became a legend.

After finishing a major face climb on the north face of Mount Assiniboine on the British Columbia/Alberta border, McKeith went on alone to the summit while his two companions belayed up the final section. When they gained the ridge, they found McKeith's tracks ending where a cornice had broken off, plunging him down the 750m east face. His body was found three days later. [1] He was aged 33 and left a wife and a six-week old daughter. The Squirrels had a small bothy in Glen Coe, above the gorge, known as The Drey, and a little higher on the hill McKeith's ashes were scattered.

The increase in good routes during the early 1960s had spread to Ben Nevis. The Bullroar had been climbed in 1961, and on 25 July 1962 it was the turn of the Creagh Dhu when John McLean, Bill Smith and Willie Gordon recorded a superb climb on Càrn Dearg Buttress. The current guide refers to this as: '*A brilliant route taking a complex but natural line up the great sweep of slabs left of Centurion.*' McLean, who early on was regarded within the Creagh Dhu as their 'great white hope', had by now matured into just that, with many fine climbs to his credit.

The route was *Torro* (215m E2), but for some reason it was not recorded until 1966. The original description includes mention of three aid pegs, on pitches one, four, and eight, but McLean later noted that the only aid point on the entire climb was a sling used for a hold on pitch four. The chase was now on for the first completely free ascent.

John Cunningham and Jimmy Gardiner made a good attempt, but missed out the last pitch (and with some intra-club rivalry, McLean was said to have been delighted at Cunningham's failure), and it was not until June 1970 that a complete and free ascent was accomplished. [2] This was by two of the Dumbarton Boys, Ian Nicolson and Ian Fulton, conveniently known to their contemporaries as 'Big Ian' and 'Wee Ian' respectively. Their climbing skills honed on the Dumbarton Boulders, both Ians were studying in Glasgow. Taking the train in daily, their major topic of conversation was a free ascent of Torro. [3] Fulton would join the SMC later in the year, while Nicolson would later serve as a Creagh Dhu president.

At the CIC hut when Nicolson and Fulton arrived were Ken Spence and John Porteous, two good Edinburgh climbers in the Squirrels who made many fine routes together. They were somewhat subdued however, having had an exciting time on Sassenach when on the chimney pitch Porteous had been pulling on a jammed boulder which decided to quit the chimney, taking him with it. His runner had used a Bonatti krab, which had stretched to the extent that the gate no longer closed. It was a sobering thought that Fulton had to sleep on, with a big route lined up for the following day.

Come morning the two emerged from the hut, blinking in the daylight; conditions were perfect.

> The sun was just above the C.M.D. arete, shining straight across on to the snow patches in Zero Gully and Coire na Ciste. The big buttress was in full sunlight, every crack and overlap showing clearly. The fine thread of the

line could not be made out, starting just left of Centurion and running up through the slabs and overlaps, until it lost itself in the shambles of overhangs above Route II. No excuses today.

Ten feet up the first pitch, below the first overhang, was an abandoned Clog peg, placed earlier by Spence. Over the next few days it would defy strenuous efforts by some of the most skilful peg removers in the country. Big Ian was soon performing wide bridges across the bulge, and Wee Ian realised that he would have to climb this section differently: *'Think what you are going to do, don't hang on your arms, work out the moves.'* This he succeeded in doing by some very delicate climbing up the next groove, leading to a five-star belay. Big Ian was happy; the first pitch had taken only 20 minutes.

The second pitch saw the rope run out more slowly as black, dusty moss floated down. Wee Ian followed on up a steep delicate groove, almost reminiscent of Dumbarton Rock, until a very thin move brought him to the edge of a smooth, mossy slab in an exposed position.

> The pulse rate quickened as I shuffled my way across the top of the slab using undercut handholds on the wall above and friction footholds. My feet kept slipping on the dry moss so a well-timed grab was made for a big jug and I quickly hoisted myself up the short overhanging groove to the belay. An interesting pitch.

The third pitch was easier, leading to the Bullroar slabs. Above loomed the double overlap on the fourth pitch, where the description suggested a peg for aid.

> Now, Ian doesn't like pegs and he is a wee bit obstinate. So up and down he went trying all the different permutations of holds until a high step up with undercut handholds allowed him to layback round the upper overlap. It looked wild and as I have already remarked, his legs are longer than mine. After a few miserable attempts to climb it free, a slight tug on the rope produced the desired effect, and I tiptoed round the upper overlap and on up to the belay.

The climbing went more easily after that, including the sixth pitch of Centurion, then Nicolson began bridging up the eighth and final pitch until level with the decaying stumps of two old pegs. He came across two loose blocks, pulling them out and watching them trundle down the slabs and over the edge, then he disappeared into a groove.

It sounded strenuous, but in due course he reappeared on the ledge above, smiling slyly and casually announcing that he had just climbed the crux. This was the 'sting in the tail' mentioned in the current guide, which regards pitch four as the hardest pitch technically, at 5c. Fulton dismantled the belay and traversed across.

Only twenty feet to go, but it was like something you meet in a bad dream. A shallow, vertical "V" groove, undercut at the base, and with no crack in the back - it would make a good boulder problem at ground level. A few tentative ups and downs convinced me I was getting nowhere.

Big Ian pulled, while Wee Ian grabbed at holds, and eventually he was landed on the ledge to complete the second ascent–and the first free ascent –of Torro. They made their way down Number Five Gully, drawn by the sound of running water, then glissaded the old snow patch.

A final toe-crunching stagger across the scree led back to my sloppy old pair of padding boots and a sac full of goodies. Ian was thoughtfully looking at his watch, only three o'clock. 'Fancy doing King Kong now?' I laughed hysterically and ran for the hut.

In June 1962, a month before the Creagh Dhu ascent of Torro, a long-standing problem on Ben Nevis was solved with the ascent of *Left Edge Route* (160m Scottish VS) by the Marshall brothers and George Ritchie. Its grade attests to the lack of attention: it may be the best rock climb on Gardyloo Buttress, but this crag really only shines under winter conditions. (See Chapter 7 for earlier summer attempts.)

Two years later, in September 1964, a pair of Squirrels were on Ben Nevis. Their intention, as devised by Brian Robertson, was to climb on Càrn Dearg Buttress, taking an intricate and improbable line through the overlapping slabs on the right of Centurion. The other climber was Fred Harper and the line would be climbed over three days, beginning with a late start on the Monday with Harper and finishing on the Wednesday with Robertson now partnered with Jimmy 'Weed' Graham of the Glasgow Etive Club.

Robertson had taken some time to spy out the possible line, and seems to have adopted an uncompromising approach. He would have preferred to start with some overhanging cracks just right of Centurion, but as these were wet he started up Centurion itself. He then needed a traverse right, and should have taken what most climbers now use, the second pitch of The Bat; instead, he made a devious, harder traverse. Fortunately, the current guide has laid out the options for any pilgrim wishing to make an ascent of what is a superb climb.

A good amount of aid was used putting up the route, the central section of which has some of the best rock climbing on the mountain, taking in beautiful overlapping slabs of reddish andesite. On the first run, Robertson and Harper succeeded in climbing the first new pitch by 8pm, fixing ropes and abseiling off.

On Tuesday they repeated the first two pitches to regain their high point. They then climbed a 5b pitch, studiously avoiding the Bat pitch, to end up belayed on The Bat. So far, so Robertson. Now it was upwards and onwards, with a 5c fourth pitch which would in later years bamboozle several parties, including the author accompanied by Fulton. (The problem was not failing to climb the pitch, rather an inability to understand or even see where the line went.) The pitch took Robertson three hours, one fall and four pegs for 40ft, after which fatigue called a halt to the day's climbing.

Wednesday saw Robertson joined by Graham, Harper having decided to withdraw. This time they sensibly took The Bat traverse to reach their gear, Robertson then re-climbing the fourth pitch. More difficult pitches followed on superb rock, but the route was done. *King Kong* (275m E2) had been climbed with about a dozen aid points. Attempting a second ascent two years later, a Creagh Dhu party including Cunningham also had a problem with the crux fourth pitch, finding another way up the slab with several aid points. It was left to Ian Nicolson and Norrie Muir, using the logical entry by The Bat, to free the route completely in June 1970. The first free ascent of the original start was that by Ken Johnstone and A Grigg on 10 July 1977.

Robertson moved to the USA in the late 1960s, and from his house in Boulder, Colorado began to make climbing harnesses. His home business expanded and finally allowed Clan Robertson Harness to be set up in the early 1970s. The harnesses were well designed and became popular with climbers in the US. The company is now Robertson Mountaineering, manufacturing a wide range of harnesses along with other rope protection and rigging equipment.

Tom Patey recorded his last new route on Ben Nevis on 24 February 1963, climbing with Joe Brown. *Wendigo* (120m IV,4) climbs Creag Coire na Ciste, lying between Number 3 and Number 4 gullies, an area which would see much activity in later years with fine routes summer and winter.

Jimmy Marshall was working on a new edition of the SMC Ben Nevis guide, and in the process found seven new routes in the latter half of the 1960s. One of these was *Thompson's Route* (120m IV,4) on Number 3 Gully Buttress, climbed in December 1963 by the Marshall brothers and Jim Stenhouse. The first two pitches take a delightful chimney, with ice for the picks and small holds on the outer edges of the chimney for the crampons.

The guide was published in 1969, in a PVC cover and what was to become a familiar blue splash of colour. It would be one of the last of the SMC guides to contain a graded list, listing all the rock climbs from Very Severe down to Easy. The top four were King Kong, Torro, The Bat, and Sassenach. It included a small selection from the Polldubh Crags in Glen Nevis, mica schist routes which provide excellent climbing.

Fortunately, a private guide to these crags was published in 1970, removing any further pressure on guidebook space. It was authored by Klaus Schwartz and Blyth Wright and published by the Lochaber Mountain

Rescue Association. The crags were popular with the RAF mountain rescue teams, whose members, including Ian Clough, recorded many of the climbs. On a sunny day in early autumn, to climb at Polldubh can be idyllic.

❀❀❀

A graded list, contentious though it often was, had been something of a life-saver over the years, before technical grades were introduced. Rock climbing in Scotland, always a step behind that in England, had persisted with traditional route descriptions for longer. In his 1949 guide to Glencoe and Ardgour, Bill Murray outlined his views in his introduction, making an argument for publishing the bare minimum for route descriptions. (See Chapter 8 for his reasoning.)

Of course Murray could not have foreseen where climbing would lead, but it is hard to avoid imagining being in the position of a novice climber in the 1940s and 1950s with no information other than what a Murray-style guide contained. One saving grace would have been the practical advice more experienced climbers would have given freely, but there would have been many an exciting and possibly dangerous experience lying in wait for a young novitiate.

Murray was right, of course, that exploration was the supreme delight–although not necessarily for all climbers, with many content to always follow existing routes. His guide did not contain a graded list; that came in the 1954 guide to Ben Nevis by Graham Macphee, which included a 'Classified List of Climbs'. This contained all grades of rock climbs where known, and was, as Macphee stated, only a general indication.

Combining a graded list with knowledge of who had made the climb added considerably to a climber's awareness of the difficulty of the route, and held off the day when the technical difficulty of a pitch would be introduced. Technical grades were not used in the 1980 Glencoe guide, nor the 1981 Lochaber and Badenoch guide (which covered Ben Nevis), though the latter did use the 'E' grading where known.

The first SMC publication to use technical grades for pitches was the 1985 Cairngorms guide, by Allen Fyffe and Andy Nisbet. As Nisbet explained, in 1977 he and Alfie Robertson were asked if they might be interested in working on a new, comprehensive guide to the Cairngorms, along with Fyffe, who was already on board. Robertson moved away from Aberdeen in 1978, so Nisbet took on his section as well. [4]

Having climbed in Wales, and liking the style of guidebook available there, Fyffe and Nisbet decided to absorb much of what they had seen and write a guide which included E grades, technical grades, photo-diagrams and action shots. It took years of work to amass information about technical grades and other details, but by 1984 they had enough information. A decision was made not to use action shots, while most of the diagrams, as in the present author's 1980 Glencoe guide, were hand-drawn and labelled with Letraset®. This was before personal computers and graphic software revolutionised publishing.

As grades rise, so the amount of information required for a safe attempt on a climb grows commensurately. On the hardest routes today it is fairly common to list what protection equipment would be useful or even necessary.

An amusing article on the Cuillin ridge traverse perhaps indicated some general criticism of Scottish guidebooks, as felt by visitors to this northern land. The article's author comes across a party of youths who were going up to the ridge. Italics are as found in the original. [5]

> Their description of the Route was in Stirring Terms, and their warning as to the interpretation to be placed upon the directions given by the *Scottish Mountaineering Club* for the guidance of Travellers was soon confirmed by the Experiences of the party. To put it plain, the guide book is a singular manifestation of the Scottish Character, reflecting as it does the capacity of that Formidable Race for understatement (carried, dare it be said, to the very Borders of Mendacity), together with their astounding Energy and Agility, neither of which can be approached, let alone Equalled, by other Races.
>
> Thus (said the Youths), a climb described in the Guide Book as *Moderate* is such as would, in the gentler hills south of the *Border*, be deemed *Severe*.

There is of course, a paradox here, as on Skye many of the classic routes were first climbed by parties from the 'gentler hills'. The guidebooks, however, would be written by members of the 'Formidable Race', and there is no doubting the frequency of frights experienced in earlier years on some of the easier climbs in the Cuillin by visiting climbers.

❋❋❋

The Greenock Mountaineering Club had been founded by Hamish MacInnes, but by the mid-1960s it had faded. At least one of the climbing groups within it kept up their mountaineering activities, led by the charismatic William Skidmore (1937-2014). Bill Skidmore, a friendly and popular man, was over six feet tall though not heavily built. He joined the SMC in 1969 and was interim president 1979-1980 after Robert Elton died. Joining Scott's Shipyard in Greenock as a draughtsman proved useful for his climbing, and many of his inventions were prototyped there; the author still has his peg carrier made from kilt pins, as well as a tiny aluminium prusik device the size of a large postage stamp.

The early 1960s saw many climbers taking to motorbikes, as cars were beyond their budget. Skidmore's steed was a single-cylinder 650cc Panther, coupled with a sidecar formerly with the Greenock Parts Department. For those interested in arcane history, after the hybrid was passed on to another member it was decoupled in an accident involving a sheep – and one of the wheels ended up forming part of a MacInnes prototype stretcher.

Skidmore preferred to lead, with his companions fairly happy to second. He had an exploratory bent, leading to the development of climbing in Arran and the Southern Highlands in particular. He and his friends soon became labelled as the Greenock Team, although their origins included Ardrossan, Gourock and other parts. Robert (Bob) Richardson was the other climber in this group with some seniority, later to be renowned as the 'Cerberus of the CIC' – he was that hut's custodian from 1980-1995 – as well as serving as SMC president 1996-1998.

The Greenock Team's early outing on Arran resulted in two good routes on the Rosa Pinnacle of Cir Mhòr, with *Anvil* (55m HVS) on 6 August 1960 by Davy McKelvie and Richardson, and *Hammer* (85m VS) by Dick Sim and Donny Cameron the following day. Anvil included a tension traverse on the second, crux pitch. The following week saw a second ascent by William MM Wallace (192?-2014) and James W Simpson, who succeeded in making a free ascent, finding the traverse *'exceptionally delicate'*.

The latter pair went on to write SMC guidebooks, Simpson for Skye in 1969, Wallace for Arran in 1970. Wallace was no relation to the accountant William (Bill) Wallace (1932-2006), who was secretary, treasurer and latterly president (1988-1990) of the SMC. The 'Arran' Wallace, who was in the JMCS and then the SMC, was a pathologist, retiring eventually to live on the island. Simpson, also in the SMC, was a longstanding custodian of the Glen Brittle Memorial Hut on Skye.

The Greenock Team's first significant new route on Arran was *The Rake* (145m Very Severe), climbed on 18 August 1962 by Skidmore and Richardson. This used two aid points and was the first route to open up the Meadow Face of Beinn Tarsuinn, with its great fan of curving, overlapping slabs. A later direct start, avoiding a turfy middle section, now makes the route 210m E2, climbed in 1988 by SMC members George McEwan and Alastair Walker.

Arran was of course a convenient playground for the Greenock group, and they were instrumental in bringing its climbing up to date and into view. Arran thus changed from being known to a small number of climbers as a pleasant holiday island with a few classic routes and good ridges, to a worthy destination for those wishing to climb on hard granite faces.

An even better line on Arran from the Greenock Team was *West Flank Route* (155m E1) on Cir Mhòr, climbed on 3 August 1963 by Skidmore, Richardson, James (Black Jim) Crawford and John Madden. This took place the morning after a night of thunder and rain when the rock was just dry enough for useful friction on the lower slab.

The fourth pitch was hard. A rounded, layback crack narrowed to virtually nothing, and without effective protection Skidmore was pushed to his limit, as with tiring arms he eyed a possible flaky hold above. Finally, as he ran out of strength completely, he swung up and grasped the flake, which luckily turned out to be good. Black Jim recalls that on a second ascent the following year they found better protection, while he led some of the pitches in big boots. [6]

Richardson, too, was happy to lead. Good enough when wielding a sabre to represent Scotland in fencing, his style on rock may have unconsciously borrowed from that sport, and was accurately described by Crawford in his SMCJ article–

> Richardson's performance on rock was assisted by explosions of a nervous energy which, when coincident with an intransigent Arran problem, usually resulted in its solution. The rest of us were in awe of him when he blew off at every fumerole, until we came to realise that it was more gas than lava.

> Skidmore's climbing […] was based on balance, great reach, an extraordinary ability to find positions of ease for long periods in the most awkward situation, and was supported by very careful attention to protection and overall safety.

By now, other climbers had been attracted to Arran granite, while a few skirmishers had visited earlier. Two of these had been JH Ashford and D Burke, who in the unlikely month of November climbed *The Sickle* (75m E1) on the Rosa Pinnacle, taking in hard slabs left of West Flank Route. The route just made it into Johnstone's 1958 SMC Guide, but almost certainly its grade had not been verified. In that guide it is given as route number 36.5, probably as the diagram and other sections were at that point set. It was an extreme example of accidental undergrading, being given as Hard Severe. The second pitch is the crux, at 5a, with a bold and serious traverse across a slab.

Andrew J Maxfield from the Climbers' Club also explored Arran rock in the 1960s, with his route *Tidemark* (75m Severe) being an exposed and enjoyable girdle on the Bastion of Cioch na h-Oighe, climbed with J Peacock on 9 June, 1960. Maxfield was back during 1968 and 1969, with R Wilde, to climb four routes on Cuithe Mheadhonach, a slabby wall on Caisteal Abhail.

The Greenock Team had attempted two lines on the Meadow Face of Beinn Tarsuinn, but had stuttered to a halt due to insufficient pegs. It should be pointed out that many first ascents of Arran routes, much as in the Cairngorms, would have involved sections of vegetation and damp rock. A few aid points were often necessary and could perhaps be deemed acceptable. The difficulty in general, found on some later routes, would be drawing the line as to where acceptable aid became excessive. In most cases, aid used on a first ascent would be dispensed with as the route became cleaner and standards higher.

The two lines attempted on the Meadow Face would later become *Brachistocrone* (230m E1), climbed on 18 September 1966 by Mike Galbraith and Bugs McKeith. The esoteric route-name has a mathematical origin, being the curve of fastest descent for a body (hypothetically frictionless) and on a plane between two points, the lower one not lying directly below the upper. It took the Swiss mathematician Johann Bernoulli two weeks in 1697 to solve the problem, whereas Isaac Newton stayed up just one night and posted off his solution next morning. The solution, incidentally, is a cycloid. Galbraith, evidently, was a mathematician.

This branch of mathematics is perhaps more relevant to hillwalkers and fellrunners than to climbers. A paper on the subject of finding the fastest route up or down a hill included the use of a critical gradient.[7] The simplest case is of a conical hill with concentric circular contours and uniform gradient; North Berwick Law is a reasonable approximation to this idealised landform. If the terrain gradient is less than the respective uphill or downhill critical gradient, the optimum route is a straight line. However, if the terrain gradient is greater than critical, the fastest route is a spiral ascending or descending at the critical gradient. Common sense really, as used by most hillwalkers.

The Greenock Team in this period, in addition to opening up Arran, stravaiged across the Arrochar and Southern Highland areas. On the Brack, the hill sitting across Glen Croe from the Cobbler, two climbers tackled the very steep wall to the left of Elephant Gully, climbing the obvious line of *Great Central Groove* (100m HVS) on 14 June 1958. The climbers, Pat Mitchell and James Morrison, were apparently unknown to Skidmore's group despite both being given as members of the Greenock Mountaineering Club in the route recording. In an article by Richardson they were *'Those two mysterious men from Greenock'*–there was probably a disconnect between the 'old' and the 'new' members, with no written records to fill the knowledge gap.[8]

Mitchell described the ascent in the SMCJ, noting that their interest had been sparked by a letter from Ben Humble, the local expert, who referred to the line as *'the Last Great Problem at Arrochar'.*[9] They came across two pitons left in earlier attempts, the upper one having a forged iron ring, presumably marking some party's high point and subsequent abseil.

Climbing in vibrams, they found the line fairly well vegetated and wet, as with much of this cliff, which sees very little sun. Jock Nimlin had twice made unaccompanied attempts on the line, in 1938 and in 1947, but it is unlikely that he left the pitons as he was very much against such use, unless of course forced to.

On one of the hard pitches, which Morrison partially cleaned before Mitchell led it, Morrison's boot jammed in a crack. Some 20 agonising minutes were then spent unlacing the boot, removing it and replacing it, all the while in danger of turning upside-down. Then on the last hard section a spare rope Morrison had coiled over his shoulder slipped down and pinned his arm. He fell off and swung away from the recess he was in before swinging back and continuing after a rest. The route was, in every sense, a classic, and their ascent was a six-hour epic with huge amounts of wet turf and mud to be removed.

I saw a hand fluttering about on the very top, followed by a wool cap set squarely above a very grim face streaked with mud. Then I realised that I, too, must look the same way, and the laughter came easily now that the tension was over...

Having missed the bus home, we spent a few minutes erecting a small cairn at the foot of the climb before returning valleywards; and at Ardgartan we got seats on a tour bus full of benevolently drunk souls, and so returned home that day, after all—wet and dirty, but incredibly happy. [10]

Mitchell also made the second ascent on 15 June 1963, climbing with David McLuckie, his 20-year old nephew. Great Central Groove had been named before its first ascent by Humble and Nimlin, and the route was revived in January 1968 when Skidmore and Richardson made the first winter ascent at V,6. They beat another party by a week. As it is a wet route, a good freeze normally suffices to build up ice. In condition, the line is certainly impressive.

On the steep wall left of Great Central Groove are two obvious cracks, the right-hand of which attracted the attention of the Greenock Team and so a campaign was begun in the summer of 1967. [11] The team knew from looking at the line that ironmongery would be needed, but even they had no warning that a sawn-off table leg would be used to overcome a bulge on the third pitch. Once they reached the foot of the main crack the realisation dawned that more table legs would be needed, along with a selection of large-angle pegs. Crawford was thus despatched to the Tiso emporium in Edinburgh to purchase all they had.

And so to September 1967, when the main crack was soon reached. Skidmore festooned himself with bongs, large-angle pegs, huge alloy chockstones and of course some table leg sections. By 1967, American equipment was easy to obtain in Scotland at a price, a leap upwards in protection and driven in part by the Yosemite wall climbs which demanded much hardware. The team found the main pitch to be mainly vertical, exposed and in the middle of an impressive wall. Despite the relatively low altitude, the crag had a real mountaineering atmosphere. *Mammoth* (80m E3), as it was named, would be climbed free by Dougie Mullin and Alan Pettit in 1978.

The Greenock Team put up routes on other hills of course, including Creag Tharsuinn in the Arrochar Alps. Later they would move north and open up an area which had been neglected for many years, the Bridge of Orchy hills, in particular Beinn an Dòthaidh. Thus began a renaissance for this mountain, from the mid-1970s onwards. Skidmore and his friends should also be remembered for their efforts at successive SMC AGMs which helped to finally make changes in the club's constitution in 1990, allowing women to join. It was of no credit to a clique composed mainly of a few prominent, elderly Edinburgh climbers who persistently opposed this change.

❆❆❆

Robin Smith was gone, but he had left The Needle on the Shelter Stone Crag as his final calling card. Across the head of Loch Avon were the Stag Rocks, on the right of which was Longbow Crag, first climbed on by Nimlin in 1930. Untouched however was a 600ft blank wall, with an overhang near its left end: the Longbow Roof. This area had attracted an Aberdeen climber, Derek Pyper, who was intent on finding a central route and had already been up the cliff to below the roof. These crags were sunny and fast-drying, but were usually bypassed by climbers aiming at bigger things across the loch. In August 1962, Pyper returned, along with Jim McArtney.

Derek G Pyper is a Cairngorms activist who worked in journalism, while McArtney (1944-1970) was described in an obituary note by Tom Patey as *'An athletic ruddy-faced lad, as large as life and radiating enthusiasm like an open furnace.'* [12] McArtney worked in the printing trade until a post came up as an instructor at Glenmore Lodge. He also worked for the Glencoe School of Mountaineering.

With the enthusiasm of his companion supporting him, Pyper reached the roof and after traversing rightwards below it for 20 feet found a way up, bypassing this major obstacle. *Longbow Direct* (140m VS) had provided pleasant climbing, and Pyper now looked at a line further to the right. The chance arose in October 1962, climbing with Sandy Sands, when slabby pitches led to a large cracked overlap where Pyper had to use a sling as a foothold. The route's name, *The Sand-Pyper* (150m HVS) attracted some criticism (Sand-Piper might have been more subtle), but the climb has become popular, particularly with its Direct Finish added by Michael (Mike) George Geddes (1951-1985) and John C Higham in July 1972.

The Cairngorms winter which followed was stifled by an excess of snow, though on 23 February 1963 Pyper and McArtney made an ascent of *Bastion Wall* (150m IV,4), an undistinguished summer Difficult on Creagan a' Choire Etchachan.

Coire Sputan Dearg on Ben Macdui is unusual in being a south-facing Cairngorms crag. Its climbs are on excellent rock which is slabby with good holds, paradise for the lower-grade climbers. McArtney was there with Brian Lawrie in September 1963, the latter leading his first new route with *Terminal Wall* (70m Hard Severe). Even better was a route climbed the following week by Lawrie, Mitch Higgins and Jim Innes, *Grey Slab* (115m Hard Severe).

Patey was sniffing around the rocks of Coire an Lochan in 1963. On 31 October, with Don Whillans, he investigated the rocks to the right of Savage Slit, where a prominent corner was an obvious target. It was raining heavily and they had to make do with a lesser line to the left of Savage Slit, climbing *Gaffer's Groove* (60m Severe). Never one to leave a good line unclimbed, Patey returned on 17 May 1964 with Mary Stewart and Robin Ford to climb the route to the right, giving *Fallout Corner* (70m VS). A wet corner at its foot was overcome using an aid peg.

A week later, Ford and Alan North made the pilgrimage to Beinn a' Bhùird, where they succeeded in climbing a much-tried problem on Coire na Ciche. *Three Step* (135m E1) took a line of slabs and overhanging walls, with the exit from an overhanging crack on the second pitch having defeated all attempts. They climbed this using aid but did not record any details – which naturally prompted the story that excessive aid must have been used. In August 1969, a second ascent by Mike Rennie and John Bower confirmed its quality, using two pegs for the exit and one peg above. It was finally freed by Colin MacLean in 1982.

In July 1964 James Stenhouse arrived in Aberdeen through his work. He wasted no time in climbing with the locals, making the second ascent of Amethyst Wall on Coire Sputan Dearg with McArtney, adding a new pitch on the upper buttress directly up the crest. The following week he was checking out potential lines on Creag an Dubh Loch with Lawrie and was struck by the Central Slabs, right of Labyrinth Edge.

Lawrie had a pair of PAs, and Stenhouse had been blooded on the Trilleachan Slabs, so from below they worked out a possible line. The slabs, they quickly discovered, could not be climbed by friction alone; cracks and grooves were necessary for upward movement and protection. Four pitches later they had gained the terrace, and due to the late hour they escaped by this. Returning the following Saturday, they climbed several more pitches before again running out of daylight, this time finishing up Labyrinth Edge in the dark. Nonetheless, they had broken new ground on this major crag. Now linked with a later route climbed by John Grieve and Allen F Fyffe on 14 June 1969, the combination of *Dinosaur/Pink Elephant* (320m HVS) would satisfy most climbers.

Also in July 1964, the following weekend, a determined ascent on a direct start to Waterkelpie Wall at Creag an Dubh Loch by McArtney and Dave Mercer started up an open groove which had been tried by several teams in the past, including Grassick and Barclay. Several steep bands of rock had to be climbed between slabby sections; McArtney led the first of these and Mercer the second, taking a short fall and using an aid peg. Shortly above this, rain could have halted progress, but pulling socks over their PAs they climbed the next 100ft to gain The Caterpillar, the sloping grass terrace which leads leftward to peter out below a prominent steep red wall.

Waterkelpie Wall Direct Start had been climbed. According to Strange's history, Mac Smith had thought that with this addition the climb would be recognised as one of the finest of its genre in the country. It was later climbed in its entirety and all freed from aid, leaving the route as *Waterkelpie Wall* (260m E1). Once again, a problem which had baffled an earlier generation had been overcome by a new wave of climbers, a recurring theme through the decades. It would be a flag to other young climbers, showing that such rock could be climbed.

❄❄❄

The use of aid pitons on first ascents would soon diminish on summer climbs, as commercially designed and manufactured chockstones, or nuts, entered the market. The practice of many modern climbers, namely abseiling down a potential hard line, cleaning as one goes, had not yet begun. There would remain the need to carry some pegs in winter, where protection in general is more difficult to find, often with some cracks filled with ice or completely obscured.

The manufacture of nuts accelerated in the 1960s, although there had been prototypes for decades before, including the very early use of natural stones carried up by climbers and inserted into cracks with the rope running behind the stones as protection. Those wishing more information can do no better than go to the *Nuts' Museum,* where original material and photographs by Stéphane Pennequin has been translated by John Brailsford and put on the website of Needle Sports. [13]

Brailsford was a blacksmith from Sheffield and a teacher of engineering technology. In 1961 he designed and created what is regarded as the first nut available commercially for climbing protection, the Acorn. Soon after this he designed a nut which was to become an early classic, an immediate favourite of climbers in the late 1960s: the MOAC (with the name taken from the MOuntain Activities Company). These worked too well on occasion, as sometimes they were impossible to retrieve. If the reader comes across one on the Nose Route on Sgùrr an Fhidleir, it's the author's.

Pitons could of course damage the rock, especially softer types such as schist and sandstone, and one great advantage of nuts was to remove this possibility. It also lightened a climber's load, as there was no longer a need to carry a hammer and pegs. The aluminium alloys used for the new nuts were much lighter than pitons.

In 1953 the German company Edelrid had introduced the first kern-mantel rope, made of nylon and with an interior core or kern protected by a woven exterior sheath, or mantle. Climbing ropes made in this manner would reach the UK in the 1960s, significantly increasing safety. Fairly soon it also became standard to climb with two such ropes, normally placing running belays alternately, depending on the rock structure, again increasing safety. It would be a few years however before climbing harnesses came on the market, courtesy of Brian Robertson in the US and Don Whillans in the UK, the latter designing a sit harness bearing his name in 1970, manufactured by the Troll company specifically for the Bonington expedition to Annapurna South Face. Bill Forrest in the US designed his own sit harness in 1968.

Before then came a small number of belts, basically beefed-up and widened nylon affairs, similar to what might now be found on a quality rucksack, though of course much stronger, with loops for hanging gear. Before that, and still in use until the mid-1960s, was the basic hemp waistline, ¼-inch diameter hemp about 20ft in length wound round one's waist. Into this the climber clipped a screwgate karabiner to which was attached the rope.

A fall that ended in a suspension could be fatal, through asphyxiation, and a good, well-fitted sit harness with leg loops prevented this, in addition to making abseils more comfortable. Add a good helmet to the pile of equipment, and with due regard given to the placing of protection–plus climbing within one's standard–it would need a high degree of stupidity or very bad luck to become badly injured or dead. Indeed, for those at the sharper end of rock climbing, good protection became so prevalent that eventually ambitious climbers began to accept falls as part of their sport. On the routes they would normally be attempting, the vertical or overhanging nature of the crag would lend itself to this practice.

❄❄❄

Weather and climbing conditions were mixed throughout January 1965, but improved somewhat towards the end of February. Patey had made a summer traverse of the Cuillin ridge in 1951, with Brooker, and had made two attempts at a winter traverse. He knew of at least a dozen other attempts, half of which had involved MacInnes with various climbers. It had become the glittering prize in Scottish mountaineering.

As Patey had learned, ideal conditions were not easy to find. In a lengthy and entertaining article in the SMCJ, later reprinted in his autobiography, he explained what he considered the necessary prerequisites:

> The essential ingredients for success appear to be a heavy snowfall without an accompanying wind and followed successively by a quick thaw and an

equally rapid freeze. A further essential is that the weather must remain favourable for at least two days. [14]

As if to prove his theory, Patey had to wait three years after his first attempt. One other major personal hazard which was part of the equation was Patey's enthusiasm for partying and of course the renowned hospitality of Skye people. All of these points would play a part in the final successful attempt.

MacInnes was certainly intent on a winter traverse, and had invested enough time and effort to deserve a good shot at it. His approach was naturally better organised than that of the Aberdonian, with local help coming from Pete Thomas who lived in Glen Brittle, ran a hostel at Carbost and sold basic climbing equipment at the Glen Brittle campsite. Thomas would keep MacInnes updated on local conditions, then carry bivouac gear up to Sgurr na Banachdich, allowing lighter loads for the climbers. There was no fixed agreement between MacInnes and Patey; whatever happened would be on the spur of the moment.

On the successful traverse, finished on 1 March 1965, the climbers were MacInnes and Davie Crabb, along with Patey and Brian Robertson. Their first night, in the glen, was an indication of the two methodologies: MacInnes and Crabb went to bed at 9pm, while Patey and Robertson attended an impromptu ceilidh and retired at 2am. Robertson thus spent his first climbing day with a hangover, retching his way along the ridge.

They were climbing solo, from north to south, with the occasional use of a rope for abseiling and on the trickier parts of the ridge, such as the Gendarme on Sgùrr nan Gillean. The first abseil was the descent from the Bhasteir Tooth, where an earlier attempt involving Patey, Robertson, Langmuir and Tiso had seen the latter almost come to grief when his cramponed foot became entangled with his abseil rope just above the ground. In his struggle to free it, he turned upside-down, not an amusing state, as human physiology is not designed for such manoeuvres. Langmuir had to slowly prussik down the rope using a special friction knot and not knowing what had happened due to a bulge in the rock, before disentangling Tiso's foot with a flick of his axe.

The four men spent the night near the summit of Sgùrr na Banachdich, where their bivouac gear had been left. Patey had been in front, with Robertson *vomiting periodically, about twenty minutes behind me*'. At least half an hour further back were MacInnes and Crabb, and Patey wondered why they were not closer. It transpired that Crabb had broken a crampon, losing the use of the front half. He then roped up behind MacInnes for safety, slowing that pair somewhat.

The next morning dawned with some light snow and a slow but easy start to the day. At the next col they dropped the bivouac gear and spare rations down the slope, except MacInnes who, cautious as ever, stashed his under a rock. The next obstacle was the Inaccessible Pinnacle, where Patey soloed up the easy long side, gaining the top in time to drop a rope down for the other three who were intent on climbing the harder short side.

The main remaining stopping-point was the Thearlaich-Dubh Gap. Robertson was on the point of attempting to climb down when MacInnes suggested he could throw a loop of the rope over a pointed flake on the other side, one which he had found while investigating in the summer. *'With his very first cast his rope wrapped itself neatly round a projection at the top of the wall. Most men would have sweated blood and tears to achieve this.'*

The only problem was that this was not the intended projection. Patey was uncertain, but MacInnes suggested he try the rope. It was, as Patey wrote, the *'throw of the dice'*, making the difference between success and utter disaster. He was very relieved when the rope was found to be securely jammed. One more abseil and the traverse was done, as they wandered silently and independently along the final scree-speckled mile to Gars-bheinn.

The Main Cuillin Ridge Winter Traverse (12km, 3000m ascent, Grade IV, 2/3 days) was, as Patey concluded in his article, *'...the greatest single adventure in British Mountaineering'*. He continued:

> It would be presumptuous to be conceited about the success of our own exploit. We can only be grateful that we were lucky to find this superb climb in superb winter conditions. If any individual honours are awarded then they should go to Davie Crabb and Brian Robertson who completed the Ridge on half a crampon and half a stomach respectively, thereby revealing – in Hamish's own phraseology – *'a determination that is truly Scots.'*

Determinedly, Tiso returned two days later for another bout with the winter traverse, climbing with Moriarty. The steps left by the first ascenders at the Inaccessible Pinnacle led him to think that they had climbed up the harder short side, so that was the route the pair took. Patey was generous in commenting that this was a sterling performance. The pair succeeded and thus completed the second winter traverse.

❄ ❄ ❄

Point Five Gully on Ben Nevis had been climbed by siege tactics in 1959, and in February 1960 Marshall and Smith made the second winter ascent in just over seven hours. The third ascent, in 1962, raised the profile of the Squirrels group, with Ian MacEacheran and Dave Bathgate climbing the gully in hard conditions which necessitated a bivouac halfway up. In an article describing the fifth ascent in 1965, Brian Robertson, a leading figure in the Squirrels, mentions that four days after the MacEacheran/Bathgate ascent a team from England had utilised their steps to make the fourth ascent. [15]

Point Five was at this time seeing around one ascent per winter, a mark of its difficulty; in hard conditions it was obviously a test piece, with only a limited number of mountaineers in Scotland capable of climbing it. Some of the tactics employed by Robertson and his climbing partner Jock Knight give an indication of the physical effort involved in such climbs.

Knight was one of the most proficient winter climbers in the Squirrels and had tried Point Five before, failing in poor conditions. He bullied Robertson into leading the first pitch. As in most ascents, the third and fifth pitches proved to be the tough ones – so Robertson was up against it. To make the leader's task easier, excess equipment was carried by the second man. Robertson was fit, as his traverse of the Cuillin ridge had come only a few weeks earlier. The pair used Salewa ice screws, only just on the market. These were tubular and hollow, making them easier to insert into ice and also stronger, as their diameter was greater than previous solid screws. As they were screwed in, snow and ice would be pushed up the hollow centre, to fall out at the end.

The first pitch being easier-angled than those higher up, Robertson climbed the initial 60 feet in a quarter of an hour, cutting only three or four handholds. On the next pitch, Knight cut large jug-handle holds in the ice, so well-fashioned that Robertson followed without needing to improve the holds with his axe.

On the crux pitch, their fifth, spindrift was flowing down its narrowing, adding to the discomfort as no progress could be made while enveloped in its icy embrace. The fine ice crystals would enter the slightest opening in clothing, and it could be difficult to breathe fully when under a strong flow. Robertson's fingers were weakening as he clung on below the top of the pitch. On a winter climb, time is a valuable commodity, not to be squandered, and he thought that the spindrift probably cost them an hour.

It would take the pair just under ten hours before Knight's powerful arms battered down the cornice and gained the plateau. They were climbing in March, and had made an early start, an important safety factor in the days of step-cutting.

❄❄❄

Haston included a brief description of the new Salewa ice screws in a 1966 SMCJ note on equipment. [16] As he put it, the most significant developments in the past year had been in hardware, including US-made pegs of alloy steel along with nylon tape and improvements by the German company Salewa in their adjustable crampons. These became very popular in the 1960s and 1970s and were ideal for mixed climbing, although more tiring, especially on the calf muscles, for long pitches of ice.

The note by Haston was of course not motivated purely by a personal interest in the development of climbing equipment; it ended with a plug for Tiso, whom he mentioned as being 'forward-looking'. This was quite true, and for some time there was nowhere else in Scotland for climbers to purchase something as basic as a pair of the new rock boots, or a new-fangled alloy chockstone.

Graham J Tiso (1935-1992), originally a salesman for Cadbury products, had spotted the opportunity and made the leap, moving from chocolate to chockstones. With no immediate competition, particularly on the hardware side, his business in Edinburgh rapidly expanded (and in 2012 celebrated its 50th anniversary). A good mountaineer in his own right, Tiso would have discussed equipment–its development, functionality and availability–with those he knew and climbed with. He died in the West Indies, following an accident when working on his yacht while ashore.

There was another side to Tiso, who as a member of the SMC became involved with the production of guidebooks. He had backed the production of a *Climber's Guide to Creag Dubh and the Eastern Outcrops* in 1967, whose authors included Robin Campbell, Haston, MacEacheran, McKeith and other Squirrels. [17] Although the present volume does not cover outcrop history, mention must be accorded to some of those who climbed on the lower crags and helped produce guidebooks to them.

Bugs McKeith must have been a busy man at this time, as in 1966 he published another useful private guide, to the winter climbs in Coire Ardair, Creag Meaghaidh (note that this seems to be the older spelling of Meagaidh, with two occurrences of 'h').

As the imprint of the 1967 Creag Dubh guide announced, it had been 'organised' by Tiso and 'reorganised' by M Fleming. The latter, Dr Michael Fleming, was SMC editor of rock climbing guides 1965-1966. The diagrams were by McKeith, who studied at Edinburgh College of Art, Glasgow School of Architecture and Alberta College of Art, where he won awards in sculpture. The publication of this guide removed some angst from the SMC, as the section on Creag Dubh, the steep crag near Newtonmore, contained many route names which were regarded as obscene.

One of its innovations was the use of a PVC cover. From start to finish it was an Edinburgh project, even being printed in that city. In turn, it would lead to the publication in 1975 of a more modest guide to *The Western Outcrops*, written by the present author and backed by Ian (Spike) Sykes, the founder with Ian Sutherland of the Nevisport Company.[18] There had been various samizdat guides to Scottish outcrops in limited circulation, some handwritten, some typewritten, some with diagrams, and both these guides did a service to climbers in bringing together these disparate crags. Many climbers new to the sport may not have been aware of some of these outcrops.

The Western Outcrops was followed some six months later by another guide, *The Glasgow Outcrops*, published by another retailer, Highrange

Sports (backed by Sam Brown). This guide, like the earlier one, included Dumbarton Rock but not, crucially, the boulder problems. There was, inevitably, some leaning on the earlier guide, but this was offset by inclusion in the latter of a hitherto 'secret' crag, Craigmore, a few miles north of Bearsden. This blossoming of guidebooks was a natural result, fertilised by the increased number of climbers through the 1960s.

In the east, the Tiso guide did not enter into any history, though some of its authors might have produced earlier descriptions of routes on their local crag. The authors of *The Glasgow Outcrops* were John Kerry, Douglas Benn, John Mackenzie, Brian Shields and John Jackson. In the west, much of the research was based on original work of Shields (who covered Dumbarton Rock), Jackson (Loudoun Hill), John Cullen of the Creagh Dhu (the Whangie) and Bill Skidmore (the Quadrocks in Ayrshire).

Mike Fleming must have been occasionally frustrated with his work on SMC guides, and in the 1966 SMCJ he vented this in a three-page note entitled '*What Happened to "Glencoe II"*? [19] Glencoe I was the guide to Buachaille Etive Mor, written by Len Lovat and published in 1959. Glencoe II was the planned volume for the rest of the Glen Coe area plus the Trilleachan Slabs and Ardgour. It finally came out in 1965 and the delay, as Fleming pointed out, was not due to Lovat, its author. Basically, the SMC was not yet sufficiently organised, and on top of this the printing industry in the UK had many shortcomings.

When the SMC became organised enough that the Glencoe II manuscript could be looked at, it was clearly out of date, as climbers had become more numerous and more active in the new-route game. As Fleming wrote:

> About this time, a complete set of new diagrams was forthcoming from Marshall, and forthwent immediately to Chambers the publishers, who forthchucked them on to Cunningham the printers, who were so fascinated by these works of art that they sat and stared in wonder for a further eighteen months, fobbing off irate enquiries with the occasional galley and page proof.

By the end of the 1950s, the SMC had in print only five climbing guides, all out of date– to the Cuillin of Skye, Ben Nevis, Glen Coe, Arrochar and, to a lesser degree, Arran. By 1970, thanks to the efforts of Fleming, Scott Johnstone (1922-2005) and William Blair Speirs (1907-1997), guides to the Cairngorms (two volumes), Glen Coe (two volumes), the Cuillin (two volumes), Northern Highlands (volume 1), Ben Nevis, Arrochar, and Arran had been published. Anyone who has an interest in the history of climbing guidebooks should refer to the superb work by Alan Moss, which covers British and Irish guides from 1894-2011. [20]

Fleming also mentioned plastic covers in his 1966 note, stating that these should be considered for the SMC guides. When it came time for a new edition of the Glen Coe guide, which was written by the author and appeared in 1980, the publisher used was West Col. The author made strenuous arguments for a plastic cover, but was told by Tiso, convenor of the SMC publications sub-committee, that according to West Col this was not possible. [21]

The SMC guide to the Northern Highlands, Volume 1, was published in 1969. It too had major problems with its PVC cover wrinkling and becoming unsightly, and was quickly withdrawn. This problem was endemic, and the cover photographs reproduced in Moss's guide to the guidebooks show that virtually all the English clubs had the same problem in the 1960s and 1970s.

In 1981 the SMC began to publish guides under its own banner, beginning with Rock and Ice Climbs in Lochaber and Badenoch authored by JR Marshall and Colin Stead. This had a PVC cover, but to date no wrinkles have appeared – except those on the authors, of course.

❊❊❊

By 1961 or thereabouts, it had dawned on Haston that he was not born to be a student. Various odd jobs kept him occupied between visits to the Alps or climbing trips in Scotland. In October 1964, he visited the impressive Great Wall on Creag Dubh with T Gooding to record *Inbred* (105m HVS), a line taking in the steepest part of this roadside crag. It was a bold lead. In May and June 1965, 18 new climbs were recorded here by the Squirrels and Haston. In 1967 came the intimidating and impressive *The Hill* (60m E2), by Ken Spence and John Porteous, just left of Inbred.

Along with Elly Moriarty, and with financial backing from the Londoner Bev Clark, Haston began the Scottish Climbing School. A VW van would be used to pick up pupils and drive them to Glen Coe and other crags. Haston was not a businessman, however, and the venture would probably have been doomed anyway – but its actual demise was sudden and tragic.

On Easter Saturday, 17 April 1965, the weather in Glen Coe was at its worst, and many hit the hotels. Haston had maintained his fondness for alcohol, and this Saturday was no exception. Coming out of the Clachaig Inn he was drunk, yet insisted on driving the van. Even sober he was a poor driver, and careering along the narrow, twisting old road towards Glencoe village he ran into a group of walkers. An 18-year old student from Glasgow, James Orr, later died from his injuries, while several others were injured to various degrees. Haston panicked, left the scene, and hid overnight in a friend's cottage. Fred Harper, Big Elly and others were passengers in the van.

The following day Haston turned himself in. He was charged with careless driving and also with driving while unfit through drink. He was found not guilty of a third charge, leaving the scene of an accident. His sentence was a £15 fine, a two-year driving ban and 60 days in prison, which he spent in Barlinnie. Some reports had him driving again illegally following his release, again after having taken too much drink. [22]

Haston did not leave Scotland immediately, and recorded several rock climbs, three on the Trilleachan Slabs, including *Attila* (200m E3) with Jim Brumfitt, using two pegs and climbing directly on the main slab between Spartan Slab and The Pause. This was in October 1965, which would effectively mark the close of his regular Scottish rock climbing. In December, with McKeith he would climb *Drainpipe Corner* (50m IV,5) on the East Face of Aonach Dubh, a short but difficult ice pitch.

At Christmas he moved into John Harlin's basement in Leysin, Switzerland, where the American climber was running the International School of Mountaineering. Haston joined Harlin for an epic winter ascent of the Eiger's North Face, and the rest is history, with other big Alpine routes leading eventually to a successful ascent of Everest which catapulted him into the public gaze.

Haston never expressed public remorse for the incident in Glen Coe, although he never drove a vehicle again after he moved to Switzerland. He died in bizarre circumstances, having just finished a novel whose main character was patently himself and who died in an avalanche while skiing down the North-East Face of La Riondaz. The following day, despite warnings of avalanche conditions, Haston went out to ski the very same face and died in an avalanche. The date was 17 January 1977.

❊❊❊

Ronnie Marshall had pointed out a major line to his Edinburgh acquaintance Dave Bathgate, a line he could hardly miss. It was a prominent corner soaring above the screes of Central Gully, Creag an Dubh Loch. Accordingly, Bathgate headed to the crag on 23 October 1965 having dragooned two other Squirrels, Arthur Ewing and Jim Brumfitt, into the project. There is a sentence in the article Bathgate wrote after the first ascent which with time acquired an ironic ring– *'The rock hereabouts is very sound; otherwise it would all fall down.'* [23]

Car problems on the Friday night had delayed their arrival and it was 2pm on Saturday before they started up the route. The line was about 600ft, more or less straight up the cliff, with black roofs and smooth pink walls, sullied only by the odd rusty peg from previous anonymous attempts. Brumfitt and Bathgate roped up, Ewing staying down as time was short. After two pitches, with light fading, they left the ropes and descended to their bivouac on the heather.

The next day all three roped up, with Ewing leading and attempting a corner. While standing in an étrier the peg came out and he had a short fall before a lower peg held. The parallel corner to the right overhung more but had better cracks, and he climbed this to near its top until he could go no further. Bathgate came up, speeded by a tight rope, and passing Ewing managed to gain a belay above using several pegs and a jammed nut.

Brumfitt now followed, but was unable to recover the étrier at the top of the corner. On the following pitch, Bathgate came across more rusty pegs and climbed a steep wall with good holds. These ran out below a little holdless slab at the top. A peg was inserted at full stretch, pulled up on, mantelshelved on to, then stood upon. A balancy move right across a void led to a good belay ledge below the last corner.

They all gathered in the gloom below the last obstacle, a superb 100ft right-angled corner. There was half an hour of daylight remaining as Bathgate moved up. After some strenuous bridging for 15ft or so a wedge was inserted, then a second, and a third, and soon he was standing in étriers again. He stood on the second-top rung and placing another wedge in a good crack hung his next étrier from it. As he was using the top wedge for balance, his supporting wedge popped out and he was flung out into space, performing a somersault.

Bathgate came to a halt upside-down and below his two companions on the belay. He had fallen 70ft and had been held by a wedge and by his belayer, Brumfitt. A little skin had been lost and he was shaken, but unhurt. Time had been lost, but he decided to carry on, pegging all the way up the final corner. About 14 pegs and other aid points later Bathgate emerged from the corner and in the last of the light found a crack for a belay peg.

Ewing arrived, and together they held a rope and helped Brumfitt climb from peg to peg.

> We were able to judge his progress by the spaces between the red marks my bloody hand made on the rope and when we could hear his heavy breathing, we knew he was almost up. One last effort from the three of us and he landed safely ashore and Arthur and I could try to straighten out our fingers.

The trio now spent a miserable ten hours shivering on their poorly protected perch, before the slowly brightening morning mists allowed a wander to the top of the buttress and down to their gear below. As for the route, *The Giant* (140m E3), sometime after 2010 the final corner fell down and added its pile of shattered rock to the gully below. It was a fine pitch of course. The route can still be climbed, taking a diversion near the top for an alternative finish. The original route had been repeated in 1970 by Wilf Tauber and Squirrel member Bill Sproul, who reduced the aid but could not free the top corner which was wet. A 1974 ascent by Paul 'Tut' Braithwaite and Nick Estcourt was reported as having been free.

Another hard climb was also finished in the dark, in the east of the country, but with perhaps less angst and certainly no bivouac. Ken Grassick, Jerry Light and Graeme Nicol teamed up on 16 January 1966 on the strength of a good forecast, bound for Pinnacle Face on Lochnagar. It was Very Severe in summer, and Grassick had visited the corrie six times in the previous four years hoping for suitable winter conditions. He had climbed the summer route three times and had actually been on the lower section twice in winter. [24] By mid-month conditions had settled after successive thaws and freezes, with thinly iced rocks.

At dawn they were at the foot of the cliffs; it was a cold morning with little wind. Most of the morning was needed to climb the first 120ft to a stance below the summer crux, with ice and névé on ledges and in cracks. Grassick and Light led through, alternating the lower section which they divided into three shorter pitches. Grassick was on the summer crux by early afternoon, overcoming it by one poor peg for aid. A few feet further on he made an intermediate belay and brought up Light, then with combined tactics continued and finished the pitch on a large ledge. By 3.30pm they were all together with Light starting up the next pitch in the gathering gloom, reaching a small ledge below the final steep corner.

Now in the dark, they had to climb this corner then find their way down Route I. Grassick tried for an hour with no luck, coming back to allow Light to have a go. They discovered that between them they had one working headtorch, with that despicable species of equipment still waiting for a breakthrough in design. As Light – an ironic surname given the circumstances – could do no better in the corner, with a huge effort they formed a human tripod, and with Nicol belaying the other two Light was able to gain a good hold above and so reach a ledge.

All that remained was a nerve-wracking traverse on narrow ledges in the dark, but the route had been climbed. Once they reached the Springboard they abseiled down Route I into the Black Spout. It had taken 12 hours of sustained climbing, and their description in the SMCJ leaves no doubt as to the difficulty. The top grade at the time was V in winter. Sustained severity, no pitch less than IV, three pegs for direct aid, steepness – it all added up to a hard route. The crux pitch alone required three hours of effort, as did the summer version.

In his Cairngorms history, Greg Strange notes that in 1966 the winter ascent was a close contender for the most technically difficult winter climb in Scotland, at Grade VI. The current guide gives it as *Pinnacle Face* (250m VI,7). Also on Lochnagar, February 1967 saw the second ascent of Parallel Gully B, climbed in under six hours by McArtney and Fyffe. With continuing good conditions, several days later Martin Boysen and Jud Jordan confirmed the quality of climbing by making the third ascent.

July that same year saw two fit Yorkshire brothers, Robin and Tony Barley, visit Creag an Dubh Loch. On 5 July they walked in from Glen Clova; the great slabs were wet, but high on the left they spied an apparently unclimbed 400ft face. This was Broad Terrace Wall, and with four aid pegs they succeeded in climbing it. Aberdonian respect for this ascent was tempered somewhat by its provocative naming as *Culloden* (125m E2). It was freed in 1975 in drier conditions by the Lakeland pair of Jeff Lamb and Pete Whillance.

Robertson the Squirrel was in action at Creag an Dubh Loch in September 1967, intending a direct route up the Central Slabs. Climbing over two days with Fyffe, and on the first day with an American, Bill Wilkins, he succeeded with *The Blue Max* (305m E1). As was Robertson's style, it had one somewhat contrived section or, as Fyffe succinctly described his companion, '*Robertson was into difficulty over logic*'.

The climbing on Creag an Dubh Loch would continue to find new lines, many of which would require some aid due to loose rock, dampness and vegetation. These factors would gradually be whittled down over the years as the routes were cleaned and standards rose, ultimately producing one of Scotland's great crags with a rich field of entertaining climbs.

References

1. Accidents in North American Mountaineering (1979). <goo.gl/uafztk> (Accessed December 2016).
2. Connor, Jeff. *Creagh Dhu Climber*. (Ernest Press, Glasgow, 1999, p.98).
3. Fulton, Ian. *Torro*. Glasgow University Mountaineering Club Magazine, 1970.
4. Nisbet, Andrew. *Personal communication*. January 2017.
5. Plint, Michael. *A Gentleman's Tour in Skye*. SMCJ 29, 159, May 1968, pp.19-22.
6. Crawford, Jim. *The Greenock Team*. SMCJ 34, 180, 1989, pp.193-209.
7. Kay, Anthony. *Route Choice in Hilly Terrain*. Department of Mathematical Sciences, Loughborough University. <goo.gl/S5Mpfv> Accessed December 2016.
8. Richardson, R. *The Brack – New Routes on an Old Mountain*. SMCJ 29, 161, May 1970, pp.227-230.
9. Mitchell, Pat. *Great Central Groove, The Brack*. SMCJ 26, 150, May 1959, pp.356-358.
10. Mitchell, Pat. *Unpublished account*.
11. Richardson, R. Op.cit.
12. T.W.P. [Tom Patey]. *In Memoriam – James McArtney, 1944-1970*. SMCJ 29, 161, May 1970, pp.330-331.
13. The Nuts' Museum. <goo.gl/lzJyll> Accessed December 2016.
14. Patey, Tom. *The First Winter Traverse of the Cuillin Ridge*. SMCJ 28, 156, May 1965, pp.69-87.

15. Robertson, Brian W. *Squirrels on Point Five.* SMCJ 28, 157, May 1966, pp.182-185.

16. Haston, Dougal. *Equipment Notes.* In: Notes. SMCJ 28, 157, May 1966, pp.232-233.

17. Various authors. *Creag Dubh and the Eastern Outcrops.* (Graham Tiso, Edinburgh, 1967).

18. Crocket, K.V. *The Western Outcrops.* (Nevisport, Ft. William & Glasgow, 1975).

19. Fleming , Michael. *What Happened to 'Glencoe II'?* In: Notes. SMCJ 28, 157, May 1966, pp.234-236.

20. Moss, Alan. *British and Irish Climbing Guidebooks 1894 to 2011 A Collector's Guide.* (BMC, Manchester, 2012).

21. Wightman, Andrew. *In Memoriam – Graham Tiso, J. 1959.* SMCJ 35, 1993, 184, pp.337-339.

22. Connor, Jeff. *The Philosophy of Risk.* (Canongate, Edinburgh, 2002, pp.81-88.)

23. Bathgate, D. *Explanation Giant.* SMCJ 28, 28, 157, May 1966, pp.190-196.

24. Strange, Greg. *The Cairngorms – 100 Years of Mountaineering.* p.160.

14

Corriemulzie (1965-1968)

By the mid-1960s, various members of the Squirrels Mountaineering Club were active not only in Scotland, but also in the Alps. Jimmy Marshall was still climbing and recording routes, particularly on Ben Nevis, where he was working on a new edition of the SMC guide which would be published in 1969. Ian Clough was also active on the Ben and continued to record routes there through the 1960s, summer and winter. One summer line by Clough was *Mourning Slab* (100m VS), on 1 June 1961 with Keith Sutcliffe. Named after a corner which often weeps on to the slab below, this route is transformed in winter, when without fail at some point in the season it forms an excellent, three-pitch ice climb known as *The Curtain* (100m IV,5).

The Curtain is on the left flank of Càrn Dearg Buttress, conveniently close to the approach path to the CIC hut. It is very popular, and in a good spell a trench can be worn up the slab on the first pitch. The first ascent in February 1965 was by Dave Bathgate and Jock Knight, two good ice men in the Squirrels. Bathgate had a moment of excitement leading the bulge on the second pitch when one of his crampons decided to detach its front half. As he noted in his SMCJ article:

> When reversing on steep ice it's comforting to know that groping boots will slip into well-placed jugs. It's no use scraping your way up an ice pitch to make fast time: sooner or later you'll have to reverse one... [1]

It was Bathgate's second attempt at the route, the first having been defeated by poor weather. The pair took six and a half hours, faster than anticipated. They had the new Salewa tubular screws, one of which Knight used for tension on the steep ice of the last pitch. The route even finishes at a convenient point–on the ramp which leads from No.5 Gully to the top of the buttress. It was one of the few winter routes which had a name before it was climbed.

To Bathgate's comments it can be added that, on occasion, a leader cutting steps would start to run out of steam before the end of a pitch. In such situations retreat was usually out of the question and the climber would either cut a large step and rest if possible, or dig deep for the last dregs of arm strength and finish the pitch.

The Marshall brothers continued working on the Ben Nevis guide, and on 4 September 1966 climbed *Knuckleduster* (120m HVS) on the right-hand section of No.3 Gully Buttress. This is an outstanding line, taking a very obvious groove, though it requires a dry period. Jimmy Marshall has commented that late summer or autumn seems to be best time for rock climbing on Ben Nevis. Early summer, by contrast, often has melting snow.

The brothers were back in March 1967, when joined by Robin Campbell they succeeded in climbing *The Clanger* (90m IV,5) on South Trident Buttress. This was a route with which Jimmy Marshall had some history, having first climbed it in June 1964 with Jimmy Stenhouse, checking out some Kellett routes. Kellett's Groove fitted with his description, although the only exit they could find was very loose, so Marshall thought it could make a good winter climb. Accordingly he was back in February 1965 with Big Elly Moriarty, the 'Gentle Giant', the mountain snowing and blowing as they moved up under The Trident. Marshall indicated the groove and Moriarty gave him an old-fashioned look – but, being gentle, acquiesced.

> The groove looked thin and hard, the forty-foot entry wall glazed and awkward, with spurts of powder drifting down, so I bashed a peg between loose flakes and offered the toil to Eli. Up he went, showing the soles of his boots, forty feet to a string runner, then leftward a little into the groove and out of sight. Winter's worries assailed me, the axe belay was useless, the peg doubtful, but at least it would save me extruding through snaplinks above! Muffled mumblings and excuses filtered down the rope; brittle ice; glazed bulges etc.; the gut began to tighten, he's an enormous bloke, must get a grip and think happy thoughts. Och, he'll be alright, he's so tall he's over most problems before they start, the happy thoughts prevail and I peer into the grim corrie below. The rope moves up, good, that's the bulge over, and then—a, great rasping, rumbling, thrashing, tumbling offends my ear. I race the rope back through the string runner, Jesus Christ! there isn't a higher runner. Eli streaks out off the groove head down like a 225 lb. torpedo, my eyes are on stalks as he smashes a crater from the ledge and bounces out into orbit. I wrap the rope tight and think of the 500-foot drop below—Whang he comes on the rope, I'm up in the air. If you've got to go.... he's got his, now for mine. [2]

Fortunately, Moriarty was made of harder material than most, and other than a tiny cut on his nose, from which much blood oozed, he was unhurt. Marshall's belay peg had wobbled somewhat but had held; the pair gave up for the day and shambled downward, where an English party timorously pushing upward were to meet an–

> ...enormous bloodstained Eli looming through the drifting snows, to have their awed enquiries treated with traditional disdain in his reply 'Never mind, but dinnae go up there, the whole bloody corrie's avalanchin'.

Two years later, somewhat calmed down, Marshall was back with his brother and Campbell. Jimmy climbed the groove, passing the ice bulge which had come off with Moriarty, and belaying above passed the lead to Campbell – who, reaching a ledge below an overhang, traversed right and out of sight. When it came turn for Jimmy to follow, he found the other two belayed above a narrow chimney crack. Marshall tried to climb this, but his more generous girth prevented progress. Furious now, he demanded a rope be thrown down, and with both men hauling he eventually spluttered his way up outside the crack. Then, months later, Marshall discovered that what they had climbed with so much effort was not Kellett's Groove at all – that was a groove further along the buttress, '...*a tiny little chimney, ours loomed and leered in splendid scale above, a classic Nevis joke'.*

In September 1967, Ronnie Marshall and John R Jackson made the first climb on Indicator Wall, the steep face to the right of Good Friday Climb and the highest rocks on Ben Nevis. Although *Psychedelic* Wall (185m Scottish VS) is not a great route, and probably best avoided in summer due to the risk of rocks from above, it would form part of a burst of excellent winter ascents made on this face in 1978.

Turning from one of the highest Ben Nevis crags to one of the lower ones, on 9 June 1970 Norrie Muir and Ian Nicolson recorded *Heidbanger* (90m E1) on Central Trident Buttress. That same summer two members of a sub-group of the Creagh Dhu, the Steam Team as they were called, Stevie Docherty and Bobby Gorman, climbed *Steam* (90m HVS) starting just left of Heidbanger. The latter received a Direct Start in 1977, *Cranium* (25m E1 5b), by Muir and Arthur Paul, while in August 1971 the rope of Docherty and Davy Gardner climbed *Metamorphosis* (105m E2), the finest route on the buttress.

Most of the above characters were hard-boiled Glaswegians or 'Weegies', and accordingly not to be trifled with. One of the most interesting was Muir. Among several legends attached to him is that he was the only climber known to have persuaded his GP to prescribe a pair of big boots for self-medication, allowing him to continue climbing. This, of course, may simply be another urban myth. He would figure prominently in the 1970s and join the Creagh Dhu.

A winter route was found on 16 February 1969, and it was a good one, on the Little Brenva Face. *Route Major* (300m IV,4) is a fine, sustained mountaineering route, climbed by Clough and MacInnes. It has a reputation for difficult route-finding – or, in other words, some parties have become lost here.

❄❄❄

Exploration of Creag Meagaidh seems to have ceased by the outbreak of World War II, with Colin Allan and Jim Bell having climbed the Centre Post in 1937. It would not begin again until the end of the 1950s, courtesy of Jimmy Marshall and others. Appropriately, it was to the Centre Post that a trio of Squirrels returned in 1964; Brian Robertson, Fred Harper and E Cairns. They were not the first, however, as before moving on to Ben Nevis (where they climbed Wendigo), Joe Brown and Tom Patey had also looked at the Centre Post, intent on making a direct ascent by taking in the massive ice pitch at just over half-height. Bypassing this on the right, as Allan and Bell had done, gives Centre Post (400m III).

Determined to make an early start, late on Friday 21 February the Squirrels left their bothy, the Drey in Glen Coe, and drove to Aberarder farm. An hour's walk saw them below the cliffs where they pitched a tent for a few hours' sleep.

> In the morning, a large breakfast was eaten in preparation for an assault on one of the last great problems of Scottish mountaineering. We were in no doubt that, if ripe, it would be picked like a plum from under the very eye of the S.M.C. and C.D.M.C. hard men.

> It took us just under an hour to cover the lower 1000 ft. to the great unclimbed pillar of green ice: the lower section consisted of snow-ice and water-ice set at a moderate angle of 45 degrees. On this section we found traces of steps, only to hear from the farmer the following day that none other than Tom Patey and Joe Brown had made an attempt on the Centre Post Direct the previous weekend. They had told him that they had climbed to within 10 ft. of the top of the central section. [3]

Robertson noted that the earlier steps, of which there were many, continued on the right edge of this section, which he considered 'a wee bit cheating'. The Squirrels' line was about 30 feet to the left and involved step-cutting on vertical water-ice, which fortunately eased back to about 80° higher up. The leader took around four hours on this pitch, with five ice-pegs for protection. *Centre Post Direct* (60m V,5) had fallen.

Creag Meagaidh would see much activity in the 1960s. Patey would be especially prominent in recording lines, with highlights including *The Last Post* (240m V,5) climbed 5 March 1962 by Patey and RF Brooke, and *Diadem* (210m V,4) 19 February 1964, Patey and Joe Brown. On 23 March

1969, Patey succeeded in outdoing himself with a massive solo girdle, *The Crab Crawl* (2400m IV,4), which crosses the Coire Ardair cliffs in four stages. Patey had 'previous' on such routes, having been on the Ben Nevis Winter Girdle (1500m IV,4) with Jimmy Marshall on 31 January 1959.

As recounted by Patey himself, the route's name derived from a comment made a fortnight beforehand, when he had tried to enlist Whillans in the attempt.[4] *"Look mate,"* he interrupted, *"do you know what you want to do? You want to team up with a crab. It's got claws, walks sideways and it's got a thick 'ead. This isn't a climb, it's a bloody crab-crawl!"*

The first two sections had been tackled earlier, by Bugs McKeith and Dennis Gray on 15 and 16 January 1966, taking in *The Scene* and *Apollyon Ledge*. Patey – who thought the grades and times for these sections excessive – climbed The Scene's 1000ft in 30 minutes and thought it merited Grade II, and not the two and a half hours and grade III it had been given. Patey did not have ideal conditions, with black ice and windslab. For Apollyon Ledge, he took one hour, so thus far he had compressed a suggested seven hours into 90 minutes. The entire girdle estimate in the guide was 15 hours, and there were four and a half hours of daylight remaining. It should be borne in mind that Patey's climbing style was all whirlwind and little grace.

The climbing was going well, with very few steps needing to be cut and Patey relying on his front points and the two picks of his axes. It was inevitable that he would continue. On the section which shares a common start with The Last Post, Patey could see a few dimples on an enormous bulge of ice, probably where Rab Carrington and Con Higgins had gone a few weeks earlier. That formidable pair had nonetheless been so delayed on The Last Post, Patey noted, that they were obliged to spend a night on the plateau. He found an alternative line, cutting steps across a smear of metallic ice. It was tiring work, but he finished the section and continued on easy snow bands to cross the South Post. Here he met a climber on a roped ascent.

A second climber was encountered in the Centre Post, who persuaded Patey to lead the next pitch and bring him up before Patey continued sideways. Heading for the North Post, Patey was probably becoming tired, and this is when mistakes creep in. He was halfway down a diagonal crack before realising it was the wrong one, and windslab almost knocked him off while he was attempting to correct the error. A small ring-spike tied off in a blind crack was the stuff of nightmares, but somehow held to allow a diagonal abseil, gaining a big ledge.

Another route-finding error further on meant he missed a ledge system and had to climb back up 300ft or so, despite the strong temptation to call it a day. Eventually even Creag Meagaidh ran out of cliff, and with the corrie floor rising to meet the last traverse, the girdle was over.

By now, Patey was involved with the media, and trailing along on the day of the girdle were Jim McArtney and Mary Anne Hudson as climbers, John Cleare as photographer and Peter Gillman as reporter. Patey had realised at the start that this was far too cumbersome a party for such a long route, so he dashed off on his own. Cleare succeeded in taking a few photographs, which provide some atmosphere.

Sadly, as Patey wrote in a postscript to his article, his friend McArtney, along with Hudson and Fergus Mitchell, died on 19 January 1970 in a slab avalanche on the Italian Climb on Ben Nevis. The sole survivor of this accident was John Grieve, who was last on the rope and had untied in order to free a snag. Patey, highly distraught over the loss of his friend, applied pressure to the Procurator Fiscal in Fort William, suggesting that there was more to this incident than a simple accident. [5]

One feature of Creag Meagaidh is that many of the prominent gullies build up fine icefalls which can be avoided; this has led to several routes receiving indirect first ascents, later climbed directly by other parties. One plus point is that parties not up to Grade V may be able to climb some routes through great scenery at an easier grade.

One such route is the South Post, now described in the guide with three different dates attached. First climbed on 10 February 1956 by Norman Tennent and Malcolm Slesser, the initial icefall was avoided by traversing in from the left via Apollyon Ledge, while an ice section on the third pitch (normally the crux) was avoided, giving *South Post* (400m III). On 5 March 1962 the initial icefall was climbed direct by Patey and RF Brooke, while the icefall forming the third pitch was climbed direct in March 1964 by Ian A MacEacheran and Jock Knight, giving *South Post Direct* (400m V,4).

❄ ❄ ❄

Patey was by now exploring stacks along the north-west coast. The repulsive Old Man of Storr on Skye had been climbed by Whillans on 18 July 1955, with his Original Route currently graded at E5 although this probably varies as bits fall off. The only confirmed later ascent was that by Creagh Dhu climber Pat Walsh in the late 1960s, having followed instructions written on an envelope by Whillans. Two others, J Barber and GJ Sutton, also climbed the pinnacle, but prusiked up the crucial section.

More popular is the Old Man of Hoy in Orkney, which was climbed on 18 July 1966 by Rusty Baillie, Chris Bonington and Patey to give *Original Route* (130m E1), with aid used on the first ascent. Encouraged by the potential for a TV spectacular, Patey drew up a portfolio which attracted the media and featured Joe Brown, Ian McNaught Davis, Pete Crew and Dougal Haston in July 1967. Two more routes were added. Since then, four other routes and a free ascent of the Crew-Haston South-East Arête have been recorded.

In June 1966, and arguably giving the best climbing, Patey had visited the Old Man of Stoer, north of Lochinver, and investigated with Brian Robertson, Paul Nunn and Brian 'Killer' Henderson. The ascent of their *Original Route* (75m VS) is amusingly painted by Patey in an SMCJ article and reprinted in his autobiography.[6]

In July 1967, Am Buachaille at Sandwood Bay received attention, with Patey, accompanied by Cleare and Clough, climbing another *Original Route* (55m HVS). A slightly better line on this pinnacle is *Landward Face* (50m VS), climbed shortly after Original Route by Nunn, D Peck, Clive Rowland and others, with the first pitch being shared.

❅ ❅ ❅

In the 1967 edition of the SMCJ, Bugs McKeith suggested an improvement to the grading system. This followed a comment the previous year by the editor Robin Campbell, who noted that '*...we detect a dissatisfaction in some quarters with the present summer grading system. Correspondence is invited.*'

At that time the top grade was Hard Very Severe (HVS), but McKeith wrote that he found the prefixes 'mild' and 'hard' very misleading. He suggested that in conjunction with the six main grade divisions then in use – Easy, Moderate, Difficult, Very Difficult, Severe and Very Severe – a more accurate picture would involve providing a numerical grade for the hardest pitch. At the same time, for a route with individual pitch descriptions, all pitches could include this grade.

Examples he provided included *Agag's Groove* Very Difficult (3+), *Whortleberry Wall* (5+) and *The Bat* (6+). McKeith was influenced by the continental system, but noted that there seemed to be about half a grade's difference. He was right to suggest a new system, as the top end had long been compressed, with Very Severe containing a much larger number of technically harder climbs than of old, but he had not gone far enough. Although the suggestion did not catch on, it probably seeded itself in a few minds. While most Scottish climbers became adept at working out what the 'true' difficulty of a Scottish VS was, understandably visitors from outwith Scotland could find it frustrating.

As noted in the previous chapter, it was not until 1985, and the Cairngorms guide by Fyffe and Nisbet, that technical grades were introduced, with an addition at the top end for summer of Extremely Severe and also a Grade VI in winter. These grades had become widely accepted elsewhere in the UK, and the authors were basically following suit. The Extremely Severe, or E grade, was further subdivided into E1, E2 etc. Grades given in this volume, using current guides, may not reflect the original grading, as many recorded as VS could well have been harder.

❄❄❄

The interest in routes girdling cliffs continued through the 1960s, with Brian Robertson expending his boundless energies on finding and making one on the Trilleachan Slabs. There is no doubt that the classic routes there, such as Spartan Slab and Hammer, are very enjoyable, but once these routes have been done and harder, bolder lines are approached, doubt can begin to creep in, with the climber facing the potential of a long and abrasive fall down a bald slab of granite.

Robertson did not describe his route on the Slabs, that would have been too easy, but wrote an article from which a description was worked out.[7] Basically, *The Thin Red Line* (460m E3 A2 5c †) was climbed in several sections over several days with several climbers, the main party being Robertson and Nunn. As it is rarely attempted, and there is insufficient information, the route in the guide is awarded the cross symbol. The interest in girdle traverses would gradually diminish over the following years.

The summer of 1966 saw a flurry of routes in Glen Coe, a few of which, it was later pointed out, had probably been climbed earlier. There was a spell when the New Climbs section of the SMCJ included the phrase '*J.R. Marshall remembers*', often when some innocent had spotted an easy line on an obscure crag which turned out to either be a route which had been climbed earlier and deemed not worth recording or, worse, had been a common scrambling line of ascent or descent for a major crag. It pays to do homework, which in addition to study of current guidebooks should also include each year's New Climbs section.

Good climbs were found on various crags on the Buachaille, for instance *Snowba's* (125m VS) on Cuneiform Buttress in May 1968 by Con Higgins and John McLean, with the name suggesting a cold day for the Creagh Dhu men. Higgins was back in August 1969 with Ian Fulton to record *Lift Off* (90m HVS). These routes lie left and right of a V-shaped corner which would be climbed on 7 August 1995 by Dave (Cubby) Cuthbertson and Jo George, *The Mighty Atom* (90m E2). Girdle traverses continued to provide entertainment, for example on the East Face of North Buttress (100m VS †, September 1967, JR Jackson and K Robson), Great Gully Buttress (120m VS †, June 1966, JR Marshall and J. McLean) and the Terrace Face on Aonach Dubh (180m VS), 16-17 September 1969, Ken Crocket, Cam Forrest and Dave Jenkins.

Fulton was one of the Dumbarton Boys, with other members of that informal group including Rab Carrington, Ian Nicolson, John Jackson, Neil MacNiven, Brian Shields and Michael Connolly. Jackson, Carrington and Nicolson went on to join the Creagh Dhu, while some, such as Fulton and for a few years Carrington, were in the SMC. As Ken Spence would cannily observe:

Ian Nicolson, a superb technician, required incentive to be led to the spot and pointed in the right direction. He did the rest. A total enthusiast, Jackson spent the first evening in the Dolomites below the North Face of the Cima Ovest gazing up with a head torch, while the wasters imbibed in the local hostelry. [8]

Fulton would also be a member of the Rannoch Mountaineering Club, one of many informal small clubs ranged across Scotland. Based mainly in Glasgow, and with a bothy in Glen Coe, the Rannoch MC would grow in the late 1960s, and would be most active through the 1970s and later, though as with many a small club there was an even earlier history, lost in the mists of time.These clubs were independent of the large, long established clubs, but nonetheless probably contributed as much exploratory climbing.

Another club enjoying use of a bothy in Glen Coe was the Squirrels, who would also send frequent raiding parties to the glen. In 1967, Bathgate and McKeith attacked the prominent pale wall on the Lower North-East Face on the East Face of Aonach Dubh– easy of access, lying as it does about 30 minutes from the main road, it has a superb crack-line splitting the centre of the wall, begging to be climbed. As with a few great routes, it has a history, beginning in 1960 with an attempt by Pat Walsh and H Swales who climbed an initial section then traversed out right.

On 1 July 1967, Bathgate and McKeith beat the crack into submission. Their description mentions that it was a grand route for a wet day, a comment perhaps offered in mitigation for the aid used. In all, the hard pitch required 15 pegs, one nut and one sling. In 1977 this was reduced to one peg by the 18-year old Edinburgh climber Dave (Cubby) Cuthbertson, then freed completely two years later by Doug Mullin and J Melrose. The route, *Freak-Out* (75m E4), was originally graded at VS (6, A3). Other good and difficult routes would later be recorded on this wall, and Cuthbertson will figure large in Volume Three of this history, making a series of very hard routes, summer and winter.

On 18 April 1968, the Trilleachan Slabs saw an impressive and bold first ascent with *The Pinch* (215m E3). The grading given here is from the current guidebook, which follows a more direct line for the first two pitches and adds a fourth pitch. The first ascent was by Jackson and Carrington, and basically the route takes a parallel line right of Hammer, up the corner and slab overlooking Agony. Three of its seven pitches are technically 5c, and it was an indication of where confident climbing on these slabs could go. On a trip to the Alps later that year, Jackson was killed by a fall on the Aiguille Noire de Peuterey.

The winter of 1969 was exceptionally icy, and many climbers grabbed the opportunity to look for first ascents. Especially well placed were the instructors on the MacInnes winter courses based in Glen Coe, and in

February and March no fewer than 35 routes were recorded, along with another five winter routes where the date was not recorded. Many were of Grade II and III, but from time to time instructors on free time could discover more chewy climbs. Allen Fyffe recalls that winter as exceptional, and he climbed for a straight 30 days at one point. Even Clough remarked one day that he was hoping for rain, so that he could have a rest day.

The routes recorded included *Sabre Tooth* (120m IV,5) on Lost Valley Buttress on 9 February by Clough and MacInnes, *Mome Rath Route* (150m V,5) on the East Face of Gearr Aonach on 16 February by Fyffe and McArtney, and on the same day *The Wabe* (135m V,5) right of Mome Rath Route, by MacInnes, Clough and John Hardie. The latter two routes are rarely in condition, particularly with changes in global climate; on The Wabe ascent a fine icefall descended the summer line. In mid-February 1969, the temperature at Newtonmore fell to -18C.

One route climbed during this good winter was ahead of its time. *Fingal's Chimney* (180m VI,7) cuts through the steep wall on the right of Ossian's Cave on the North Face of Aonach Dubh. It was climbed by Wilf Tauber and Davy Gardner in March 1969 and is a classic line, with four hard pitches. Wilfrid Joseph Amadeus Tauber, a St Andrews University graduate who joined the SMC in 1970, was drowned after a fall while climbing solo on the sea cliffs at Gogarth on Anglesey. The Glen Pean bothy was renovated in 1973 as a memorial.[9]

Ian Clough, a very modest and popular mountaineer, was killed on 30 May 1970 while on an expedition to climb Annapurna by its South Face. The approach route had to pass under seracs which were clearly dangerous, but Bonington the expedition leader knew that the danger window lasted about three minutes, and it was deemed an acceptable risk. The ascent was a success, with Haston and Whillans reaching the summit, and the expedition had almost cleared the mountain when a tower of serac ice fell on Clough, killing him instantly. He was buried at base camp.

❄❄❄

With better access and cheaper transport, it was easier in the 1960s to discover new winter climbs, especially if exploring the Northern Highlands. Clearly, living there made this much more convenient, and for a mountaineer like Tom Patey it must have been idyllic. He was happy soloing, as has been seen, and the frequent necessity of doing this would rarely have been a burden. His extrovert nature also meant that he would climb with anyone, whether invited or found by chance.

In the early years of the decade Patey made some routes in the west with his friends from the Cairngorms: on Ladhar Bheinn in Knoydart, for example, with *Gaberlunzie* (280m IV,4) and *Viking Gully* (360m III/IV), climbed respectively on 14 April 1962 with AG Nicol and RWP Barclay and on 15 April with AG Nicol. If alone, Patey would solo routes such as *Nose Direct* (140m VS) on Fuar Tholl, which he did on 7 October 1961. This mountain, on the north side of Glen Carron, would later grow in status as many of its rock climbs produced superb winter climbing.

On the Mainreachan Buttress of Fuar Tholl, a breakthrough route was a 1970 winter ascent of *Sleuth* (240m VII,7) by MacInnes, Fyffe and Spence. At the time, it was regarded as the hardest winter climb in Scotland, and had been climbed the previous summer at VS by Clough and MacInnes who evidently spotted its winter potential. MacInnes was involved in five new routes on Fuar Tholl in 1969, climbing variously with his then wife Catherine and Clough.

The Applecross peninsula was another happy hunting ground for Patey. There were three mountains here: Beinn Bhàn, Meall Gorm and Sgùrr a' Chaorachain. Patey had climbed on the latter in 1952 and 1953 with his friends from the North East, and he was back in 1960 to record the popular Cioch Nose with Bonington (see Chapter 12). On Meall Gorm, across the glen from the South Face of Sgùrr a' Chaorachain, Patey and Co. had found *Blue Pillar* (180m Severe) and *Cobalt Buttress* (140m Very Difficult) on 2 May 1953. These would later provide excellent winter routes, the former climbed by Patey and Joe Brown in February 1958 at V,6 , the latter by Clough, G Drayton and C Young on 10 February 1970 at IV,5 .

In Coire na Poite of Beinn Bhàn, Patey opened up this vast winter face with an ascent of *March Hare's Gully* (300m IV,4), climbed with Bonington on 1 March 1969. Beinn Bhàn, being on a west coast peninsula, tends to dive in and out of condition during winter, but when its terraced face is laced with icefalls it cannot fail to impress. Following Patey's Sword of Gideon ascent on the South Face of Sgùrr a' Chaorachain in 1961, other parties would begin to record climbs on this roadside crag. An adventure centre located on the peninsula was a source of climbers who recorded climbs here, and there were visiting climbers too.

The great crags of Coire Mhic Fhearchair on Beinn Eighe demand a longer approach, but there was much potential. Development was slow and it was five years after Smith's route Boggle that the Squirrels, in the form of Jim Brumfitt and Bill Sproul, arrived on 30 May 1966 to climb *Kami-Kaze* (100m VS) on the Far East Wall, and on the same day *Samurai* (110m HVS) on the Eastern Ramparts.

As with many other summer routes, imminent advances in techniques and equipment would see some of the hard rock climbs here receive winter ascents. The guidebook notes encouragingly that:

> ...in winter the corrie is a paradise for modern style mixed climbing, and comes into condition very quickly. The steep blocky quartzite provides good axe placements, reliable protection and sensational lines.

Further north, the great crag of Carnmore in Fisherfield continued to produce quality routes. On 28 May 1967, Geoff Cram and Roelof Schipper climbed *St George* (90m E1), taking a fine and steep crack-line to the right of *The Sword*. Cram was a Lakes climber who was active in that area's renaissance in the mid-1960s. He wrote the FRCC guide to Pillar in 1968 and continues to have an interest in rare books including those on mountaineering.

The following month, a strong Mancunian team arrived. Seven routes were produced, of which the best were *Penny Lane* (70m HVS) by Richard (Dick) J Isherwood and Eddie Birch, *Trampoline* (100m E1) by Robert (Bob) Jones and Gordon MacNair, and The Sword (see Chapter 11). Three aid points were used, and its first free ascent was made by G Duckworth and R Kerr in May 1980.

A highly visible and valued line was the corner on the Upper Wall, but a hollow at the top contains a spring, so a long spell of dry weather is required. *Carnmore Corner* (65m E2) was climbed by Carrington and Jackson on 19 May 1968, with the spring rumoured to have been dammed temporarily, allowing some drying to take place. One aid point was used.

One centrally placed area in the far north gave its name to the Corriemulzie Mountaineering Club, formed in the Nest of Fannich Bothy at New Year 1965. Many of its members originated from St Andrews University MC, including Alistair RM Park, Pete Baker, Blyth Wright, Will Fraser, John Wedderburn, Jadwiga Kowalska, Chris Doake, Colin Martin, Peter F MacDonald, Ken McLean, Neil Travers and Ian Rowe. A prominent member was Philip Nigel Lakin Tranter (1939-1966), son of the author Nigel Tranter.

Philip Tranter was a civil engineer renowned for his ability to drive for considerable distances, a useful attribute in an area where long journeys were usually connected to long walks and the ensuing late-night drives back home. He was a prodigious walker, the first to form the concept of climbing all the Munros surrounding Glen Nevis – the Mamores, the Grey Corries, the Aonachs, Càrn Mor Dearg and Ben Nevis – within 24 hours.

Tranter's Round, as it became known and which he completed in June 1964, involves 36 miles with over 20,000ft of ascent. Appealing to hill runners as well as mere mortal hillwalkers, a recent record for the round was the 10 hours 15 minutes taken by Finlay Wild (Lochaber Athletic Club) on 1 October 2016, while Jasmin Paris of Carnethy Hill Running Club holds the women's record having taken 12 hours 41 minutes on 26 July 2014. Tranter was also the first person known to have visited all the Munros twice, completing his rounds on 14 April 1961 and 26 September 1964, on Ben Hope and Ben More Assynt respectively.

Tranter and three friends mounted a small expedition to the Hindu Kush in 1965, driving 6,000 miles by Land Rover. They made first ascents of eight mountains, which they graced with Scottish names, and also climbed Koh-i-Krebek (20,500ft) by its South-East Face. He was killed in a road accident in northern France in August 1966, returning from a shorter climbing trip to Turkey. From his diaries, his father edited a book based on the Hindu Kush expedition.[10] Alistair Park had also been killed, on 4 April 1966, in a climbing accident on Foinaven while with Tranter. His double rope held when he fell while attempting a new route on Creag Dionard, but his head hit a rock and he was killed instantly. The Corriemulzie MC restored Camban bothy in Glen Affric in memory of the two men.

In 1960, the Corriemulzie area had just one recorded climb, but by the end of the decade there were 40. The burst of activity had prompted Park and Tranter to produce *An Interim Guide to Easter Ross* in 1966: this had 44 pages and five diagrams and also included a 29-page Foinaven supplement. Park, apparently, was briefly an editor for the new SMC *Northern Highlands Volume I guide to Letterewe and Easter Ross*, which was eventually published in 1969 by West Col, edited by Ian Rowe following Park's death.

Living in Ullapool, Patey had plenty of opportunity to make the most of good conditions in the Northern Highlands. Two easy rock climbs on Beinn Dearg in 1962 were followed by a good winter route on 29 March 1964. Climbed with Bill Murray and Norman Tennent, *Penguin Gully* (350m III,4) has become a classic. It remains hidden on the approach until one is almost upon it, and has a wonderful feeling of remoteness. One of the best routes at its grade, it cuts through the West Buttress of Beinn Dearg and gives varied climbing.

In March 2002, two climbers were killed by an avalanche in the gully.[11] The avalanche forecast in all areas of Scotland was then at Category 4 (High), and rescue team members described walking waist-deep in snow while winds reached 80mph.

Nearby, *Emerald Gully* (200m IV,4) was climbed in March 1970 by Nunn, B Fuller and A Riley, and several of the easy winter lines were climbed by the Squirrels in the late 1960s. Later years would see good routes at harder grades, but the Gleann na Squaib area is rarely in condition

Many of the routes recorded in the far north of Scotland from the 1970s onwards have been on outcrops and crags, these having been largely ignored by earlier climbers who had at their disposal unexplored or rarely visited mountain crags. Sgùrr an Fhidhleir had been an obvious target with its superb Nose flaunting an obvious edge visible from the road. It had been attempted as early as 1914 by two experienced alpinists from the SMC, Ling and Sang, and it was not until 1962 that it finally fell to Neville Drasdo and Christopher Michael Dixon (1931-2004), the same Dixon who had climbed with Brooker, Patey and other Aberdonians on Skye in the 1950s (see Chapter 9).

Neville Drasdo was the brother of Harold Drasdo, a Bradford boy later to became a professor and research scientist in optometry. Dixon wrote a popular book on rock climbing in the *'Know the Game'* series. It seems that various climbers have had problems with the route descriptions of *Direct Nose Route* (245m HVS). The first ascenders gave Patey a verbal description and three months later Dixon sent written details to the JMCS.

It is more of a mountaineering route, with vegetated pitches low down leading to cleaner and spectacular finishing pitches. It was later climbed in winter, at VII,7 , and is now a sought-after classic when in condition.[12] On the first summer ascent, which like many others in these years had been suggested after an encounter with Patey, the climbers experienced unusual meteorological conditions. Nearing the crag, they were surprised to be showered with water, picked up from the loch and hurled high into the air. Drasdo recalled that the air would be still for periods of about one minute, followed by violent gusts lasting about 30 seconds.

Beyond the vegetated pitches, there was some enjoyable slab climbing. After about 600ft, they arrived at a belay on the arête where the rock was steeper and the difficulty increased dramatically. Following a hard move in a corner requiring friction for the feet, difficulties eased gradually from HVS to Severe.

Drasdo now had to face the unusual wind problem, as every time he tried to make a move up a crack of about Hard Severe the cyclical gusts threatened to blow him off, forcing him to descend very rapidly. This happened numerous times and eventually, with no nuts for protection, he was forced to insert a peg. He clipped into this and when the gusts subsided again quickly finished the moves at the top of the crack.

From the summit, they could see great rain squalls approaching. A figure loomed out of the mist as they made their way across boggy ground towards their car: Patey. He had feared the worst and had come out to look for them. A note written on the back of a prescription form had been left on the car, but the rain had washed the ink down, lending a curious *'Sherlock Holmesian'* appearance. It read: *'I have gone to look for your bloody bodies. Back shortly. Tom.'*

This indicates fairly closely Patey's character, in that he was generous to others. He had a bothy next to his house and would happily invite passing climbers to stay there. This had happened to Drasdo and Dixon, and to many others. Whisky, cigarettes and route suggestions would flow along with the conversation.

Patey climbed *The Magic Bow* (195m E1) with Martin Boysen on 1 June 1967, and returned to solo *The Phantom Fiddler* (215m HVS) the following year. MacInnes, who climbed with him, would in time write as one of several contributors to a lengthy obituary that–

He was outstandingly capable; capable of soloing up to his top standard on an unknown and remote crag in the Highlands. Only a handful of men in the history of climbing have had this ability.'[13]

On Quinag, the mountain on which Raeburn and friends climbed Barrel Buttress in 1907 (see Volume One), Patey was involved in six new routes. On its western cliffs, the guidebook mentions that *The Waste Pipe* (150m II), climbed with R Ford in March 1965, *'would be one of Scotland's best at its grade if it were in good condition more often'*. On Stac Pollaidh, little climbing was recorded between the visit of the Clark family in 1906 and several routes being put up on the South Face of the West Buttress. Worthy of mention were *Enigma Grooves* (70m E1), by Patey and R Barclay in August 1965, which avoided the final 5b corner by moving right; this last pitch was added on 18 August 1979 by John R Mackenzie and P Goodwin, upping the grade to E1.

On 26 August 1964, *Jack the Ripper* (75m E1) was climbed by MG Anderson and G Mair, with direct starts and finishes added later. The rock here is typically a rough, reddish pebbly sandstone. It pays to be good at jamming and bridging, while for protection a climber should take all the camming devices they have. In the late 1980s many good routes would be recorded on this peak.

Foinaven lies in the Reay Forest, and its highest point, Ganu Mòr, falls three metres short of Munro status–making the mountain that much quieter. The rock is quartzite or gneiss, and there are numerous crags. Exploration here began with Ling and Glover in 1910, but with its location in the very far north and its long walks for access it was not until 1950 that *Original Route* (300m Moderate) was climbed by James A Parker (not the pioneer of the same name mentioned in the early chapters, who died in 1946) and James Reid Young.

In 1954, Tom Weir, Len Lovat and ADS Macpherson climbed three long routes on Creag Urbhard, the biggest crag in the massif, some 200m-350m in height and over a kilometre in length. As with many a crag in the Northern Highlands, there was confusion over what went where and what was done by whom – a situation abetted by a short break in reportage by the SMC in the 1960s. An excellent article by Peter F Macdonald in the 1977 SMCJ helps clear some of the fog.[14]

Harder climbing on Creag Urbhard began in 1959, with Terry Sullivan, a friend and RAF rescue colleague of Ian Clough, recording two routes on the south ridge, of which *Gargantua* (170m Hard Severe) is the better. Route discrimination here is also not helped by the rock formation, while protection on the quartzite can be hard to find. All of this makes climbing in this area more serious than might be expected.

Zigzag (300m Very Difficult) was found by Drasdo and Dixon and climbed a few days before their ascent of the Fhidhleir Nose in 1962. By June 1962 it is known that Patey had joined the hunt, soloing *Fingal* (300m Severe), recommended in the current guide as a *'...mountaineering adventure with "difficult route finding"'* – and that despite Patey's detailed route description.

Inevitably the Corriemulzie MC arrived, and in 1965 Rowe and Tranter climbed *Chicken Run* (200m Hard Severe), amusingly noted as *'A natural line, with plenty of nature involved.'* The same day saw *Boreas* (150m Severe) by Park and Macdonald. In 1966 it was the turn of the Squirrels, with McKeith and Mike Galbraith avoiding some vegetation to climb a cleaner, exposed arête. The route was *K.W.H.* (280m Severe). The name came from the party's only comment on the route: *'Kilroy Was Here.'*

In 1968, MacInnes and wife Catherine, working assiduously on what would become a two-volume guide to climbs in Scotland, climbed *Three Tier Route* (280m Severe). Clive Rowland visited Creag Urbhard in June 1969, recording *Tortoise* (260m Hard Severe) with Nunn. Using Rowland's nickname, it starts close to a mound resembling a tortoise at the foot of the cliff. These early explorations were understandably cautious, due to the nature of the climbing; future years would see routes which were not only harder, but often higher in quality.

The guidebooks by MacInnes must be mentioned here.[15] They were hard-bound with dust-wrappers and subtitled *'A mountaineer's pictorial guide to climbing in Scotland'*. There were no line diagrams: in their place were monochrome photographs, either action shots or crag photographs with dashed lines indicating routes. Consistent with his maverick character, MacInnes used the International Union of Alpine Clubs grading system, with Roman numerals from I to VI including + and – subdivisions. Many climbers bought the guides, but with various reactions, often unhappy. They were of use in showing the more obscure crags, some not yet mentioned in an SMC guide, but the marked lines were not always to be relied on. Winter routes were also graded differently, from Easy to Very Severe. As one indication, perhaps a slightly cruel one, here is a footnote from the Macdonald article on Creag Urbhard:

> In the photograph on page 169 of MacInnes's Scottish Climbs, Volume 2, the line shown for K.W.H. is in fact that of Chicken Run; the line shown for Chicken Run is not a route at all; the line shown for Crawlie Mouzie is approximately that of K.W.H.; Crawlie Mouzie itself is not marked; and the line shown for Fingal is much too far to the left.

There was however much to say in praise of the guides: they had good notes on first-aid, weather, avoiding midges and so on, but climbers in the main learned not to rely too heavily on the photodiagrams, instead using some of them to seek out new rock. Graeme Hunter, who drew the maps and prepared the photographic artwork, noted that many comments concerning the photodiagram lines were made to MacInnes, who blithely ignored them.[16] With modern technology, and using high-resolution colour photographs, photodiagrams now have a place in guidebook production, showing perhaps that the '*Fox of Glencoe*' was yet again thinking ahead.

Coastal climbing was becoming popular, both in the far north and on the Hebridean islands. A general increase in prosperity allowed car ferries to be used more often, with costs offset by using camping as cheap or free accommodation. The huge cliffs of St John's Head on Hoy in Orkney saw a media-enriched ascent on 6-8 April 1966 of *Original Route* (400m XS/ E3) by Ed Drummond, Al Evans, Jack Street, Leo Dickinson and Ben Campbell-Kelly. This was filmed, and the route was later freed by Mick Fowler and Caradoc Jones.

A notable victim of the continuing interest in sea stacks was Patey, who was killed abseiling from The Maiden, a stack off Whiten Head on the Sutherland coast, on 25 May 1970. With Nunn, B Fuller, C Goodwin and Rowland, he had made the first ascent on Eastern Stack of *Original Route* (55m HVS). Patey was notorious for his indifference to dress, equipment or technical points, and on the day he died it seems he was using a sling and a karabiner borrowed from MacInnes, who wrote:

> The previous weekend I had been climbing with Tom and he had forgotten his belt, so I gave him an old sling and an old Pierre Alain [sic] carabiner (a swing gate that was recalled due to safety issues) that I just used for hauling rucksacks. I told him, 'Don't use that carabiner for climbing,' but these things didn't register with Tom. That was the carabiner he used for the abseil.[17]

It is highly likely that Patey's sweater caught in the karabiner, and while attempting to free the jam the gate opened, allowing the rope to exit. He was 38, and was buried in his home town of Ellon, in Aberdeenshire.

✸✸✸

Creag Meagaidh continued to provide new routes through the 1960s, from the Squirrels and from a new group with Dundonian accents: the Carn Dearg Mountaineering Club. On 14 April 1968, Bob McMillan, Gerry Peet and Neil Quinn entered the inner corrie to find *The Pumpkin* (300m V,4), its name following a theme set earlier on Creag Meagaidh, the naming of routes from the story of Cinderella.

The party was lucky with the weather: bright, clear and cold. When they gained the inner corrie the route stared them in the face, with an initial open corner of ice rearing up nearly 300ft, finishing with an impressive bulge of blue-green ice. Two short pitches led to a very steep section, where an ice screw was used for aid. Further up, they met a 150ft iced-up chimney:

'Gerry cut up the first 60 ft, then passed the buck. Over the steepest part it was impossible to get any artificial aid and several sorties up and back again for a rest were needed.' [18] The route is longest in the corrie and has become a popular classic, often in condition.

On 2 February 1969, Quinn was joined by Quintin T Crichton (1934-2007), Douglas (Doug) Fairgray Lang (1941-2011) – who was from Dundee, though born in Dumfries – and Graeme N Hunter, another member of the Carn Dearg MC. They climbed *The Wand* (210m V,5), again in the inner corrie and one of two parallel ice features about halfway up the Grade II route The Sash. Lang and Quinn had looked at this line the previous weekend, but in atrocious weather had retreated after 100ft of the icefall. They had then ended up crawling on all fours down parts of the track.

The following weekend their steps on the icefall only needed cleaning to be useful, with Hunter leading the first pitch of 60ft, then Quinn the next of 40ft, which gained the abseil peg and belay from their earlier attempt. Lang then came up and leapfrogging Quinn led another bulge using an ice screw and slings for aid. Some bridging by Quinn brought the top of the icefall with easier ground above. Lang, Quinn and Hunter, along with MacInnes, later produced one of the best mixed winter climbs on Creag Meagaidh with *Trespasser Buttress* (300m IV,5), climbed in March 1969.

The Carn Dearg MC was formed in Forfar in 1949, originating through ex-service personnel who enjoyed the outdoors, particularly in Glen Clova which was easy to access by bicycle or bus. The club's name comes from the Red Craigs of Clova, *dearg* being Gaelic for red. It later became centred on Dundee and included such members as Crichton, Lang, Quinn and Hunter. Crichton had joined the SMC in 1959 and would be instrumental in feeding several of the others into that club. Both Lang and Quinn would serve as SMC presidents. Lang, according to Quinn, had only two interests in life: his work, and climbing. He died in March 2011 while on a solo outing to Glen Clova, avalanched in poor conditions in A Gully in Corrie Fee.

Gerry Peet was originally from Lincoln and joined the JMCS, then the SMC in 1966. Climbing in Skye, where he met his future wife, persuaded him to remain in Scotland. He would become the custodian of the CIC hut on Ben Nevis, from 1967-80, and stood as a list candidate for the Scottish Senior Citizens Unity Party in the 2007 Scottish Parliamentary election.

Quinn would join the SMC in 1968, followed the next year by Lang and Hunter. The latter pair developed Binnein Shuas, Hunter having recognised its potential during a wet walk in 1965, and in June 1966 they climbed its classic route *Ardverikie Wall* (190m Hard Severe). Patey had visited in 1964, also on a wet day, climbing the easy upper section of The Fortress, but perhaps missed the crag's full potential. Lang and Hunter then went into stealth mode, climbing a further ten routes before their secret emerged. It is a micro granite outcrop in a fine setting, latterly with a forestry road ideal for bike access.

In November 1971 there was a tragedy when five children and the leader's assistant died of exposure on the Ben Macdui plateau. A Fatal Accident Inquiry would lead to formal requirements being set up for leaders of school expeditions, along with the removal of three mountain shelters. It is regarded as Britain's worst mountain accident, and there are several accounts of what was named the Cairngorm Plateau Disaster.[19, 20, 21.]

An interesting reference to belaying in snow appeared in the SMCJ of May 1972. It was written by Graham Tiso and described snow anchors developed by climbers from their experience while serving with the British Antarctic Survey. Used to anchor dog teams, huts and even aeroplanes, these anchors were pieces of marine plywood which had a length of heavy rope threaded through their centre. Buried in the snow, they had remarkably good powers of anchorage and could withstand heavy pressure before being pulled out

Tiso mentioned tests which had been performed in the Cairngorms in February 1969 on three different sizes of these anchors, known in the UK as deadmen. It had also been realised that aluminium alloy and wire cable would be better suited for climbing purposes, with the plate having a slightly pointed lower edge and a strengthening bar on the top, so that the plate could be hammered more easily into firm snow. The best size was found to be about 20cm x 25cm. That these worked was personally verified by the author during an attempt on a new climb in Glen Coe, when he held a leader fall twice using a deadman belay. Later, they were slowly superseded by other devices such as newer designs of ice screw.

On 11 June 1967, a new route was recorded on Lochnagar, climbing the frontal wall of Tough-Brown Ridge – and surprisingly, it was the first new summer route here for a decade. This triangular face was the largest area of virgin rock on Lochnagar, and accordingly had begun to attract attention. It drew two Mikes, Forbes and Rennie, on to its steep rock, with one pitch up a vegetated corner leading to an obvious crack they had spotted from the ground. Around 30 feet up, the crack cut through a prominent roof with twin cracks.

Overcoming the roof needed three aid pegs and gained a smooth slab where a poorly protected mantelshelf led to a narrow rib of rock. Crossing this to enter the left-hand crack and gain a ledge above took another four aid pegs. After some moves along the terrace the groove was re-entered, with four more pegs used to gain easier ground. *Mort* (110m E1) is high in the grade and is now cleaner, with no pegs needed. Greg Strange comments that technically it was a significant advance for the mountain.

The remaining years of the 1960s saw more new areas being opened up, and in his Cairngorms history Strange appropriately entitled his chapter on 1966-69 *'On To The Big Blank Spaces'*. Among the Creag an Dubh Loch highlights was *King Rat* (220m E1) by Allen Fyffe and John Bower on 9 June 1968, which took the previously climbed pitches on Central Gully Wall, leading in 50m or so to a roof which impeded further progress. Fyffe tired himself trying to climb this free, but eventually climbed up one side of the roof with four aid pegs, after which the remainder of this fine route went without problem. The roof was eventually completely freed in 1977 by Mick Fowler and Phil Thomas, who gave it an E1 grade.

The very next weekend in 1968, Mike Rennie and Yorkshireman Paul Williams returned to a line they had been working on since early May, the left-facing groove near the right end of Central Gully Wall. The groove was blocked by a large overhang, forcing a logical move to its left. Rennie reached a hidden, grassy corner which needed four pegs, finally reaching a belay 30ft below the huge hanging slab. From a small stance at the foot of this slab they could clearly see the next stage, hopefully to be reached via the only weakness in the slab, a single crack, then on to rocks which looked desperate. Meantime, however, the two abseiled off, leaving behind a new Perlon rope belonging to Rennie.

The next weekend was wet, but Rennie prusiked up the rope and replaced it with an old 9mm laid nylon one. Finally the weather improved, and Rennie and Williams returned to the fray, prusiking up the old rope, boldly hoping it was undamaged. Rennie followed the crack leftwards on the great slab and found a short, overhanging corner. Using aid, he landed on a small slab then moved up and left.

Rennie continued leading and found the next pitch to be the crux: a shallow crack with a protruding stone. Seven pegs were needed, mostly tied off, before this scary pitch could be climbed to reach easier ground leading to a terrace. Rennie was enamoured with this form of climbing and had few scruples about using aid on a new route. The pair named their route *Cougar* (135m E3), and after further ascents and cleaning all, aid was dispensed with by Edinburgh climbers Murray Hamilton and Dave Cuthbertson in June 1977, pushing the grade of this four-star route up from HVS, A2 to E3.

The Shelter Stone Crag, too, was seeing plenty of action in 1968, with the great Central Slabs being the arena. In early August four climbers left Glen Coe and converged on the Shelter Stone: Ken Spence and Michael (Mike) Leonard Watson from the Squirrels, along with Rab Carrington and Jimmy Gardiner of the Creagh Dhu. Spence, an art teacher, is one of the most underrated mountaineers of this period, making fine ascents not only in Scotland but also in the Alps, including a gruelling multi-day first ascent of the North Pillar of the Eiger in August 1970 with McKeith and MacEacheran. On Ben Nevis in 1986, on his third attempt, he made the first winter ascent of Centurion (VIII,8), climbing with John (Spider) MacKenzie. Maintaining his interest in art, Spence has an interesting series of hand-drawn rock climbing picture books online.[22] He often climbed with John Porteous, who later emigrated to Australia.

Mike Watson was a medic who later became president of the Mountaineering Council of Scotland (subsequently known as Mountaineering Scotland). He received an OBE for services to medical education. Jimmy Gardiner played chess at competitive level and became a headmaster in Dunblane. Rab Carrington went on to found his company Rab, manufacturing outdoor clothing and sleeping bags of high quality. Born in Glasgow in 1947, he eventually decided that it rained too often in Scotland so moved to Sheffield. The company was sold in 2003 and Carrington now roams the world, climbing in the sun.

The line Carrington and Gardiner were chasing was on the Central Slabs, where there was, as Carrington wrote, *'a long straight wire of a crack on the right of the slab'*.[23] The pair quickly made their way up the rubbish to reach the steepness, finding a peg and carabiner left by the last party. The first pitch was steep, with very small holds and a scarcity of protection. Gardiner took the lead and it looked easy to an overlap – from where he observed that it was anything but easy. Carrington didn't believe him and suggested he was off form, at which point he was offered the lead and soon found that it was nothing to do with form and all to do with a lack of holds. He placed a good American peg, a leeper, and continued.

The next pitch was just as deceptive, as Gardiner headed up to a dripping overlap where after a few attempts–and some difficulty–he inserted a nut and pulled on a sling. A total of 150ft had taken them five hours: enough for the day, so they abseiled down for their doss and dinner.

> The new morning was born its usual dull self and it had just stopped raining. While two Sandhurst fellow-dossers argued about who buttered the bread and who got the butter out of the pack we settled down to a lazy day. Approaching afternoon we roused ourselves and decided to have a look from the top. It was too wet for climbing and courage and nerves needed a day to recover.

They scrambled up a loose gully then traversed right to overlook the slabs. A hanging garden of slipping slimy vegetation barred their way to the top. Roping up, Carrington climbed across this, fixing runners as he went, to gain the exit crack after about 450ft. They now had to learn how to prusik, as they fixed abseil and safety ropes. Carrington slowly lowered himself down the cliff, trying to clean the crack as he went. Although he couldn't quite reach the previous day's high point, what he saw worried him.

> Slowly spidering my way up the cliff I had ample opportunity to survey the difficulties. Not vertical, but steep and with very strange holds and little choice. Back across the grass and rubbish, then up to the top instead of risking our bodies in the gully. Down to the doss and a large meal and more cards.

> Now Jimmy's a wee bit wee so I had a go thinking I might be able to use the nut hanging there 15 ft. above my head. I moved up and, semi-laybacking from three fingers, I grabbed the nut and out it popped. Sticking my fingers in the now vacant pocket I explored the next pocket—no joy. My strength flew out through the soles of my PA's. The only way out now is to swing on to the wall and rely on friction once there. A quick move and I'm over, but mud doesn't help the friction and as I take one foot off to clean it the other slips.

It was like trying to stay in the same place on an escalator, but somehow Carrington had to keep going and hope for progress. It worked, and he succeeded in reaching a belay. Gardiner followed with a bit of grunting, and *The Pin* (70m E2) had been climbed. The two men decided to abseil down rather than suffer from '*P.A . foot*'.

Malcolm Smith's 1961 guide to the Cairngorms (Northern Area) had stated that the great Central Slabs on the Shelter Stone Crag were '*manifestly impossible*'. Carrington had earlier climbed The Pinch, a hard line on the Trilleachan Slabs, and was also just recently back from the Alps, so he was fit and confident enough. The partial cleaning of the top pitch from above was one of the earliest instances of this in the Cairngorms, though by now it was a widespread practice in the south for hard climbs. The route was freed in the early 1970s.

What of the other pair of climbers? The intended route for Spence and Watson was also on the Central Slabs, a central line about 100ft to the left of The Pin. They ran into difficulties after Spence gained the foot of an S-shaped groove, where he made some progress but was finding it difficult to insert pegs and eventually gave up. They descended, leaving their gear before removing it the next day, which was wet.

On the day The Pin was climbed, Spence and Watson headed up for a new line, the lower of two prominent right-facing corners, just left of the starting gully to the route Postern. Cracks in the corner needed cleaning, while a nut for aid was required at an overlap. Watson needed three hours for this 100ft pitch. The next two pitches led through a bulging wall, then up a narrow ramp, to a good stance and belay at the top of the fourth pitch of The Needle. They had solved the link between the lower corners and the upper bastion. Above was the great corner splitting the upper crag left of The Needle, and they reached the foot of this by a pitch up and right, taking an obvious line of layback cracks avoided by Smith and Agnew when on The Needle.

Much time had been lost through their attempt on the other line and due to the weather, while the initial part of the corner looked very hard. Darkness would have fallen before they finished the corner, assuming of course that they could climb it. The pair had a brief look at the start and were pleased to find a hidden crack inside the main corner. They then traversed rightwards across The Needle and descended to the doss at the Shelter Stone. All four then returned to Glen Coe.

On 16 August Spence and Watson returned, joined by John Porteous, Spence's regular climbing partner. They abseiled down the Needle crack and reached the foot of the big corner. Spence aimed for a small niche visible about 50ft above, reached by strenuous laybacking. He found some good nut belays before being lowered, Watson then taking over the lead. He managed to gain the niche, where he made an awkward belay. Spence then took the lead again, climbing up the now-widening corner, to finally gain a big ledge just as the rain came on.

Until that point, the corner had been sheltered and had remained dry; now the rock was more exposed and becoming greasy. The race to finish was on as Watson tackled a difficult crack in an exposed position directly above the corner. Easier climbing then led to the top of the crag, and *Steeple* (250m E2) was in the bag. The two nuts for aid were freed in 1975.

All of these recent harder routes were first recorded as Very Severe, there having been as yet no move to introduce the new grades being used in Wales, despite the attempt by McKeith.

The breakthrough in climbing the central part of the Shelter Stone Crag had been the ascent of The Citadel in 1958, by Sellers and Annand, and now, with The Needle, The Pin and Steeple, the crag had no need to feel inferior to Creag an Dubh Loch. The Needle saw a second ascent in 1967, by Forbes and Rennie, while Steeple received its second ascent a week or so after its first when George Shields and Robert Doig, unaware of the first ascent, used its top corner as an alternative finish to The Needle. A few days later they returned and climbed the lower pitches of Steeple, finishing by the Needle crack.

Spence would continue to find good routes, including in 1980 a much sought-after winter ascent of The Citadel, but of all the routes he climbed in Scotland, he stated it was Steeple which brought the most satisfaction.[24]

References

1. Bathgate, D. *First Ascent of The Curtain.* SMCJ 28, 156, May 1965, pp.108-111.
2. Marshall, J.R. *In The Groove.* SMCJ, 29, 162, May 1971, pp.378-382.
3. Robertson, Brian. *Creag Meagaidh: Centre Post Direct.* In: Notes. SMCJ 28, 155, May 1964, pp.41-42.
4. Patey, Tom. *Creag Meagaidh Crab-Crawl.* SMCJ 29, 161, May 1970, pp.231-238.
5. Grieve, John. *Nowhere To Fall But Off.* SMCJ 32, 173, 1982, pp.246-250.
6. Patey, Tom. *The Old Man of Stoer.* SMCJ 28, 158, May 1967, pp.261-267.
7. Robertson, Brian. *The Thin Red Line.* SMCJ 28, 158, May 1967, pp.300-304.
8. Spence, Kenny. *Scottish Climbing since 1945 – A Squirrel's eye view of the West.* Mountain. Jan/Feb 1986, No.98.
9. Sang Award I: *Pean Bothy.* In: Miscellaneous Notes. SMCJ 30, 165, 1974. pp.280-281.
10. Tranter, Philip & Nigel. *No Tigers in the Hindu Kush.* (Hodder & Stoughton. London. 1968).
11. '*Two climbers killed in avalanche.*' <http://news.bbc.co.uk/-1/hi/scotland/186-5047.stm> Accessed May 2017.
12. Richardson, Simon. *Chasing the Ephemeral.* (Mica Publishing. Glasgow & Edinburgh. 2016.)
13. MacI, [MacInnes] H. *In Memoriam – Thomas Walton Patey.* SMCJ 29, 162, May 1971. p.439.
14. Macdonald, Peter F. *Creag Urbhard.* SMCJ 31, 168, 1977, pp.148-152.
15. MacInnes, Hamish. *Scottish Climbs.* (Vols. 1 & 2. Constable, London. 1971.)
16. Hunter, Graeme. *Personal communication.*
17. Hedgecoe, Guy. *Tom Patey: The Tiger of Yesterday.* Rock & Ice Magazine. <http://www.rockandice.com/climbing/epics/tom-patey-the-tiger-of-yesterday?page=5>. Accessed September 2017.
18. Quinn, N. *More on Creag Meaghaidh.* SMCJ 29, 161, May 1970, pp.271-273.
19. Wikipedia. *Cairngorm Plateau Disaster.* <https://en.wikipedia.org/wiki/Cairngorm_Plateau_Disaster> Accessed January 2017.
20. Allen, John; Davidson, Robert (2012). *Cairngorm John: A Life in Mountain Rescue* (eBook). Dingwall: Sandstone Press.
21. Duff, John (2001). *A Bobbie on Ben Macdhui: Life and Death on the Braes o' Mar.* Huntly: Leopard Magazine Publishing.
22. Spence, Ken. *Climbing Tales.* <www.kenspence.co.uk> (Accessed February 2017.)
23. Carrington, Robert. *The Pin – A New V.S. on Shelter Stone Crag.* SMCJ 29, 160, May 1969. pp.128-130.
24. Spence, Ken. *Personal communication.* February 2017.

15

Product Placement (1968-1971)

George Shields (1930-2012) was a Creagh Dhu member from Dunfermline. In 1952, he and Mick Noon climbed Kipling Groove on Gimmer Crag in the Lake District, onsight and without knowing it had been climbed by Arthur Dolphin in 1948. It was thus the second ascent, which for some time was wrongly ascribed to Joe Brown. A cobbler by trade, Shields switched to ski instruction, moving to Aviemore in 1962. His climbing was reinvigorated in July 1968 when, aged 38, he teamed up with John Cunningham to record several routes including *Ventricle* (95m E1) on No.1 Buttress of Coire an Lochain. Cunningham had likewise moved to Aviemore, and had started working at Glenmore Lodge as a full-time climbing instructor.

Shields also partnered Sydney Wilkinson, the chaplain at HMP Peterhead, who had climbed with many of the Cairngorms legends. On 25 July 1968 they went to Ewen Buttress in Coire an Lochain and climbed the impressive right edge of an overhanging recess, *The Vicar* (70m E1). Both Ventricle and The Vicar used some aid, with the latter starting up a *'vile overhanging corner'*. The Vicar was climbed in five short pitches.

Shields and Cunningham had spotted the parallel line right of Ventricle, and agreed to climb it together. However, Shields badly dented the trust between the pair when he returned in August with Brian Hall, a ski instructor at Glenmore Lodge. They climbed the line, *Daddy Longlegs* (70m HVS), again in five pitches and with five aid pegs and six nuts for aid according to the guide (or 12 aid points in the Strange history).

The Cairngorms climbing community seems on the surface to have been fairly relaxed about this amount of aid being used to grab a new route; one suspects it would have raised a few howls had it occurred in the west, where admittedly it was often easier to find holds and some natural protection. According to Strange, when Shields was asked about the aid he replied that he found the climbing in grooves and cracks more difficult than he was used to in the west, where there were more holds. [1] It was nothing to do with wet rock or vegetation.

Cunningham was livid at this breach of trust, but was climbing again with Shields the following year. On the south flank of Cairn Gorm there is a glaciated slab of granite in two parts. Stac an Fharaidh received one ascent in 1952, a Difficult at the far left end, but when Mac Smith visited the crag and climbed the route, which he named Rectangular Rib, he described the slabs in his guide as being holdless. No one disputed this, and the slabs slumbered on until Cunningham chanced by with a party from Glenmore Lodge.

Having realised their potential he returned in June 1969, and with a 'voluntary instructor' from the lodge picked the obvious plum line on the eastern slab, a clean crack shooting upwards for 150ft to below an overlap, the crux of the route. *Pushover* (140m HVS) was presumably named from the mantelshelf move needed to cross the overlap, and it would be the first of a good number of pleasant routes. Cunningham returned on 1 July with Shields to record *Après Moi* (150m VS), described in the guide as a rather wandering line, but better the same day was *Whispers* (135m VS). A further 26 or so routes would follow from various ropes, once the secret was out.

The commission from Constable Publishing for MacInnes to produce a climbing guide to Scotland–using photographs for topos and in two volumes–meant that he was now having to dash around the country filling in the blanks in his collection of crag shots. Realising that Creag an Dubh Loch was seeing much activity, MacInnes grabbed the opportunity with several of the climbers working in Glen Coe as instructors. These included Allen Fyffe, who was between the winter courses run by MacInnes and the summer ones run by Ian Clough, John Hardie and John Grieve. The party was boosted by Graeme Hunter and Doug Lang.

Of this team, only Fyffe and Grieve were staying on after the weekend, to which end they staggered in to the Dubh Loch with a week's supply of food. The food was later used by Grieve as a vehicle for his article in the SMCJ, describing some of the antics on the crag. [2] They were blessed with great weather.

McArtney had an incomplete line adjacent to The Giant, and– *'Earlier, Fyffe's eyes had waxed large as he lovingly spoke of The Dwarfie (self-identification?) that half-finished line'*. Lo and behold, as Fyffe rushed uphill to make sure no one else could bag his line, he discovered Rennie and Findlay were already halfway up it, posing for MacInnes.

A real bonanza day: Hunter and Lang are on a vicious line right of False Gully (Bannockburn), Mike Rennie is almost up his route —a great line named Goliath, the A team is slowly fighting up very unlikely rock between Giant and False Gully, and B team is now well up a direct route right of Blue Max (Black Mamba).

This was on Saturday 7 June 1969, when three first ascents were climbed: *Falseface* (90m E2), Hunter and Lang, using 13 pegs, was freed in 1977 (Grieve's article confusingly has this as Bannockburn, and perhaps Hunter and Lang changed the name later); *Goliath* (150m HVS), Findlay and Rennie, using four pegs and freed in 1970 by Ian Nicolson; and *Black Mamba* (320m VS 4c), Fyffe and Grieve. The last route is described in the guide as the classic of the slabs. Goliath was selected as an entry in Ken Wilson's Hard Rock collection, along with King Rat. [3]

There was more to come from the Dubh Loch granite, and the dynamic duo of Fyffe and Grieve made the most of the great spell of weather. As Fyffe recalled, it only ended when they were completely out of food. On the Sunday they climbed King Rat, making its second ascent and posing for the MacInnes camera. Monday saw them on the other side of the Dubh Loch, climbing on Eagle's Rock where they recorded *Gibber* (120m VS). Climbing here had only recently begun, after McArtney and D Duncan recorded a Severe in 1967.

Tuesday saw a day of rest, followed on Wednesday with Fyffe and Grieve going up the crack system immediately right of The Mousetrap, naming it *The Kraken* (180m HVS). On Thursday they made a girdle traverse of the Central Gully Wall with *Catwalk* (400m HVS); most of the climbing was VS. Their last two days were employed in working out a new line up the Central Slabs, where the colour of some of the rocks suggested the name *Pink Elephant* (320m HVS). This appears in the current guide as a combination of the earlier Dinosaur and Pink Elephant pitches; the upper crux groove is slow to dry, but when in condition it provides the best route on the left side of the main slabs. The week had given Fyffe and Grieve six first ascents, climbing some 5000ft of good rock, and impressively and refreshingly free of any aid. It cemented Creag an Dubh Loch as one of Scotland's major crags.

Two more major rock climbs were recorded here in 1970, first on 18 June when Ian Nicolson and Dave Knowles climbed *Dubh Loch Monster* (200m E1). Knowles (1947-1974) was from Preston and was working as an instructor on the MacInnes winter courses. A fine alpinist, he was killed by rockfall on the Eiger (which he had climbed in 1970) while working on the film set of *The Eiger Sanction*. The route on the Dubh Loch was recorded as having used a peg handhold on the second pitch; Nicolson didn't like using aid.

This was in marked contrast to the other route, climbed two days later by Hunter and Lang. *The Sword of Damocles* (100m E2) is described as providing a strenuous climb of great character. It also has a top chimney very slow to dry and repulsive when wet, but luckily this can be avoided by a variation. It was originally climbed using 14 pegs and three bolts, and then graded VS and A3. The pair made eight visits to the crag for this route, so presumably obsession had set in: they were by now determined to climb the line by any means. It was freed in July 1977 by Dougie Dinwoodie and RA Smith. The route name arose from a huge and loose-looking block lodged at the top of a chimney pitch and later trundled by Smith.

Greg Strange remarks that the summer of 1970 had seen the last major new routes employing all-out aid, and– *'...with the benefit of hindsight, it can be seen that this style of climbing was inappropriate for Scotland, as all these routes were eventually climbed free'.* [4] With respect to climbing ethics in Scotland, all interested parties were later involved in an extensive consultation process, followed by the issuing of a policy statement by the Mountaineering Council of Scotland. [5] This was endorsed by the SMC, which now includes the summary with every guide. On the subject of bolts, it was agreed that these should be limited to sport climbs– *'Bolts are unacceptable to the majority of Scottish climbers on established (documented) mountain cliffs and sea cliffs, in both summer and winter.'*

❊❊❊

The rise in activity in the 1960s affected Skye as well as the mainland, and it has already been noted that the first winter traverse of the Cuillin ridge halfway through the decade provided one major landmark. On 23 July 1965 John Harwood and Hamish Small found *Gail* (95m E1) on the South-West Buttress of Sgùrr Thuilm: the first ascent required three pegs on the corner pitch with loose rock which has latterly been largely cleared. Small followed the profession of his father, Alex, by becoming a school teacher, working at Tarbet, Loch Lomond. Harwood would later be active in the Climbers' Club. The route was running with water and had a very dirty crux pitch.

As in other areas of Scotland, the Squirrels were active on Skye and in August 1965 *The Snake* (110m HVS) on the Eastern Buttress of Sròn na Cìche was climbed by Bill Sproul, Jim Renny and J Hall of the JMCS. This steep and exposed route follows one of the numerous Cuillin basalt dyke lines.

By now, a new SMC guide to Skye was being researched, with Jimmy Simpson as editor. Despite more or less living in the new Glen Brittle Memorial Hut, and by various accounts working hard on research, he seems to have had a cavalier attitude to some routes, quite a few of which were omitted from his two-volume guide published in 1969. The author recalls meeting him around then on Skye and perhaps naively asking him to recommend an easy route, which request went unanswered. He presumably had distractions enough.

In 1968 came what became known as the Coruisk Affair, which threatened this wonderful wild area and became a major *cause célèbre*, one which still rankles in the memory of those active at the time. Basically, a Manchester-based Territorial Army unit was about to build a two-mile-long Land Rover track from Kilmarie to Camasunary, while a wire suspension bridge would be built across the Camasunary river, the footpath from there to the Scavaig river 'improved', and another wire bridge built over the Scavaig river. The Bad Step on the coastal path would be blasted to make a three-foot wide pathway.

No approach had been made to the Countryside Commission for Scotland, the Scottish Countryside Activities Council, the Ramblers' Association, the Association of Scottish Climbing Clubs, the Mountain Bothies Association, the JMCS, the SMC or the Mountain Rescue Committee of Scotland. As a letter from Lt. Col. D Barker-Wyatt stated that the work was originally asked for by the police, rescue organisations and Skye council, this would seem to have been something of an oversight.

The only reason that this 'project' became known to those with an interest in this area was that Barker-Wyatt had been requesting use of the Loch Coruisk Memorial Hut. Sandy Cousins of the JMCS was on the case immediately, and began to communicate with the aforementioned bodies, in addition to which other key personnel were contacted. As for the rescue argument, MacInnes was the secretary of the MRCS at the time and replied that the scheme would not be of very great value. The MRCS was almost unanimous in its opposition to the project in its stated form.

The revelations which emerged from this sorry episode were very well covered and described in a lengthy article in the SMCJ, but in essence it can be summed up in the conclusion by Cousins–

> An unnecessary intrusion into one of the few remaining remote mountain areas of Scotland has been pushed through by insensitive and ill-advised authority despite requests for democratic discussion of better alternatives, in the interest of mountain safety, search and rescue, by an overwhelming number of well-informed people who know and love Coruisk. [6]

In the end, the plan to blast the Bad Step was dropped but the track and bridges were built. Work was completed for an official opening on 20 June 1968, but by October 1969 both bridges had been badly damaged by gales, with one being swept away soon afterwards, while the track was unsuitable for transporting a casualty in a vehicle. The second bridge disappeared some years later. Various public bodies were often unhelpful, deaf to suggestions and advice, and even obstructive. It was an eye-opener for the outdoor-loving public. To provide just one example, the Skye mountain rescue team was told by a police representative at their AGM that they should not come to any decision on the project as this would be made in Inverness. They had not been consulted earlier.

Returning to the rocks of Skye, Bealach Buttress of Coireachan Ruadha had been somnolent for some time, until J Barraclough and JB Cooper came along in June 1969 to record *Tinn Lamh Crack* (105m E1). This climbed a striking vertical crack, and while the English translation of the Gaelic *tinn lamh* is 'sore hand', it might also have been a play on the phonetic 'tin lav' version, in other words an outside lavatory with a tin roof. The first ascent used a sling to overcome the crux, where the crack narrows on the final steep wall. John Harwood freed the route in 1972.

As Mike Lates notes in the history section of his fine 2011 SMC guide to the Cuillin, Elly Moriarty ran some courses for the Mountaineering Association in the early 1960s, based in Glen Brittle. Harwood was a pupil on one such course in 1963, and returned as an instructor for the next two years. Ian Clough also worked as an instructor in 1965, climbing *Shan-gri-La* (130m VS) on the Eastern Buttress of Sròn na Cìche. In a harder vein were the two excellent routes by John McLean, Bill Smith and Willie Gordon on the South Face of Sgùrr Alasdair: *The Asp* (105m E2 5b/c) and *Con's Cleft* (60m E1).

Another good find on Skye at the end of the 1960s came on Blàbheinn. Clough had been active on Skye for several years, and by September 1968 had been developing much of the unclimbed rock on Blàbheinn. Some 14 new routes were recorded that year, including *The Great Prow* (105m VS), by a party from St Andrews University comprising TW Band, Philip WF Gribbon (1929-), NS Ross and Wilf Tauber. The latter party had beaten Clough and his friends from the Yorkshire Cave Rescue Team to the Great Prow by two months, while the other 13 routes at least gave the Yorkshiremen some consolation.

As the route was first reported by Clough's team, their name was retained, otherwise it would have been called The Splinter. It is a spectacular, jutting rib of gabbro. Although a great line, the rock could be better, and in compensation there are adjacent routes which are of a higher quality. One of these was climbed in May 1969. *Jib* (130m E1) tackles the large wall left of The Great Prow and has a difficult, bulging band of rock at the start, taken by several possible first pitches. The climbers were Clough and MacInnes, with Martin Boysen and Dave Alcock, with the two ropes taking different starts.

❊ ❊ ❊

The first winter route of 1971 on Ben Nevis was *Comb Gully Buttress* (130m IV,4), on 3 January by Ian Fulton and Davy Gardner. This buttress has enjoyed a mixed history, as part of it was first climbed on 8 January 1960 by Clough and John M Alexander, who followed the summer route then traversed right below a bulging ice pitch to finish by the upper half of a prominent, left-curving chimney. The lower half of this chimney was climbed by the French climber Godefroy Perroux (1957-2002) and partner in the 1990s, while combining these two halves gave Simon Richardson, Robin Clothier and Rosie Goolden a complete ascent of *Clough's Chimney* (130m VI,6).

The Fulton/Gardner ascent took the logical finish to the buttress and was made by cutting steps. The final chimney was the crux and took several hours of cutting in hard ice. This is worthy of mention as 1971 saw Scottish winter mountaineering poised on the cusp of a technological breakthrough. Not all climbers at that time would have been aware of this, but even in those pre-internet days the 'bush telegraph' could spread a message fairly effectively. The revolution began, as many do, with a single action, namely the first winter ascent of the Direct Finish to Raven's Gully on the Buachaille, a 50m stretch of desperate bridging graded at VI,6 with the coveted guidebook four-star rating. The climbers were from sunny California, Yvon Chouinard and Doug Tompkins. Born in 1938 in Maine, Chouinard was brought up speaking only French, his forebears having been French-Canadian. In 1946, his mother organised a move to Burbank, California, and Chouinard would start climbing when he was 16, eventually joining a group in the Sierra Club.

In 1957, Americans were using European pegs; these were not only expensive, being 'soft' they deformed in use and became very difficult to extract. Chouinard bought a used forge along with an anvil and the necessary tools and began making chrome steel pegs. These sold well, and borrowing money from his parents he had Alcoa, the Aluminum Company of America, build him a drop-forging die, with which he made carabiners. This was the beginnings of Chouinard Equipment, with partners Tom Frost and Frost's wife Dorene.

Eventually, concern regarding the damage to rock by 'hard' pegs forced the commercial manufacture of aluminium chockstones, (discussed in Chapter 13) and other pieces of hardware such as ice axes, including one using bamboo wood for the shaft. In the mid-1960s, some Yosemite-trained climbers started looking for more challenges and became intrigued with climbing ice. From December to March there were plenty of frozen waterfalls spread across the continent to keep them happy. This meant looking harder at ice-climbing equipment.

In 1966, Chouinard visited the Alps, testing ice axes to see which worked best on the current French technique of moving up steep snow, known as *piolet ancre* (literally 'ice axe anchor'). This involved using all points of a ten-point crampon, which of course was hard work for the ankles. The

Germans and Austrians however had 12-point crampons, and in particular used the four front points of these, two pointing vertically down, two angled upwards and forwards. The argument raged for a few years, before the French tacitly admitted defeat and switched to front-pointing. By 1971, Chouinard also tested which axes were better at cutting steps.

He then, with some help from Donald Snell, the owner of a climbing shop in Chamonix, persuaded the Charlet factory to make him an axe 55cm in length and with a curved pick. Chouinard had assessed that a curved pick would work better with the trajectory of its swing, and be more efficient at remaining fixed in the ice. As climbers knew only too well, the traditional straight pick was too easily pulled out of a snow or ice slope, making it useless for pulling on.

At the same time, Chouinard and Frost were also working on an alpine hammer and rigid crampons, both of which were manufactured and sold by 1967, with the ice axe becoming available in 1969. The axe shaft was initially made of hickory wood, with a switch to bamboo in 1972 as it was felt to provide a warmer and lighter shaft. Ash shafts were also available in Europe. The head was of chrome-nickel steel.

MacInnes, meanwhile, had been designing all-metal axes, available from the early 1960s. The manufacturer was Massey, and the advertising slogan claimed that they could hold an elephant. This was possibly a reasonable claim, as the axes had been built to NATO specifications, but they were far too heavy to use on a mountain without fatigue setting in rapidly. They did however sell thousands, and MacInnes was probably the first person to design an all-metal axe.

Tiso wrote a review for *Mountain* in 1971, listing the ice climbing tools then available. In addition to Chouinard's alpine hammer and axe, there was a Salewa Alpine hammer, this being the tool which the author used in Raven's Gully during one of his winter attempts. Having just managed to make the crucial move on the crux chockstone, the end of the pick snapped off when it hit a rock under the snow slope above, precipitating him back down to hang under the chockstone on a runner.

The Salewa company was formed in Munich in 1935 by Josef Liebhart, registering a corporation for Saddler & Leather Wares– in German **Sa**ttler, **Le**der, **Wa**ren, hence the name of his company– SA+LE+WA.

This Salewa alpine hammer was of course not designed for hitting Scottish rock, and it seems that the original batch of Chouinard hammers sold in the UK had also been modified from the existing stock of peg hammers, by having the pick re-forged to stretch it into a downward curve with notches added. The pick became quite slender, and breakages using Chouinard hammers were also not unknown. Better was the 'Universal Classic' crampon designed in 1962 by Salewa's Hermann Huber, an adjustable, hinged 12-point crampon, punched rather than hand-forged. This sold well over a third of a million pairs, rapidly becoming their best-selling product. Two years later Huber produced his tubular ice screw.

In 1979, following concern from the UIAA that wooden-shafted axes were not strong enough, a 'synthetic' material called Rexilon appeared (also used by pole vaulters before fibreglass became available). Rexilon was actually a wood 18-piece laminate, stronger than bamboo but heavier. Chouinard axes were made by CAMP in Premana, Italy. (The name CAMP comes from **C**onstruzione **A**rticoli **M**ontagna **P**remana, which translates as Articles for Mountaineering made in Premana.)

One important point concerns the teeth cut into the underside of the pick. Initially there were several teeth at the pick end, and more were later added closer to the shaft, apparently to help ensure that the pick did not pull out when a layer of ice had been broken through, with the mid-pick teeth holding firm.

A later axe, the Chouinard Zero, had less of a curve and teeth all the way along the pick. It was designed to complement the North Wall Hammer, for use on vertical ice. It was not meant to replace the Chouinard Piolet, and was 55cm in length with a bamboo shaft, later using a laminate of beech. Chouinard bought out Frost in 1975; before then, axe heads would be stamped either Chouinard or Chouinard-Frost, but this again became just Chouinard.

In use, Europeans tended to prefer a shorter axe of 50cm. They also found that the Piolet axe could sometimes be somewhat disconcerting, going in with a swing then coming out slightly, just enough to worry the sensitive. It certainly worried the author, who quickly decided they were not for him.

The new Chouinard tools were used in earnest in the winter of 1967 in California, often in combination with rigid crampons, which were more secure in steep ice and gave less muscle strain. For protection, the new Salewa tubular ice screws were the best available.

So, armed with their innovative tools, Chouinard and Tompkins came to Scotland. Theirs was basically a commercial trip: they had new gear, it worked, and they would like to demonstrate this. Product placement in snow and ice was not the only name of the game, however–it also included being business-like. The pair duly entered Raven's Gully on the Buachaille in February 1970.

There is a one-page article on their ascent, and this records them having enjoyed perfect 'styrofoam' snow, which they soloed in the initial pitches.[7] The first giant chockstone, which would have been the normal crux, was mounted with a mere couple of grunts. They continued on more snow-ice to find themselves in the dark confines of the direct finish. The title of the article is *Salsipuedes*, which is Spanish for '*leave if you can*':

Escape was now defined in a fading shaft of light coming over a Great Stone stuck between two icy walls. The verglas was too thick for boots and too thin for crampons while the distance between the walls was a bridge—or more. The game was to maximize your body and scratch up as high as you could before your legs gave. At least there was a nice soft snow bottom to the chimney. Spread eagling with his crampons, Doug managed ten feet before he jumped. Trying a Nureyev split, I did fifteen and lost it. Doug got to twenty and [...] at thirty feet the tip of a knifeblade held for a tie-off just before my legs accordioned. The thin ray of light was growing faint as I was winched up to the peg for one last effort. Taking a wee rest in a sling I swore that next time I came back to the Scottish Winter I'd be better fit for climbing rock! The next thirty feet to the stone was indeed a shaky endeavour.

MacInnes intimated that their climbing not only included several falls but even jumping for icicles. [8] All that was left was the MacInnes slot, where that tough legend had waited for over eight hours, his back against a wall and the two front points of his crampons on a narrow hold. In this chimney Tompkins defeated the thin ice and powder snow with tied-off screws and delicate moves to finish the climb. *Raven's Gully – Direct Finish* (50m VI,6) remains a hard variation and is rarely climbed.

One recent ascent was on 8 February 2013 by three instructors from Plas y Brenin, Keith Ball, Tim Neill and Dave Rudkin, who were reported as having thoroughly enjoyed the experience. [9] As Neill noted on his website, they knew that Crowberry Gully was in superb condition the day before, and in Raven's they were very impressed with the crux chockstone, noting that it would be very easy to fail on the first four metres of the climb. As for the Direct Finish–

> To say the direct looks intimidating is an understatement, and it's much harder than it looks. Wild. It's a good job for most climbers who climb big winter grades that this one isn't a benchmark testpiece. [10]

The Direct Finish was attempted the following week by Stephen Reid and Caradoc (Crag) Jones, who had trouble following the line – the final pitch was ridiculously wide and they did not realise it had to be bridged. Instead, they abseiled down to the fork to finish by the original route. They also found that the Direct Finish was at least 75m in length, and not the guidebook 50m.

In 1970, John Cunningham and Bill March met Chouinard and Tompkins at Glenmore Lodge. On the same trip, the Americans also met several prominent climbers at the Clachaig Inn. Ken Spence, who worked at the MacInnes Winter School for four years, was present, as were Cunningham and March again. It had been Cunningham who had recommended Raven's Gully. Chouinard showed his new design of axe, and the downward-curving picks were immediately picked up as being the crucial feature.

It should be noted that, with Cunningham being at Glenmore Lodge and several Creagh Dhu climbers working on the skiing on Cairn Gorm, many of the axes used for instruction had their picks bent down at the Cairn Gorm workshop. Pupils being instructed on winter climbing had footwork emphasised as being central to good, safe climbing, and many would have used curved picks even before the new tools were commercially available. Having been trained as a joiner, Cunningham had a practical nature.

What is important to understand is that several mountaineers, Cunningham included, had already been experimenting with ways to climb steep ice. With good opportunities when he was working in the Antarctic, Cunningham found that with practice he could balance his way up on front points on angles of up to 70°. Vertical ice, effectively anything over 80°, needed some sort of support from above, whether from holds or driven-in ice pegs such as used on the first ascent of Zero Gully. Once the great leap was made to use picks which were inclined downward, whether on an axe or hammer, the way was open to making steep ice easier, faster and safer to climb. As mentioned earlier, some winter pitches were finished by front-pointing, if only because the leader was too tired to cut any more steps.

While instructing at Glenmore Lodge, Cunningham teamed up with March; in late January 1970 they went out looking for steep ice and found it on Hell's Lum Crag, where a steep icefall had formed on the left wall of Hell's Lum itself. Cunningham was armed with Salewa 12-point crampons, four ice screws and two daggers. On the wall of vertical ice, he front-pointed upwards, using the daggers as alternate handholds, hammering one in at full stretch, moving up on his front points until the dagger was at arm's length below, then repeating the move with the other dagger. The ice screws were used as runners. The ice plated under one dagger, precipitating him off to be held by March and a screw runner. It was not a technique for the faint-hearted or those with average balance and strength.

Named *The Chancer* (90m V,6), the route was an early technical winter 6 grade in Scotland, but not the first. On Lochnagar there was *The Stack* (150m V,6) by Mike Taylor, Goggs Leslie and Leslie Fallowfield, climbed in 1952, while on Meall Gorm in Applecross, *Blue Pillar* (180m Severe) was climbed by Patey and Brown in February 1958 at V,6, and Patey soloed *Western Route* (120m IV,6) in Coire an Lochain in February 1959. There was of course Pigott's Route on Ben Nevis, February 1960, by Smith and Marshall at V,6, and finally *Great Central Groove* on The Brack in January 1968, when Skidmore and Richardson made the first winter ascent at V,6, with three aid pegs. These grades were given years after the first ascents, after the new grading system had been introduced. It was a few weeks after The Chancer that Chouinard and Tompkins arrived in Scotland, and it was probably the first ice climb to be given this technical grade, as opposed to the Grade 6 for the mixed routes mentioned above. Cunningham and March immediately saw the potential provided by the curved picks.

MacInnes, when he saw the Chouinard alpine hammer and axe, was also on the case with a view to producing his own design. The first sketch, with a straight, inclined pick and shorter shaft, was probably produced within 24 hours. Graeme Hunter, who assisted MacInnes in its design, remembers making quite a few cardboard cutouts for a pick mock-up. [11] There were several attempts before the best pick angle was arrived at.

MacInnes named his new axe the Terrordactyl, a play on the ancient flying reptile *Pterodactylus antiquus*, which had a head somewhat similar in outline to the pick. Two models were produced: one with an adze, one with a hammer. Some climbers, the author included, found the hammer too heavy and unbalanced, but many took enthusiastically to the adze version. MacInnes also committed immediately to using sheet metal, having seen at first hand the tragic failings of wooden shafts if used for belaying.

As the adze version shaft was very short, the author also bought a MacInnes axe, with its longer shaft, then had its pick bent down. This allowed a longer reach to be used if necessary on a mixed climb, or perhaps a good pick insertion to be gained over a bulge of ice. It was not the over-heavy Massey axe, rather a newer design, similar to the Terrordactyl but with a straight pick. A peg hammer then had to be carried. The short shafts and steeply angled pick gave rise to a new form of minor injury to winter climbers– Terrordactyl knuckle. If slightly careless in driving in the pick, or when using it on an ice slope which was uneven, it was easy to bang one's knuckles on the slope.

The swing used was often slightly different from a classic hold-cutting swing, with an element of a hooking-down motion. The 'Terror' also had a bright orange nylon sling which was narrow and uncomfortable for hanging one's weight on – and it also looked somewhat dubious, so most climbers removed this and replaced it with a broader tape sling. The coldness of a metal shaft could be alleviated slightly by taping.

The change to front-pointing was certainly not uniform, nor did it happen overnight. There was a psychological hurdle to be crossed, switching from a slow, tiring, but usually reassuring use of foot- and hand-holds, which allowed the occasional rest and which in extremis could often be reversed, to what initially could feel like a committing lead up steep snow or ice with no immediate harbour in sight. Some climbers became fully committed to it on their first route, others needed longer.

There were early experiments in front-pointing by other climbing ropes. Let it be stated more clearly–these were not full front-pointing, with hand tools designed to be pulled on safely with secure placements; rather, various intermediate experiments were being trialled. One of these was adopted by Patey and MacInnes, where they used two axes and moved up by alternately pushing in the picks, or on easy angled slopes the shafts. As the picks were straight, they pulled out easily except on lower-angled ground, where they could be pushed down from above. Cunningham and March as described above experimented with ice daggers. These could be stabbed into ice and used for balancing upwards, but this method too was fraught with danger and basically insecure. Norrie Muir tried a variant on this in 1970, using two Salewa half-round ice screws, again insecure, and failed on The Curtain.

Experiments became more advanced and certainly safer once climbers heard about inclining the pick, and many workshops saw axes which climbers already owned being heated and bent down. One of the first to make the transition was Michael (Mike) George Geddes (1951-1985), born in Edinburgh and educated at Daniel Stewart's College (now Stewart's Melville College). In 1967 he went to study chemical engineering at Cambridge University, where he met Harold Gillespie and Alan Rouse. Both Geddes and Gillespie, who had attended George Heriot's School, were in the Edinburgh JMCS.

Geddes was an enthusiast for the Scottish mountains, and in the published list of Munroists became number 100 in 1970, completing the Munros and Tops at the age of 18 years and 315 days, a few months after having left school. At the time he was the youngest compleater. (That distinction now belongs to a nine-year old!)

Geddes and his friends, who included Alan Paul Rouse (1951-1986), would become renowned for making the long trip from Cambridge to Fort William by hitchhiking. On some occasions a pre-arranged lift could be taken, but often it was by 'rule of thumb' all the way to the Fort and back, leaving late on a Friday and hopefully returning in the small hours of a Monday. The trips alone required determination, which Geddes had in full. As for training, Cambridge was somewhat flat, but Geddes scrutinised maps of the area for disused railway lines and found some useful locations, similar to the Currie Wa's.

An article in *Mountain* at the end of 1970 by the alpinist Rob Collister had stimulated Geddes' interest in the techniques of winter climbing, and he began to look at alternative ice tools, buying a Chouinard alpine hammer and persuading a blacksmith to make a copy of its head, which he then fitted to his own shaft. On ice Geddes used two hammers and Salewa 12-point crampons. As for an axe, he probably used a Chouinard-Frost model, which he was certainly using in the Alps in 1972.

On their New Year holiday in January 1971, Geddes and John C Higham climbed Penguin Gully on Beinn Dearg on 2 January by front-pointing.

The previous month they had bought Chouinard tools, each climbing with a Chouinard axe and hammer. Two days later they front-pointed Glover's Chimney on Ben Nevis, along with Alison Lamb. She later married Higham and would have been one of the first women to front-point a route in Scotland.

Geddes was on Ben Nevis for a week in March 1971, the occasion being the President's Meet of the CUMC. On Monday 15 March, with Higham, he recorded *Aphrodite* (200m IV,4) on No.3 Gully Buttress, to the right of Green Gully. Described in the guide as *'A good but wandering snow-ice route'*, it starts up the middle of the buttress and goes up and left towards Green Gully, before heading upwards more directly.

Tuesday, 16 March saw an ascent of Point Five Gully. Geddes led the lower, difficult pitches in Point Five Gully with his three companions – Higham, Gillespie and Rouse – prusiking up behind. In the upper section they split into two ropes and dispensed with the prusiking. Gillespie remembers, with great clarity, *'Mike powering up the 4ᵗʰ pitch of Point 5, the shaft of the home-made hammer bending alarmingly every time he moved up.'*[12] The shaft was wooden.

The entry in the CIC Climbers' Log reads–

16/3/71 Mike Geddes & JC Higham, H Gillespie & Alan Rouse - as a rope of 4 on the lower section, two teams above. Conditions quite good, no spindrift epic, although rather poor ice on pitch 3 & 4. Front-pointed throughout, 4 steps for resting! Times MG & JH 7½ hrs, HG & AR 8½ hrs.

On Thursday 18 March, with Gillespie, Geddes climbed *The White Line* (300m III) on Goodeve's Buttress, the buttress area to the right of Glover's Chimney. In Volume 1, a case is made that The White Line may in part correspond to the line taken by Goodeve's party in 1907, trying to climb to safety during a 29-hour epic after a series of errors on Tower Ridge. Geddes and Gillespie would not have been aware of this, however. Since 1971, a number of other winter routes have been recorded in this area.

On 21 March, and climbing with Edinburgh climber Nigel Rayner, Geddes made the third ascent of Observatory Buttress (Original Route, 340m V,4), in excellent condition, taking five hours, another of the Smith-Marshall 1960 classics. With a grand climax to this week of climbing, Geddes shattered the air of near-invincibility surrounding Smith's Route on Gardyloo Buttress, making a second ascent with Rayner on the 22 March, 11 years after its first ascent by Smith and Marshall, and taking four and a half hours.

Continuing this fine burst of activity, the first known new climb using Terrordactyls occurred at the end of March that year on Ben Nevis, with *Astronomy* (300m VI,5), by Fyffe, MacInnes and Spence. The precise date is uncertain. They had recently been climbing on Creag Meagaidh, and on driving south to Glen Coe the clear weather allowed a view of the Ben Nevis cliffs from the road. They spotted that the Minus Face was not completely plastered in snow and ice: some rocks were showing through. Looking for a big mixed climb to try out the new technique, and with the end of the winter season approaching, at least in the west, they were becoming anxious. Astronomy in summer is a straightforward climb, with most of its difficulties low down. The route was almost certainly done the following day.

The party was slow in starting, gaining the foot of the climb at about 11am. Thinking that they might not have sufficient daylight, they carried bivouac gear. MacInnes handed out Terrors for their ascent – and collected them afterwards! Spence recalled that there may not have even been six between the three climbers. They were not all prototypes, though mostly very early designs, perhaps the second batch. One was a prototype, the hammer version, used by Spence the following summer on his first ascent of the North Pillar on the Eiger.

Conditions on the Minus Face were excellent, and to help save time the leader would climb up and belay, to be followed by the other two using Jumars, prusik devices which allowed a fixed rope to be ascended. [13] The third man would have the worst task, as he would have to remove any protection. They alternated the leads, but even so they ran out of time near the top and spent the night on the North-East Buttress, finishing up the final part of this next morning.

MacInnes and Fyffe returned to the climb in 1974, to make a BBC film of a winter ascent. This included a bivouac at half-height. A ten-minute clip can be found on YouTube, but it appears that the original film was destroyed by the BBC. The following month, April 1971, saw Cunningham and March on Ben Nevis, attracted by reports of good conditions. Point Five Gully retained enough snow and ice to be climbable, and the pair took a total of six hours on the route.

In 1972, Geddes returned, and by front-pointing made the second winter ascents of Minus Two Gully and Orion Direct. A week or two later Quinn and Lang made the third ascent of Orion Direct, but the Dundonians had yet to convert to front-pointing; when asked about this delay, Quinn explained that they had not yet come to trust the technique. [14] Their ascent was therefore the second by step-cutting, and took some time. On the chimney pitch, Lang had an attack of hypoglycemia and barely managed to reach the belay.

A fairly typical example of how active climbers in Scotland moved from step-cutting to front-pointing comes courtesy of Spence and Fyffe recalling this period:

…we both remember a short intermediate period probably lasting only one or two seasons at most where ascents were made using only one Terror in conjunction with another more conventional axe. So steps were cut which might be smaller than normal and the Terror used for extra security and also when arranging protection. For very short steep sections, front pointing with Terror and conventional axe could be employed. And although limited, it definitely had advantages over traditional step cutting. [15]

Cost naturally came into it as well, and the new tools bit deep into any pocket money working climbers would have. When Spence and Fyffe went to the Alps to climb Les Droites in 1971, they had one Terror borrowed from MacInnes, another borrowed from Bill March, one prototype Salewa borrowed from Ian Rowe and one Curver axe owned by Fyffe. The Curver was a British ice axe made by Snowdon Mouldings, a company set up by Mo Anthoine (1939-1989) and Joe Brown. It had a curved pick and a fibreglass shaft, and was heavier than the Terrordactyl.

As with most new technologies, there would be teething troubles. Some picks would start to bend, perhaps in protest at the cold stressing they underwent, while some of the rivets in early Terrors were of the aircraft design and would work loose. Over the following decades many new designs would emerge and new companies would appear. This, and the continuing evolution of climbing on both rock and ice, is a story to be continued in the third volume of this series, under the authorship of Simon Richardson.

We have seen how the foundations of Scottish mountaineering as a discrete and distinct style of climbing was formed, from its earliest years when it was basically a winter pastime for the professional and upper classes, to be taken up between the two world wars by the working classes escaping from the cities, and then morphing into a sport with all its paraphernalia, literature, ethics and even governing bodies. Happily, most of these aspects have been quietly incorporated, leaving a game remarkably open to personal expression.

Research for this volume has led to one dominant conclusion above all others– advances have been made by the efforts of individuals, not all of whom can be mentioned due to space limitations. Some have become legends. They have left their own personal works of art, some equal to the great works in other fields such as literature, fine art, sculpture, music. These unique works are open to the elements and will, through the millennia, be altered. Some are ephemeral, morphing every winter depending on the vagaries of climate. Go and seek these works, repeat them as no other artist can, and even find your own raw material, to leave something for others who come after.

References

1. Strange, Greg. *The Cairngorms – 100 Years of Mountaineering*. (2010, SMT.) p.183.
2. Grieve, J. *Creag An Dubh Loch A La Carte*. SMCJ 29, 161, May 1970. pp.264-266.
3. Wilson, Ken. *Hard Rock – Great British Rock-Climbs*. (Hart-Davis, MacGibbon. London. 1975.)
4. Strange, Greg. Op cit. p.217.
5. <https://www.mountaineering.scot/activities/outdoor-climbing/ethics>. Accessed February 2017.
6. Anon. *The Coruisk Affair*. SMCJ 29, 160, May 1969. pp.111-120.
7. Chouinard, Yvon. *Salsipuedes*. SMCJ 30, 163, May 1972, p.20.
8. MacInnes, Hamish. *Personal communication*.
9. *Raven's Gully – Recent Ascents*. February 16, 2013. <http://www.scottishwinter.com/?p=3544> Accessed February 2017.
10. Raven's Gully Direct. *Tim Neill Guiding*. February 2013. <goo.gl/rTJhdw> Accessed February 2017.
11. Hunter, Graeme. *Personal communication*. January 2017.
12. Gillespie, Harold. *Personal communication*. February 19, 2017.
13. Jumar Pangit was a Swiss manufacturer, founded by Adolph **Ju**esi and Walter **Mar**ti. Juesi was studying eagles for the Swiss government and needed to ascend on ropes in order to perform his work, so Marti developed the ascender for him. In 1958, they introduced the first jumar to the climbing market.
14. Quinn, Neil. *Personal communication*. February 2017.
15. Spence, Ken. *Personal communication*. February 2017.

Appendix A - Ice Tool Development

Ice Dagger. © John Cleare

Chouinard Ice Tool. © John Cleare

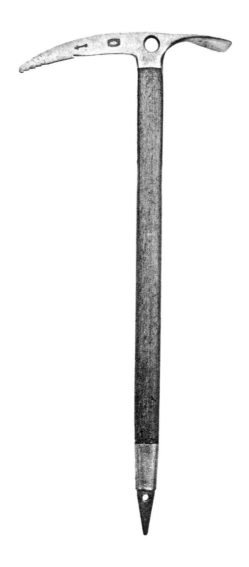

Chouinard Alpine Axe. © John Cleare

Chouinard Ice Hammer. © John Cleare

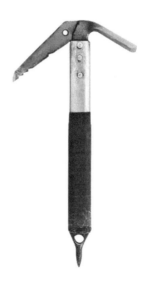

Terrordactyl Adze Ice Tool. © John Cleare

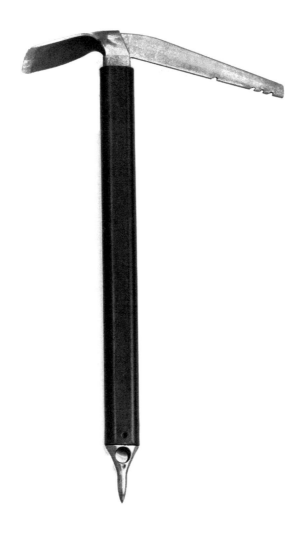

MacInnes Peck Axe. © John Cleare

Appendix B - Maps

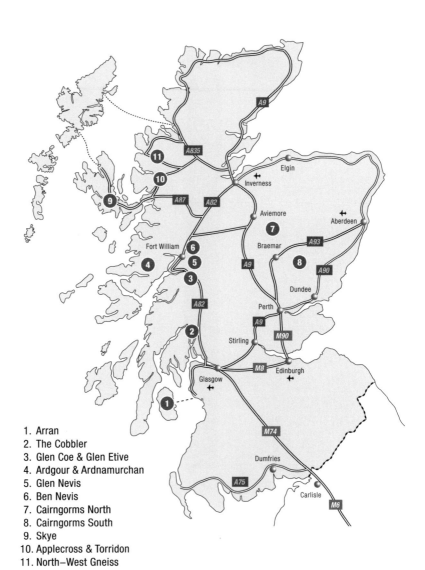

1. Arran
2. The Cobbler
3. Glen Coe & Glen Etive
4. Ardgour & Ardnamurchan
5. Glen Nevis
6. Ben Nevis
7. Cairngorms North
8. Cairngorms South
9. Skye
10. Applecross & Torridon
11. North–West Gneiss

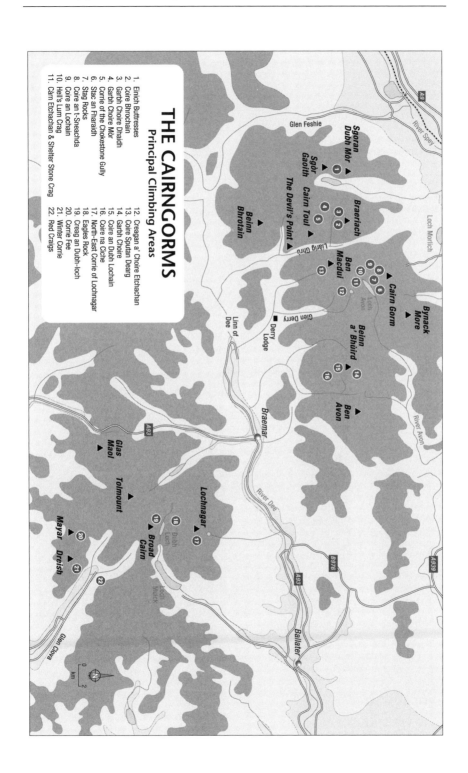

THE CAIRNGORMS
Principal Climbing Areas

1. Einich Buttresses
2. Coire Bhrochain
3. Garbh Choire Dhaidh
4. Garbh Choire Mòr
5. Corrie of the Chokestone Gully
6. Stac an Fharaidh
7. Stag Rocks
8. Coire an t-Sneachda
9. Coire an Lochain
10. Hell's Lum Crag
11. Càrn Etchachan & Shelter Stone Crag
12. Creagan a' Choire Etchachan
13. Coire Sputan Dearg
14. Garbh Choire
15. Coire an Dubh Lochain
16. Coire na Ciche
17. North-East Corrie of Lochnagar
18. Eagles Rock
19. Creag an Dubh-loch
20. Corrie Fee
21. Winter Corrie
22. Red Craigs

General Index

Note: routes have been indexed firstly under under the general area in Scotland, then under their respective mountains, with the route name italicised if denoting a first ascent as in the main text.

Scottish Mountaineering Trust

All profits from the sale of this publication go to fund the Scottish Mountaineering Trust. All grants given by the Trust benefit mountains or the people who enjoy them.

Since 1990, the Trust has granted more than £1.3m for causes such as:

- Renovation of Club Huts
- Footpath construction and maintenance
- Land purchase, such as John Muir Trust acquisitions
- Supporting visually impaired people to attend Glenmore Lodge courses
- Mountain Rescue
- Supporting young people to go on expeditions
- Supporting access
- Supporting environmental conservation

Our funds come from Trust publications, such as Scottish Mountaineering Club guidebooks, as well as donations and bequests from the public.

If you would like to donate to the Trust, or to see how the Trust could help you or your organisation, please go to http://www.smc.org.uk/trust/

Scottish Mountaineering Trust

SCOTTISH MOUNTAINEERING CLUB
SCOTTISH MOUNTAINEERING TRUST

Prices were correct at time of publication, but are subject to change

Hillwalkers' Guides

The Munros	£23.00
The Corbetts and Other Scottish Hills	£23.00
The Grahams & The Donalds	£25.00
North-West Highlands	£22.00
Islands of Scotland Including Skye	£20.00
The Cairngorms	£18.00
Central Highlands	£18.00
Southern Highlands	£17.00

Scramblers' Guides

Skye Scrambles	£25.00
Highland Scrambles North	£19.00
Highland Scrambles South	£25.00

Climbers' Guides

Highland Outcrops South	£28.00
Inner Hebrides & Arran	£25.00
Northern Highlands North	£22.00
Northern Highlands Central	£25.00
Northern Highlands South	£25.00
Skye The Cuillin	£25.00
Skye Sea-cliffs & Outcrops	£25.00
The Cairngorms	£25.00
Ben Nevis	£22.00
Glen Coe	£22.00
North-East Outcrops	£22.00
Lowland Outcrops	£22.00
Scottish Winter Climbs	£25.00
Scottish Rock Climbs	£25.00
Scottish Sport Climbs	£28.00

Other Publications

Ben Nevis – Britain's Highest Mountain	£27.50
The Cairngorms – 100 Years of Mountaineering	£27.50
Rising to the Challenge – 100 Years of the LSCC	£24.00
Hostile Habitats – Scotland's Mountain Environment	£17.00
Munro's Tables	£16.00
A Chance in a Million? Avalanches in Scotland	£18.95
The Munroist's Companion	£16.00
Scottish Hill Tracks	£18.00
Scottish Hill Names	£16.00
Mountaineering in Scotland (The Early Years)	£24.00
Ski Mountaineering in Scotland	£18.00

Visit our website for more details and to purchase on line:
www.smc.org.uk

Distributed by: Cordee Ltd, 3a De Montfort Street, Leicester LE1 7HD
(t) 01455 611185 (w) www.cordee.co.uk